Retelling a Life

ROY SCHAFER, Ph.D.

RETELLING A LIFE

Narration and Dialogue in Psychoanalysis

BasicBooks
A Division of HarperCollins*Publishers*

For credits regarding previously published chapters, see pp. 317–18.

Designed by Ellen Levine

Library of Congress Cataloging-in-Publication Data

Schafer, Roy.
Retelling a life: narration and dialogue in psychoanalysis / Roy Schafer.
p. cm.
Includes bibliographical references and index.
ISBN 0-465-04811-0 (cloth)
ISBN 0-465-06938-X (paper)
1. Psychoanalysis. 2. Psychology—Biographical methods. 3. Discourse analysis, Narrative. I. Title.
[DNLM: 1. Psychoanalysis. 2. Psychoanalytic Theory. 3. Psychotherapy—methods. WM 460 S296r]
RC506.S292 1992
616.89'17—dc20
DNLM/DLC 91-44125
for Library of Congress CIP

---

94 95 96 97 ❖/RRD 10 9 8 7 6 5 4 3 2 1

For Rita

Contents

ACKNOWLEDGMENTS

I WOULD like here to express my indebtedness to a number of major modern thinkers who have deeply influenced the conception of psychoanalytic interpretation used throughout the book and particularly in chapter 9. Listed alphabetically, not in order of influence, they are Mikhail Bakhtin, Wayne Booth, Jacques Derrida, Stanley Fish, Michel Foucault, Jurgen Habermas, Frank Kermode, Paul Ricoeur, Gilbert Ryle, Hayden White, and Ludwig Wittgenstein.

I thank my wife, Dr. Rita V. Frankiel, for her enthusiastic personal support, her confidence and patience, and her helpful critiques of the scope, organization, and much of the content of this book. Dedicating the book to her is small thanks for all she has done.

I also thank Jo Ann Miller, my editor, for her encouraging interest and guidance. And I am grateful to Susan Zurn, project editor, and Debby Manette, copy editor, for first-rate assistance at Basic Books, and to Barbara B. Frank for her secretarial care and readiness to help out.

INTRODUCTION

RETELLING A LIFE rests on the foundation of my work on action language (1976, 1978, 1983). I presented action language as "a new language for psychoanalysis," one designed to replace the mechanistic language of Freud's metapsychology. Metapsychology features an obsolete theory of mind as a mental apparatus. Yet the language of metapsychology has continued to shape much of the thinking and many of the expositions of mainstream, mostly North American Freudian analysts.

In my proposed new language for theory, I use *action* in the broad sense that characterizes much of its use in the philosophy of mind, action, and ethics. In its broad sense, action refers to far more than overt behavior; it refers as well to whatever it is that people may be said to do, and in this respect it stands in contrast to *happenings,* those events in which one's own human agency plays no discernible or contextually relevant part (for example, a rainstorm or receiving a misaddressed letter a week late). Among the things that people do is perceive, remember, imagine, love, hate, fear, defend, and refrain from overt activity. In psychoanalytic discussion, special emphasis is then placed on what people do unconsciously and conflictually (fantasize, remember, love, defend, and so forth).

Subjective experience itself is viewed as a construction of human agency. Experience is not simply "there in the mind" waiting to be found and retrieved by objective introspection. Different people tend to construct experiences of the same event differently, each for reasons of his or her own. Many of these reasons originate early in life and therefore give rise to primitive forms of emotional and cognitive experience, and these persist unconsciously and influentially into adult life. They also add individual coloring to otherwise standardized responses to the conventions of one's culture.

Actions are performed by a person, not by a "mind" or "personality" and not by "drives" or "defense mechanisms." Repression, for example, is an action of a person, and so are an angry tirade, an erotic approach to another person, and the solving of a puzzle.

Narration enters into it as soon as we take into account that, as philosophers say, actions exist only under one or another description. That is to say, we may describe the same event differently depending on our aims, such as approval or condemnation; our context, such as being among strangers or intimates; our level of abstraction, such as setting up broad categories or developing individualized accounts; and other such discursive variables. The action of projecting, for example, may be variously described as defensive, a constituent of empathy, a refusal to take responsibility, a distortion of reality, self-deception, or an early form of defining external reality. Indeed, to speak of "projecting" is already to present an action under a description; it is not an unmediated report of a fact, and it can be named differently.

In the context of narrative theory, therefore, it would be emphasized that actions are always told by someone and that each telling presents one possible version of the action in question. (It may be argued that we are never absolutely right to say that it is the "same" action when there are only distinguishable versions of it; however, that argument introduces a philosophical problem that does not bear on the present theme and so need not concern us here.)

I invoke the idea of narration precisely in connection with the inevitability of alternative descriptions. Using the term broadly, I designate as narration whatever qualifies as a telling or as the presenting of a version of an action; also, whatever qualifies as a version of a happening or an event or scene of any kind, as each of these, too, is always presented under one or another description.

In the sense used here, narratives are not made-up stories (fictitious in the established sense) with beginnings, middles, and endings. Narrating, giving an account, presenting a version, developing a storyline, telling: These terms and others like them make up the core vocabulary of the narrational approach.

It is especially important to emphasize that narrative is not an alternative to truth or reality; rather, it is the mode in which, inevitably, truth and reality are presented. We have only versions of the true and the real. Narratively unmediated, definitive access to truth and reality cannot be demonstrated. In this respect, therefore, there can be no absolute foundation on which any observer or thinker stands; each must choose his or her narrative or version. Further, each narrative presupposes or establishes a context, and the sentences of any one account attain full significance only within their context and through more or less systematic or consistent use of the language appropriate to the purpose.

Psychoanalysis is conducted as a dialogue. However much the analyst may remain silent as she or he listens patiently for suitable opportunities to define themes of unconscious conflict, the process still qualifies as dialogue, for each of the analyst's utterances and meaningful silences counts heavily in the course of the work—sometimes far too heavily owing to the influence of powerful transferences. In this dialogue, actions and happenings (for example, traumatic events) are continuously being told by the analysand and sooner or later retold interpretively by both analyst and analysand. Closure is always provisional to allow for further retellings. In many instances the tellings are nonverbal enactments: showings that are yet to be transformed into tellings. Often the analysand's responses to the analyst's interventions are themselves regarded as material to be retold (clarified, interpreted) in order to progress toward insight. Insight itself refers to those retellings that make a beneficial difference in a person's construction and reconstruction of experience and adaptively active conduct of life. Each retelling amounts to an account of the prior telling as something different or, more likely, something more than had been noted. In this dialogic way, each analysis amounts in the end to retelling a life in the past and present—and as it may be in the future. A life is re-authored as it is co-authored.

Narration has no necessary connection to literariness or self-conscious ornamentation. Although literariness (such as deliberate building of suspense, conventional poetic diction, conspicuous use of stylistic devices) may be an aspect of some narrations, matter-of-fact reportage qualifies as narration just as much as an account presented by a flowery orator.

These introductory remarks merely indicate—they certainly do not expound fully—the narrational and dialogical approach to psychoanalysis. The chapters of this book containing numerous clinical examples, will, I hope, fill in many of the major details of this approach. They should help the reader to see more clearly the usefulness of narratological and dialogical considerations in grasping the theories and practices of psychoanalysts and the diverse, often dramatic, bodily and mental phenomena to which they give rise and which, in the end, exemplify them.

Although these chapters cover a wide range of topics, they can be arranged in four parts: "Narrating the Self," "Narrating Gender," "Theories as Master Narratives," and "Versions of Practice." The parts are not altogether distinct from one another; for example, self narratives are considered throughout the book as are versions of practice and of theories (master narratives). At times the discussions confront major philosophical problems, such as those pertaining to knowledge of self and others, personal identity, and theory construction; at other times, and often, they are deeply engaged with clinical observation, interpretation, and technique.

With reference to the self, after introducing aspects of self narratives in relation to the goals, processes, and especially endings of clinical analyses, I go on in chapter 2 to argue that, for the individual subject, the self is always a narrative construction, always open to flux, and so never totally settled once and for all; on the same argument, this generalization also applies to others in a person's life—the objects so-called. Thus, unlike some other current and popular positions, my position on the self is anti-essentialist; I do not regard the self as an entity found in nature and available for detached study by nonparticipant observers. Selves are told through dialogue, in words, images, and enactments, and they are retold by observers whose narrative preferences and strategies express specific aims, values, and competencies. This first part ends with my considering narrative aspects of the philosophically thorny question of self-deception, and, with that, of defense, multiple-self theories, and other issues of concern to ego psychology, self psychology, and object relations theory.

In the second part on gender, I take up the inherently narrative nature of gender in five different, though related, contexts: the frequently masculine bias in Freud's psychology of women; sexist rhetoric in clinical discussions of impotence and frigidity and its consequences for our conceptions of heterosexual relations; problems of men and women in dealing with success and happiness; men's problems with emotionality; and disruptive aspects of power and rage in male-female relationships. In an effort to shrink the frequently emphasized gap between feminists and psychoanalysts, I emphasize the interaction between sexist factors in social reality and women's unconscious conflicts and identifications, recognizing always that the latter do not develop in ways that are altogether independent of our phallocentric social order. Clinical illustrations are distributed through these chapters.

Aspects of the third part, "Theories as Master Narratives," have been anticipated in the preceding parts; nevertheless, major and direct discussions are presented through, first, a review in modern terms of Freud's legacy; second, an examination of the role of narration in clinical as well as applied psychoanalytic interpretation; and third, a short survey of the many problems encountered by any attempt to find common ground shared by the major, competing schools of psychoanalytic thought. Psychoanalysis emerges as an array of master narratives that dictate specific and incommensurable storylines for the interpretive work of analysts.

In the final, heavily clinical part, and with the aid of detailed examples, I first take up numerous narrational aspects of the clinical interpretation of defense and resistance and the clinical uses of narrativized life experience in the past and present. Then, in an effort to clarify further my story of what psychoanalysis "is," I take up in sequence the difficulties, ambiguities, and limits of training analysis and of the attempt to differentiate analysis from its imitations and from psychotherapy. With psychotherapy now in the text, I take up next some crucial dialogic issues involved in practicing psychoanalytic therapy. And I conclude this wide-ranging story of narration in psychoanalysis by discussing "analytic love"—the analyst's sublimated love for his or her patients as it is expressed through the analytic work itself, taking my cue from Hans Loewald's several published references to this phenomenon.

A number of the chapters in this book have already been published. For the sake of coherence and consistency, I have revised that previously published material, in some instances only slightly, in others more noticeably. I have done so by cutting in order to reduce repetition; by clarification, to improve the argument; by change of terms, to coordinate the chapters; and by highlighting, to bring out the places of narration and dialogue in the argument where they had been left obscure or merely indicated in passing.

My goal was not unity at any price; however, with the benefit of hindsight, I now see considerably more coherence among these chapters, the writing of which has extended over a number of years, than I could have recognized during the production of each of them. In one way or another, these pieces are about interpretation. As I now conceive it in narrational and dialogic terms, interpretation is always a way of either telling something that has not yet been put into words or retelling something already told. In sum, we may say that it is a life that is being reworked beneficially through analytic dialogue.

PART ONE

NARRATING THE SELF

The case studies presented in this book are based on real individuals; however, the names and identifying characteristics of those individuals have been changed to protect their privacy. The material for some of these examples has been gathered from supervisees, whom I thank for their contribution and their willingness to remain anonymous in order to ensure their patients' privacy.

CHAPTER 1

Self-interest, Self Interest, and the Termination of Psychoanalysis

IT is one of the enduring popular burlesques of psychoanalysis that at its conclusion, the analysand is a moral monster. Self-interested to the exclusion of all considerations of decency, tact, and mutuality, guilt-free and shame-free in unbridled appetitiveness, the analysand prowls through the world seeking opportunities for self-assertion and self-revelation. And to boot, does all this with instantly displayed and usually boring, if not offensive, insight into the self and others. In a word, this person is selfish: maddeningly and tediously selfish. So the burlesque goes.

One dictionary defines selfish as "concerned *excessively* or *exclusively* with oneself: seeking or concentrating on one's advantage, pleasure, or well-being *without regard for others*" (my emphases). Is this the business that analysts are in? Is it the analyst's mission to help people to be selfish? Is the attainment of unconflicted selfishness a criterion for successfully terminating analysis? It seems rather that that mission could bespeak only poverty of spirit on both sides of the couch.

It must be admitted at the outset that this burlesque can be properly applied to the way some people behave in the thick of their ambivalent analytic transferences. Sometimes it can be applied to analysands who have interrupted their analyses or who have completed what they or their therapist mistakenly or pretentiously call analysis or successful analysis. Additionally, the caricature may not be far from the mark in describing some people as they are when they begin analysis and as they may continue to be or to seem, even if in diminished form, as their analyses make substantial progress. None of which should be surprising, and all of which should, upon reflection, give the lie to the burlesque. But the burlesque persists, and we must ask why that is so.

Analysts know to how great an extent this conventional lampoon of analysands originates in the irrational attitudes of not-so-innocent bystanders and observers. Knowing this, thoughtful analysts make it part of their job, especially as termination approaches, to help genuinely progressed analysands recognize and withstand the pressures exerted by this attack or by one of its many variants. They do so by continuing to promote insight—in this respect by analyzing analysands' denials of what they are up against and their regressive responses to it. This facilitation of insight might begin by taking up denials of an analysand's own ability to understand what prompts the hostility or the regressive shift; that they are denials is made plain by the abundance of available evidence of the burlesque's origins, and, that they are regressive shifts is made plain by the patients having more or less vigorously returned to modes of response that appear to have been worked out or given up in the course of analysis.

Let us consider, first, three outstanding origins of the burlesque: frustration, envy, and defensive insecurity. The three go together and essentially imply one another, but each can be singled out for purposes of exposition.

FRUSTRATION AS THE SOURCE OF THE BURLESQUE

Analysts know that many of those who share their lives with analyzed people prefer them as they were preanalytically. Especially those analysands who used to be inhibited, undemanding, and masochistic in attitude were liked the better for it. Once they had been good company: good losers and ever ready with the knowing looks, the sympathetic shrugs, and the self-pitying and bitter jokes that convey a sense of togetherness and passive resignation to a life that offers little and deprives one of much. Once they had been ready to make the expressive movements and to emit the sighs and groans that grease the wheels of communality. Male and female, they played the basic Woody Allen role with considerable ingenuity. Now unappreciative friends, relatives, and lovers view these progressed analysands with a sense of frustration, for they had grown accustomed to the patients' self-effacing faces. In these faces they had seen the victims of the spontaneous, provoked, or simply imagined sadistic exploitativeness of others. They are the prisonerlike faces of those who share the passive and not uncommon ideal of living unhappily in shame, guilt, weakness, helpless rage, and failure.

Progressed analysands have already understood this dynamic. They have developed that understanding largely through analysis of their own transferences, and that understanding has been crucial in whatever progress they have made. Now for the most part they no longer play these victim games as seductively, expertly, or insistently as before. With some consistency they convey a strong sense of pride combined with realistic assessments and expectations. They also convey a strong sense of self-love and self-respect combined with continued strivings for further development. By changing in these ways, they not only frustrate the desires of others, they stir up envy.

ENVY: THE SECOND PRESSURE ON PROGRESSED ANALYSANDS

Envy is the origin of the second sort of pressure that progressed analysands must withstand. Poisonous envy: Surrounding the progressed analysands like poison gas, it takes the form of little digs, malicious and too readily believed gossip about the analysand or the analyst or promising life situations, and other such efforts to spoil the goodness that analysands have newly found in themselves, in their analysts, and in the surrounding world. In response, they are tempted to, and in fact do regress—slowly, rapidly, grossly, or subtly; it is not the first time in their lives they have responded so, and, as before, they feel that their survival depends on this defensive shift. The vigilant analyst picks up these shifts in level of functioning, recognizing how in large part they are regressive responses to envy, and helps work out their connections with current real and imagined interactions with others. Imagined interactions must be taken into account, for the analysand's fear of envy and other defensive dealings with his or her own inner grandiosity and shame may lead the analysand to project envy as well as frustration and a sense of insecurity where there is not very much supporting evidence.

At this relatively late stage of analysis, that which has been imagined will be readily linked up in the analytic dialogue with two sets of factors: (1) influential infantile prototypes of envious responses by siblings, friends, parents, and others in the immediate environment, and (2) a guilty sense of the analysand's own unconscious, infantile, ruthless greed and grandiose competitiveness, intensified perhaps by comparable qualities in others. Much of the analytic work will throw into sharp relief the extent to which an analysand's progress has stimulated defensive insecurity as well as frustration and envy in others around them.

BURLESQUE OUT OF DEFENSIVE INSECURITY

Well-analyzed people are felt by others in their lives to be threats to the defensive solutions that they have come to count on. These analysands no longer consistently support prevailing neurotic compromises and no longer consistently endorse and participate in the preferred but severely compromised pleasure possibilities in the lives of these others. Out of defensive insecurity, these others may then experience the analysands' hard-earned and owned pride as nothing more than insensitive egoism, their unconcealed self-confidence as merely callous exhibitionism, and their unhampered though not exclusive attention to pursuing their own interests as ruthless exploitativeness or self-indulgence. What, they will then ask, has happened to these analysands' stoicism? Where is their ethical responsibility? Have they lost their sense of decorum? What has happened to their sweetness? Why do they not just go along in order to get along?

Adding to the problem in all three respects, progressed analysands may have reached a point where they continue in analysis not out of dire need and abject humiliation but because they want to, even if not without noteworthy ambivalence. To the extent that they do want to continue, it is because they view analysis as having added life to their lives and as fortifying them in their efforts to do the same for themselves in the future. They see analysis as having strengthened their integration and enhanced their future prospects. Now they are not so inclined to think of analysis negatively; in their psychic realities it is far less a crutch, a trap, or a life sentence than it is a release, an opportunity, a source of autonomy. Worse still, from the standpoint of these frustrated, envious, defensively locked-in others, progressed analysands may even have the nerve to say that, on balance, however arduous analysis remains, they enjoy it! They enjoy it even while recognizing ever more clearly and with expectable mixtures of foreboding and regret that the time is coming when it will no longer be in their own self-interest to continue in analysis. As one analysand said, "It doesn't get any easier, but it does get better." These analysands are experienced as threats not only to the defensive order of things but to the social order in general. Clearly, they must be stopped!

ANALYSANDS' RESPONSES TO THE REACTIONS OF OTHERS

Small wonder then that they encounter efforts to undermine their gains. Small wonder, too, that they anticipate and experience some painful loneliness as their relations with at least some of the important others in their lives become more and more estranged and less and less worth the cost to them. They sense the withdrawal of others or their own withdrawal from others, or most likely both at once; or the emphasis may fall more on disapproval on both ends of the relationship than on direct withdrawal. Analysands must feel the pressure to regress, to "fit in" once again, in circumstances like these. Terminating analysands will have many other reasons to revive problems that already have been effectively analyzed; nevertheless, it is important to the completion of the analysis to help analysands confront, in an analytic way, this kind of appeasement of others through flight from progress.

Postanalytically, too, analysands may respond regressively when they encounter the reactionary pressures I have described. And they may not see the connection for what it is, perhaps partly out of the wish to regress back to being an analysand for other reasons. In any case it is not unusual for some analysands to return for postanalytic consultation with some kind of flare-up of previously mastered problems or symptoms. Upon analysis, it may soon become apparent that these flare-ups are designed unconsciously to appease others. In analysands' fantasies, the analyst may be among those to be appeased—the analyst they have "left behind," "discarded," "abandoned," "used up," "fooled," or "surpassed" in youthfulness, success, pleasure, or what have you. Guilt may play a major part in these returns. At such times, further analysis is likely to establish that the need to appease is greatest where there had been deep-seated vulnerabilities not so much to others as to guilty reactions to the analysands' own special achievements and richness of experience. Residual fears of their own greed, competitiveness, and grandiosity may also be involved. And some of these regressing former analysands may be undergoing a variant of survivor's guilt in relation to others in their lives: not sure they deserve their gains and so fearing that what they have gained will be taken away from them. In all of this, analysts will encounter the play of transference residues, negative and positive.

Appearances may be deceiving at a time like this, for it is not necessarily true that analysands' gains are predominantly unstable. The likelihood is that, unexpectedly, their gains, their advances to higher levels of functioning and interaction with others, have brought them into new difficulties or new versions of old difficulties. It may prove that their continuing personal development after termination has evoked further manifestations of central infantile conflict and unresolved transference. It may be that, as Freud (1937b) surmised, these conflicts were not active enough or accessible enough during the main period of analysis to be worked through adequately. Even so, postanalytic work will be based on the considerable working through that was accomplished earlier, for analysts today understand that personalities are not so compartmentalized that some major issues never enter a sustained analysis in one guise or another. This newly encountered conflictual experience may, for example, center around getting married, divorcing, becoming a parent, losing a loved one, or achieving high-level success at work, no one of which can be altogether removed from infantile fantasy and its conflictual aspects. With some analytic clarification of current pressures, these former analysands may be ready to be on their way again without undergoing a second lengthy analysis. Unanalytic perfectionism on the part of the analyst may, however, dictate otherwise.

In any event, the terminating analysands' secured and enhanced self-interest must be seen as both an important asset and a potential source of new problems. The new problems appear at the interface of internal object relations and relations with others in the environment.

SELF-INTEREST VERSUS SELF INTEREST

Thus far I have been merely approaching the intrapsychic and interpersonal complexities of the enhanced self-interest of terminating analysands. I have been using the term *self-interest* in its conventional sense of protecting and promoting one's own best interests in whatever way one defines them. There is, however, another kind of self interest [unhyphenated] that we must attend to: interest in constructing, maintaining, and extending a self to which one can feel committed. This interest may be benevolent or malevolent or, as is often the case, a mixture of the two. In the progression toward termination, the balance shifts slowly but surely toward benevolent self interest. In the following text I discuss the two poles of self interest, giving some clinical examples along the way. Subsequently I attempt to show that benevolent self interest must include interest in the selves of others.

In certain respects this turn in the discussion runs parallel to Erikson's discussion of ego identity formation (1956); in other respects, as when I invoke certain aspects of Kleinian thought about the depressive position and reparation, and also when I invoke Hartmann's discussion of the testing of inner reality, I more or less diverge from Erikson. And when, in conclusion, I take up the self as one kind of psychoanalytic narrative, I shall be far from Erikson's essentially naturalistic presentation of ego identity: a presentation in which the development of identity is described as simply observed in nature by an objective observer rather than as an account delivered by a narrator from a particular psychoanalytic point of view. What lies immediately ahead, then, is consideration of the two kinds of self interest and discussion of clinical examples. Finally, I develop a metatheoretical view of this entire presentation as psychoanalytic story or narrative.

Malevolent Self Interest

The best starting point now is a focus on malevolent self interest. Certainly, analysts are extremely familiar with self-scrutiny that ranges from nagging reproachfulness to outright persecution. Typically, this harsh and painful self-scrutiny is stereotyped in content and fragmenting in its effects. Typically, those who are inclined to burden themselves with this malevolent gaze directed inward promptly do so in spades whenever they begin to experience or express benevolent self interest. Almost instantaneously at those times, they turn the benevolent narrative around into new charges against themselves, say, of smugness, overconfidence, showing off, or destructive competitiveness. By projection, they may charge others with being persecutors, and in order to externalize their own conflicts completely they may readily go on to provoke others into being persecutors.

Whatever the extent of the distortions, analysts bear in mind that, first of all, it is the patients themselves who are the malevolent critics. Primarily, they have already been doing the dirty work intrapsychically either by raising their own voices against themselves or by conjuring up the experience of hostile introjects who examine them hatefully. These are people who will not take yes for an answer. They say such things as these: "I don't want to give in to my good feelings," "I have trouble feeling depressed today," and in an apparent slip, "You've got to learn to take the good with the bad." In these cases, the self is not the party of the first part; it is the party of the worst part.

When it is done malevolently, the construction of a self is consistently restricted and warped. A self-victimizer elaborates one-sided, often grotesque fantasies about the self that, however, are presented as reports of incontrovertible reality testing. Should the analyst mistakenly attempt to argue against these reports, he or she is likely to be regarded with some suspicion if not contempt. However negative it may be, this self-portraiture does manifest sustained self interest; it is not helpful to analysis to think of this material merely as showing problems with self-esteem or fixation on passive suffering or something of that sort. Those points of view have their own important place in analysis, but they may not fill the place occupied by the recognition of a malevolent form of self interest.

The clinical examples that follow show different types of malevolent self interest, and some also indicate transition to benevolent self interest over the course of analysis. For purposes of exposition, I present these case examples mainly in terms of the single storyline that concerns us here; many other storylines were, of course, consistently noted and elaborated in each case.

Case Example

After five years of treatment, one young woman reported that she was really beginning to look at herself in the mirror in order to see what she looked like. And she liked what she saw. It was not that previously she had had no visualized self; rather, she had visualized herself as ugly. This malevolent fantasy picture was disconfirmed by her beginning to look at herself realistically, and it was the new look that was consistent with the way her friends had been seeing her all along. For the analyst, too, it seemed that ordinary reality testing would not support the extreme attributions of ugliness she had been making. Upon analysis, it seemed that a large part of the patient's previous self-narrative had been being used as one of her archaic defensive precautions against intimacy; this was one element of a masochistic strategy that she had worked out and maintained from her earliest years. Previously, she had not dared to test out that self-narrative by conventional means and to revise it accordingly. She had no reality-tested self and precious little benevolent self interest; in her psychic reality, she could not afford to have them.

As could be expected in a case like this, the analysand had grown up with parents who, owing to their own plainly apparent, severe conflictual existence, had not taken an objective and appreciative interest in the physical and emotional child she had been and for the most part had remained, both in their psychic reality and in hers. She was seeing herself through their eyes. There had been no benign parental mirror—only her parents' aversive and critical stereotypes of what she was as compared to what she should be and was failing to be, only their fixed and destructive ideals of anhedonic conformity and flawlessness. They had never framed the open-minded questions, the mirroring questions, the benevolently interested questions: What have we here? How can we respond to it genuinely? How can we help it along? Their interest in her self was malevolent. Such at least was the lifelong experience reported by this young woman during much of her analysis. However exaggerated her account of her past—and it did require important modifications later on (for these see below)—these painful details were well documented, and they were prominent influences on her development up to the present.

In her attempt to compensate for the absence of benevolent parental interest and subsequent self interest, this young woman had tried to develop a public image of flawlessness and unreachability. In this effort her subjective success was limited, but this did not stop her from persevering. Accordingly, she had precluded mirroring and caring responses by others; she had perpetuated the problem of continuing to feel that she was living among uninterested others. On his part, the analyst had shown consistent analytic interest in her through his careful and caring attention to enactments that entered into her transferences; these enactments included much oppositionalism and much displacement into the trials and tribulations of her daily existence outside the analysis. So far as he could, he had avoided showing such *un*analytic interest in her as providing her with explicit, socially conventional reassurances. As time went on, it seemed that it was his analytic interest, combined with the suitable interpretations it made possible, that was helping to bring about moderating changes in the superego prohibitions she had been enforcing, the damaging ideals she had been holding up, and the unconsciously sexualized pain that had been involved.

The patient showed these changes by beginning to take an interest in having a viable self of her own. This was to be a self that encompassed needs, appetites, sensuality, individuality, and the assets of attractiveness, intelligence, generosity, and other such benevolently conceived qualities, qualities that are a delight to behold and a pleasure to live out once the attendant dangers and despair have been reduced. It was noteworthy that these excursions into benevolent self interest were accompanied by some sexual arousal in her sessions and that this arousal regularly frightened her and stimulated regression. In my analytic experience, some sexual arousal often accompanies explicit and new self-affirmative advocacy, and it often seems to be the cause of some immediate backing off; I believe the patient backs off because feeling sexually stimulated or feeling alive in that way is itself viewed malevolently as something to be condemned and suppressed.

Concurrently, the patient began to take an interest in the actual, extremely conflicted, and pain-inducing selves of her parents. At times in her analytic sessions she even allowed herself to empathize with them; the empathy seemed genuine enough in that it was experienced without minimizing or disavowing her rage and sense of deprivation. Only then could she dare to peek into an actual mirror, even if only briefly and anxiously; that is to say, she began to tolerate peeking into the psychic lives of others with some real curiosity and even some compassion at the same time as she began to look more deeply and empathically into her own psychic life and into her face as its visible manifestation.

Case Example

The next example is that of a woman who, although she was appreciated by everyone in her field as an extraordinarily talented person, could find no way to participate in their judgment. She had grown up with a nebulous mother—an unreflecting mirror, one might say—and so had developed no adequate foundation for a benevolently affirmative self interest. This simplistic causal connection seemed to hold up, but only as one factor contributing to her problems; the final account of the origins of her problems, developed over the course of the analysis, was far more complex than that. As is usual in such cases, it was not just a question of lack of self interest; not having felt herself to be an object of interest, she had developed prohibitions against affirmative self interest. To wish for benevolent interest was bad and to feel it was bad.

This important consequence is another example of how children who grow up under adverse developmental conditions establish severe moral self-condemnations on the grounds of their deprivations and traumas and thereby play an active part in the organization of depressive and masochistic positions and in the compensatory grandiose inclinations that often go along with those responses.

Because benevolent self interest had become bad as well as dangerous, this analysand had to be consciously bewildered and troubled by the esteem she commanded in her current life. She professed not to know what all the commotion was about. She could only shrug off praise and catalog the reasons why she deserved criticism or at least no response at all. Thus, she could respond only in frightened and guilty ways to the acclaim she received. These negative responses were not just surface responses; they went deep into her—without, however, altogether replacing the latent compensatory grandiosity that had become part of her make-up, too. As she progressed toward termination, she was able to moderate all this malevolence to a significant extent and to reduce her latent aloofness.

Case Example

A third patient reported that, on looking at himself in the mirror each morning, he responded with shock and a tendency to duck out of his reflection with aversion. He was not seeing the reflection of the good-looking and capable man that, by all conventional standards, he was. We can say that, strictly speaking, he was not looking at himself or his self and in that sense was not seeing a reflection at all. Instead of seeing, he was enacting his mother's reacting with dismay to his birth and his presence in her life. And by ducking out of the mirror, he was, among other things, ducking out of her life—compliantly dying, submissively suiciding in this symbolic way. Later on in the analysis and as a result mainly of analysis of corresponding transferences, he could tolerate some benevolent self interest; then he was able to give some independent account of his mother's failure to thrive as a mother and to go on from there to experience consciously the mixture of helpful, guilty, and devastated reactions to her failure he had had when a child and to some extent still had. Earlier it had been more than he could bear to recognize and sort out these reactions and thereby to become truly able to look and see. Earlier the failure had to be his, not hers. Looking and seeing were tabooed activities.

Case Example

In the words of a fourth patient—words he was capable of only late in his analysis—"I had to be a moving target, a chameleon, a nothing; if I exposed myself even to myself, I'd be killed or I'd kill them. So I became a mush; I had no edge." By "them" he was referring to extremely persecutory and neglectful figures in his early environment, but also, to a very great extent, as shown by his transferences, to internal versions of these figures that had been greatly magnified in their destructiveness and were imagined to be lurking in the shadows of his inner world.

Although analysts do not minimize the destructive consequences of parental failures, they realize that they cannot hope to work through the problems being presented unless they also attend closely to the many ways in which the analysands, already when they were children, began creating actual failure or accentuating it in fantasy. They also remain vigilant to the many ways in which these analysands cling to the problematic consequences of these real and examined failures and the many ways in which they continuously re-create them in feeling if not in fact. Analysts focus on this unconsciously insistent, provocative, and inventive repetitiveness. They focus, too, on the veiled inclinations toward, and compromised expressions of, hateful, frightened, ashamed, guilty, and reclusive reactions. Additionally, they focus on their patients' turning passivity into activity by identifying with the real and imagined aggressors. In these ways they establish grounds to interpret the self-perpetuated inner-world battle of the malevolent self interest against the positive. Benevolence, it seems, had become the enemy.

In this complex situation, analysts face forbidding technical problems. Large parts of the existing textbooks on technique are directed at just these problems, though often in other terms. I shall not attempt to survey them here, even briefly; however, I shall mention one essential caution: Benevolent analytic self interest can be faked, consciously and unconsciously, and it may take an analyst some time to get beyond defensive pseudointerest or false-self posturing. The painfulness of primitive guilt and depression begins to act as a powerful deterrent just as soon as analysands feel the first faint stirrings of benevolent self interest. Analysands may then become quite ingenious in taking in the analyst by seeming to be wholeheartedly and progressively "in analysis."

In some instances, the analyst may become part of the problem by being all too ready to be taken in by this show of the patient's. That analyst may do so owing to his or her own fears of dealing with the extremely painful, primitively depressive episodes that the analysand must live through in order to participate genuinely. Indeed, the patient's mounting a semblance of benevolent progression toward termination may be a reparative gesture stemming from just those deep, unanalyzed depressive problems. In other words, in part, an analysand enacts in the transference a guilty attempt to undo the effects of destructiveness without dealing with the destructive wishes and fantasies themselves. Kleinian analysis has much to teach us in this connection, and I shall include some notes on that below.

BENEVOLENT INTEREST IN OTHERS

This part of the discussion is organized around two questions: Should the idea of benevolent self interest include benevolent interest in others? And is it only a matter of enlightened self-interest—self-interest in the narrow, conventional sense—to take an interest in others, that is, to do unto others as you would have them do unto you, or in other words, to work out trade-offs in which everyone gets his or her back scratched?

Trade-offs do have their place in the conduct of life, and at the termination of a helpful course of analysis, the analysand is not likely to react in ashamed or guilty ways when tacitly making some such accommodations in a context of ordinary enlightened self-interest. But it would be to leave too much out of the story of human affairs to give an account of relatedness to others *only* in terms of narcissistic utilitarianism. In particular, that account would leave undeveloped the analysis of what mediates these trade-offs and thus of what makes some of them binding, exhilarating, and successful and leaves others indiscriminate, tedious, and doomed to failure.

The evidence that accumulates as termination approaches supports an affirmative answer to my first question. Benevolent self interest does go hand in hand with interest in others. As termination approaches, analysands report ever more frequently that they have had experiences with parents and others that show that there was an unexpectedly or unremembered good side (in some sense of the word *good*) to these others and in the analysands' feelings for them. Reports of this kind became prominent even in the first and extreme case I sketched earlier—the young woman who insistently thought herself ugly. Later on in her treatment, others who had been consistently portrayed as cold, self-absorbed, competitive, or destructive began to be portrayed as acting differently. They were beginning to show benevolent interest in, tolerance of, and satisfaction with the analysand. Sometimes they even helped out: the father in a more conventional "fatherly" way and the mother, warmly even girlishly, in a conventionally more "motherly" way. They tried to help with the patient's career; to be helpful with matters of grooming, marriage, and play; to come to the rescue in a nice enough way when crises developed. They commiserated. Previously limited to monologue or muteness, they entered into dialogue. They phoned and they wrote. They shared confidences. Not always, of course, not necessarily frequently, and not always successfully, for they were still manifesting deep-seated and provocative ambivalence. Nevertheless, they acted differently enough to make a difference.

Usually it seems that analysands are not just presenting less distorted versions of these others. Nor does it seem that these others have just begun to act differently for reasons of their own. Upon analytic investigation, it typically turns out that the analysands' activities have been an important stimulus to these changes. Even though acting and responding to the positive results with much anxiety, analysands have played a significant role in bringing about these new gratifications. It becomes evident that patients are approaching parents and others in a different way: showing interest, anticipation and planning, forbearance, firmness, appreciation, and understanding. Patients are no longer so easily put off by the initially negative responses of others. Patients do not rapidly withdraw or get into a fight, nor do they provoke quarrels in order to cut off the possibility of affection, disclosure, embrace, apology, and gratitude. More than one analysand has said, "I was able to let them love me."

As these modified accounts of relatedness develop, analysts gain a sense of parents, siblings, and friends beginning to be uncovered or rediscovered and of families beginning to be reunited. Some analysands even seem to move emotionally into their family's control center while feeling at the same time that they can also let themselves be cared-for children once again or, as far as they recall, children for the first time. Also, they can do all this without denying their recognition of the fragility and potential malevolence that continues to pervade the family.

To put it more exactly: Those who seem to allow themselves to become children for the first time may actually be doing it for the third time; the first time was perhaps in their unremembered prehistory and the second time certainly in earlier developments within the transference. But even the scope of prehistory may begin to change, for often these analysands begin to bring up parallel memories of previous positive behavior by these significant others and by themselves. Earlier in analysis, these memories of very early times were either just not there or were not there in sufficient quantity or distinctness to be used to question analytically the repetitively one-sided portrayal of others. In part the analysands are now viewing past interactions in a new light and in a more rounded way; these changes in perspective should qualify as another form of recovery of the past.

Thus, as termination approaches, the life history is sometimes revised radically. Voids are filled in, stormy weather is replaced by partly sunny, and the temperature rises from subfreezing, progressing at least to the point where the ice can begin to thaw. It feels like spring (rebirth, adolescence, first love) is in the air. From the standpoint of benevolent interest, analysts can say that, in these instances, the analysands are now being benevolent enough to others to allow or even encourage them to be benevolent in return; at least these others let up on their malevolent interest, which, in the patients' subjective experience, is felt to be no small gain in benevolence. Another analysand put it this way: "I see now that if I give more, I get more," and he made it clear that he was not talking about a trade-off of gratifications so much as a generally expanded sense of pleasure possibilities in reciprocal enhancement of selves.

We may say that the analysands are helping others to feel better and do better and to feel better about doing better. And it will all have been made possible in the forge of the analysis of transference; that is where all these changes must be hammered out in whatever form is possible, that form not necessarily being the one that characterizes the restoration of relationships with others. I emphasize the greater rapidity of change in many of these cases as termination approaches, but I do not imply that changes of this sort are absent until then in any analysis that is progressing satisfactorily.

THE ROOTS OF BENEVOLENT SELF INTEREST IN THE DEPRESSIVE POSITION

I turn now to the last part of my discussion of benevolent self interest: its foundations in the depressive position as described in Kleinian psychoanalysis (M. Klein, 1964; see also Segal, 1964). At this point, the plot thickens; the benevolence is seen to be rooted in conflicts of its own.

We must picture young children as possessed by frightening and remorse-inducing destructive fantasies and unable to differentiate these from conventional reality on the basis of well-developed reality testing and consistently mature feedback from the environment. On this account, children need urgently to keep making reparation for their destructiveness; reparation must be made perhaps especially in relation to the mother, although it can certainly include many others as well. This reparative urgency is not simply a phase of early childhood; rather, it enters into our finest adult achievements in human relations and into all our cultural attainments. Further, if it is granted that the establishment of certain defensive strategies is a necessary part of civilized life, then it can be understood that these reparative needs also foster the development of appropriate defenses.

When reparativeness is well integrated into a person's character, he or she derives a sense of goodness from it. The core of the goodness, however, seems to derive not from that development alone; to a significant extent, it derives from incorporated good parenting and the child's pleased and pleasing responsiveness to it. Together, these reparative and identificatory elements provide an antidote to the poisons of greed, ingratitude, and apprehensiveness that otherwise have pervaded these subjects from childhood on.

I have already mentioned that, frequently, analysts see in their analysands a bitter struggle against allowing this goodness any play in their relationships. They see this in the transference especially. Analysands cling to hatefulness and mistrust (characterized in fundamental respects as the paranoid-schizoid position in Kleinian thought). They insist that it is only realistic to limit themselves to guardedness and coldly calculated trade-offs. They rationalize greed, exploitativeness, and ingratitude, anticipating that if they depart from this policy they will become slavish, more victimized than before, and perhaps even melancholically depressed. Fearing that they are sheep, they put on wolf's clothing. Later on, however, as they progress in analysis, they may begin to change their lines and say of others, in the words of one analysand, "They want to be friends and now I let them; I let them come along with me in my feeling, and I don't try to make them be one way or another. It's better for all of us." Another analysand said something similar: "I feel more responsible and less guilty. Before, I felt like a kid. Now Henry makes me feel good because of the way I make him feel. I don't shut it down like I used to because I felt like it was too much for me. And I love it."

It is, however, not only the Kleinians who are so concerned with the internal world. It is just that they have their own rich and useful way of conceptualizing it. Ego-psychological analysts have not lost sight of that world. In this regard I refer to Heinz Hartmann's (1956) emphasis on the testing of inner reality. Hartmann was trying to develop an adequate concept of reality testing from an ego-psychological point of view. He argued that an essential part of ego-oriented analytic work lies in enhancing reality testing in its inner-directed as well as its outer-directed aspects. In the context of my discussion, one of the fruits of the testing of inner reality is the recognition that that reality contains reparative goodness and that it is crippling or impoverishing either to deny that goodness expression or to avoid finding it in others, despite manifest appearances, assuming that it is there to be found.

Also, the testing of inner reality makes it plain that, in addition to reparativeness, patients have established powerful identifications with the parents and parent surrogates as their more or less idealized *caretakers* during early childhood. Having been building blocks of the personality, these identifications cannot be denied expression except at very great personal expense. During analysis, it may well be that, first, the transference must be opened up to benevolence and the correlated recovery of relevant but hitherto repressed memories from early childhood of the "good" side of the self and the selves of others; only then will it be possible for positive infantile identifications to be recognized, tolerated, expressed, and integrated.

No longer defending rigidly against these aspects of inner reality entails acting on them without great ambivalence and continuing to do so even when the returns are far from what might be wished for. Benevolence, as we know, is not always rewarded, as terminating analysands repeatedly discover or rediscover. Nevertheless, in many cases, to the extent that other conflictual positions have been worked through and other aspects of self interest have been liberated, it will have become clear to analysands that discriminating reparativeness and integration of feared identifications entail no great danger of being "taken over" by slavishness, exaggerated and self-injurious altruism, pure malevolence, or deep depression. Thus analysands are ready to make those second efforts when first benevolent actions are rejected or fall flat; often the second or perhaps even the third effort brings the desired result. Sustained reality testing of other selves finds the goodness, such as it is, that is available.

Progressively, it becomes established that self interest requires a person to take a benevolent interest in both the self-interest and the self interest of others, to empathize with them, enjoy them, respect them, and protect them, and to show them whatever measure of interest and gratitude is their due rather than showing only frustration, envy, and defensive insecurity. In some instances, however, it can and does become clear that in spite of all of a person's best efforts with important others (spouses, parents, old friends), the cost of keeping a relationship nondestructive is too high. When the entire effort seems at last to be futile, the best course to follow will be to limit that relationship drastically or end it.

As termination approaches, the changes I have just been describing become particularly conspicuous in the transference. Analysands may become more and more reliable collaborators and even on occasion good supervisors—that is, participants who do not regress when the analyst seems not to have acted well. Instead, such analysands tend to find a way that is neither obscure nor self-injurious to let the analyst know what is disturbing the analytic work at one moment or another. Also, as I mentioned, terminating analysands may show a stable and relatively relaxed interest in being in analysis and may take a deep interest in it. They may act appreciatively, gratefully, or excitedly, with no significant anxiety or guilt and no hypersensitive concern with being pleasing—and may do all of this without foregoing further expression, if necessary, of more dismal, archaically hostile, and sexual tendencies.

Although competitive, envious, possessive, and prurient interest in the analyst keeps coming up all through the analysis, its forms usually become much more temperate, and they do not undermine the intense and benevolent collaborative spirit that usually characterizes the final phase of analysis.

This mature self interest will be evident at the very end of a beneficial analysis when progressed analysands depart, smiling or crying or both, convinced not only of a better and truer set of storylines with which to give an account of a past life, including a past analytic life, but convinced that there are better and more truth-making sets of storylines with which to organize and conduct a life among people in the future. Analysands recognize the inseparability of self-interest and self interest and the inseparability of both from interest in the self-interest and self interest of others. For the most part it will no longer seem to serve well or to be necessary to keep saying or implying of self and others, "I don't care," "I don't dare," and "It's no use trying," and also "You don't care," "You don't dare," and "You're not trying." There are other and better stories of human relatedness to construct and tell.

CHAPTER 2

Narratives of the Self

THE concept of the self can be approached in two ways: as posing a significant problem for theory construction in psychoanalysis and as a significant feature of the self psychology of everyday life. Herein I attempt to show that the terms and the results of these two approaches need not be as different as might be expected. That is, the self psychology of theory may be shown to have a good deal in common with everyday self psychology as it appears in ordinary language, such as analysts hear from the couch. In particular, both approaches may be characterized as the construction of narratives. Grossman (1982), it should be noted, took up some of these problems under the aspects of individual *fantasy* of a self and individual *theory* of a self and considered both aspects in relation to psychoanalysts' theories of the self.

THE SELF IN CONTEMPORARY ANALYTIC THOUGHT

The self has become the most popular figure in modern, innovative psychoanalytic accounts of human development and action. Usually the self is presented in these accounts as an active agency: It is the source of motivation and initiative; it is a self-starter, the originator of action; it is the first-person, singular, indicative subject, that is, the "I" of "I come," "I go," "I will," "I won't," "I know," "I wonder," and "I do declare!" This is the self that exhibits itself and hides itself and can love or loathe its own reflection.

There is still more to the usual presentation of this active self. The self appears in these accounts as the subject of experience: It constructs and participates in an experiential world; it is the self of taste and value, impression and emotional direction; it is the sexual self, the private self, the fragile self, and the bodily self.

Furthermore, this featured active self is the central organized and organizing constituent of the person considered as a structured psychological entity. In this aspect the self is the unity, the essence, the existential core, the gestalt, and the mastermind of a person's life.

In modern times this self or some selective version of it has been called by many names: the self and the self-system by Sullivan (1940), the action self by Rado (1956), the true self by Winnicott (1958), and the cohesive or nuclear self by Kohut (1977). Additionally, it is the superordinate self of Kernberg (1982) and the self as agent of the philosopher Macmurray (1957).

Concurrently, however, this self is not always and only active. Usually it has been presented as also being the object rather than the subject of action and experience. And often, as in reflexive locutions, this self appears as the object of its own action and experience, as when we speak of self-observation and self-esteem. Moreover, the self as object is not just a reactive agency or an observed agency; it is also the ensemble of self-representations. That is, it is the core content of all of a person's ideas about him- or herself, the self-concept or self-image. In this mixing together of agency and content, there is, I believe, some serious overloading of the conceptualization of self and possibly some theoretical incoherence as well (Schafer, 1976, 1978). Despite this, modern theory has it that the object-self is impinged upon by internal and external stimulation, and as a result of this impingement, both the functional self and the represented self may be fragmented, shriveled, inflated, chilled, and so forth.

Even in a brief and incomplete introductory survey of the self in contemporary analytic thought, which is all I claim for this section of this chapter, it is mandatory to mention that this self has also been presented, at least implicitly, as a force. In one respect this force is very much like an instinctual drive the aim of which is full selfhood or self-realization; in another respect this force is very much like a growth principle that vies with or replaces Freud's (1911b) pleasure principle. I believe this obviously teleological self principle or self drive is at the center of Kohut's (1977) self psychology; there it plays just as essential a part in explanations of psychopathology and cure as it does in explanations of normal development and personality organization. And I believe there can be discerned a similar teleological thrust in Erik Erikson's (1950, 1956) "ground plan" of development and its particular manifestation in a close relative of the self, namely, ego identity.

To continue establishing the terms for a narrative account of the self, I discuss, first, the self as active agent and second, the experiential self.

THE SELF AS AGENT

It is intrinsic to any psychological theory to present the human being as an agent or actor in certain essential ways and to some significant extent (Schafer, 1976, 1978, 1983). Even an extreme tabula rasa theory must include an account of how the person who has been written on by the surrounding world and by bodily processes becomes, in turn, an author of existence. Although the person may be a repetitive and largely preprogrammed author, he or she cannot be that entirely, for there is no one program to be applied to everything identically. The person must select and organize in order to construe reality in one adaptive way or another or one maladaptive way or another. Certainly, the theorist who is advancing a new set of ideas about human psychology must be viewed as a selective and organizing agent.

An author of existence is someone who constructs experience. Experience is made or fashioned; it is not encountered, discovered, or observed, except upon secondary reflection. Even the idea of experience as that which is turned up by the introspecting subject introduces an actively introspecting subject, an agent engaging in a particular set of actions, and thus someone who may introspect in different ways and for different reasons (Grossman, 1967). The introspecting subject extracts from the plenitude of potential experience what is wanted; in one case it may be sense data and in another case a self or, as is more usual, an array of selves. Introspection does not encounter ready-made material. For these reasons, developmental theories cannot avoid giving accounts of the different ways in which experience is constructed as advances take place in the child's and adult's cognitive and psychosexual functioning. Analysts refer to this as phase-specificity.

All this has to do with the self, for in their necessarily presupposing an agent, psychological theories of the self usually equate agency with selfhood. These theories then speak of what the self does. This is a permissible move in the game of theory construction. Once agency and selfhood have been equated, however, at least two new problems will have to be dealt with.

Self or Person?

The first problem is explaining what advantage is gained by saying that a self engages in actions rather than saying that a person does. Why speak of activity at one remove from the person—from him or her or, for that matter, from you or me? Might there be some misguided need on the theorist's part to add an air of detachment to the discussion, an air that spuriously gives it an appearance of scientific legitimacy or clinical objectivity? Is it demonstrably more plausible or heuristic to say that a self can be organized and organizing than to say that a person can be?

But perhaps it is not an image of scientific detachment and of clinical objectivity that is at stake; perhaps it is a culturally reinforced need to retain in our psychologies some extrapersonal source of agency and thereby some implicit passive stance toward life. Although the self that is set apart from the person is not quite a soul or a god, it may be viewed as an idea that is not quite free of the kind of disclaiming of personal agency that most of us associate with souls and divine visitations. This is so because in adequate accounts of human action the person is retained alongside the self as a necessary activating figure.

Self psychologies retain the person in this way. They tend to exempt the "I"—the first-person pronoun, singular indicative—from the self in order to make the theories work; for the "I" is the informative witness to its own self and the source of the theorist's data. Comparably, when Freud talked of psychic structure, he still found it necessary to refer to the person or subject, for the structural theory could not do all the work; it needed a psychological being to stand behind it and to contain it, and it is that being that I call the person. In "The Ego and the Id" (1923a), for example, Freud introduced the person through blatant personification of the ego (see, for example, p. 58).

Doubling and Multiplying the Self

The second problem encountered by a psychological theory that attributes agency to the self rather than to the person follows on the heels of the first. If the theorist tries to deal with the first problem by making every effort to include the "I" within the self, then he or she is required to speak of that self as being self-constructing, self-maintaining, self-containing, and self-evaluating. That is, the theory is committed both to self as mental mover and to self as mental content, or to self as subject and object simultaneously—and thus to a self that includes itself. There occurs at the least a doubling of the self. This doubling is a feature of Kohut's (1977) self psychology: The Kohutian self is not only an experiential self, it is also a center of initiative that establishes and repairs self-experience in general and self-esteem in particular. Additionally, in order to account for the profusion of diverse tendencies that characterizes each person's life, the self psychologist must sooner or later, and more or less officially, propose the existence of various subselves (for example, the grandiose self, the true and false self). Each of these subselves is supposed to be viewed as acting as a more or less independent agent even while it is still to be regarded as part of one basic self.

What is the result of this doubling and multiplying of selves? We seem to end up with a mind that is located both *within* and *outside* its boundaries and that contains numerous little minds that are *within* itself and at the same time *are* itself. This odd turn in self theory is a sign that it is in deep trouble. It has become fluid if not weakened. In contrast, it is less artificially detached and perhaps theoretically and scientifically less pretentious to think more plainly in terms of persons constructing and revising their various experiential selves of everyday life and ordinary language. Then each person is taken to be a narrator of selves rather than a non-Euclidean container of self entities. In the next section I hope to strengthen the case for a narrative approach to the self.

THE EXPERIENTIAL SELF

I begin with a puzzle and my solution to it. The puzzle is analogous to the one where you look for hidden faces in a sketch of the landscape. Here is the puzzle: How many selves and how many types of self are stated or implied in the following account? A male analysand says to his analyst: "I told my friend that whenever I catch myself exaggerating, I bombard myself with reproaches that I never tell the truth about myself, so that I end up feeling rotten inside, and even though I tell myself to cut it out, that there is more to me than that, that it is important for me to be truthful, I keep dumping on myself."

I count eight selves of five types. The first self is the analysand self talking to his analyst, and the second is the social self who had been talking to a friend. These two selves are similar but not identical in that self-organization and self-presentation are known to vary to some extent with the situation a person is in, and in many ways the analytic situation is unlike any other in life. The third self I count is the bombarding self; the fourth, the derogated self that exaggerates; and the fifth, the exaggerated self itself. The sixth is the truthful self the man aspires to be; the seventh, the conciliatory advisor of the bombarding self, the self that advises cutting out the reproaches; and the eighth is the defended self, the one with redeeming features. As to type, there is what is presented as the actual self (whether exaggerated, reproached, or defended), the ideal self (truthful), the self as place (the one with the rotten inside and the one that can be dumped on), the self as agent or subject (the teller, the bombardier, the aspirant, and the advisor), and the self as object (the self observed, evaluated, reproached, and defended).

My answer to the puzzle introduces once again my thesis that there is value in viewing the self in narrative terms. I suggest that the analysand's experiential self may be seen as a set of varied narratives that seem to be told by and about a cast of varied selves. And yet, like the dream, which has one dreamer, the entire tale is told by one narrator. Nothing here supports the common illusion that there is a single self-entity that each person has and experiences, a self-entity that is, so to speak, out there in Nature where it can be objectively observed, clinically analyzed, and then summarized and bound in a technical definition—as if Humpty Dumpty could be put back together again. Whether the material is rhymed, brief, and cute like Humpty Dumpty, or prosy, long, and difficult like most analytic material, we analysts may be said to be constantly dealing with self narratives—that is, with all the storylines that keep cropping up in clinical work—such as storylines of the empty self, the false self, the secret self, and so on.

SELF NARRATIVES

I must point out first that it is consistent with ordinary language to speak of self *narratives*. In ordinary language, we refer to ourselves or to the self of another person in a variety of ways that derive from the different vantage points that we occupy at different times and in different emotional contexts. Implicitly it is accepted that, except for certain rhetorical purposes, there is no one way of telling it "like it is." For example, in my puzzle, it comes across as perfectly acceptable to produce what appears to be one narrative that includes a self that never tells the truth and another self characterized by other and more estimable tendencies within which self is situated the self that exaggerates. It is taken for granted, it is common practice to converse on the understanding that, whether in the role of observer or observed, a person can only *tell* a self or encounter it as something *told* (Schafer, 1983). Or, as the case may be, tell more than one self. The so-called self exists in versions, only in versions, and commonly in multiple simultaneous versions.

For example, to say "I told myself to get going" is to tell a self story with two characters, an admonishing self and an admonished self, or perhaps with three characters if we include the implied author who is telling about the admonishing. To say "Deep inside him there is a grandiose self" is also to tell a story about two selves, this time about one self contained within another. And smacking one's head after making a mistake is to make a show of punishing a dumb self. This last example also makes it plain that some of these versions of self are nonverbal. That is, they are versions that are shown in expressive movements or life-style rather than told verbally; however, showing or enactment may be regarded as a form of telling, so that it is warranted to treat nonverbal manifestations as self narratives in another form of our common language, say, as charades of self narratives.

To debunk the idea, as I have been doing, that personal experience discloses a single self-entity and that theory must include that self is not to maintain that all self narratives are inherently unstable and inconsistent; nor is it to maintain that all these narratives are on the same level; nor yet that the content of these narratives concerns only chronic flux or chaos. Many of our actions may be presented noncontroversially as differentiated, integrated, and stable, and these presentations themselves may share these organized and enduring qualities. In many instances, certain self narratives are so impressively stable in organization and content and so clearly superordinate to others that it seems a matter of simple observation to say that there must be, or we must be seeing, psychic structure. There must be nuts and bolts somewhere, we feel, or good strong glue to make it possible. But in reacting thus we are, I submit, following the good old storyline of primal chaos: This chaos is the baby with only an id to start life with, the seething cauldron of instinctual drives that must be curbed and contained by psychic structures. This is not the account of a preadapted baby in a world of prepared objects or others, the account that today seems much more adequate to express the way we make sense of humanness and its development.

Furthermore, through developmental study and analytic reconstruction, we can often impressively claim to trace a progressive differentiation, integration, stabilization, and hierarchical arrangement of self stories.

At the same time, however, it must be said that in daily life we seem to have acquired an exaggerated impression of single and unvarying self-entities. This results from our unreflective attitude toward the heavy use we all make in our ordinary language of first-person singular pronouns and of such reflexive terms as self-esteem and self-control. Also, as we have self as agent available to us as a culturally or linguistically well-established narrative possibility, we gain an apparently experiential conviction that we possess a unitary and enduring self that may be experienced directly, unmediated by language and story. Locutions such as "be yourself" and "divided self" are instances of what I mean. Our common language authorizes us to think and speak in terms of single, stable self-entities. And so we want to protest that the self is not a matter of language, theory, and narrative mediation at all: The self is something we know firsthand; it is (in that marvelously vague phrase) the sense of self, a self we feel in our bones. I submit that it is correct to reply that "to feel it in your bones" is to resort to yet another good old storyline of the knowing body or the body as mind; the "sense of self" does not escape the web of narration.

In addition, from the psychoanalyst's point of view, there are still more and differently told experiential selves to take into account than my first answer to my puzzle suggested. I referred only to selves that appear to be consciously or preconsciously available at the moment. Yet unconsciously, the analysand in my puzzle may also be regarded as experiencing and presenting to the analyst *in the transference* a helpless self—that is, a child-self that cannot run its own affairs and so must appeal to a parental figure for help. Additionally, the puzzle statement may be indicating to the analyst that, unconsciously, the speaker is maintaining, among other experiential selves, a cruel and totalistic moral self, a grandiose self without blemishes, and an anal self that defiantly makes messes by lying.

I have just named only a few of the narrative retellings of the troubled analysand's self stories that the analyst may have to develop in the form of interpretations. Even what I called his actual self may have to be retold. For example, it may turn out that, for this analysand, his actual self is given very little to exaggerating; he produces no impressive analytic evidence in his sessions that he does exaggerate to any notable degree; and the significant problem may be that, fearing the envy of others, he has suppressed the presentation of a justifiably proud actual self and has substituted for it an unconvincing defensive account of an outrageous braggart. The self that is claimed to be felt in one's bones could not possibly encompass all of these experiential selves, even if it could think; neither could the "sense of self" encompass all of them.

At this point, we might ask whether, in the interest of our own mental safety, we should not avoid this milling crowd of narrated selves in which we could easily get lost or trampled. Should we not instead mingle with only a few well-behaved self categories? My answer is, first, we do have available superordinate self categories, such as the actual self and the ideal self (Schafer, 1967). Second, we should be careful not to lose sight of the proliferation of selves in each person's construction of experience lest we begin to mistake our superordinate categories for entities discovered in Nature and observable without narrative mediation. In principle, no limit can be set on the number of experiential self constructions that it may be profitable to discuss in one or another context of inquiry. It is no good saying that we already have enough concepts to do the job of interpretation, for to do so is to close the book on new approaches and the new phenomena made available by these approaches. As I have argued in connection with prisoner fantasies (1983), each proposal in this realm should be assessed on its merits.

STORYLINES

Although I have alluded to the storylines of self narratives, I have neither attempted to define them nor provided examples. In this connection, however, we must ask not only "What *is* a storyline?" We must also ask "What is the relation of storyline to self-representation, fantasy, and metaphor, the three apparently germane concepts that clearly occupy more or less established or at least familiar places in analytic thought?" It is around these questions that I have organized this next section of my argument.

First, then, what is a storyline? By "storyline" I refer to whatever it is that can be used to establish a set of guidelines and constraints for telling a story that conveys what convention would certify as having a certain general kind of content. These guidelines and constraints may be derived from one or more symbols, metaphors, similes, images, themes, or dramatic scenes, or some combination of these. This storyline serves as a tool for working out ways to retell other stories in its terms, and so it makes it possible for narrators both to generate many versions of what is conventionally regarded as the same basic story and, through reduction, to create faithful repetitions of these versions out of apparently diverse narrative materials. In one respect, for example, we have the storylines of imprisonment, rebirth, and odyssey that are commonly developed in the course of analytic work.

Take, for example, the instance of using rebirth as the storyline: The analyst may understand an analysand's references to new growth, new beginnings, glowing embers among the ashes, emergence from water, revival, and so on, as references to rebirth. In other instances, analysts develop narratives of oedipal victory and defeat and of masochism: When using the oedipal storyline, analysts may take a negative therapeutic reaction in part as a frightened retreat from oedipal victory and in part as a switch to the negative oedipal position. In contrast, when using the masochism storyline, analysts may take a negative therapeutic reaction in part as a sign of powerful reluctance to give up preferred forms of compromised and painful gratification and in part as a bid for their pain-inducing, preferably sadistic response to the dashing of their own therapeutic hopes.

With this sketchy account of storyline and its uses in analytic interpretation, let us now compare and contrast storyline with self-representation, unconscious fantasy, and metaphor. In this way I hope to bring home what I mean when I speak of the storylines of self narratives and why I give storyline the central position that I do.

Self-representation

Self-representation is a concept with a complex history and current status in psychoanalysis. As one of its most relevant features, the concept of self-representation is intended to announce the writer's assumption or realization that the self, like the object, is knowable only through more or less individual, partial, or whole versions of it. These are the versions the analyst encounters or defines in the analysand's psychic reality, and they may have little to do with conventional or putatively true versions of the self.

There is nothing mutually exclusive about the concepts of storyline and self-representation. Storyline may, however, be regarded as the more inclusive concept of the two. This is so because in practice single representations are not identified and analyzed as static and isolated mental contents. Rather, they are dealt with thematically, that is, as being significant insofar as they actually or potentially play parts in basic stories of the self. For example, the prisoner storyline includes a large array of not necessarily glaring representations of the self as deprived, confined, or punished; at the same time, it includes a large array of more or less subtle representations of others as judges, jailers, or fellow prisoners. It is the job of interpretation to show that those are the representations it will be important to define more sharply and relate to one another in a thematically unified rendition of the analysand's diverse associations. Seen in this light, storyline pulls together and develops important aspects of the conceptualization of self-representations—and object representations, too.

Unconscious Fantasy

Unconscious fantasy is another concept with a complex psychoanalytic history and current status. Arlow (1969a, 1969b), in two discussions that seem to have become the standard references in modern Freudian literature to unconscious fantasy, came close to the idea of basic storyline. He took note of the aspect of unconscious fantasies he called "plot line." However, Arlow was not concerned, as I am now, with working out a narrative approach to psychoanalytic topics. He referred to these plot lines, such as Sleeping Beauty, in a way that was conceptually subordinate to fantasy, and he mentioned plot line only in passing, in a footnote (1969b, p. 47); obviously, he was engaged in making another kind of contribution.

As I see it, we must go beyond the consideration that to speak of a fantasy is to imply that we are referring to mental content organized by a storyline; we must also note that storyline has a more obvious generative connotation than emplotted fantasy does, for it is forward-looking or anticipatory. It is on this basis that storyline can more readily encompass the many variations of basic stories we conventionally recognize in daily life and analytic work. Fairy tales, too, have many versions; indeed, they have so many that it becomes unclear at what point we may no longer speak persuasively or confidently of a specific story as an unusual version of the same basic story (Smith, 1980). The same is true of any of the storylines I mentioned earlier: Odyssey, for example, which can encompass many variations, has the generative advantage and at the same time the disadvantage of unclear outer limits. In practice, it can become unclear when the analyst is forcing the same storyline on material that is extremely varied.

Metaphor

Have I been talking of metaphor all the while, and also of metaphoric entailment (Lakoff and Johnson, 1980)? Metaphoric entailment is exemplified by the basic spatial metaphor, Good is Up. This metaphor entails that, among other attributes, intelligence, good taste, and wealth are Up, while stupidity, vulgarity, and poverty are

Down. These are entailments insofar as consistency and coherence of discourse are being aimed at, which they often are. Thus, for example, very intelligent is "highly" intelligent. These few remarks on metaphor and entailment seem to suggest that metaphor says the same as storyline.

Again, however, it seems to me that storyline is the more inclusive term of the two. As I noted earlier, metaphor may establish a storyline, and what is called unpacking a metaphor is in certain respects much like laying out the kinds of story that are entailed by the metaphor. For example, "Analysis is Hell" entails the analyst being experienced as the devil. The analyst's attention to departures from the fundamental rule are experienced as the heat being put on. Perhaps in analogy with "War is Hell," the analyst's discipline is likened to Sherman marching to the sea. The stress of the analytic process becomes punishment for past sins; and so on. It is understood that the manifestly metaphoric "Analysis is Hell" is to be used as a set of latent instructions or rules for telling certain kinds of story about being analyzed. Analysts who can work through a core conflict show that they understand the narrative regulations of metaphor; they show it by their steady sense of relevance as they listen to apparently diverse communications.

A Clinical Example

There are many ways by which children are provided with storylines for the construction of self narratives and at the same time the construction of narratives concerning others. The dynamic content involved in these transactions is well known to analysts, but because that content has not usually been conceptualized in narrative terms, I should like to present a clinical example of consequential storylines and to bring it into relation with the topic of childhood memories.

The example concerns a successful, hard-driving, loveless career woman in her forties, once-divorced, who had never managed to establish a lasting, intimate, and gratifying relationship with an adequate and assertive man. From her early years on, she had been warned emphatically by her mother never to let herself be dependent on a man. That warning may be retold as having conveyed to her a number of interrelated storylines, only some of which I shall mention here.

It was being conveyed to her that as a girl and woman she was fated to be vulnerable to helplessness in relation to any man with whom she got deeply involved; further, that the only way to develop and maintain significant strength and dignity was to cut herself off from heterosexual love. Thus, she was being told that a heterosexual female self is a weak and degraded self and, also, that to love her father was to make herself vulnerable to this fate. In the broadest terms, she was fated to live in a world of powerful, dangerous, and certainly untrustworthy men. Although this woman had by no means renounced her heterosexuality altogether, she had repetitively developed and played out many versions of this set of storylines in her relationships, and ultimately she did so in her transference to her male analyst. Penis awe and envy, fantasies of castration and of a hidden penis, and primal scene themes were woven into the grim stories of her life that she both elaborated and enacted.

Before going any further, I should make it clear that I am not suggesting that her parents and others around her were the only conveyors of storylines for her life. As I mentioned, analysts assume that the child, too, is a storyteller from the onset of subjective experience. For example, there is the storyline "I once had a penis and lost it." The usual analytic term for childhood constructions of this sort is fantasy. I have been saying that fantasy is a story and that children manufacture stories that interweave what they are told and what they imagine. There is nothing analytically new in this point except my emphasis on narration. And, of course, there is always our culture with its stock of established storylines.

To return to the analysand: An additional and congruent burden had been imposed on her explicitly during her adolescence and her early adult years by her father's admonishing her never to have children. In this way, he authorized and reinforced her own guilty, anxious, and defeated account of her childhood oedipal romance. This romance included in the usual way wishing to bear her father's child. Thus, from her father's side, too, she was being pressed to renounce her heterosexual femininity. In large part she was to construct stories of marriage as offering extremely limited prospects of satisfaction and fulfillment; there was little to hope for even in the ordinary marital form of displaced and matured forms of oedipal love. Furthermore, her father's admonishment could not fail to add weight to her own storyline that she was an unwanted and burdensome child who somehow was responsible for her parents' unhappiness and lack of fulfillment. As was to be expected, she repetitively applied and elaborated this self story in her transference. For example, the repetition began with her earliest appointments when she insisted on paying for each visit at its conclusion. It turned out that she did so in order not to be a financial burden on the analyst, and, in addition, in the terms of the storyline of dangerous dependence on men, so she would not be indebted to the analyst in any way. The storyline she was acting on was this: The only good woman is a good man; more exactly, a tough, utterly self-reliant man in drag. In effect, by paying as she did, she was saying "This is the story of my life." This enactment included some other major storylines, too, such as those touching on anality, concerns with social status, and so forth.

My intent in this summary of a few aspects of this analysis is theoretical clarification primarily rather than revision of the dynamic variables analysts customarily invoke to understand clinical phenomena. My theoretical point is that so-called self-concepts, self-images, self-representations, or more generally the so-called self may be considered to be a set of narrative strategies or storylines each person follows in trying to develop an emotionally coherent account of his or her life among people. We organize our past and present experiences narratively.

On my reading, this perspective on experience as a narrative construction is implied in Freud's final comments in his 1899 essay, "Screen Memories." There, after commenting on the "peculiarity of the childhood scenes" in that the child is portrayed as an outside observer of scenes in which he or she is an involved participant, and thereupon taking this peculiarity as "evidence that the original impression has been worked over," Freud soon concluded:

> The recognition of this fact must diminish the distinction we have drawn between screen memories and other memories derived from our childhood. It may indeed be questioned whether we have any memories at all *from* our childhood: memories *relating to* our childhood may be all that we possess. Our childhood memories show us our earliest years not as they were but as they appeared at the later periods when the memories were aroused. In these periods of arousal, the childhood memories did not, as people are accustomed to say, *emerge;* they were *formed* at that time. And a number of motives, with no concern for historical accuracy, had a part in forming them, as well as in the selection of memories themselves. (P. 322; Freud's italics)

I further believe that Freud was indicating the view, subsequently developed in ego-psychological terms by Ernst Kris (1956b) and that I am now recommending in narrative terms, that theoretical clarification of this sort *does* make a difference in practice. It encourages analysts to be aware that the life-historial material being worked with may be usefully approached as a series of tellings and retellings constructed and reconstructed over the course of development—indeed over the course of the analysis itself. In this light, what we call free association may be retold as the production of bits and pieces or even larger segments of life stories being constructed and related in the here and now of the analytic relationship.

Speaking in terms of memory, Freud said, "the raw material of memory-traces out of which it [the screen memory] was forged remains unknown to us in its original form" (1899, p. 322). I am adding that we do best to think of the raw material itself as having, to begin with, become *psychic* material in narrative form, however rudimentary the narrative. In other words, the clinical questions we put to whatever we hear from the couch are these: Of which story is this now a part or a version and for which further stories has it served or is it now serving as a storyline? With regard to the self specifically, the questions become these: Which self stories are now being hinted at or disclosed or are now in the process of being constructed or revised and for which purposes?

CHAPTER 3

Self-deception, Defense, and Narration

SELF-DECEPTION AND DEFENSE

Freudian analysts have not established the idea of self-deception as a problem with which they should be concerned. They do not focus on self-deception in their formal propositions, and they do not mention it with any frequency in their informal discussions of theoretical and clinical matters. However, some casual versions of self-deception do crop up within the clinical dialogue—for example, when the analysand says to the analyst, "My mind played tricks on me," and when the analyst says to the analysand, "You are kidding yourself."

Traditionally, analysts have taken up the phenomena presented in these self-deception locutions under the description *defense.* The idea of defense, however, is not simple and straightforward. It has been embedded in the complex, technical vocabulary that Freud introduced and dubbed metapsychology. Consequently, before considering self-deception as narration, it will be necessary to review at some length both the place of defense in traditional analytic discourse and the assumptions that secure it in this place. And this review requires a comparative discussion of defense in the mechanistic terms of Freud's metapsychology and the nonmechanistic terms of action language. In order to situate this chapter in the context of the analyst's daily practice, I refer frequently to clinical problems, practices, and ambiguities; it is in practice that the foundation has been laid for the psychoanalytic understanding of defense. At the same time, however, the complexity of the conceptual problems to be dealt with requires a measured, formalistic, unhurried mode of exposition and also some familiarity with the argument of chapter 2.

Freudian psychoanalysts take up defenses under two headings. The first is the mechanisms of defense. Included here are, for example, repression, projection, and reaction formation. The second is defense, or defensive measure, operation, or function, terms that connote a virtually limitless number of actions, any one of which may, after adequate clinical investigation, be said to be engaged in, or to have been engaged in, defensively. Included here are, for example, altruistic surrender as a defense against greed and envy, hostility as a defense against clinging dependency, and clinging dependency as a defense against hostility. The limits on what can be subsumed under this meaning of defense are set only by the analysand's inventiveness and the analyst's perceptiveness and narrative skills.

When the description *defense* is being used appropriately, the claim is made that in some sense (one analysts usually leave vague or unspecified) the subject—say, a woman—both knows and does not know that she sees, remembers, desires, believes, or feels something that she believes does or will involve her in some kind of dangerous situation, X. We cannot attribute a defense to her without attributing to her the knowledge (in some sense) that there is a danger to defend against. Further, not only is it assumed that the subject believes that because of X, she is in danger or is about to be; it is also assumed that she believes in this threat unconsciously and that she engages in defense against it unconsciously. Accordingly, she cannot be expected to explain as defensive those actions or changes of action (including reconstructions of experience) that she is aware of in this connection, such as an impulsive gesture of generosity or a flattening of emotional responsiveness. In one way or another, she will describe and explain these actions and changes of action in ways that skirt or deny their defensive employment and significance.

Freud (1926) laid out what he considered to be the four major danger situations of early childhood: loss of the love object, loss of the object's love, castration, and superego condemnation and punishment. He proposed that in psychic reality, where whatever is thought or imagined is taken by the subject to be real or actual, these dangers are the prototypes of all later dangers (even of death). That is, all later dangers in psychic reality are considered to be derivatives of these early ones and are potentially and usefully reducible to them through interpretation. In Freud's terms, when that part of the "mental apparatus" he called the ego unconsciously recognizes that one of these danger situations or one of its derivatives is developing, it responds with anxiety. Under ordinary circumstances, the ego then uses the first phase of this anxious reaction as a signal of impending or mounting danger, and it invokes one or more mechanisms of defense or defensive measures against this danger or its consequences. In one account, the ego makes this defensive move to prevent the danger situation from materializing full force (for example, it represses certain fantasies in order to curb "immoral" sexual inclinations). In another account, the ego aims to avert panicky dissolution of its own organization. The essential phases of this defensive process are passed through unconsciously, and its essential constituents operate unconsciously.

These accounts of defense require the subject to deceive herself twice (at least) as to the dangerous state of affairs, X: (1) She manages somehow not to know consciously part or all of what she knows and believes unconsciously; (2) she manages somehow not to know consciously that and how she is effecting this split between knowing and not knowing. For example, by unconsciously employing the mechanism of projection, she attributes an unacceptable hostile impulse of her own to someone else. In another defensive context, she might resort to any of the countless defensive measures that make it possible to block, divert, misrepresent, or obscure her knowledge of X. For example, by defensively exaggerated optimism, cheerfulness, and initiative, she might represent in glowing terms both herself and her experienced situation. Thereby she avoids consciously experiencing her life in the exceedingly painful terms of the profound and chronic passive-depressive mood with which she feels herself to be continuously threatened. And for this ruse to be successful, she must take the defensive measure unconsciously. To be successful, the deception must be immaculate.

I will assume from this point on that when psychoanalysts refer to defense, they are also referring (among other things) to multiple self-deceiving actions that are performed unconsciously. But when, why, and how they refer to defense requires some clarification.

DEFENSE: SOME DISTINCTIONS, QUALIFICATIONS, AND ELABORATIONS

Freud's Metapsychology

Freud (1915a), ever interested in developing a model of mind to help him explain psychoanalytic phenomena, tried in a number of ways to explain this knowing/unknowing defensive split in the subject's mental processes. (Because he did not deal with all the phenomena that today's analysts define and deal with, his discussions are not always as refined and comprehensive as would now be required. Accordingly, they are no longer as authoritative as they once were.) All of his explanations were essentially nonpsychological in that he based them on his mechanistic-energic metapsychology. That is, he based his explanations on shifts, accumulations, and expenditures of unmeasurable and qualitatively varied psychic energies (libido, aggression, attention cathexis) and on other factors that were holdovers from his earlier, neurologically conceived "Project" (Gill, 1976). Additionally, these energic explanations were, in one way or another, redundant or gratuitous (G. Klein, 1975). Subsequently, other analysts, among them Hartmann (1964), Kris (1975), Jacobson (1964), and Rapaport (1967), made noteworthy efforts to follow in Freud's metapsychological footsteps.

Notwithstanding these efforts, typical Freudian analysts in the course of their daily practice do not concern themselves with asking "How is it possible for someone simultaneously to know something and not know it?" and "How is it possible to defend and not know that one is doing so?" They just take it for granted that it is possible to effect this split unconsciously and that the split is probably present in what they hear and see in their clinical work. They do not seek a philosophically secure account of defense, and they do not justify their doing without that account. They try to pinpoint the occurrences of defensive transformations; they try to investigate their origins, their occasions, and their reasons or "determinants"; and in their own thinking perhaps, they try to sort out all the "mechanisms" involved. All this they do in order to interpret as precisely as possible the conflicts that necessitate self-deceiving actions, the compromise formations or attempted solutions that rest on self-deceiving actions, and the defense-serving characterological rigidities that must be both explained and modified for therapeutic purposes.

Wishful Thinking

Analysts distinguish between defense against X and simple wishful thinking to the effect that Y, something desirable, is the case. In simple wishful thinking (for example, in the presumably simple case of a very young child's idealization of a parent), the subject is assumed to be altogether ignorant that anything but Y could be the case. There is nothing to suggest that the subject is trying to rule out some other unconsciously known account of things (the dangerous X) owing to the intense anxiety that would be experienced should it consciously be recognized that X is, or is threatening to be, the case.

But analysts do frequently follow two other possible lines of interpretation of wishful thinking. The first is that there are complex forms of wishful thinking, as when the defense mechanism of denial is being used (for example, in a later phase of idealization, the child idealizes the parents defensively in order not to experience the insecurity that it feels upon recognizing its relative helplessness and their shortcomings). The second is that there are complex forms of ignorance, as when the subject evinces anxiety over finding things out (for example, the subject actively maintains ignorance of family secrets, an ignorance that not rarely is dispelled solely by clinical analysis of anxiety-based situational avoidances and both gaps and contradictions in remembering). Thus, in their work with adult analysands, modern analysts typically are skeptical of the idea of simple or nondefensive, conflict-free wishful thinking. In keeping with the principle that psychoanalysis is a conflict psychology, they look for defensive or self-deceiving features routinely, and usually they are not disappointed in the results (Fenichel [1941], A. Freud [1936], Schafer [1968c]).

Defense Mechanisms

With the possible exception of repression, the mechanisms of defense are not held to be inherently and exclusively designed for defense. For example, projection and introjection, which are believed to operate as malignant defense mechanisms in certain forms of psychopathology, are also presented as playing central roles in the highly adaptive process of empathy. Even though repression may never be taken to be entirely without defensive uses and consequences, it may on occasion be interpreted as being used to implement aims that are not exclusively defensive. For example, repression may help a young child bear up under conditions that otherwise would be intolerable. Later in life, this use of repression may be established by reconstructions during analysis, reconstructions according to which "forgetting" psychic wounds and their occasions seems to have been the only way to endure excruciatingly painful phases, situations, and relationships of childhood. When recounted in contexts of this sort, repression will be presented as an adaptive resource or process; the analyst then will able to anticipate with some confidence that any sudden relinquishing, relaxing, or failure of specific repressions could be traumatic or lead to traumatization. In psychic reality, the analysand appears to view these modifications of repressions in just that way and will, accordingly, approach analysis in the most gingerly or defensive manner.

It makes no sense to pigeonhole any one of the myriad activities thay may be used defensively—such as being altruistic, clinging, or hostile—as inherently and exclusively designed for defense.

Self-deception

Self-deception need not be linked to mechanistic conceptualization just because it is linked to defense. It is not necessary ever to invoke the term *mechanism* when speaking of defense. Speaking nonmechanistically, which is a linguistic option being taken by more and more analysts as they discard the model of a "mental apparatus," we can just as well put the matter in this way: In times of apparent danger, and in order to be able to function less anxiously and in a less restricted or damaging manner, the subject (not the ego) will aim to develop or restore subjective feelings of safety and confidence by employing forms and contents of thought whose nature it is to transform threatening conceptions of the current state of affairs and threatening courses of action, or both, into less threatening ones. This occurs in the case of denials, idealizations, and reaction formations. In this, the subject will be self-deceiving.

Rather than acting less anxiously, a person may, of course, act defensively in order to function less guiltily, in a less ashamed or depressed manner, or in some other less painful and restrictive fashion. These variations of affective tone and action do not alter the criteria as to what is the best way to conceptualize defensive actions.

Defense by the Analysand

Defense is, of course, defense *by* as well as defense *against.* Everything that has already been mentioned about the types and instances of defense and defense mechanisms indicates the often bewildering variety of factors the analyst must take into account. On a higher level of abstraction, defense is, mechanistically, instituted by the metapsychological "ego" or, nonmechanistically, *by* the person or agent.

Defense of the Ego

Defense is also defense *of.* The traditional Freudian analyst regards defense as defense of the ego, the adaptive "organ" or "structure" of the mind. There are many aspects of defense of the ego, and which of these aspects the analyst emphasizes depends on the specific intersystemic or intrasystemic problem he or she is placing in the foreground. Problems in the ego's relations with the id center on intersystemic boundaries; specifically, they center on protecting ego functions against the dangers of sexualization and aggressivization. The function of perceiving, for example, may be said to be excessively sexualized (invaded by the sexual drives of the id) when it is being used to implement voyeuristic aims. Similarly, remembering may be said to be excessively aggressivized (invaded by the aggressive drives of the id) when the faults and errors of others are relentlessly and remorselessly cataloged and rehearsed. Self-deception might implicitly enter this intersystemic interpretive context when, for example, although the subject defensively believes consciously that she is engaged in reading purely for scholarly purposes, the analyst is able to interpret that she is also reading sexually, perhaps mainly in order to bring herself into a sexually excited state. In another instance, she might be reading not for scholarly purposes alone, as she maintains consciously, but also and unconsciously aggressively, perhaps mainly in order to violate or destroy certain familial or general social conventions or to prepare an "overkill" critique of a hated rival.

Problems in the metapsychological ego's relations with the superego and the ego ideal center on reducing the need for self-punishment, making restitution to others, and recovering from loss of self-esteem, all seemingly in response to, or as manifestations of, the subject's painfully experiencing guilt and shame. Self-deception enters this intersystemic context when, for example, reading, ostensibly undertaken for pleasure, competition, or profit, is interpretable at least partly as an unconsciously carried out, weighty act of self-punishment or penitence (for example, as a way of forgoing certain social or erotic pleasures).

In the metapsychologically based structural theory of psychoanalysis, the ego also has organizational or intrasystemic problems of its own, and it uses defensive measures in this connection too. It may even be said to be engaged in defense against defense, as in the case of a conscious Pollyanna stance of denial that defends against projective paranoid mistrust of others. Analysts usually discuss these conflictual actions as reflecting the ego's problems both in preserving its own organization against potentially traumatic threats in the environment and in resolving the difficulties inherent in coordinating or synthesizing its multiple aims, functions, and contents. Garden-variety instances of intrasystemic problems are confronting and resolving contradictions among beliefs, values, and personal loyalties. For example, self-deception may take the form of representing oneself as being more interested in social relationships than one actually demonstrates to be the case, as when one does not, despite ample opportunity to do so, do things with other, presumably interesting or enjoyable people.

Complete analysis of significant clinical phenomena will include some reference to all the intersystemic and intrasystemic problems that have just been reviewed. Analysts speak in this regard of multiple function (Waelder, 1930) and compromise formation (Freud, 1899). Typically and repeatedly, they focus their attention on a number of such problems until they are satisfied that they have developed and worked through with the analysand the needed insights.

To emphasize that defense is defense *of* is, in part, to point again to the adaptive aspect of self-deceiving actions. However, it must be borne in mind in this connection that what an analysand may be defending adaptively might not conform to any conventional use of the term *adaptive.* For example, in a seemingly unadaptive way, the analysand might be protecting a rosy view of a terrible occupational situation; only after analysis will the analyst be able to understand that rosy view in its adaptive aspect (for example, it makes it possible for the analysand to go on working). Analysts do not use adaptation to mean conventional adjustment or conformity (Hartmann, 1953). They mean something closer to socialized survival values and the means-end relations these values imply and are used to support, any or all of which may be highly individualistic or conventionally disapproved.

Goals of Psychoanalytic Interpretation

Analysts assume that the more desperate the conditions under which defensive action is initiated, the more rigidly will the defenses be deployed. In less extreme circumstances, when defenses are being less rigidly maintained because they are less desperately resorted to, they can sometimes be modified by the subject herself. For example, in one context, the subject might notice that she is rationalizing her envy of a strong rival by thinking she is merely expressing a sense of decorum and then stop being defensive in that way. In another context, she might calm down after being upset and realize that it was because her pride had been hurt that she had been trying so hard and even arbitrarily to find fault with others in order to humiliate them and thereby, she hoped, restore her own self-esteem; whereupon she might reestablish with increased stability her usual more tolerant and less self-deceiving outlook.

Among its many potential accomplishments, psychoanalytic interpretation prepares or assists the analysand to be independently and regularly self-correcting or less self-deceiving. Through interpretation, it reduces the desperateness of the prototypic danger situations of childhood in terms of which, unconsciously, the analysand has continued to construct experience. It also familiarizes the analysand with her characteristic, hitherto unconsciously employed repertoire of defensive activities and their histories and fantasy content. It does so in order to help her recognize signs that she feels endangered and is already beginning to respond defensively in a way that now she mostly does not want. And it reduces the multiple, more or less irrational aims and emotional positions that have, over time, come to be served by these defensive activities, a development that has made them seem even more indispensable than they had seemed initially. (It does so, for example, when the need to be pleasing through defensive reaction formation against hostility has come to serve effectively other, maladaptively restrictive functions, such as gaining attention and sympathy by presenting oneself and conducting one's affairs in an overly pliable or "spineless" manner.)

SELF-DECEPTION AND NARRATION

In defense, the subject restricts what can be represented and experienced consciously, thereby excluding X, the threatening content, from her idea of . . . of what? Her self? Her personality? Her ego? Her being? Her consciousness? There is no single, correct, and exclusive answer to the question. Each of the answers I suggested is permissible, each covers a somewhat different range of phenomena, and each has had its uses within one or another philosophical, literary, or psychological framework of assumptions and concepts.

In the preceding sections of this chapter I have tried to establish the legitimacy of claiming that, for psychoanalytic purposes, what conventionally could be presented as one and the same action may be described as defense, wish fulfillment, punishment, and adaptation. The description to be used should depend on the analytic observer's aims and on the context of method and attribution of significance that has been established by, or in keeping with, these aims. For example, consider the repression that appears to have enabled the subject to endure terrible events of childhood. It might be said, *within a social-developmental context,* that that repression had been an essential means of adaptation at that time and under those circumstances. Then repression is presented not as a defense merely but as a process of adaptation as well. In contrast, *in a clinical context,* later on, when this victim's suitability for psychoanalytic treatment is being assessed, the analyst wants to emphasize the current, pathological rigidity and scope of the defensive repression that once had had that psychological survival value. Then the analyst may present that repression primarily as an extremely costly and forbidding defense.

I am applying the familiar proposition that no single designation of an action may be presented as final, definitive, exclusive, or conclusive. Narrative priority may be given to a particular description of an action only after carefully spelling out a context of aims, conventions, circumstances, and practices, or at least when there is ample reason to assume that the listener or reader knows this context very well. The description to be given of an action depends on the kind of account one wants to give of it. No action can be presented intelligibly or usefully if it is not in the context of an implicit or explicit narrative. The narrative context helps readers understand the description being employed at the same time as the description contributes to the further development and persuasiveness of that narrative account. Part-whole interactions of this sort seem to be intrinsic to informative or clarifying communication.

It may be argued that it is incoherent to refer to "*an* action" or "the same action" under different descriptions, for different descriptions present different actions. "The same action" loses all meaning or all power to constrain or verify what is being said. Yet it can be asserted that this argument does not take into account the fact that, in order to communicate at all, we abide provisionally by conventions with regard to sameness or identity. Convention provides minimal accounts of actions—for example, kissing or hitting. A minimal account makes possible the beginning of an answer to the question "Just what are we talking about?" It is only a beginning in that the minimal account does not provide an explicit and developed context in which to consider the action in any useful way. Contexts for action descriptions are established by an emphasis on motivation, pragmatic consequences, ethical import, historical circumstance, or whatever else would relate minimal descriptions to our interests. In turn, the significance of each such context derives from still larger contexts; depending on what kind of inquiry is being undertaken, those larger contexts might or might not have to be specified. Closure on contexts is endlessly deferrable.

I am not claiming that the minimal account is not conceived narratively itself, for even an extremely terse description of an action may be viewed as being the expression of a choice that is in accord with an implicit narrative design. Nevertheless, in each instance of minimal description we are left to ask: What are we to see it as and why? The regulative and generative influences of the description are minimal. We are left with many degrees of freedom—even if, under the prevailing conditions, not with total freedom. There are constraints, even though it is characteristic of psychoanalytic and some kinds of interpretation in the humanities to show that these constraints are far fewer than the conventional narrator would feel comfortable with. For example, some kissing may be retold as an attack that is close to hitting and some hitting may be retold as a sadistic form of loving that is close to kissing.

Briefly, then, I am claiming that—provisionally and always open to critical review and revision—we may speak of different descriptions of the same action, even though we can work only with the different versions of that action and in principle can never get to *the* action itself. (This is true except for certain conventionally acceptable minimal descriptions whose narrativity it is not usually to the point to consider.)

Returning now to defense: No instance of action is, therefore, to be limited in presentation only to being (1) a defense—or self-deceiving. In principle, it is always possible, and it may be more to the point, to present it also as: (2) one or more wish fulfillments, (3) one or more adaptations, (4) one or more punishments, (5) any combination or compromise of the four sets of possibilities, (6) any other description of these possibilities, combinations, or compromises, and (7) any other description of defense or self-deceiving action (for example, in some circumstances defensive reaction formation can also be presented as an instance of defensive identification).

Also, for certain narrative purposes, we might give an account of an action that contains less than we could include. For example, the accounts that analysts give in their writings are not always as complex as they could be, for an action might be considered merely under the description of a specific defense or a specific wish. That many of Freud's examples of wish fulfillment in dreams are of this optionally simplified sort may be inferred readily from the contrast between them and the examples of the complex approach to dreams he used in his work with Dora (1905a), work in which he was engaged at about the same time he wrote his dream book (1900). Simple in one narrative context, he was complex in another; indeed, there is a considerable range of complexity within the dream book itself. A similar range of complexity characterizes the interventions and the written examples of any adequate clinical analyst.

Because so much describing, relating, and explaining depends on the kind of account of action that is desired, the topic of defense and, with it, self-deception may be placed squarely in the interesting and evocative realm of narration. In this narrational realm, questions are asked that differ from those asked in Freud's mechanistic and objectivist metapsychological realm. Now, usually implicitly, it is asked: What kind of story do I as observer want to tell? What kind of story am I now committed to tell (assuming I concurrently have made the commitment to provide a consistent and coherent account) by my beginning to organize a clinical or theoretical report around a specific description, that is, as my implied storyline? For example, in using the description of *defense,* a warlike storyline is established, and in the interest of narrative consistency and coherence the writer makes a commitment to follow that storyline. Such terms as *abwehr, warding off, attack, infiltration, breakthrough, collapse, strengthening,* and *rebuilding* may be used: terms that have figured prominently in conventional psychoanalytic discussions of defense, and all of which may be said to be entailed and regulated by commitment to the same bellicose storyline. Elsewhere (see, for example, chapter 14), I have tried to show that the term *resistance* (a close relative of defense) establishes a commitment to the same adversarial storyline and that it may misrepresent or limit the technically desirable impartial and affirmative aspects of psychoanalytic practice.

I have already pointed out in chapter 2 that "storyline" is to be favored over "metaphor" and over unpacking metaphor or working out metaphoric entailments because, in my estimate, it has more obvious generative and regulatory connotations. Storyline suggests that there are a number of versions of the story that may be actualized, provided only that the storyteller observes enough of the conventional constraints (follows the "line"). These conventional constraints are not ordinarily extremely limiting, but there is usually a point beyond which attentive readers or listeners will begin to question whether a different story is now being told; for example, a consistent emphasis on experiences of relaxed pleasure in the context of giving an account of defense will be thought to be changing the story unless it is made clear that and how that relaxed pleasure is necessary to the story of defense.

Also, to favor "storyline" entails no neglect or exclusion of metaphor. Along with theme, image, dramatic scene, and expressive movement, metaphor is now to be regarded as one of the ways of introducing a storyline, one that is undeveloped or only implied. Unpacking a metaphor or working out its entailments should be regarded as making explicit its implications and defining its narrative consequences.

Consequently, self-deception may be considered a description that derives from and invites the further development of two storylines combined: *the self* and *deception.* Next I give an account of the problems raised by, and the generative potential and regulative effects of, this combination of storylines.

The Self Storyline

Let us consider the issues first from the side of the *self* storyline. Upon taking self-deception to be laying down the storyline of the self lying to itself, we encounter the same problems that reside in those accounts in which the mechanistic ego, when defending itself, seems to be deceiving itself and, equally odd in Freud's (1926) account, to be doing so after signaling to itself with blips of anxiety that defense (deception) is in order. Freud noted that the ego's deception is practiced unconsciously. As he developed his ideas, he seemed to argue that this unconscious aspect of the deception is both a necessary inference from analytic "data" (analysands give no sign of knowing they are defending) and a commonsense requirement (a deception cannot succeed if it is known to be a deception). In his studies of defense Freud proposed that he seemed to have encountered another kind of unconscious, that is, an unconscious that had *not* been repressed (1923a). With this proposition, he tried to avoid that infinite regress in explanation according to which there would have to be defenses against defenses against defenses ad infinitum. But in introducing another kind of unconscious into his model, in saying that one unconscious set of mental operations may deceive another such set, Freud was establishing another mind within the metapsychological mental apparatus. Thus, at least in this respect, a multiple-ego narrative took the place of the story of the ego's deceiving itself.

A version of this second mind or ego appears in the storyline of *self*-deception. Not that we are obliged to tell the odd and necessarily unconvincing story in which the self deceives itself; rather, we are to tell the story of one self in the act of deceiving another self. Self-deception is an event in a narrative that features multiple selves. In this multiple-self narrative, we are to present each self as able to act autonomously and at least one of these selves as able to act secretively. A story of this sort can be told in much the same way as a story of one person deceiving another. Thus, the account "I was kidding myself" differs little from "He was kidding me." The storyline's generative and regulating roles are the same. Whether the story will feature one or more persons should not affect its development. All that is needed is a pair of selves, belonging either to one person or two, each self having its own capabilities, initiatives, and reasons. If one person may have or does have at least two selves, the story of self-deception may continue unhampered. It is just that another kind of mind—actually multiple-mind—must be featured in this story. And it is not thrown into question that only one person is the subject of this story; the philosophical problem of how the identity of one person is established is not raised (nor, of course, is it settled).

As I argued earlier, there are many narratives of self, and many selves have been named to fit the tales in which they are to figure. There is the true self, false self, cohesive self, fragmented self, public self, secret self, sexual self, ideal self, and so on. There are also implicit multiple selves in the notions of self-control, self-love, self-hatred, self-esteem, and so on (Schafer, 1978). Consider, for example, the multiple selves (including the self of the speaker) in these locutions: "I won that fight with myself"; "My feelings washed over me like a giant wave"; "I can't forgive myself for showing myself off so."

Are we bound to reject multiple-self narratives? Is there any compelling reason to disallow psychological narratives featuring a proliferation of selves? The criterion of parsimony is no help in setting limits on multiple-self narratives or in excluding them altogether, for that criterion is always more treacherous to apply than seems at first to be the case. Simply to posit fewer selves or just one self is not sufficient to establish parsimony, as it may be necessary then to make many additional assumptions in order to accommodate the smaller cast of characters. Was Freud really being parsimonious when, to locate anxiety in the ego, he invoked the problematic idea of the ego's sending itself anxiety signals?

To the objection that multiple-self narratives introduce something like a demonological model to explain human action, it may be countered that at present there seems to be no other satisfactory way to provide for the following: (1) the accounts of multiple personality in which one personality observes another but not vice versa; (2) the accounts of posthypnotic suggestion, in which the subject acts as if he or she were maintaining a second, distinct self that independently complies with the hypnotist's suggestions; (3) the accounts of the subjective experience of introjects, that is, figures that seem to be in the subject's "inner world" and to observe, judge, and otherwise influence him or her (for example, a consciously experienced maternal figure that seems to operate as an independent persecutory or reassuring presence); (4) the accounts of splitting, said to be particularly prominent in so-called borderline personalities, according to which there are distinct and totalistic "good" and "bad" selves organized around positive and negative affects and with corresponding "good" and "bad" others or "objects" (Kernberg, 1975) and, in Kohut's (1977) self-psychological theory, apparently autonomous subselves, such as the "grandiose self." We do not yet have a way to discuss these accounts that avoids altogether the use of manifest and latent multiple-self narratives. On this basis, we continue to develop multiple-self stories, like it or not. I am proposing that it is useful to consider these "phenomena" under the description of complex narratives and, further, that we should not ignore the often cumbersome consequences of using the multiple-self storyline (Thalberg, 1977).

Matters are not easier when considering the alternative storyline of a single self. Some problems arise out of a misunderstanding. Typically, those analysts who insist that there is *only* a single self, like those who employ accounts of multiple selves, do not recognize that they are making a narrative choice. Consequently, their accounts of a self that is simply *found* have a naïvely empirical tone. They seem to reify *the* self as a concrete mental entity. According to this sort of monistic view, there can be only one self (or mind, or ego, and so on) per person. Only one is demonstrable, and only one exists. The self is not a construction made by observers—that is, one way of telling about mental and behavioral actions; it is an entity in Nature that may be observed directly by the objective or the "empathic" observer, who may be the subject whose self it is. This a priori account is holistic. It establishes a narrative of basic mental unity. Typically, that narrative features the progressive differentiation and integration (except under pathological circumstances) of that one entity and also its regressive fragmentation and fluidity under conditions of stress. Additionally, this entity is presented as retaining its identity over time even though every one of its elements may change, and it is supposedly capable of regaining its mature identity after it has lost it through stress-induced regression.

In the history of the psychological study of human beings, the possibilities and the advantages of this holistic story have been developed extensively (Werner and Kaplan, 1963). It has probably been the dominant narrative in psychology. The story is very well documented. Because the story is so familiar, we are not ordinarily prepared to recognize it as a story. We do not automatically view it as just one way of telling about personality development and action. Other ways of telling about development and action, such as the multiple-self way, are brushed aside. The phrase "I am not myself today" or "be yourself" is regarded merely as a manner of speaking. Either the accounts of multiple personality, posthypnotic suggestion, and so on, are ignored, or tortuous monistic versions of them must be developed in order to remain consistent theoretically.

In my own case (1976, 1978, 1983), before I recognized the consequences of the view that we are always and only dealing with implicit or explicit narrative presentations of reality and never with reality pure and simple, I deplored the (often implicit) proliferation of selves. I saw that proliferation not only as theoretically cumbersome; I saw it also as an instance of defensively disclaimed action and of importing into theory the phenomenon that that theory intends to explain. I favored the monistic narrative.

I continue to favor the monistic narrative and for much the same reasons. However, the storyline I favor is not that of one self or one mind, but of *one person* as agent. And I propose that that person be viewed as a narrator, that is, as someone who, among other noteworthy actions, narrates selves. One person narrates numerous selves both in order to develop desirable (not necessarily "happy" but at least defensively secure) versions of his or her actions and the actions of others and to act in ways that conform to those selves. In this account, there is no self that does anything. Instead, there is one person telling stories about single selves, multiple selves, fragments of selves, and selves of different sorts, including *deceiving* and *deceived selves*. The narrator may, of course, attribute selves or self-states of these sorts to others, too, and others may (and do) reciprocate.

This single-person program seems to have an important heuristic advantage over the multiple-self program. The multiple-self narrative always allows the narrator-theorist to slip by some important theoretical problems by introducing one more self into the cast of characters; this is what instinct theorists used to do when they added to their lists of instincts new ones to deal with difficult phenomena. These ad hoc improvisations offer little prospect of sustained dialogue about self-psychological "phenomena." Additionally, a simple multiple-self choice introduces all the fruitless problems of arranging those selves that do get official recognition into some kind of stable, hierarchically organized structure. This structure is bound to be controlled or regulated by a super-self once due recognition is extended to commonly accepted accounts of large-scale coherence and consistency of functioning. In this way, the concretized monistic self returns through the back door, and we witness a failure of the entire enterprise.

To summarize, self-deception is but one instance of a set of problematic ideas that are introduced by self theories or grand self narratives. It is advantageous to regard self-deception as a story that people tell in order to present themselves or others as their own dupes or in order to make a psychoanalytic interpretation. In this story, the person is constituted by more than one self. The self-deception story is consistent with numerous other conventional multiple-self stories that are always being told by parents, friends, teachers, poets, philosophers, psychologists, analysts, and so on. By common consent, it is a story that "works": It communicates effectively and it helps construct experience. But it is only a version.

For those who do not accept this multiple-self version, the critical problem is not that of establishing one definitive, presumably nonnarrative account of what self-deception *is*. Rather, what should be examined are the origins, the occasions, the reasons, and the consequences of the variety of self narratives that may be rendered in connection with the study of what seem to be knowing/unknowing splits and corresponding reports of self experience. On this basis analysts consider the cast of self characters in the accounts people give of action as similar to the cast of characters in a dream; upon analysis this cast of dream characters gets to be retold as distributed versions of self: the self in desire, the self sitting in judgment, the self as child, the self as opposite gender, and so on.

The Deception Storyline

Let us take the following instance as an example around which to organize an examination of the storyline of deception. By all conventional standards, S.M., a teacher, derives pleasure from regularly treating his students cruelly; that is, he is a sadistic teacher. He, however, thinks that he treats his students fairly, dispassionately, professionally, and he is pained to think that he might ever have to do something in his role as teacher that any of his students might feel or any witness in the classroom might think to be cruel. His pleasure, he maintains, is in being a dedicated teacher. Surely, an ordinary observer would be inclined to say, S.M. is deceiving himself. Isn't the discrepancy of accounts as plain as can be? How can S.M. not see it?

The attribution of self-deception is, however, based on a number of unstated assumptions, interpretations, and evidential claims. Far from this deception being an unmediated perception by an "objective" observer of what S.M. is "really" doing, it is a rather elaborate construction.

The construction begins with the assumption that there is (or certainly there could readily be established) a firm consensus of informed and competent observers to the effect that S.M. is sadistic to his students. It is assumed that there exists a conventional description of that sort of conduct on the part of a teacher that fits S.M.'s conduct to a *t;* the consequence of this consensual validation is that a sadistic account is true or adequate while any other is false or inadequate. To tell it otherwise would violate our common sense of social coherence and ordinary reality. The burden of proof is not ours.

The construction continues with the assumption that S.M. knows the conventional account or is capable of using it appropriately in other situations, and does use it so, perhaps with reference to the actions of other teachers or other authority figures or even his own actions outside the classroom. It is also assumed that S.M. knows unconsciously that the sadistic account does fit his conduct in the classroom and that he will not admit this knowledge consciously to himself. We will make these assumptions if we are in possession of enough "evidence" of the following sort (in addition to S.M.'s inconsistency or incoherence in his use of "sadistic"). To the least suggestion that he is being sadistic to his students he overreacts: He protests his benevolent intentions more frequently, indignantly, anxiously, or desperately than would be expected. Also, he is impervious to rational confrontations by others that his conduct does fit a conventional description that he does accept in other contexts. Further, he behaves in a conspicuously frustrated or otherwise troubled manner when circumstance prevents his continuing to act cruelly to his students and derive pleasure from it. He exaggerates, minimizes, forgets, jumps to conclusions, contradicts himself, and so on, in ways that are not typical of him when he gives accounts of the relevant situations and actions. A psychoanalytic examination of his life history, fantasies, dreams, conduct in love, and so forth, strongly supports "sadistic" as the description that best fits his personality picture. These are the kinds of "evidence" psychoanalysts hope to obtain in order to justify attributing noteworthy sadism to some people and attributing correlated defensive measures (and self-deceptions) to them. In S.M.'s case, analysts can then say that he has a stake in not seeing himself as he is (that is, as sadistic) and latently believes himself to be; he is bound to be fooling himself.

We cannot fail to notice how obtaining this warrant and making this attribution depends entirely on the observer's adhering to conventions of description, interpretation, contextualization, and reduction of one account to the terms of another. Specifically, there are judgments to be made about types and degrees of inconsistency, competence, overreacting, imperviousness, frustration, and so on. There are other judgments to be made as to which accounts adequately convey a life history and personality make-up and additional judgments as to whether specific accounts of events fit these general ones and how well they do so relative to alternative psychoanalytic accounts. The evidence does not consist of simple, narratively unmediated, objective facts. What is called the evidence is, like all other evidence, theory-laden. It is constructed in that uncertain area between what is found and what is created, and it is that "evidence" that is used to support reasoning which, unreflectively, is taken to be simply logical, factual, and conclusive.

Two more sweeping assumptions go into the construction of the deception story: First, individuals are best regarded as being naturally and primarily truth-seekers; second, they engage in truth-seeking primarily consciously. These, however, were not Freud's (1911b) assumptions. He assumed that gratification (the pleasure principle) is natural and primary, while truth-seeking (the reality principle) not only is secondary but is difficult to attain and sustain and is clearly a compromise with harsh necessity; it is a compromise that is entered into in order to guarantee as much gratification as is compatible with security or, in extreme cases, survival. Freud (1915a) further assumed that unconscious mental processes—fluid, concrete, illogical, wishful, timeless, contradictory—are primary, while conscious rational mental processes not only are secondary but normally are merely the fragmentary result of selective endorsement and attention. Certainly, conscious mental processes are not in themselves the best guides for making sense of the decisive features of anyone's cognitive and emotional development and present functioning. Thus, for Freud the problem was not to explain social and personal incoherence; it was to explain the attainment of socialized, objective, and coherent mental processes. In his account, we start out with mercurial wishful thinking; we never give it up altogether; we work out ingenious compromises, including especially those that provide for us, in the derivative form of social conformity and consensus, everything that we wished for so urgently as children, such as a secure and gratifying place in a secure and gratifying family.

For Freud, then, deception was not the preferred storyline of personal development and everyday functioning. His story goes from the nonveridical unconscious id to the rational, realistic conscious ego. In contrast, the story of self-deception seems to be the story of a rational, realistic conscious ego that is somehow losing its supremacy.

Those who tell the deception story ignore the availability of more than one convention to describe or explain a situation or course of action. They also ignore the way some available conventions contradict others, rather like those proverbs that seem to work well enough when taken singly but begin to look untrustworthy when paired with other well-working proverbs that more or less contradict them. Additionally, a sweeping consensus in human affairs is pretty hard to come by unless the issue is so impersonal and conventionalized that it is irrelevant, trivial, and uninteresting. Further still, conventions change over time, and what we regard as desirable social change often stems from gross breaks with convention. We cannot depend uncritically on convention and consensual validation in making claims about what is real or true.

Prepared with these qualifications, let us return now to S.M. If we say he is acting cruelly to his students in order to derive pleasure from doing so, we are initiating the construction of a story that depends on many other stories, among which is the story that there is an overwhelming coalition of real and safely imagined witnesses who would give a sadistic and self-deceiving account of S.M.'s conduct. This coalition would agree on the judgment that S.M.'s conduct meets enough of the criteria of sadistic action and self-deceiving action to leave little room for doubt. Further, the coalition would reject both the idea that S.M. is unmotivatedly and incompetently missing the point and the idea that he is secure in another conventional account, such as that he is trying to bring out the best in his students by holding up and strictly enforcing high standards of achievement and decorum, not being put off by their juvenile and manipulative howls and protests, and so on. They refuse to acknowledge that they might be making value judgments in the realm of legitimate and competing educational psychologies and philosophies. But would they be arguing fact or preferred storylines?

The answer I propose here is that it is the storylines that establish the facts of the case, which of these facts are to be taken as significant (for example, as evidence of sadism), and how these facts are to be situated in an account of the situations and actions in question. Like the self, deception can be taken as a storyline, and it is useful to do so. And self-deception can be taken to be a complex and coordinated elaboration of two storylines. The case of S.M. could be told differently; it often is. Owing to ambiguities that are encountered all along the line, it is not easy, though it is not impossible, to discredit alternative, nonsadistic versions of the case of S.M.

I am not proposing that any account is as acceptable as any other. Rather, I am proposing this—when we speak of true and false accounts of actions, we are positioning ourselves in a matrix of narratives that are always open to examination as to their precritical assumptions and values and as to their usefulness in one or another project. Some versions of S.M.'s conduct, such as that he is totally permissive, would depart so far from the conventions and uses of social or clinical discourse that they would founder from the start, except perhaps if they were being developed with obvious irony. Of them we say that they are false, inadequate, or illogical in any comprehensible discourse. Some accounts will be judged to be better or closer to the truth than others on the basis that they show a higher degree of consistency, coherence, comprehensiveness, and common sense than the others. But in the complex instances that concern us the most, we cannot count on incontestable proofs of superiority and we resort to, or submit to, rhetorical, ethical, and esthetic persuasiveness to decide what is better or best. Such, at any rate, is the account being used here of the way narratives of action are constructed and used.

SUMMARY AND CONCLUSIONS

Analysts deal intensively with defense in their clinical work. As defense implies self-deceiving actions, analysts have a lot to say about the when, the why, and the various forms and transformations of these actions. However, none of this gives them a basis outside a narrative project to say anything in response to the question of how it is possible in the first place for anyone to be self-deceiving. Self-deception itself is a description of action that inaugurates an explicit or implicit narrative; it lays down a complex storyline of multiple selves interacting. Like self-deception, defense, too, can be taken to lay down a storyline. Thus, it is open to examination as a term that both conforms to a version of mental development and functioning and prescribes certain ways of maintaining and extending that version. I presented the contrasting versions of defense in Freud's mechanistic metapsychology and my action language. I did so to support my thesis that it can be illuminating to approach self-deception in the terms of narration, that is, as a matter of choosing a storyline and observing such constraints as it exercises on narrators working within the conventions of how these deceptions are to be presented.

PART TWO

NARRATING GENDER

CHAPTER 4

Problems in Freud's Psychology of Women

PROLOGUE—1991

Except for a few minor changes, I have left chapter 4 in its original 1974 state. The reader who has been attending to my major argument for a narrational perspective on psychoanalytic theory and practice in part 1 (and also in parts 3 and 4) will readily see how the lexicon of narration can be introduced at key points in the argument. In contrast, I have revised chapter 5, on impotence and frigidity (originally written in 1978), so that it is more in keeping with my current narrative perspective. Chapter 5 should help the reader estimate the difference that my perspective makes in the flow and impact of my discussions of gender. Narrational considerations are more in the foreground of chapters 6, 7, and 8.

Psychoanalytic ego psychology has established as its proper subject of study the whole person developing and living in a complex world. No longer is psychoanalysis a theory simply of instinct-ridden organisms, turbulent unconscious dynamics, and the like. All aspects of development are to be seen as being profoundly influenced by learning in a context of object relations that are, on the one hand, biologically essential and biologically directed and, on the other hand, culturally molded and historically conditioned. Analysts also emphasize the clinical as well as theoretical dangers to psychoanalytic understanding represented by any simple and immediate reduction of manifest content to infantile dynamics.

On this basis, ego psychology has helped establish lively two-way interchanges between psychoanalysis and modern biology, psychology, anthropology, history, linguistics, philosophy, aesthetics, and other disciplines. Proceeding with justified caution, psychoanalysis has begun moving more freely within the history of ideas, of which it is itself, of course, a significant part. And within the history of ideas, sooner or later it comes to pass that well-established answers are found to require reconceptualization or replacement by new answers, framed to deal with different and possibly better questions.

Consequently, psychoanalysts who genuinely appreciate ego psychology will not shrug off the current great discussion of the making, warping, and exploiting of women in our society. In this discussion, fundamental Freudian propositions about psychological development are being challenged from all sides while the entire psychoanalytic enterprise is being widely discredited as the child and now the servant of the male-dominated, bourgeois social order. Simply interpreting these criticisms as militant rationalizations of penis envy being put forth by neurotic females and their male supporters is a flagrant instance of reductionism and intellectual isolationism and is equivalent to shrugging off this discussion, which, it should be noted, concerns the allegedly distorted development of men as well as women. Analysts should be prepared to rethink the concept as well as the role of penis envy in female development. This can be done without dismissing or minimizing many findings concerning its psychological importance.

My focus here is on some problems in Freud's theoretical generalizations concerning women's development and characteristics. These generalizations deal with typical conflicts and typical rational and irrational attempts to solve them. They have, of course, been of incalculable value both in understanding the varieties of female development and, through clinical psychoanalysis, in greatly alleviating neurotic disturbances in individual instances. But problems there are, and my strategy in getting at them is to focus on the type of theorizing Freud used in this connection. I examine the logic and internal consistency of his ideas; I try to sort out the preconceptions that went into the making of the theory, the empirical evidence it deals with, and the rules by which this evidence was established. Additionally, I attempt to identify the confusions between these three features of the theory. These are the theoretical features and the confusions that determine what are certified as the facts of gender, how these facts are related to each other, and whether and where there are factual errors and failures to make sense.

It is legitimate to begin by limiting the discussion to Freud alone. One reason for doing so is that much of the current criticism is directed specifically against Freud and relies heavily on allegedly representative quotations from his writings. Another reason is this: Although Freud's psychoanalytic descendants have made many major theoretical and technical advances, his basic assumptions—indeed the very mode of his thought—are still very much with us in modern psychoanalysis. Consequently, we may concentrate on Freud without being altogether ahistorical. At the same time, we must bear in mind that, over the years, Freud modified many of his ideas. We must ask, therefore, whether he modified his psychology of women.

It seems that he did. Not only did he finally emphasize how little, after all, he really understood female development (1931, 1933); he also began to emphasize, along with the vicissitudes of penis envy, the major and continuing influence of the girl's active preoedipal attachment to her mother. But Freud was not altogether consistent in making this change, for, in his final discussions of the subject (1937b, 1940), he pretty much reverted to his earlier, simpler, and patriarchal viewpoint (1923b, 1925). To put it plainly, this is the viewpoint from which Freud's propositions seem to imply that female development is both second best and second rate: second best in the experience of the girl and woman and second rate in the judgment of patriarchal spokesmen of civilization at large. Freud never did consolidate and develop a fundamental change in this regard. From this fact follow many of the problems in his psychology of women.

I discuss some major and representative problems under three headings: "The Problem of Women's Morality and Objectivity," "The Problem of Neglected Prephallic Development," and "The Problem of Naming."

THE PROBLEM OF WOMEN'S MORALITY AND OBJECTIVITY

What sense, if any, could Freud have been making when he characterized women as being less moral than men? Consider what he said:

> for women the level of what is ethically normal is different from what it is in men. Their superego is never so inexorable, so impersonal, so independent of its emotional origins as we require it to be in men. . . . that they show less sense of justice than men, that they are less ready to submit to the great exigencies of life, that they are more often influenced in their judgments by feelings of affection or hostility—all these

would be amply accounted for in the modification of the formation of their superego. (1925, pp. 257–258)

The Freud who wrote this passage was also well aware that many or most men manifest serious deficiencies in conventional moral rectitude. He saw this in their personal lives: Think of the men in the Dora case (1905a). He saw it in their professional lives: Consider the scandalous way in which he was treated by his colleagues in medicine and psychiatry. And he saw it in the lives of men as citizens: Recall his gloomy remarks on World War I (1915d). More than once he expressed plainly his low estimate of the morality of most people in the world he knew. Consequently, in his generalizations about women's morality, he could not have been contrasting them with *most* men, at least not in *that* sense of the word *moral*. What then was he doing?

In one respect, he seemed to be referring to a certain quality of moral rigidity characterizing men more than women. Men's moral stands seemed to him much less easily swayed by emotional appeals or so-called subjective impressions than those of women. Men seemed more consistently to affirm and abide by abstract and so-called objective principles. Although it could be argued effectively that the idea of this quantitative sex difference rests on a selection of criteria that is biased in favor of men, and so more or less begs the question, I shall bypass this issue in order to stay close to Freud's explicit line of thought, and I shall grant, *though only for the sake of critical analysis*, that this difference is real.

As clinicians, most psychoanalysts would, I think, infer from the "fact" of this quantitative difference that men have a greater capacity for isolation of affect. Like many others, Freud did estimate that hysterical proclivities are more commonly encountered in women and obsessive proclivities in men, and he did portray isolation of affect as a peculiarly obsessive mechanism (1926). Consequently, what seems to follow from Freud's generalization is that obsessive natures are more moral than hysterical ones. But that conclusion makes no sense for two reasons. One is that, although obsessives differ from hysterics in at least certain aspects of their morality, it is meaningless to suggest that it is possible to measure such differences on a single scale or indeed on any scale, for no scalar quantities are in question; obsessions and hysteria are modes of response or configurations of attitude and behavior. Instead of quantification, we would only be imposing a value judgment in the guise of making an empirical comparison. Apparently following the conventional patriarchal approach of his time, Freud was *in this sense* confusing values and observations. (In another sense, which is irrelevant here, there can be no value-free observations.)

In addition to this logical objection to the individious comparison, there is a psychoanalytic objection to be raised. Even assuming this isolation and this rigidity to be true differentiae, a psychoanalyst could never accept the obsessive as a more definite morality or a firmer one. This is so because obsessive morality is founded on reaction formation against anal-sadistic tendencies, intellectualization, irrational and savage unconscious guilt, and much devious immorality for which atonement must continually be made or that must be "magically" undone. Additionally, obsessive tendencies toward scrupulosity serve as unconscious equivalents of masturbation and torture. The obsessive model is, according to psychoanalytic understanding, a poor model of morality, indeed. And to argue on behalf of milder or more neutralized versions of this morality, we would still have to compare them with milder or more neutralized versions of hysterical morality; so the other problems I have just raised would still have to be faced. The charge of reductionism or genetic fallacy would have to be made against *both or neither* of these references to the infantile psychosexual prototypes of morality.

Thus far, Freud's quantitative comparison of the morality of men and women does not seem to stand up. Let us go on to examine it from another viewpoint. Freud also seemed to be assuming that holding to moral stands once taken, regardless of consequences in one's own personal relationships, is a sign of firmer morality, and that men clearly surpass women in this regard. There are additional grounds for entertaining this interpretation of Freud: He did think the predominant danger situation in the lives of women is loss of love, whereas in the lives of men castration is the main danger situation (1926); and since castration anxiety is considerably more narcissistically detached a concern than fear of loss of love, in that it is more remote from the immediate vicissitudes of love relationships, it provides a more impersonal foundation for moral activity. In Freud's final theory of development, this castration anxiety is the chief incentive for the renunciations and identifications that constitute the influential superego organization (1923a). Freud concluded that girls, already believing themselves to have been castrated, lack the same incentive as boys to become moral, and consequently seek solace and restored self-esteem in being loved by men and receiving babies from them (1925).

In this context Freud was clearly not appreciating two factors. One is the part played in the girl's development by the example of the active, nurturant mother who has her own sources of pride, decency, and consolation, and the other is the part played by the great variety of positive environmental emphases concerning girls and women. His attention was fixed on the decisive part played in the girl's development by one set of unconscious equations: My lost penis = father's actual penis = the baby I wish to be given me by father's penis.

Freud's conclusion seems inevitable. It is not only that women crave unconsciously to be loved, invaded, and impregnated, but that they bend their morality all too readily in order to fulfill these cravings; their fear of disapproval often overrules whatever independent sense they may have of what is right for them and others. No Freudian psychoanalyst would deny the applicability of these propositions to many segments of the significant problems presented in analysis by typical neurotic women in this culture. But surely every such analyst would affirm as well that, whatever the castration anxiety of men might have to do with superego structuralization, typically that anxiety is so unresolved, so persistent, and so intense that it continuously incites men to violate conventional morality and to do so often in an egregious manner. Consequently, when Freud cautioned against overestimating the degree of true superego formation in people in general, he must have meant men in particular.

More remains to be said about superego morality. For Freud, the unconscious infantile superego is the foundation of individual morality and establishes its character. His immediate *developmental* concern in working out his superego theory was to give an account of how and why the incest taboo is established and secured. He did not address himself particularly to the concept of reality-attuned, organized, adaptive moral codes; later on, Hartmann did so (1960). Many places in his writings suggest that Freud had some definite ideas along this line. These ideas are also implied in the dictum that Hartmann says Freud was fond of quoting: What is moral is self-evident. But in his psychoanalytic writings, he did not, as he should have, sharply distinguish between superego and moral code.

Generally speaking, the consequences of drawing this distinction have been insufficiently appreciated. One such consequence is a radical alteration of our idea of superego, for now we are able to see that superego is not morality at all, nor can morality grow out of it alone, for superego is fierce, irrational, mostly unconscious vindictiveness against oneself for wishes and activities that threaten to bring one into archaically conceived, infantile danger situations. As Freud described it, unconscious superego is mostly a demonic aspect of mind,* and as he developed this theory of it, it is his Death Instinct enshrined in psychic structure (1923a, 1930). This is the sense of Freud's conclusion that one aim of therapeutic analysis is to reduce superego influence on ego functioning (1933); by this he did not mean any reduction of morality.

This severe superego authority does generally enforce respectful observance of certain fundamental personal, familial, and societal taboos. In this respect, it is a powerful, societally oriented set of primitive prohibitions and policies of self-punishment. But Freud also demonstrated that this same internal authority may be subversive of people's achievements, their love, and even their moral codes, for, like any harsh and arbitrary authority, it continuously incites rebellion, hatred, and self-destructiveness. In its extremes, superego can even make criminals of people. Whatever superego does contribute toward eventual morality requires considerable tempering before that morality can be secured, and certainly superego cannot temper itself; it cannot become independent of its being and its emotional origins.

It follows that Freud may have drawn exactly the wrong conclusion from his developmental psychosexual theory. If, because of her different constellation of castration concerns, a girl does not develop the implacable superego that a boy does, then at least in this respect she might be better suited than a boy to develop a moral code that is enlightened, realistic, and consistently committed to some conventional form of civilized interaction among people. And perhaps that is the truth instead and the basis of another widely held view of women that Freud ignored in this connection: women as the guardians of civilized conduct and morality. I shall not argue here for or against the logical inevitability or empirical truth of either of these conclusions or of any other. Before doing so, we would have to scrutinize various types or styles of moral code—the assumptions, articulation, flexibility, scope, and applications of each—and that would be to study qualitative differences as such. Also, we would have to compare the developmental sequences of relaxing initially severe superego policies with consolidating a moral code despite initially insufficient superego formation. Clinically, analysts see both sequences. Probably no one factor or description could state the whole truth in this regard. We must

*I say unconscious superego is *mostly* demonic, for Freud also pointed to a benign, loving aspect of superego (Schafer, 1960). But that aspect, too, is archaic in its magical, grandiose, and absolute attributes, and so cannot amount to a moral code; like the punitive aspect, it can constitute only part of the history of that code.

remain dissatisfied both with Freud's estimate of men's and women's moralities and with his assumption that analysts may measure and generalize in this respect.

Can we be satisfied with Freud's related view that women are less objective, lucid, and acute in comprehension than men (1920b)? Here Freud was implying that, besides manifesting less superego development than men, women manifest less ego development (though when he said this, in 1920, he had not yet formulated his structural theory; but see also his paper of 1931). The derivation of this generalization is the same one I presented of Freud's estimate of women's morality: briefly, that an already castrated being's incentive for development is weaker than that of a being fearful of castration; that is to say, as it is to superego development, castration anxiety is also the greatest spur of all to ego development.

If we again agree *provisionally* that there are or may be sex differences in ego development, how are we to construe them? As in the case of morality, I suggest that these are not measurable differences in degree of development. Certainly the degree of development of single skills or functions can be measured according to the rules for applying specific scales to performances elicited by standardized methods. And certainly informal estimates of this circumscribed sort can be made, with the naked eye as it were. But, taken as a whole, such differences between men and women in ego functioning as there may be would be qualitative, corresponding to *modes* of functioning rather than to *amounts*. Contrary to Freud, there can be no final authority on the question of whether one mode of functioning is superior to another, for the question makes sense only in a context of values. Modes may be described, and different modes may be contrasted, but only a taken-for-granted patriarchal value system could lead to Freud's unqualified statement about women's relative mental incompetence.

Furthermore, there are contradictions to be noted. For example, if women are, as Freud believed, more intuitive and keenly empathic than men, are they not thereby manifesting another *kind* of acute comprehension? The difference then would not lie in acuteness at all, but in the judge's estimate of worth. Additionally, there hovers over all these considerations the major questions of whether or in which respects these differences do exist, and, if they do, whether they are inevitable or are enforced or at least exaggerated by methods of rearing and educating boys and girls differently in and for a phallocentric world.

There is also the hard question posed by wide individual differences *within* the sexes.

Here I should point out that Freud's feminist critics are close to Freud in a fundamental sense. Freud, too, presented the world as phallocentric, though he had in mind the world as it exists in psychic reality, whereas his critics are referring to the actual formative and normative environment. And yet, what of it? Let us grant the primary or tremendous importance of psychic reality. Then we would expect it to shape the comprehension of social reality, to constitute a significant part of the social reality we encounter in the form of other people, and, historically, to determine much of the content and organization of social reality—to all of which real adaptations would have to be made. Consequently, the child's sexual identity would be defined by that "complemental series" of inner and outer influences that Freud regularly invoked in his developmental propositions. A one-sided approach to reality cannot stand up to close inspection.

Additionally, Freud relied heavily, in his final theory of ego and anxiety, on the idea of the infant's prolonged helplessness and the consequent importance of the environment, both as it really is and as it is in psychic reality; this idea entails the recognition that external reality and psychic reality shape each other. In this light, Freud's more thoughtful feminist critics may be viewed as exploring the following questions concerning sexual identity: To what extent does societal indoctrination shape psychic reality and regulate the development of skills, attitudes, and ideas and values about oneself in relation to others? And how are any such societal influences mediated by family roles, schooling, and the actualities of later existence as well as by anatomical-physiological differences between the sexes? These questions are not alien to Freudian inquiry, especially when it is informed by ego-psychological adaptive considerations. What is problematic is the patriarchal bias in Freudian conceptualization and emphasis, a bias involving taken-for-granted models of masculine and feminine roles in our society.

In some early and illuminating Freudian papers on female sexuality, Karen Horney (1924, 1926, 1932, 1933) identified patriarchal bias in the then-existing psychoanalytic literature on the sexes. However, her mode of thought—that of the authoritative scientist laying down definitely the properties of a species—continued the patriarchal tradition of formulating sweeping generalizations about the sexes. It is unlike the nonpatriarchal mode of that exciting and evocative mixture of observation, impression, discovery, perplexity, and reservation that we encounter throughout Freud's case studies and clinical papers, that part of his *oeuvre* which, patriarchally, Freud seemed to regard as merely his "novels" or preliminary scientific data (I might say, in his terms, the feminine side of his work). Here I can only allude to the idea that phallic prototypes and values play major roles in traditionally esteemed modes of knowing used alike by many women and men.

We must conclude that Freud's estimates of women's morality and objectivity are logically and empirically indefensible. In large part these estimates implement conventional patriarchal values and judgments that have been misconstrued as being disinterested, culture-free scientific observations.

THE PROBLEM OF NEGLECTED PREPHALLIC DEVELOPMENT

Because Freud tried to account for women's personality characteristics and problems mainly in terms of the phallic phase, he neglected to assess adequately prephallic development. It is necessary to put this problem in theoretical perspective before coming to the problem itself. Accordingly, I first discuss in some detail certain general features of Freud's theorizing that seem to account for his having based so much of his theory of psychosexual development on anatomical genital factors.

The fact that Freud adhered to a biological, evolutionary model for his psychology (Schafer, 1970b) led him to neglect, in his theorizing, and thus in his comparative views on men and women, prephallic development. His model requires a teleological view of the propagation of the species (see, for example, Freud, 1933, p. 131). That is, it requires the assumption that individual human beings are destined to be links in the chain of survival, and this assumption necessarily implies that genital sexuality is the culmination of psychosexual development. In turn, that idea necessarily implies that anything else is an arrest of development and so must be, in some sense of the so-called natural order of things, unnatural, defective, or abnormal. Accordingly, pregenital pleasures, being nonprocreative, belong at best to foreplay in adult sexual life; otherwise they are perversions. And homosexuality, being similarly nonprocreative, is to be viewed not as an alternative to genital heterosexuality but as a so-called inversion. In this entire line of thought can be observed the operation of an implicit but powerful *evolutionary value system.* According to this value system, Nature has its procreative plan, and it is better (healthier, more normal) for people to be "natural" and not defy "the natural order." The propositions are not neutral.

Here is one of the great ironies in the history of psychoanalysis:

Even after Freud gave up the idea of an instinct of self-preservation and in general deemphasized his ideas about very specific instinctual drives, he continued to think along similar lines in some respects and, in so doing, contradicted his major clinical observations and conclusions. Clinically, even as early as his "Three Essays on the Theory of Sexuality" (1905b), he had come to realize that genital heterosexuality is a difficult, imperfect, more or less precarious achievement, and that this is so because it is a psychological task as well as a biological eventuality. Biology provides chiefly the stimuli, especially the insistent, pleasurable, and potentially painful stimuli of bodily needs and the sensuous zones; it is experience in human relatedness that defines and emphasizes specific aims and objects. The attainment of genital primacy is therefore very much a matter of the child's learning certain lessons about sexual pleasures and dangers and its developing some type and degree of mastery of both of these. Because of the child's immaturity, this learning and striving for mastery will involve many animistic, illogical, unrealistic, and symbolic infantile mental processes; these processes, usually ignored or underestimated by the revisionist schools of cultural analysis, are among the phase-specific features of early psychosexual development. And this learning will be very much under the influence of bodily experience in the context of some caretaking presence. But however crude it may be, it *is* learning.

In effect, Freud had shown that for human beings there is nothing inevitable about propagating the species. This was truly a revolutionary discovery! Because we know only societies that, owing to various combinations of need and tradition, are geared for creating children, we tend to take it for granted that procreativity is a central and inevitable aspect of human beings, as of other animals. It need not be argued here that, in crucial respects, human beings differ fundamentally from other animals, and it was Freud's clinical contributions that made it possible to realize in how many ways and how insistently societies steer children from their infancy toward procreative male and female roles. However imperfectly, we are continuously preparing children in our society to become fathers and mothers in nuclear families. Freud also showed, and especially emphasized, that, from the standpoint of the child, this indoctrination impinges on, and to a large extent is understood in terms of, the child's own wishes to be in the procreative role; these are wishes based on the child's identifications, rivalry, love, infantile fantasies, sensuous desires, and other variables familiar from clinical work. But there is no sense of assuredness among the members of our society that the child's own procreative wishes would or could by themselves finally establish their own primacy; and so, implicitly and explicitly, we plan the child's psychosexual development. We try to turn out men and women who will aspire to have children in nuclear families, too, and who, in turn, will prepare their children to continue this pattern and will think it good and natural to do so and live so.

Although it is fruitless to speculate about how children would develop in this respect if left to their own devices, we are able to consider the place of learning in procreative genitality because there are other and real types of control situations. For instance, in our society we often observe children and adults who have been indoctrinated by parents to hold ideal conceptions of sex roles other than the traditional procreative ones. These are the psychologically masculinized daughters and psychologically effeminized sons. Moreover, procreation is not an inevitable consequence of the pleasure of sexual excitement and orgasm; nor is hetersexual genital intercourse the only route to these pleasures.

Considerations such as these highlight the centrality of learning in the human being's movement toward procreativity. Consequently, we need not and should not assume a self-fulfilling instinctual drive toward propagation of the species. Nor is it logical to argue that some drive of that sort has to be operative, even though it is not amenable to our isolating it and studying its action; if it cannot be studied, we have no right to speak of its existence or to build it into the foundation of our developmental theories, as Freud did. That it might have a place in preliminary or informal speculation, which might then lead to significant discovery, is another matter altogether. I have discussed logical problems in psychoanalytic theory elsewhere (1972, 1973a, 1973b).

Finally, with regard to *unlearned* influences on psychosexual identity, it must be noted that Freud never really integrated his references to constitutional differences in the strength of masculinity and femininity with his psychological propositions about sexual development. Furthermore, he did not—indeed, could not—demonstrate that he regularly encountered these differences in the neurotic people with whom he was working. He just assumed their existence.

Thus, it is one great consequence of Freud's discoveries that psychoanalytic explanations may no longer presuppose any natural or preestablished culmination of human psychosexual development. Another consequence, a corollary to the first, is that psychosexual outcomes other than reproductive genitality are called illnesses and arrests in development *only from the standpoint of the values and associated child-rearing practices common to the dominant members of a society.*

In speaking of perversions and inversions and their cure, we are operating in the realm of societal value systems concerning taken-for-granted evolutionary obligations; we are not operating in any realm of biological necessity, psychobiological disorder, or value-free empiricism. There is no established relation between these value systems and psychoanalytic insights, though there may be between these value systems and religion or existential choices. None of which is to deny, of course, that clinical psychoanalysis can and does often greatly reduce profound and painful conflicts in these areas, or that it may be legitimate or even inescapable to define illness in terms of value systems. But analysts should know that this is what they are or may be doing.

The argument may be pursued by emphasizing Freud's helping us to understand the socially widespread intense revulsion toward, and derogation and persecution of, so-called sexual deviants. He showed that these violent reactions are founded on three factors: a degree of precariousness in the heterosexual genitality attained by most nondeviant people; a greater or lesser dread common to these people of succumbing to modes of gratification that would disconfirm their heterosexual genitality; and some readiness on their part to project their repudiated desires onto others and then persecute them. This *precariousness* expresses various unconscious fixations on, and regressions to, homosexual and pregenital pleasures, and this *dread* and *persecution* reflect the intense, partly incorporated social pressures against adopting these deviant sexual roles. These pressures have, of course, impinged on the child's archaic fantasies of pleasure, destruction, castration, loss of self and others, and loss of love and security; and they have been understood in terms of these fantasies and gained much of their great power from them.

Along the same line, Freud helped us to see through and beyond our society's many hypocritical moralistic attitudes toward pleasure of all sorts and its usually excessively confining sense of decorum, especially with regard to sexuality. But this understanding of sexual development and sexual attitudes must be predicated on the proposition that human sexuality is indeed *psycho*sexuality. The concept psychosexuality excludes a sexuality of blind instincts culminating in propagation of the species, as in nonhuman organisms (though even for them this simple statement is no longer really acceptable); and it excludes a sexuality simply of erotic techniques and orgasmic adequacy. Psychosexuality means mental sexuality, that is, a sexuality of meanings and personal relationships that have developed and been organized around real and imagined experiences and situations in a social world.

Freud disregarded this consequence of his own revolutionary clinical discovery. He persevered with the biological, evolutionary model and value system. Just as his doing so greatly confounded his metapsychological theorizing (Schafer, 1976), it limited his clinical view of development prior to the phallic phase; thereby it interfered with his developing an altogether satisfactory developmental psychology of girls—and of boys as well. The fact that psychoanalysts, in following Freud, tend to regard and name these early phases the *pre*genital and *pre*oedipal phases betrays the relevant bias and limitation in traditional thinking.

In Freud's major systematic statements, he repeatedly indicated that real mental development begins and is crystallized during the time of the passing of the Oedipus complex, which is the very time when the foundations of procreative genitality are being decisively laid. For example, Freud spoke of the ego as at best a rudimentary organ before this time. Also, he seemed to underestimate the influential fantasies of incorporated parental figures and other "presences" that seem to abound during the very early years and to persist to some extent thereafter. Further, Freud held that it is not only the superego structure which is established during the resolution of the Oedipus complex, but the structured and structuring ego as well (1923a); for only then, on the strength of its new identifications and the desexualized energy now available to it for sublimated activity, does the ego begin to function as an organized, independent, and influential agency.

In his structural theory of mental development, Freud provided no fully adequate and integrated treatment of the acquisition of language, habit training, oral and anal fantasy life, consolidation of narcissism, rudimentary character formation, and many other early factors. Despite his tremendous discoveries concerning just these prephallic factors, Freud still put the phallus, oedipal fantasies, castration anxiety, and procreation in the center of his developmental theory. And yet we can only begin to comprehend the development of the phallic phase and the Oedipus complex and the possibility of their coming to any resolution whatsoever on the basis of considerable prephallic ego development (Schafer, 1968b).

This centering on ultimate procreative genitality explains some of the imperfections of Freud's psychology of women. The essential point may be developed through consideration of Freud's having pretty much taken for granted the girl's catastrophic response to her discovering the anatomical difference between the sexes and her basically implacable envious attitude thereafter. Freud was remarkably incurious about the background of these reactions. He did refer (almost in passing, it seems) to speculative ideas put forward by others concerning the girl's being primed to respond thus catastrophically by prior losses of breast and feces; otherwise he was silent. Similarly, with regard to the danger situations of loss of love object and loss of love, which precede the era of castration concerns, Freud's comments remained schematic as well as isolated from considerations of the girl's intense reaction to the anatomical difference.

We encounter the same problem even in Freud's major revisionary efforts of 1931 and 1933. Although there he stressed the pregenital girl's activity, her mother's "sexual seduction" of her through bodily ministrations, the girl's natural ambivalence toward her mother and her struggle with her over masturbation, he did not present these variables as the foundations of the castration shock. These variables remained isolated. Soon they would be superseded by the beginning of the "feminine [phase] to which she [the girl] is *biologically destined*" (1933, p. 119, emphasis added). Here there is no sense of developmental continuity.

To mention only one more problem: Freud was too quick to favor the designation *penis envy* for the complex array of feelings, wishes, and fantasies of which penis envy is, after all, only a part, though often a most intense and consequential part. Here the influence of Freud's phallocentrism can hardly be overlooked.

Insofar as it is the hallmark of psychoanalytic investigation, and particularly of Freud's thinking, that it always presses its questions further and further in the interest of establishing the fullest understanding possible of the particularity of response on the part of individuals in specific circumstances, especially when these reactions are intense, disturbing, profoundly formative, and enduringly influential, it is all the more remarkable that at this point Freud asked virtually no more questions. It is as if it is sufficient just to know that girls assume they are phallic in the way boys are and that they pursue active as well as passive aims until the terrible time of revelation, mortification, and envy. But it is *not* sufficient. The psychoanalytic clinician as well as theorist must remain curious and so must go on to ask: Why *is* the girl so mortified and envious? Her mortification and envy are not explained by the fact of her simply seeing the difference; nor are they explained by her having previously maintained unchallenged her assumption that she and the boy are anatomically alike.

To begin to answer the question at all satisfactorily, we must assume that, before the time of mortification and envy, it was already terribly important to the girl that there be no differences between herself and boys. And to make that assumption is to land smack in the middle of so-called pregenital mental development. At this point, this phasic location can no longer seem quite so *pre*genital, in any case. In effect I am arguing that we cannot have a simple, self-evident *shock theory* of the girl's mortification and consequent penis envy. That the girl reacts this way indicates that she is already heavily invested in and worried about genital comparison and intactness. Freud's consistently restricted view of these developments is evident in the way he contrasted to the boy's initial "irresolution and lack of interest" the girl's response to having to face the anatomical difference: "She makes her judgement and her decision in a flash. She has seen it [the penis] and knows that she is without it and wants to have it" (1925, p. 252).

The problem of the readiness for castration shock is not the whole of the difficulty. In their quest for particularity of explanation, psychoanalysts must also ask about the apparent precariousness of the girl's self-esteem in the face of the genital discovery, however and whenever it is made. Indeed, in Freud's theory this precariousness is presented as so great that the collapse of self-esteem in the context of the castration fantasy is held to be a decisive and permanent influence on the woman's entire mental development and organization. As Freud was to put it much later on, penis envy was the "bedrock" of her neurotic problems (1937b). But, again, where are Freud's questions in this regard? It was he, after all, who taught us how to establish through psychoanalysis the historical background and the complex determination of psychological trauma.*

Even after making allowances for due restraint on speculation, it may still be argued that Freud was in a logical and methodological position to at least raise these questions about the girl's readiness for mortification and envy and the precariousness of her self-esteem. The answers, about which I have more to say later, would have to center on the girl's relationship with her mother during the first years of her life, and they would establish the profound importance of this relationship throughout the remainder of the daughter's existence—as of the son's. *That Freud did not raise these questions seems to be in large part an expression of his being preoccupied with the organs of reproduction, in consequence of his commitment to an evolutionary model and value system and a patriarchal bias.* Freud neglected to a noteworthy degree two interrelated psychological variables, one the manifestations of mind prior

*Methodologically, *at the time he was writing,* Freud was wise not to press his questions too far. He cautioned against formulating propositions concerning mental processes during the earliest phases of development, for the relevant data from clinical work were, at best, extremely fleeting, fragmentary, and ambiguous, and it was primarily through analytic work proper that his developmental propositions were framed and tested (1931).

to the time of the phallic phase and the Oedipus complex, the other the powerful role played by learning in the development of sexual attitudes, roles, and subjective experience. Far more than it should have, anatomy had become Freud's destiny.

Anatomy and reproduction, and anatomy and mind: The links were forged. Despite Freud's keen awareness of early mental functioning, he developed no *psychological* way of taking it into account. Mostly he biologized the early mental processes by relegating them to instinct, instinctual energy, processes, and principles, such as the pleasure principle, the primary process, and the repetition compulsion; and he viewed each of these as seeking to gratify its own aims in its own way. Thereby he anthropomorphized them, that is, reintroduced psychological propositions by the back door of biology (Grossman and Simon, 1969; Schafer, 1976).

A psychological approach to the prephallic period must center on the girl's primary, mind-formative, certainly intensely and complexly physical, and ultimately indestructible relationship with her mother. Freud, however, was mostly concerned to explain the girl's turning *from* her mother *to* her father as lover and sire of her children. In this effort, he portrayed the girl as having simply turned against her mother and, together with that, against her own identification-based active orientation and her clitoris. But, to be consistent with psychoanalytic propositions and findings, the girl and, later, the woman must be seen as being in a profoundly influential, continuously intense and active relationship, not only with her real mother but with the idea and imagined presence of her mother, and with her identification with this mother; she must also be seen as integrating her clitoris firmly into her sexuality. Whatever the girl's narcissistic vulnerability at the time of the castration shock, it would have its history and find its meaning in this matrix. Although Freud approached this consistency in some of his later papers, he did not achieve it.

Freud's value-based interpretation of his investigations is further evidenced in a limitation of his approach to the problem of the analysis of transference. Typically, he construed the transference he had observed as being based on the ambivalent tie to the father of early childhood. Even in his 1931 paper, in which he was reconsidering his psychology of women and beginning to emphasize the importance of the pregenital relation to the mother, he suggested that it would be *female* analysts particularly who would be the ones to work out the child's early relation to the mother. Thereby he continued to neglect the essentially androgynous role of the psychoanalyst in the transference; for the male analyst this means his female as well as male identity in this central aspect of his work. There is little evidence that Freud was alert to or impressed by maternal transference to the male analyst—or, for that matter, by maternal countertransference on the part of the male analyst.

It is not inaccurate to say that Freud tended to neglect bisexuality, even though that concept and the relevant observations are such central elements in his theory of development. This neglect is evident in his discussions not only of transference but of resistance, ego and superego formation, and other topics as well (Schafer, 1976). He was preoccupied with the father's position in a way and to a degree that stunted his conception of the mother's status in the family and thereby her stature in his theory. Again, for his theory of development, the important thing was to get the girl to become *feminine* and ready to receive love and babies *passively* from an active man, thereby to continue to propagate the species. For this, Freud thought he needed a sustained phallic perspective. But that perspective is not inclusive enough for his own psychoanalytic discoveries.

THE PROBLEM OF NAMING

Now we must consider how such designations as feminine, passive, and active behave in descriptive and explanatory propositions. This is the problem of naming.

To designate is also to create and to enforce. By devising and allocating words, which are names, people create entities and modes of experience and enforce specific subjective experiences. Names render events, situations, and relationships available or unavailable for psychological life that might otherwise remain cognitively indeterminate. Consequently, whether something will be an instance of masculinity or femininity, activity or passivity, aggression or masochism, dominance or submission, or something else altogether, or nothing at all, will depend on whether we consistently call it this or that or consistently do not name it at all, hence do not constitute and authorize its being. Similarly, to the extent that we link or equate such names as, for example, femininity and passivity, we exert a profound and lasting formative influence on what it is said to be like to be feminine or passive. Logically, there is no right answer to the questions of what is masculine and what is feminine and what is active and what is passive. There are no preconceptual facts to be discovered and arrayed. There are only loose conventions governing the uses and groupings of the words in question. And these conventions, like all others, must manifest values.

For example, in our society we often merge words pertaining to social values such as status and so-called breeding with words pertaining to sexual identity. To be a lady in the sense of a fine lady and to be feminine may be set up as equivalents, with the consequence that a woman who does not act ladylike, according to a certain conception of that word, may be said to be not feminine. In this instance, not feminine might mean rude, loud, socially too forward, sexually too adventurous, intellectually too serious, or cosmetically too casual or vivid. Thus, to say that a woman is not feminine is often a way of saying that she does not act or look as a woman "ought to" act or look. An additional part of this poor lesson is the implicit idea "She is bad." In this way, verbal conventions that implement value judgments are passed off as simple and unequivocal facts—and are so learned by children (Hartmann, 1960).

Clinical psychoanalysts have much occasion to observe and modify the disturbing influence of cultural, familial, and individual conventions regarding the valuative use of words or names and of their groupings and equations, especially in the case of words pertaining to sexual identity, aggression, and personal worth.

In this third and final (and all too-brief) section of my discussion, I concentrate on one strategic problem of naming: how Freud used the words *active* and *passive* in relation to the words *masculine* and *feminine*. Freud showed some awareness in this regard—that he was using and devising verbal conventions. In one place he said, "Maleness combines [the factors of] subject, activity and possession of the penis; femaleness takes over [those of] object and passivity" (1923b, p. 145). In another place he said, "We call everything that is strong and active male, and everything that is weak and passive female" (1940, p. 188). Except for his reference to the penis—which, being an empirical rather than a defining proposition, is out of place in the first statement—Freud seemed to know that he was not making empirical assertions about how women really and necessarily are. In many places he even insisted that women come in all kinds, as do men. What he wanted was merely a suitable rubric for such personal characteristics as weakness and passivity. The names he chose were masculine and feminine (or male and female), and so, within this verbal convention, a woman is masculine to the extent that she is active and strong, and so on (see, for example, 1933, pp. 114–117).

Whatever our criticisms of this choice of names, such as that it both implies and enforces a derogation of women, it seems thus far that Freud was proceeding logically. In fact, however, he repeatedly lost his bearings and did not keep definition distinct from observation.

Freud's logical sophistication did not stop him from making all sorts of conventional patriarchal statements about what women are actually like and should be like (for example, submissive to their husband's authority). Such statements suggest that all kinds of "right" answers about sexual identity are being dictated by a pair of biological principles—the masculine and the feminine. Freud's repeated remarks about constitutional strength of masculinity and femininity reveal this to be so.

This same confusion can be traced in the course of Freud's chapter entitled "Female Sexuality" (1933). What was masculine and feminine, like what was moral and objective, seemed to be self-evident to him. His attempt at definitional rigor succumbed to this complacency. For Freud, then, feminine comprised passive, submissive, and masochistic; it meant the willing object of the man's biologically natural sexual and aggressive activity. This thesis must have seemed to Freud a scientific way to guarantee the continuation of the species. Looking back, we can see now that it served the continuation of the patriarchal social order, which, in his theories at any rate, Freud seemed to take uncritically as Reality. To put it another way, Freud assumed there to be normative links between, on the one hand, female-feminine-passive-submissive-masochistic and, on the other hand, male-masculine-active-dominant-aggressive. If this is so, a change of any one term would necessarily imply a change of all the others linked to it.

In trying to explain how women get to be as they allegedly are, particularly in terms of their attempts at resolving their penis envy, Freud made many fundamental and grand discoveries. Nevertheless, he was begging the question in at least two different ways. One was his presupposing that in fact women get to be *essentially* passive, submissive, and masochistic. The other was his presupposing that it is their psychobiological *destiny* to get to be as he said they are. Consequently, he worked with a simplified view of women, and he paid scant attention to the questions whether and to what extent girls are continuously being seduced and coerced into being "that way" by members of a society committed unconsciously, if not consciously, to guaranteeing that outcome.

Much of the argument turns on the meaning of passive. For Freud, masochism is the passive complement of sadistic aggression; submission is the passive complement of dominance; being loved, of loving; being looked at, of looking; and being impregnated, of impregnating (see, for example, Freud, 1915b). If all these passivities add up to femininity, we had better be clear about how Freud was using the word *passive.* The trouble is that Freud was not clear or consistent in his use of that word. At times he was even self-contradictory. First of all, he confused phenomenological passivity with passivity in the eyes of the psychoanalytic observer of behavior (Schafer, 1968a).

A clear example from psychoanalysis is the so-called fate neurosis in which, phenomenologically, a person repeatedly experiences him- or herself as the unfortunate passive victim of circumstance. At the same time, the psychoanalytic observer of behavior sees the person in question as actively bringing about his or her own misfortunes, say as symbolic castrations for incestuous wishes or as abandonments that are punishment for unconscious oedipal triumphs.

Second, when Freud generalized about women's passivity, he neglected such factors as unconscious identification with the partner in any significant relationship. Yet he had been the very one to establish the importance of these factors through his psychoanalytic method. In this connection, for example, the masochist is understood to be also unconsciously identifying with, and thereby vicariously enjoying the activity of, the sadistic partner. To this I must add that moral masochists, at any rate, not only actively seek out and provoke the abuses they seem to suffer passively but use their suffering to torment others.

Third, Freud repeatedly demonstrated how extraordinarily subtle and complex the interweaving of active and passive themes can be in any one person's life. From this fact it follows that one-sided or simple characterizations of any significant project as active or passive hardly makes sense, once a given person and situation is known well enough. Yet Freud was not deterred from generalizing on the basis of such simplistic characterizations. Again, he dealt inconsistently with his own discoveries and conceptual perspective.

Perhaps most fundamental to the analysis of this problem of naming is that, in many crucial instances, the decision whether to speak of behavior or of aims or attitudes as active or passive is like the decision whether to say of a certain glass of water that is half full or half empty. For example, to be exhibitionistic a person must find a real or imagined audience and show him- or herself off, which is to be active; and it is to be looked at, which is to be passive. Another example: To be loved is to be passive, and yet there are so many ways of getting to be loved and of receiving love, all of which are forms of being active. One more example: Does the penis penetrate the vagina or does the vagina receive the penis? Here I should point out that, immediately after the sentence I quoted earlier in this section, in which Freud grouped subject, activity, and possession of the penis as the referents of maleness, he went on to say "The vagina is . . . valued as the place of shelter for the penis; it enters into the heritage of the womb" (1923b, p. 145). Can a human place of shelter be passive? Can a womb be passive? To put it in terms of persons-in-relation, which are the proper ones, we must ask whether it makes any sense to say of a woman engaging in sexual intercourse that she is simply passive and whether it makes any sense to say of a caretaking mother that she is simply passive. Although Freud raised this last question (1933, p. 115), he did not draw its consequences for his general theory.

That Freud was not prepared to think about mothers very far is, as I noted earlier, evident from how little he said directly about them and about relationships with them, and, correspondingly, how little he said about how they appear in the transference, the resistance, and the formation of the ego and superego systems. Additionally, in his writings he showed virtually no sustained interest in their subjective experience—except for their negative feelings about their own femininity and worth and their compensatory cravings to be loved and impregnated, especially with sons. Consequently, Freud dealt with the feminine trends in men chiefly in terms of the two factors of castration and "passive" homosexuality, and he failed to consider in depth and systematically what more is entailed by being a woman and feeling like one in our society and how it might be different under other conditions. It seems that he knew the son, the father, and the castrate in himself and other men but not the daughter, the mother, and the woman.

To return to the idea of a fine lady: There is a Victorian precept that in sexual relations "a lady doesn't move." The modern psychoanalyst has to recognize this role not as passivity but as a desperate form of activity: a drastic inhibition required to play this inactivated part. The inhibiting may be carried out unconsciously and supplemented by conscious aversion, and the groundwork for this behavior would have to have been laid in early childhood, but it is activity nonetheless, at least as much as anything else is. It is from Freud particularly that we have learned about this unconscious activity. Yet although Freud the clinician was ever alert to the many forms unconscious activity takes in the lives of women, Freud the theoretician, when dealing with the development of sexual identity, named this inhibition passivity and made it the crux of femininity.

CONCLUDING REMARKS

Freud was working within a nineteenth-century biological-medical tradition that was not of his making. He merely applied and extended the conventions that constituted that tradition which was marked by a fusion of mechanistic and evolutionary modes of thought and patriarchal complacency. It based itself on ruling principles of nature, such as activity-passivity and masculinity-femininity, and other broad generalizations designed to take nature by the throat. Additionally, it was a tradition of belief in the idea of value-free empiricism and of pride in the achievements of the utterly objective scientist, and so was philosophically too immature to appreciate what is better established today: the pluralistic, relativistic, linguistic, and inevitably valuative aspects of the various forms of knowledge. Against these odds, Freud's achievement is all the more impressive. Nevertheless, at this historical moment we are obliged to identify and clarify the problematic aspects and limitations of Freud's contributions to the psychology of women. Much remains to be said on this subject and on the correlated subject of the fear that haunts the lives of men, pervading their relationships with women as well as with men: the fear of being second best and second rate themselves.

CHAPTER 5

The Phallocentric Narrative of Impotence and Frigidity

IMPOTENCE and frigidity, whether actual, imagined, or anticipated, are two of the most pervasive and abiding concerns of men and women. And there is hardly another human concern that is so imbued with irrational thinking. As a rule, impotence and frigidity are taken to be failures of the worst kind. Esteem for oneself and others rides precariously on sexual performance and one's idea of what this performance signifies. Some who live in the shadow of these concerns desperately avoid sexual intercourse and even social relations, while many others desperately keep proving to themselves or to the world that they are not impotent or frigid or that they have no reason to fear being so. These concerns with impotence and frigidity also disrupt relations with friends of the same sex, owing to the shame, bravado, competitiveness, and plain dishonesty to which they ordinarily give rise. Moreover, through displacement, men and women manifest these sexual concerns in other areas of life, such as physical, occupational, intellectual, and social fitness and worthiness. Although these areas seem far afield from sexuality, unconsciously they are more or less invested with sexual significance. In the end, there may remain few aspects of life that are not haunted, unconsciously if not consciously, by these concerns.

Psychoanalysts have learned a great deal about direct and displaced expressions of these actual, fantasied, and anticipated disturbances. Simply describing the phenomena in question and summarizing what has been learned about them would require a series of books, not only because there is so much to cover but also because psychoanalysts differ among themselves as to what it is most important to describe and explain and how to do so. But as I want to do a different job than that, I devote the first and introductory part of this chapter only to some well-established descriptive and explanatory highlights.

Mainly in this chapter I want to show how phallocentrism may be discerned in the conventional ways observers construct the narratives that define and appraise the phenomena in question. These narratives feature discriminatory ascriptions of personal agency that conform to the traditional sexist ideas of what it is to be a man and a woman or of the differences between the masculine and the feminine. In that way they bias our observations of sexuality from the first, perception never being divorced from our master narratives.

It is beyond the scope of this chapter to focus on sexual relations other than heterosexual genital intercourse.

PSYCHICAL IMPOTENCE AND FRIGIDITY

Nothing will be gained for present purposes by agonizing over strict clinical or descriptive definitions of impotence and frigidity; no one attempt can be successful because the narrative possibilities that yield up these definitions are so numerous. It is, however, important, for reasons that will emerge, to avoid importing into our definitions presuppositions about ability, capacity, achievement, success, and failure.

In the main, *impotence* refers to the absence or disappearance of a penile erection or the absence of ejaculation during a man's ostensible attempt to perform the heterosexual act fully. When used more loosely, *impotence* may also refer to premature or minimal ejaculation and to partial erection, in which descriptive respects the notion of *degree* of impotence seems to be appropriate. Those instances of impotence that have clear organic etiologies need not concern us here.

Freud used the term *psychical impotence* to cover all instances of psychological origin, but also and mainly in a narrow sense to cover the far more common instances of *selective* impotence. Selective impotence refers to a man's being limited to completing the sexual act with only certain types of women; typically these are "degraded" women in relation to whom the man may exclude tender, affectionate, and respectful feelings. Of these men Freud (1912a, p. 183) said, "The whole sphere of love . . . remains divided. . . . Where they love they do not desire and where they desire they cannot love." Selective impotence is the form most frequently encountered in clinical practice, particularly if we take account of the fact that it is observed as an intermittent phenomenon just as often in relation to one woman, perhaps the man's wife, as it is in relation to a type of woman.

As customarily used, *frigidity* refers to a woman's lack of sexual desire, ardor, and pleasure in sexual intercourse; it may include conscious aversion to the act. We may speak of *degrees* of frigidity. Corresponding to the man's difficulties with erection and ejaculation are the woman's vaginal tightness and dryness, which, because they usually occasion pain and fear of pain during intercourse, further decrease her sexual arousal and increase her aversion to the act. The term *frigidity* is used by some to refer to the regular absence of orgasm. What Freud said about psychological impotence in the narrowed sense applies, with appropriate changes, to frigidity: Psychological frigidity refers commonly to selective frigidity, whether it is with one type of man or with one man at different times. If nowhere else, this selectivity is likely to be evident in the excited and orgasmic masturbation that is often practiced by otherwise frigid women.

Freud (1910b; 1912a, p. 183) observed the following of the restricted sexual activity of the selectively impotent man: "It is capricious, easily disturbed, often not properly carried out, and not accompanied by much pleasure." The restricted sexuality of the selectively frigid woman shows the same features.

Through Freud's investigations and those of generations of analysts after him, it has been established that a multitude of factors must be taken into account before an explanation of individual cases of impotence and frigidity can be claimed. There is no one, simple, causal explanation for it and no one, simple account of the reasons for it. Indeed, it may be said that there is no significant aspect of personal development and existence that cannot sometimes figure as a condition of, or reason for, these disturbances. Foremost among the factors emphasized by Freud is the unconsciously maintained incestuous significance of the sex act. In cases of impotence and frigidity this significance is enlarged, unduly threatening, and dealt with by splitting the person's affectionate and erotic feelings and directing only the latter toward "degraded" or otherwise unsuitable persons. For the man, unconsciously, there is also the interfering influence of the castration anxiety associated with his oedipal rivalry with his father. For the woman, there is in addition the unconsciously imagined shameful fact of her castration, her mixture of longing and bitterness with respect to her frustrated wishes to bear her father's children, and her envious, appropriative, or destructive attitude toward her partner's penis.

Further, the disturbing influence of exaggerated, unconsciously maintained homosexual attachment to the parent of the same sex—the inverse or negative Oedipus complex—is often carried into heterosexual relations, rendering them threatening and unsatisfactory on that count, too. Disruption may stem as well from special concerns with the so-called voyeuristic and exhibitionistic aspects of sexual intimacy. These aspects usually originate in infantile observations or imaginings of the primal scene, that is, the parental coupling. They are likely to involve fear of, and shame at, exposing or viewing sexual excitement and confronting the imagined damage and threatening potential of the female genitalia.

Today psychoanalysts realize more than ever that, in addition to oedipal and genital influences, *preoedipal* or *pregenital* influences also figure significantly in the heterosexual life of a man or a woman. To the extent that the preoedipal is a disturbing factor (it need not be so), a person may, for example, unconsciously view the sex act as devouring and persecutory or excrementally dirty and explosively destructive. Disruption may stem from the imagined unacceptable requisites of cruelty and suffering in sexual activity. The sexual disturbance may then serve to protect the partner and stave off guilt. Confusion associated with early and unstable phases of the differentiation of the self (or ego) from others in the environment may be the occasion of a person's greatly fearing that he or she will lose both the self and the world through increasing intimacy, mounting sexual excitement, and orgasm.

From one case to the next, analysts attribute different degrees of importance to these and other, usually unconsciously operative factors. In some cases, some of these factors may be present with no obvious disruption of sexual performance and no dissatisfaction. In fact, often it is found that for certain people, some of the frequently disruptive factors are necessary features of sexual performance and satisfaction. In some instances of this kind, such as those involving staged cruelty and suffering, analysts speak of perversions. Freud numbered these so-called perverse features among the many "conditions for loving," grouping them thereby with the splitting of feelings and persons that I mentioned earlier. In these instances, analysts are likely to have occasion to interpret enactments of impotence and frigidity in areas of life other than the directly sexual. However, it is more often the case that these "perverse" features retain the status only of unconsciously elaborated and repudiated fantasies, and that they act as disturbers of the sexual peace rather than as overt "conditions for loving"; simultaneously, they may disturb the peace of working and conducting other aspects of a person's life. In many cases an analyst's weaving a web of interpretation of these consciously repudiated perverse fantasies goes a long way toward reducing or eliminating both direct impotence and frigidity and displaced or symbolic versions of them in work and elsewhere, particularly as they get to be enacted in the transference.

Before concluding this introductory survey, I must mention two more sets of common observations. First, many men and women carry through the sexual act on the strength of conscious fantasies they construct during its performance. Typically these fantasies involve someone other than the actual partner and sometimes they exclude the self as well, or instead. Also, these fantasies often represent relations that are not copulatory and may not even be sexual by ordinary standards; for example, threatening or adventurous interactions or situations may serve the purpose. And the fantasy during heterosexual activity may be homosexual. Recourse to fantasy as a condition for sexual loving is so common that I hesitate to speak of it as merely disguising impotence or frigidity. But in psychoanalysis, the hypothetical ideal has usually been total involvement in the immediate personal relationship—that is, in the actual erotic and affectionate interactions through which it is manifest. This is what psychoanalysts mean by *genitality*. With reference to the ideal of genitality, therefore, intercourse based on conscious fantasies falls closer to masturbation than to loving sexual relations, and so it may mask impotence and frigidity of considerable proportions. Also short of the ideal are the many instances of sexual intercourse that are simply not very satisfying; it is not unusual for men and women to feel pent up and to masturbate not long after "completing" these sex acts, as if they must meet their conditions for loving in the isolation of fantasy after the act rather than in the physical closeness during it.

The second addendum is this: On close analysis it often emerges that the actions of a person's partner have been playing a key role in the person's own impotence or frigidity. What has been getting in the way may be, for example, some subtly conveyed lack of ardor or tenderness or some aversion or rage. But analysts will not be content to stop asking questions once a strong case has been made for the existence of this kind of disturbing factor. Analysts will go on to try to understand why the analysand has chosen and stayed with that kind of sexual partner or why he or she has refrained from taking steps to improve the situation, or why the designated patient has not even noticed consciously the partner's provocation.

Relationships of this kind are unconsciously imbued with meaning of many kinds; typically they serve certain purposes rather than being plain bad luck. To the extent that this is so, the actions of the sexual partner imply choices of a person's own. As a rule, it takes two to make a chronic sexual problem. However, what will be decisive finally is not the partner's overt behavior in itself, but the way it fits and confirms the analysand's unconsciously maintained infantile imagoes, such as that of the abandoning mother or prohibiting father. In this light, the relational sexual problem gets to be seen as a route to what is centrally and anciently conflictual for the individual; and following that route, with the invaluable help of transference analysis, will contribute to alleviating that problem, for it will rest on a frank reconsideration of the person's lifelong human predicaments rather than on the technological adjustments of his or her sexual conduct that may be effected by sex counseling.

PHALLOCENTRIC NARRATIVES OF SEXUAL PERFORMANCE

The extended connotations of the words *impotence* and *frigidity* make it clear that a masculinist conception of heterosexuality is built into our thinking about heterosexual activity. "Impotence" means lacking in strength, force, drive, or power; it is a word specifically suited to describing a person as agent. "Frigidity" means extreme coldness; it is a word specifically suited for describing a milieu. Together, the words entail the proposition that in sexual relations a man is acting in a milieu. It is implied that there is only one agent. Although a milieu may be said to have effects, it cannot be said to act. Only people act. It follows from this pair of designations that the woman is by nature an inactive or passive object: If frigid, she is an unsuitable object; if ardent, she is a suitable object. Strength, force, drive, and power are not for her; nor are intent, initiative, interaction, and control. And in the same vein, the properties of milieu are held to be alien to the man's nature. The words lay down a host of potential storylines, all of them imbued with phallocentrism.

Of the various ways open to me to tell this phallocentric tale, I have chosen to make extensive use of the figure-ground terminology of perceptual organization. According to the conventional terminology for sexual performances, the man—especially his penis—is the figure in the sexual act; the woman—especially her vagina—is the ground. In figure-ground relationships, it is the ground that sets off the figure and never the other way around. The figure imparts some properties to the ground; visually a gray ground becomes whiter if it contains a very dark figure and becomes blacker if it contains a very light figure. It is also possible to say that the ground imparts some properties to the figure; for instance, a dark ground makes a light figure look whiter and a light ground makes a light figure look darker. Although reciprocal influences are exerted by figure and ground, this reciprocity does not obviate the fact that one is figure and the other ground.

According to the master narrative established by the words *impotence* and *frigidity*, a man may arouse a woman sexually without thereby establishing her as a figure in the sexual act and certainly not as *the* figure of the act. Instead, he will have changed the temperature of his milieu, and it will be a change that sets him off all the more as figure through his enhanced and confirmed potency. In clinical work it is often observed that a man's anxiously striving to bring his partner to orgasm has less to do with concern for her as a person and more with self-centered confirmation of his being a potent figure or agent acting on an object. Sometimes men use impregnation for the same kind of self-reassurance.

The figure has definition, boundaries, articulation, structure, prominence, and impact; it is that which is seen as such; it is what is looked at; it shows itself by standing out; it is remembered. The ground or milieu is amorphous, unbounded, unarticulated, unstructured; it is seen only through what it does for or to the figure; it is necessary for the sake of something else; it is modest, recessive, anonymous, set back or behind; it is not remembered, at least not for itself. Thinking along similar lines, Virginia Woolf likened the woman to the flattering mirror that shows off the man. From the standpoint of writing, the woman is the page on which the man writes his story of power. Thus, the phallocentric tale of what it is woman's nature to be and what she ought to be, if she is to be feminine, corresponds closely to the correlated terms *milieu*, *object*, and *ground*.

This sexist idea is shared by the mass of men and women, and it covers much of the conventional role of motherhood as well. Typically, male chauvinism or phallocentrism is the condition of both sexes, even if not equally so in every respect. When I say *sexist*, therefore, I am not referring only to men; nor am I referring only to its crudest forms. Elsewhere (see chapter 4), I have tried to show how sexist thinking influenced for the worse Freud's formulation of his otherwise profound, though partial, insights into the psychology of women.

The ground receives and incorporates the figure; the figure intrusively occupies the ground. The woman receives the man who intrudes into her. As the child is told, Daddy plants the seed in Mommy. The man has sexual drive; the woman sexual appetite. Consequently, the woman who assumes the prerogatives of the figure, as conventionally described, can expect to be viewed by others as aggressively masculine or as hostile to men or competitive with them. In psychoanalytic work, we often observe that, unconsciously and *in part,* a woman of this sort *is* attempting to depose the ruling man and be a man herself and, more specifically, to acquire symbolically a penis for herself by taking it away from the man. One familiar clinical instance of seizing the conventional male prerogative is encountered in the sexually tantalizing, exhibitionistic but frigid woman who, unconsciously and totally, equates her body and its sexual prominence and influence with the phallus. For her, the male's arousal is ground to her figure.

FANTASIES OF THE VAGINA DENTATA AND THE PHALLUS AS BREAST

The fantasy, shared by men and women alike, of the vagina dentata—the mutilating, castrating, devouring vaginal mouth—is frequently found to play a major part in impotence and frigidity. In the man's case, the fantasy of being unmanned by this vagina is in large part a way of wishfully projecting what he wishes: to turn into a woman, *for men envy women, too.* In the fantasy, the frightening female organ will do to him what he secretly wishes to bring about, even while fearing that outcome. Alternatively, the vagina dentata fantasy may be the man's way of regressively retreating to the imagined ultimate milieu: the mother's womb or the postnatal, pregenital configuration of the mother's holding arms and lap, nourishing breast, and smiling face. By such imaginings, the man hopes to merge into the ground and become one with the passive object. Thereby he will exist only through or in an indefinite other; no longer will he be required to be a person in his own right or to deal with another figure in its own right. Never again will he be alone. Perhaps thereby he will also avoid that brute annihilation of the woman as person that he unconsciously believes to be the consequence of his having to be a rapacious figure in the sexual relationship.

On the woman's part, the vagina dentata fantasy is a typical correlate of the unconsciously maintained fantasy that she has been wronged and humiliated by having been denied a penis or by having had it taken away from her, and of her having accordingly adopted an envious, rivalrous, castrating attitude toward the phallic, rapacious man. Implied in this retaliatory orientation is her wishing to become, or become once again, an assertive figure or agent. Analysts differ among themselves in how they rank order penis and power. As an assertive figure, the woman will have definition, structure, visibility, power; she will count as a person. But at the same time, in one of those unconsciously conflictual or paradoxical actions, her dentalization of the vagina may well also imply a regressive movement, specifically a returning to the role of the biting infant at the breast.

The breast enters the fantasy in this way: Psychoanalysts have defined a widespread, if not universal, fantasy in which, unconsciously, penis and breast are equated; and correlatively, semen and milk. These equations are especially salient in the analyses of those people who have centered their sexual interest in fellatio fantasies and practices, no matter whether they have done so in an overexcited, repulsed, or paralyzed fashion. Much gagging and vomiting of psychological origin can be attributed in part to a person's engaging in these fantasies conflictually and unconsciously.

This equation of breast and penis implies that the shadow of the mother has fallen on the penis and on the man whose organ it is; accordingly, the sexual act is, unconsciously, oral as well as genital. The equation of breast and penis undercuts the idea that sexism and phallocentrism are synonymous, for the bodily presence or absence of the penis as penis is now only one part of the story. Psychoanalysts would generally agree that the breast-penis equation is a lasting monument to the influence of the mother who necessarily both feeds and deprives. For this reason, figure-ground relations may be said to start at the breast and to remain there to a considerable extent. The denial of this pregenital substratum serves the defensive needs of both sexes, and in my opinion it has also served the defensive and conformist needs of many psychoanalysts of both sexes. I shall return to this point shortly.

In one of his last major contributions to the topic of femininity, Freud (1933) finally acknowledged the enduring primacy of this maternal figure in the lives of women. However, he did so only in a limited context: He ascribed many of the difficulties women have with their husbands to their importing into the marital relationships unresolved problems with their mothers; not just that they are identified with their troubled mothers, but that they unconsciously set their husbands up as unsatisfactory mothers. They establish maternal transferences to their husbands. Had Freud taken a more general view of the matter, he might have gone on to emphasize the positive potential of this same transference. A woman can, and often does, find a good mother as well as a good man and father in her husband, and to that extent has a richer and more gratifying relationship with him. Carrying this narrative line a step further, we may say that a man's integrated and balanced identification with some kind of good-mother image contributes to the warmth, generosity, and stability of his heterosexual relationships; the intent of this kind of female identification in a man is not primarily self-castration.

Sexism, whether blatant or unconsciously insidious, denies these insights and opportunities to men and women. Even more so does it deny the positive paternal potential in a woman's being the figure in relation to a man. There is little or no reference to this factor in the psychoanalytic literature. Most analysts seem to be content to stop at the idea of the phallic woman as *woman;* they view that imagined figure primarily in relation to castration anxiety; they dwell on people's unconsciously needing to reassure themselves that there is no anatomical difference between the sexes and thus no imagined castration to fear and no irreparable genital damage or deprivation to come to terms with. Useful as this view is in many cases, it is too narrow in that it does not encompass the idea that the phallic woman also contains the fantasized and perceived paternal potency, authority, and personhood. Insofar as a woman's activity and authority is unconsciously portrayed as masculine or phallic, it implies the father's potency in action. In relation to this potency, a man may become unconsciously passive, objectified, feminized, but he just as well may be paternally supported in being manly. For the man, both are consummations devoutly to be wished for as well as feared.

THE SUBJUGATION OF THE MOTHER

The significance of the infantile fantasies of the phallic and paternal mother and the vagina dentata cannot be overestimated in considering impotence and frigidity. Of equal importance is the mutual envy that exists between the sexes with its correlated wishing for and fearing the imagined castrated status. These contradictory representations and orientations pervade unconscious fantasizing. But the earliest, pregenital phase of psychological development involves other great problems that contribute to the personal and social issues with which we are here concerned. One particularly important issue is the difficult, stressful, and unstable differentiation of oneself as an active figure—a person—in relation to the caretaking and terribly powerful maternal figure. Through reconstructive analysis of dreams and transferences, which is paralleled by psychoanalytic child observation, it appears that the young child imagines loss of individuation to be a kind of devouring engulfment or annihilation that is perpetrated either by the mother or on the mother. It is a fantasy that, paradoxically, is experienced both excitedly and with shuddering horror—as is the castration fantasy.

This archaically conceived struggle for and against individuation seems to remain a lifelong project. Although some people continue this struggle more conspicuously, erratically, and anxiously than others, the fact of the struggle must be taken into account in any effort to understand problems of gender identification and its role in relations between the sexes.

In the case of girls there is the later problem—the first to have been securely established in psychoanalytic interpretation—of the struggle they carry on anxiously and guiltily against their rivalrous oedipal identification with the mother; this is the identification by means of which a girl hopes, unconsciously—though often consciously—to take the mother's place with the father. This later problem appears differently in the case of the boy. For him it is necessary to devalue the oedipal mother as one way of moderating his desiring to win her and his fearing that he will be inadequate to the task of winning her or satisfying her sexually. For the girl and boy alike, and both preoedipally and oedipally, the mother, far from being the ground or the passive object, emerges experientially as a gigantic figure to contend with and come to terms with. Speaking of the problems of the female writer in *A Room of One's Own*, Virginia Woolf (1924) recognized this phenomenon when she said, "A woman writing thinks back through her mothers." She would not have been wrong to say this of men, too, and not only when writing, for mothers continue to influence eating, dressing, loving, giving lectures, and so forth.

One of the important vantage points for viewing analytic data, then, is the one that looks squarely at the developing person's struggle for individuation and for an independent sense of adequacy, wholeness, safety, power, and worth. In this struggle, it seems to the child that the imposing figure of the mother, which is the prime representative of womanhood, must be cut down or cut up in order to be subdued or made manageable. She must be rejected, derogated, set apart, or consciously ignored. Here then is a set of powerful, unconsciously maintained reasons why, later on, both men and women are ready to participate in the socially reinforced discrimination against women, or at least to assent to it passively. For the same reasons, however, this figure must also be protected or repaired with special care—often by idealization, often by the person's own enslavement.

Critics of our sexist society find much to support their position in the fact that many or most mothers have more or less accommodated themselves to this state of affairs. These are women who, consciously, have given up aspirations of their own other than serving as a favorable ground or flattering mirrors for their husbands and children; they have neglected their own competences and potentialities of other sorts; they are disillusioned and discouraging figures who depend for self-esteem on defensive idealizations of them and enslavement to them. Today, many thoughtful young women scorn their conventionally sexist mothers and women of their sort. They regard them as wives who have declined into domesticity. They are disturbed, unconsciously even more than consciously, by their inevitable and lasting identification with these mothers. Although they seek desperately to escape, deny, or cancel out this identification, they make the effort so totally that they are bound to fail, achieving rather a radical discontinuity in their sense of themselves. Moreover, they cannot grasp the full meaning of that attempt at disidentification unless they take into account the problems, dating from infancy, of individuating from the archaic mother-figure and establishing a two-person relationship with her. They must also take into account the problems posed by the oedipal mother imago and the disillusioning mother imago of later phases of psychosexual development, and additionally they must see what they have gained by their identifications with her and what they can and do still value.

Thus, even though a demoralizing figure, the mother is still maintained as a forceful presence in the woman's own life. She is a figure to be reckoned with in her subjective inner world. The subjugation of women, in which women play a part that is more complex than that assigned in simple feminist theories of social reinforcement for male advantage, is also the subjugation of the powerful mother-figure of childhood. Unconsciously, it can get to seem that a woman's (a man's, too) life depends on that subjugation and the social world seems organized to lend its support to that project. Reparatively, that subjugation, of the mother-figure is given the appearance of adoration.

It is not sexist, as some radical feminists claim, to spell out, and work with, these insights into the relations between the sexes. It is sexist to maintain that the disruptive dramatization and proliferation of these familiar fantasies are altogether unmodifiable, that is, are simply and totally built into human development and have nothing to do with a social reality that encourages and reinforces them in countless ways and does so also for male advantage. It is sexist to think that a girl would naturally, totally, and permanently feel inferior and envious simply because she lacks a penis. It is sexist to say that nothing can be done about the reinforcing social reality, and even more so to assert that nothing should be done about it. Those feminists who have been making the developmental and social distinctions I am making—and there are some—are, I think, in a better position to attack both the societal and the therapeutic problems, for they have a more intimate knowledge of the enemy, within and without.

THE WHOLE PERSON

Developing the narrative further, we must go on to consider next what it means to be a whole person. From the standpoint of narrative action, what makes a person whole? I am referring now to an ideal definition, recognizing that in life and at best we approximate our ideals only intermittently. One of the fruits of effective personal psychoanalysis is that the analysand affirms this ideal and on the average lives closer to it than before the analysis.

A whole person is the one who acts, the agent. A whole person acts knowingly without profound reservations about the fact of acting, and so acts with presence and personal authority and without anxiously introducing serious disclaimers—such as the claim of being passively moved by natural forces, by the mind, or by a split-off self. In sexual relations, as elsewhere, a whole person acts the role of agent while refusing to deny personhood to the sexual partner, and accepts it as a psychological fact of life that *there cannot be only one whole person in the relationship.* In contrast, those who engage in extreme fantasies of omnipotence, such as paranoiac patients, implicitly sacrifice their own personal wholeness while denying that wholeness for others. Those who are thoroughly egocentric make the same double-barreled assault on self and other.

Guaranteeing the personal wholeness of others entails a readiness on a person's own part to serve on numerous occasions as object, ground, or milieu in relation to them, for they, too, must be given scope to exercise and confirm *their* personal agency and wholeness. A good conversation exemplifes what I am referring to: Can there be good conversation with only one person communicating in words, sounds, and gestures? Here we encounter the phenomenon of the *reversible* figure-ground relationship (the Necker cube, the Rubin vase/two profiles, and so on), and we come to the problem of changing the terms in which we understand the relations between the sexes.

We know that adamant rebellion does not change the terms of a problem with authority; the terms remain the same except that they have now a minus sign placed before them. Nor does a rigid role reversal change the terms of a problem. The miser who becomes a spendthrift, the mouse who becomes a lion, the homosexual woman who acts more like the stereotypical man than most men and the homosexual man who acts more like the stereotypical woman than most women: None of these has changed the terms of the problem; each is attempting to achieve what has been called in psychoanalytic discussion a change of content without a change of structure. A flip-flop is only a change of content; it accepts the structure of things as they are. Money, majesty, or macho remain the important structuring factors. Analysts have learned to be wary of such changes when, as often happens, they observe analysands abruptly and dramatically reversing their characteristic patterns of manifest action.

Traditionally, a fundamental change of the terms in which a problem is defined has been called a structural change. With regard to sexism, however, the change of terms that is called for is not limited simply to changing by conscious decision that which is to be designated *masculine* and *feminine* or *active* and *passive;* nor is it limited to consciously reallocating the prerogatives of the two sexes. Changes in both of these respects, though important and possible, depend for their force on a necessary and consequential change in the idea of a whole person who can enter into reversible figure-ground relations with others as co-agents.

A whole person allows the reversibility, in a relatively conflict-free fashion. He or she refrains from insisting on being only agent or object, only figure or ground, only active or passive, or only masculine or feminine, as conventionally defined. The reversibility is itself a form of action in that both refraining and allowing are actions. A whole person is neither threatened by reversibility nor incapable of enjoying either position in a relationship. The mutuality or reversibility of being a person not only matters more to a whole person than conventional ascriptions of masculine-feminine and active-passive; to a considerable extent, adopting the idea of persons-in-relation renders the other ideas unwelcome interferences in the business of living. Sometimes the reversibility includes projecting one or the other side of a person's bisexuality into the partner and enjoying it there: the man projecting what he regards as his feminine side or his masculine side; the woman, the same.

It must also be remarked that the reversibility, once established securely, no longer entails the threat or experience of loss of personhood. The reversible figure-ground model implies different and concurrent modes of agency; the tension between the alternating figures is essential to the phenomenon.

None of what I am saying discounts differences in degree and style of reversibility; for to state an ideal is not to prescribe absolute uniformity in its realization. To those who would cry "*Vive la différence!*" thinking of the pleasures of heterosexuality, I can only point out that nothing in my argument minimizes the different and complementary conformations, roles, and pleasure possibilities of male and female bodies; if anything, my argument should go some way toward enhancing the possibilities of loving unanxiously, unconflictedly, inventively, and without drastic confusion of stereotyped roles.

Consider, for example, the burden of always being pleasing, which weighs on most women in our sexist world and contributes to their masochistic and depressive proclivities. This burden of being first and foremost a reassuring milieu can be lifted and replaced by the pleasurable option, open to both sexes, of pleasing others of either sex—and of displeasing them, too, especially but not necessarily when it is in a good cause. A change of this sort—not a change to unmitigated hostility—is difficult to achieve; among other things, it means coming to terms with the incorporated, terribly powerful mother of infancy and of the oedipal period, the figure who ordinarily is felt to be hidden behind the ready smile and yielding empathy and who, it is hoped, is pacified and controlled thereby. Psychoanalysis facilitates this change while affirming that infantile tensions are never overcome entirely and that they increase their influence at times of crisis.

"GOOD," "BAD," "CAN," AND "CAN'T"

Some other changes in the terms of the problems of sexuality and sexism that can be accomplished through psychoanalysis concern narratives of the good and the bad, the innocent and the guilty, the safe and the dangerous; under a different and crucial aspect, these changes concern narratives of success and failure. The proper understanding of these changes depends on narratives of personal relations that do not obscure the range of agency or action.

Modification of the idea of the good and the bad, the innocent and the guilty, and the safe and the dangerous can for the most part be subsumed under the traditional psychoanalytic heading of modification of the superego. This modification is said to relieve the ego of the pressure to be as defensive as it may get to be in relation to the varieties of sexual desiring and other action. This is a familiar and crucially important chapter of psychoanalysis and will not be summarized here.

Suffice it to say that the analysand may come to accept it as an inescapable part of being a whole person that a person continues to be, in some measure, an orally receptive and biting baby, an anally sensuous and dirty baby, and a bisexually incestuous young child who is identified with both parents and desires each of them erotically. Through analysis, these continuities may get to be seen as the inescapable heritage of growing up human, which means developing into a person in the context of a family and a society composed of men and women. It also means growing up with a male or female body that has its own pleasure possibilities and vulnerabilities; moreover, it means reclaiming one's own body from the internalized parental figures, making it one's own by asserting the right to decide on its uses in sexual relationships, and enjoying the pregenital residues in lovemaking. This set of modifications typically has the effect of reducing the unconsciously maintained dominance of many of the infantile carryovers that have been most disturbing in a person's relations with a partner. These carryovers have remained disturbing because they are the ones that have been most anxiously, guiltily, and uncompromisingly fragmented and repudiated and so have never been mastered, integrated, and put to good use.

As superego condemnation diminishes, what once could only be desperate adventures, engaged in surreptitiously or in fantasy or else sternly prohibited, now become possibilities of play. The sexual act as a whole becomes a possibility of play. The claim that this is so is in no way incompatible with the claim that sexual loving is also a possibility of intimacy of the most serious kind. Play and seriousness are themselves freed from the trap of either/or judgments. These either/or judgments bear the mark of a person's own archaic, unconsciously enforced superego categories. As Freud noted (1921), this type of moralistic enforcement is frequently increased in scope and severity upon marrying and having children, for these are transitional actions in connection with which people often consolidate further their identifications with the conventionally prohibiting parental imagoes. If these imagoes are particularly forbidding, problems of impotence and frigidity may increase from then on, and so may sexist attitudes. Advancing into middle age is, I would say, another transition that favors shifts toward sexual conservatism.

Changing the narratives of success and failure at sex—the storylines of making it or not making it—comes under another aspect than does modification of superego identifications. What it requires is a new appreciation that, in the most fundamental psychological sense, impotence and frigidity are not failures at all. Here we arrive at the importance of correcting, by analytic working through, presuppositions that we are dealing not with actions but with abilities, capacities, or achievements—with cans and can'ts. Like other symptoms, impotence and frigidity are more correctly and profitably retold interpretively as complex actions corresponding to complex psychological situations. Even though their final manifestations are physical and physiological states of muscular, circulatory, and secretory unpreparedness for the complex sex act, these manifestations are appropriate features of the intentional actions and situations they unconsciously imply. They are not happenings—events to be suffered passively: So psychoanalysis teaches or tells in its narratives of sexual behavior; so it interprets to the analysands the problems of impotence and frigidity

To put what I mean concretely: If, for example, unconsciously, one partner in a marital sex act is fleeing a scene of incestuous sexuality, that person is neither in a marital sexual situation nor moving more deeply into it, nor is anything happening to a passive victim; unconsciously, that person is fleeing. Similarly, if, unconsciously, one partner in a sex act is tightening up mentally and muscularly in order to avoid an orgasmic anal explosion, an imagined eventuality that will make a mess or be destructive and in either case threaten loss of love and painful shame, that person is not to any appreciable degree interacting erotically and genitally with another person, nor is that person an unfortunate passive object; unconsciously, that person is holding in. And if, to give one more example, a man is doing all he can not to show himself off or see the other, owing to the still influential prohibitions or shame connected with infantile exhibitionism and voyeurism, then he is hiding his body and his excitement, or he is blinding himself or imaginally turning his back on his lover, and in either case hardly qualifying as a lover himself; far from finding himself out of it, he is unconsciously making sure to be out of it.

Whatever the explanation, it is psychoanalytically wrong to tell it as a story of failure. In the psychoanalytic narrative, the impotent or frigid person is doing exactly what is right to do under the unconsciously defined, fantasized circumstances that count the most at that moment. When those circumstances are sufficiently understood, no plausible alternative account is available. The storyline of failure makes sense only with respect to some inaccurate *conscious* idea of what kind of situation a person is in and what he or she wishes to do in it. That limited conscious idea precludes insightful change.

In contrast, the implicit or explicit action narrative makes insightful change possible: change, not success; change through recasting the fundamental terms of the problem. Accomplishing any such change in the social realm will require overcoming or mitigating the societal seduction of boys into uneasy representatives of pure masculine force and of girls into demoralized representatives of pure feminine milieu. What is required is a social psychological theory of the narrative seduction of children. That theory would, however, have to take account of what clinical psychoanalysis and child observation have established: the eagerness and the frightened acquiescence with which children participate in these seductions owing to the thrilling and terrifying features of their infantile fantasy life. In the light of this new, complementary seduction theory, we may hope to reclaim many disclaimed sexual actions and thereby to help people be whole, responsible, reciprocally related persons. Although that kind of reclamation work might in time do a lot more than enhance pleasurable, consummated sexual relations, it can at present help diminish much needless sexual frustration and humiliation.

CHAPTER 6

The Idealization of Unhappiness and the Pursuit of Failure

PSYCHIC suffering is more than the motive for analytic therapy. It is the problem for the therapy as well, in that the analysand has probably established psychic suffering as a fixed and necessary feature of his or her mode of living. Upon analysis, entrenched suffering often turns out to be, unconsciously, a compromise formation with multiple and contradictory constituents, meanings, or functions.

Usually discussed as masochism, entrenched suffering must in each case be analyzed in terms of themes or storylines. These themes are more particular than would be suggested by the abstract term *masochism.* These particular themes or storylines serve as organizers of interpretations. Inevitably, more than one such organizer must be applied to any one analysand's material. Few of these organizers are mutually exclusive. In the present context, they include (in traditional terms) an extravagant ego ideal with respect to which the self must always fall short; a severe superego with respect to which every pleasure must be paid for with painful guilt and self-destructiveness; and the sexualization of suffering itself, that is, suffering as what Freud (1915c) called a "precondition for loving."

In this chapter I propose two organizing themes or storylines of entrenched suffering: the pursuit of failure and the idealization of unhappiness. As well as making some general clinical remarks, I offer brief and partial case summaries that illustrate some of the major meanings of, or functions served by, failure and unhappiness. Finally, I remark on what appears to me to be a relative difference between the sexes with respect to the pursuit of failure and the idealization of unhappiness. In this connection I take up some implied fundamental problems in the theory and the psychoanalytic interpretation of unconscious mental processes.

GENERAL CLINICAL REMARKS

Typically, those who suffer from repetitive failure and chronic unhappiness present themselves dismally as afflicted or victimized. Upon analysis, however, the reported failures prove to have been pursued at least as much as they have been the result of inescapable adversity. Similarly, the unhappiness frequently proves to have been self-inflicted at least as much as it has been an expression of the inescapable miseries of everyday life. It is the unconsciously arranged and perpetuated portions of psychic suffering that the analyst should clarify and modify through interpretation. Freud (1920a) made essentially this point in his discussion of the fate neuroses.

Certainly our analysands do not simply bring all their unhappiness on themselves. But even when the analyst makes due allowance for sheer adversity, of which there is usually more than enough in everyone's life, there is ample room for him or her to show neurotic analysands not only that they are being inappropriately self-blaming for this adversity but are adding to the adversity itself, thereby increasing the failure and unhappiness being reported. It is a distinguishing feature of psychoanalytic work that emphasis is placed on unconscious activity of this sort. This feature of the work is actualized through the analyst's paying close attention to psychic reality, particularly as it is discernible in the here and now of transference and defense. In this context, "psychic reality" refers to the private, largely unconsciously maintained, infantile meanings of success and failure and of happiness and unhappiness. The term also refers to the way in which the analysand repetitiously uses these archaic meanings to construct current painful experience. Experience is always to be regarded as constructed rather than simply introspected. Transference and defense demonstrate the construction of experience in the analytic situation.

THE PURSUIT OF FAILURE

Freud (1916) approached some major aspects of the pursuit of failure under the heading "Those wrecked by success." That the phenomena to which Freud referred are widespread may be asserted all the more confidently if we take into account the wreckage associated with the mere anticipation of success and also if we allow that being wrecked may be a matter of degree, as in the case of neurotic mediocrity. Freud also noted that commonly, though usually unconsciously, analysands fear "getting well" as a form of success, that is, success as analysands. Consequently, we may recognize that what Freud (1923a) called the negative therapeutic reaction, which in varying degrees also bedevils analytic work, is a variant of being wrecked by analytic success or the prospect thereof.

In his explanations, Freud typically emphasized the unconscious oedipal triumph signified by worldly success and the guilty self-punishment for this triumph that is signified by the ensuing personal and occupational wreckage. However, the pursuit of failure is far more complex than would be suggested by Freud's typical focus on oedipal dynamics, even though we can only be impressed by the interpretive success of that focus throughout the history of psychoanalysis.

Strictly speaking, the characterization of certain people as being wrecked by success is made descriptively; that is, it is made from the standpoint of the outside observer rather than from the standpoint of the subject's own psychic reality. Looking on as outside observers, we are limited to considering dramatic overt instances, such as the depression that follows on the heels of a long-desired promotion or the panic that follows on the consummation of a long-desired love relationship. Descriptively, the subject appears to be a passive victim of achievement. In contrast, working within psychic reality, analysts seek to establish in each instance just what constitutes success and just what constitutes being wrecked by it. The individual, subjective, mostly unconsciously maintained conceptions of success and failure are not always what convention or common sense would lead us to expect.

This divergence from commonsense expectation is not surprising once we take into account that, as a rule, people are more or less unconsciously conflicted with respect to their goals in life. Due to this conflict, what is success from the point of view of one set of aims is failure from the point of view of other aims that conflict with them. Freud (1900, p. 604) established this principle in another connection, that of pleasure, when he observed that what is pleasurable for one psychical system may be painful for another. In the terms of the structural theory he developed later on (1923a), he had in mind particularly those instances in which id gratification conflicts with the ego's defensive and adaptive aims and the superego's archaic moral aims. Thus, analysts view symptom formation, for example, as combining pleasure and pain as well as success and failure. In this perspective, a subject cannot be a passive victim of achievement; unconsciously, the subject has made failure a project and frequently has become ingenious in achieving it. As one analysand once said, after having crystallized insight into his artful and unrelenting pursuit of failure, "If I put ten percent of this energy into really succeeding, there is nothing I could not achieve."

Failure as well as success must be looked at in the same complex and superficially paradoxical way. From the standpoint of psychic reality rather than conventional reality, failure may represent more than painful defeat or punishment. For example, failure may also represent the triumphant fulfillment of archaic moral aims in opposition to infantile libidinal aims; similarly, it may represent the triumphant fulfillment of a person's ego aims of reducing psychic pain to a minimum by withdrawing from situations of worldly success that threaten to bring on intolerable anxiety or guilt. Consequently, analysts must keep on asking: What is the failure in success? and What is the success in failure? It was in this vein that Theodore Reik (1941) emphasized the concept of victory through defeat in his analysis of masochism.

I have organized my case examples of the pursuit of failure largely around pathological formation of the ego ideal, as the ego ideal is an essential component of character structure. Success and failure cannot be discussed psychoanalytically without considering it. However, for reasons advanced and developed elsewhere (Sandler, Holder, and Meers, 1963; Schafer, 1967), I prefer to speak of the ideal self rather than the ego ideal. Traditionally, the ego ideal has been tied too closely to superego theory, and so it does not adequately take into account the primitive wishful, defensive, and adaptive aspects of ideal formation along with its archaic moral aspects—that is, its id and ego aspects along with its superego aspects. It is easier to take account of antisocial, utilitarian, or primitively wishful ideals when working with the concept of ideal self. I use that term to refer to a guideline for activity rather than to denote an active force or agency in the mind.

Identification, too, must be seen as central to the development of the ideal self, provided that we take into account the fantastic, infantile elaboration of the idea of the person with whom the child is identifying. Ideals are often based on identifications with figures who, in conventional terms, are far from moral or well sublimated.

Case Example

Consider a young man whose ideal self features being an underachiever. That underachievement was his ideal was established only after analytic exploration of his trials and tribulations in school, at work, and in the analysis. In his psychic reality, to be an underachiever was to conform to the role his family appeared to have assigned to him early in his life. This role warded off envy and disparagement by his siblings; it also earned parental love in the form of his father's compassionate help when, but only when, the boy was in trouble. Typically, feelings of being a "good kid" were associated with lack of achievement and steady self-disparagement. His self-esteem rode on his being an underachiever. Thus, disturbed formation of his ideal self had to be counted as a major variable in his repetitive pursuit of failure. Erikson (1956) discussed similar phenomena in terms of negative identity formation.

To present this young man's problem as one of a disturbed ideal self is not to ignore the castrating oedipal defeat that was entailed by his meeting negative ideals. Nor is it to ignore his conflictedness with respect to the negative features of his ideal self, for it also became obvious that he had not entirely renounced his positive oedipal strivings and other, more positive ideals associated with them. In self-contradiction, he also rebelled against the negative ideals he maintained unconsciously; however, owing to the painfulness of acting otherwise than self-destructively, he could not sustain his rebellion. In his analytic sessions, for example, he could hardly finish a sentence in which he said something that was even slightly positive about himself; he had to interrupt with self-criticism.

Thus, for this young man, failure was also a success of a kind, while being a success was also a failure. In his transference, he mostly worked energetically to invite the analyst's compassionate help by presenting himself as stupid, ineffectual, and desperate. And while consciously he professed to be ashamed of himself for his inadequacies, it developed over the course of the analysis that, unconsciously, he was being a "good kid," was feeling like one, and was expecting the analyst to be pleased with his failures and his need for help.

Case Example

In another instance, one of the dominant ideas of success was based on the analysand's having unconsciously identified with an asocial and antisocial gambling father, a man who had had more than his share of worldly success and worldly failure. The son felt most alive and manly when he was working alone, recklessly and unnecessarily at the brink of failure. He felt most feminine and castrated when he had to work within a group and when he was a loser. Being an isolated loser was a position he unconsciously desired and feared simultaneously.

Case Example

A third young man's pursuit of failure served unconsciously to protect the self-esteem of his apparently weak, unsuccessful father. But this unconsciously repetitive activity also served other important functions: In one way, it amounted to rebellion against his father's demands on him for a conformist type of dedication to success; in another way, it amounted to compliance with his family's general tendency to romanticize emotional distress. Emotional distress was a condition of being interesting, and the setting of this condition appeared to be based on the powerful sadomasochistic pattern of family interaction. Thus, for him, failure was a way of being sadistically and masochistically lovable as well as defiant. In contrast, being successful in a neutral and well-organized way was to invite painful exclusion from the family drama and from the opportunity for oedipal thrills and perhaps ultimate victory.

Case Example

Yet another young man had identified himself with a pretentious, egoistic father in a way that could only lead to failure in his own conventional undertakings. With this paternal identification, the young man had to be intolerant of his own limitations; he had to be a pretentious, self-undermining poseur himself. At the same time, however, in going to extremes he was enacting an angry mockery of his father. Additionally, he was not challenging his father on psychically real oedipal grounds. The real challenge would have been to be a solid, sincere, aesthetically sensitive achiever of the sort that he knew his unhappily married mother responded to romantically. Thus, for this young man to be manly in character and not castrated psychosexually was tantamount to repudiating his identification with his father, and this we know to be a difficult feat for any man under any conditions. Analysts should not be misled by analysands' consciously and vehemently asserted aim of disidentifying with paternal models—or for that matter, maternal models as well. Consequently, this young man could repudiate only partially this damaging paternal identification. Moreover, not only was the father an achiever in his own right, whatever his pretensions, but, as always, there lay in the background of these derogated images of the pretentious father the unconsciously maintained imago of the powerful phallic father that the analysand had developed during the years of very young boyhood. This is the omnipotent, idealized father who, in psychic reality, is never seen in all his complexity, conflictedness, insecurity, and limitation.

The powerful primordial father should never be forgotten. Analysands tend insistently to represent only the scaled-down father of later periods of development. They hope thereby to get the analyst to accept these shrunken representations as psychically accurate and complete. These derogated representations also have their place in personal development—they, too, are psychically real—but the analysis of the pursuit of failure, as of so many other problems, depends on getting beyond these limited and later representations to the early father imago. The primordial father is always sexually powerful enough to overwhelm, satisfy, and impregnate the mother and to castrate the oedipally rivalrous son. He can handle anything. But this primal father is not just a threatening figure; he is also a latent source of a strong and successful ideal self. Only the analysis of transference and defense enables the analyst to get securely beyond the later, problematic, consciously asserted, derogated representations of the father and thereby to tap into developmental strengths that have been given no secure place in the analysand's character structure.

More now about this pretentious young man. Early in his analysis, while he still consciously idealized his father, he felt that he could never be as cool, witty, literate, and daring as his father. He promptly engaged in a similar idealizing of the analyst, and he elaborated an extravagant, superficial identification with him. His self-esteem shot up with his analytic pretentiousness. Consequently, he was hardly approachable through analytic interventions. This father-son repetition in the analytic relationship was his initial transference, and at the same time it was obviously his initial major form of defense. Technically, therefore, it was necessary to conduct some close and patient examination of contradictory ideas and feelings concerning the idealized father of later and disturbed phases of development. This preliminary work outside of transference and defense was necessary to show the analysand that, as a son, he also felt betrayed, enraged, and despondent, and that the ideal self he was playing at was flimsy, exhausting, and painful. This phase of the work required some forceful confrontations on the analyst's part. Only subsequently could the more fundamental aspects of transference and defense be taken up analytically and a similar account of his relationship to the analyst be developed. This work opened the way to an analysis of the influence of the primordial father imago, and thereby it opened a way to alternatives to being a success only at failing.

As I mentioned, I organized the preceding examples largely around disturbed development of the ideal self; however, during analysis, the pursuit of failure gets to be organized around many other themes as well. For one thing, there is the obvious problem of warding off envy. Of the many variants of envy that could be elaborated in this connection, I want to emphasize especially the psychically real envy directed by one or another parent at the child's promise and attainments. I refer here to the envious father who feels less well endowed and less attractive to his wife than his son and to the envious mother who feels less feminine, less competent, and less attractive to her husband than her daughter. The promising or successful child faces the threat of experiencing some form of unconsciously maintained, envious, filicidal desire and sabotage. In these settings, any strong positive emotional response of the nonenvious parent is experienced as threatening in its incestuous implications.

Thus, it is not only that too much harm seems to be threatened by one parent's envy, but that too much gratification of the most problematic kind seems to be threatened by the other parent's positive response. In instances of this sort, we are probably always dealing with fantastic infantile parental imagoes resting on a fragment of good reality testing. Technically, the analysis may be blocked if the element of reality testing is totally ignored; at the same time, the analysis may miscarry if only reality testing is emphasized while the infantile fantastic elaborations are ignored. It is a delicate and taxing problem to sort out and balance these factors.

Before I move on to idealized unhappiness, I should mention other organizing themes. For example, success presents the danger that unconsciously maintained grandiose ideas of the self will be experienced consciously. Kohut (1971, 1977) had some significant points to make in this regard. Some analysands experience significant and even panicky disorientation of an incipiently manic or paranoid sort once they dare to recognize and assert their own special achievements or the special talents that are implied by these achievements. During these moments of truth, they may convey a sense of loss of reality and contact with others, sometimes even a sense of being crazy. Body-image distortions may occur. Consequently, they retreat in panic from these recognitions and assertions, and they do so repeatedly until their frightening fantasies, expectations, and reactions are more fully defined and worked through. Here, too, issues of reality testing must be taken into account, now in relation to adequate appraisals of the self.

In my view, this crisis of narcissism is not resolvable in terms of Kohut's self psychology alone. Self-psychological considerations may help gain access to fear of a latent grandiose self and of patent exhibitionism, but, as a rule, this crisis of narcissism also seems to imply the oedipal crisis that served as Freud's central organizing theme. The crisis may also imply a disruption of a preoedipal symbiotic tie or a disturbing sense of merging with the grandiose imagoes of the parents of very early childhood. Annie Reich (1953, 1954, 1960) was among the first Freudians to show a keen attentiveness to the mix of oedipal and preoedipal factors in these narcissistic crises.

To continue with self-psychological themes, sometimes the path to success seems to be blocked unconsciously by the fantasy of irremediable deficit or defect. Ideas of deficit and defect do often seem to refer to mothering that was not "good enough" or empathic enough. But that this deprivation seems to have taken place does not mean that there is no network of oral, anal, and phallic-exhibitionistic fantasies or fixations, and of defenses against them, that have served as latent sources of the idea of having been damaged by poor care. However important parental empathic failure may have been, it does not preclude the central presence of fixed and pervasive ideas of being damaged and of many infantile wish fulfillments and defenses. If the analysis is not confined to self-psychological issues, it often does prove a useful next step to reinterpret the unempathic mother, for example, as the fantastically exaggerated, powerful, and retaliatory oedipal rival or the rejecting or unsatisfied oedipal and preoedipal object. It may turn out that it is oedipal threat and defeat or preoedipal abandonment or torture that have been giving their apparent force to the ideas of defect and deficit.

An individual may use these ideas of being crippled to cope with problems of bisexuality: The male may so use psychic castratedness; the female, the repudiation of phallic aspirations. In addition, the idea of a defect may be used unconsciously as a malignant phallus or breast to triumph over the world, and in this way it may represent victory exhibitionistically and omnipotently snatched from the jaws of defeat (see, for example, Shakespeare's *Richard III*). I have argued elsewhere (1983) that some analysands may use unconsciously maintained and elaborated ideas of being imprisoned or empty in the same way that others use ideas of being damaged or defective.

Whatever the case, to those in hot pursuit of failure, conventional or analytic success inevitably means giving up a lot. For this reason, analytic accomplishment may be an occasion at least for painful mourning and more likely for periods of painful depression. In psychic reality, what is lost is the mother's breast (however bad), the secret penis, the omnipotence, and so on, that make up the fantastic assumptions on which character is based. The acutely distressing aspects of success and failure are primarily infantile in origin rather than contemporary. Certainly any contemporary success of a conventional public sort does give rise to many new problems of personal synthesis and interpersonal relationship, and those problems are not to be ignored. Yet all these new stresses and strains derive whatever devastating force they have from being construed unconsciously in the terms of infantile attachment, loss, seduction, defeat, damage, and other dangers. For those who appear to be wrecked by success, there may be much of value that is hidden among the ruins.

THE IDEALIZATION OF UNHAPPINESS

Here I lead off with a few case examples of the idealization of unhappiness and the implied construction of an unhappy ideal self.

Case Example

A woman in analysis made the following slip of the tongue. Intending to say that upon having been confronted by a threatening situation, she had experienced cold chills going down her spine, she said, "Cold thrills went down my spine." This woman had a lifelong history of attempting to relieve others of their unhappiness by absorbing it into herself. Unconsciously, as many women in our culture seem to do, she incorporated their unhappiness and suffered for them. In so doing, she felt that she was being a good girl, that is, kind, compassionate, supportive, undemanding, even self-sacrificing. From a young age, she had done this to an extreme degree with all members of her family. This Christlike role, itself a kind of excellence for her, also supported and restored good feeling to the others involved. It certainly had this effect in her fantasies, although as the analysis proceeded, evidence accumulated to suggest that often her family members were most comfortable with her when she was unhappy. The consequence of her incorporating the unhappiness of others in her family was that she could then more easily idealize them as secure, kind, compassionate, and supportive to her as a girl and later as the woman with whom we are here concerned. In her psychic reality, she gained love and importance by being unhappy, and by this means, too, she added worth to her idea of herself. In line with analytic expectation, she attempted to play this role in the transference: If she could not perceive some discomfort or distress in the analyst for her to incorporate, she invented it; thus, it was part of her transference that she was protecting or healing the suffering analyst by suffering herself and thereby reaching toward her ideal self.

Technically, it was necessary to interpret this chronic unhappiness as being designed unconsciously to enhance her own self-esteem at the expense of the analyst, as earlier it had been at the expense of her family members. The strategy also had to be analyzed as an attempt to love and be loved by an idealized figure, albeit through suffering. Additionally it emerged that, unconsciously, she also enjoyed punishing others by being miserable to the point of being inconsolable. Her idealization of unhappiness was, in its relation to others, an ambivalent or conflictual strategy. The various gratifications she achieved through this strategy rendered it extremely difficult for her to contemplate or undergo change. Signs of improvement were conducive to dramatic negative therapeutic reactions; that is, she lost analytic ground whenever she began to feel better.

Her slip of the tongue in substituting "thrills" for "chills" pointed to a sexual masochistic theme for which there was other evidence, including extensive and exciting fantasies of abuse and humiliation. That it was *cold* thrills pointed in two directions. On the one hand, "cold" pointed to that aspect of the unhappy ideal self that was ruthlessly self-serving, envious, and competitive and that was cold in the everyday sense of a "cold heart" or "cold person." On the other hand, "cold" pointed to her defending against consciously experiencing the erotic heat of her masochism (see, for example, Freud, 1919) by maintaining instead a sexual coldness in her relations with others. Indeed, this woman had been described by a friend as a come-hither spinster.

Thus, her idealization of unhappiness could be retold analytically in terms of sexuality, aggressiveness, defensiveness, adaptation (at least in the family setting of her childhood), and archaic morality. Morality was involved because, unconsciously, she not only lived her love life and hate life through suffering, she also secretly paid for living out her ambivalence by suffering even more painfully.

Case Example

Another woman made a similar slip of the tongue. Intending to say how heavily burdened she was by her mother's negative attitudes, she said instead, "I am so heavenly burdened by her." In this woman's psychic reality, she had experienced the best parental caretaking when she was most discontent and self-disparaging, and she had experienced the worst combination of neglect, disparagement, and envy when she was effective, enthusiastic, and proud. It had seemed to her during her development that she was supposed to be an object of contempt, and she had concluded that it was presumptuous of her to think or speak well of herself or to do well by herself. Thus, in her analysis, as was true in the case of one of the men discussed earlier in the section on the pursuit of failure, she could not sustain a positive self-narrative. Typically, right after she would begin a positive narration, she would break it off, calling it silly, irrelevant, offensive, bragging, or boring. She would then go on immediately to groan over a flood of humiliating associations, or she would bring up memories of personal disasters for which she was responsible, or she would at great length detail problems with respect to which she was helpless. Sometimes she never even began the positive story. Sometimes she just switched from one type of narrative to the other without transitionally derogating what she had just been saying. Occasionally she would, as it were, break in on herself indignantly, saying, "Who do I think I am anyway?"

Unhappiness was what others wanted and, through identification with her parents, it was what she now wanted for herself. It seemed that her ideal self was an unhappy one. She felt rotten when her story was positive, and she felt desirable, estimable, and secure when it was negative. During the analysis she became aware that she expected the analyst to prefer, if not require, this unhappy self.

In one respect, her "heavenly" burdens were the alleged personal defects that guaranteed that her parents would be accepting, attentive, and consoling caretakers. In another respect, the word *burdens* referred to the infantilizing and disparaging parents themselves, along with her identification with them. As always, many other influences of an unconscious nature were also involved in the construction of this unhappy ideal self.

Case Example

In another instance, an ascetic, spartan, self-absorbed, and mute unhappiness seemed in large part to be a young woman's way of appealing to a father who, it seemed, lived his life in just that way. Her unhappiness was also a way of identifying with him. As a girl, this woman had gained his companionship and admiration by modeling herself on him. As a woman, she regulated her own self-esteem in the same way. Unconsciously, for her, this mode of existence was also a way of being defiantly and proudly masculine, for in her psychic reality she could escape from humiliating femininity through masculine inaccessibility. It is by no means unusual to encounter this father-daughter configuration in analytic practice—again, however, as part of a larger complex of factors.

In the three cases I just summarized, it was possible to see that these women had also defined constituents of conventionally positive ideal selves. There was a good deal to suggest that they had been exposed to many influences that could only have been conducive to their developing more positive ideal selves. Consequently, they could only experience with great distress the consciously miserable ways in which they were constructing their current lives. It was with reference to these positive ideal selves that it became meaningful, if not imperative, for these women to throw their unhappiness into question and to undertake analysis. But for the most part, once they were in analysis, they kept these happier ideal selves secret; they found it very difficult to present and sustain them consciously. One reason for this difficulty was their struggle against identification with a devalued mother figure (Greenson, 1954). In this struggle, they were repressing the early, active, caretaking, and powerful mother figure. It was a case of throwing out the primary mother with the bathwater.

At the same time, however, there was, as usual, a good deal in their self-stories to suggest that the widespread victimization of women in our society, the discrimination against women and their brutalization, not to speak of the many subtle forms of seduction of women into debased roles, had all played significant parts in these women having taken in, developed, and rigidified the unhappiness that they subsequently had come to idealize. But, as this development is not equally conspicuous in, and disruptive for, all women exposed to these inimical social pressures, it seems that we must still give considerable weight in our explanations to infantile fantasy and other early developmental influences. An adequate discussion of these issues would require a lengthy treatment in its own right, some of which I have offered elsewhere (see chapters 4, 5, and 7).

Suffice it to say here that no amount of analytic interpretation of the unconsciously active, repetitive, idealizing search for suffering implies any preconception or conclusion that, after all, women simply bring their unhappiness on themselves. With our current understanding of all relevant factors, this idea of women is untenable as well as damaging. Furthermore, the deidealization of unhappiness that is often accomplished through psychoanalysis tends to bring with it an increased readiness to develop what are, for these women, lively critiques of our sexist world and adequately assertive means to resist and combat the seductions into suffering with which they are constantly surrounded.

CONCLUSION: REMARKS ON PSYCHOANALYTIC INTERPRETATION AND NARRATION

When I discussed the pursuit of failure, I drew my examples from analytic work with men. When I discussed the idealization of unhappiness, I drew my examples from analytic work with women. The selection of cases reflects my impression that the theme of pursuing failure is relatively more conspicuous in analytic work with men, while the idealization of unhappiness is relatively more conspicuous in analytic work with women.

But what does it mean to say that one theme is more conspicuous in certain cases than it is in others? Does it mean that I simply find it to be so in the same sense that one finds more snow up north and up high? Or does it mean that I employ a certain theme more actively in work with one sex and another theme in work with the other sex? By raising these questions, I am introducing into our considerations a major issue in psychoanalytic epistemology. The issue is one of deciding whether what Freud (1915a) called the unconscious and what he described as its contents are discovered or created, encountered or imposed, found or made. Freud can be quoted on both sides of this thorny issue. Elsewhere (1981, 1983) I have attempted at some length to develop a case for regarding "the unconscious" as both found and made; more exactly, for regarding it as the product of dialogue or as a co-authored text produced and progressively revised by two members of the same narrative and interpretive community. I shall not review the details of that discussion here, nor shall I review similar discussions by others (for example, Ricoeur, 1977).

I introduce this epistemological issue for two reasons. One is to be able to assert that the two themes—the pursuit of failure and the idealization of unhappiness—are not mutually exclusive. Few psychoanalytic themes are; hence the frequent invocation in analytic discussions of the concepts of overdetermination and multiple function. For the most part, the examples I have presented under one heading could have been presented under the other; indeed, both themes were developed in all of the cases mentioned, even though to different degrees.

My second reason for introducing the issue of whether "the unconscious" is found or made is implied by my use of the word *theme.* As I said in my introductory remarks, I am using the word *theme* in the sense of storyline or narrative organizing principle. In following this usage, I am making the following assumptions. Analytic therapy is a process of constructing by analytic means life histories that have been dominated by the analysand's own unconscious mental processes. Histories are narrative constructions, each history being controlled by storylines. The historian chooses the storylines that make sense in the narrative and interpretive community of which he or she is a member. In the course of analytic therapy, as in the course of all historical work, more than one history can be constructed, and usually more than one is. It requires several basic themes at least to help retell a life story adequately along analytic lines.

To say that this work requires narrative choices is not to say that the analyst's lines of interpretation are sheer fabrications or are selected at random. It is to say that what we analysts accept as the facts of current and past reality are necessarily rendered in the terms of one or more themes that serve as our controlling guidelines for inquiry and formulation. In this way, and only in this way, do facts acquire significance for the analysis. The significance of facts is established by and within a context of questions and methods that are consistent with a set of narrative choices. These choices are usually called theories (see also chapters 9, 10, and 11).

Taken together, all of these assumptions make it possible to understand that the nature and content of unconscious mental processes have been defined variously by alternative schools of psychoanalysis. In the same way, though to a lesser degree, these processes are defined variously by the members of any one school of psychoanalysis.

I believe that my relatively greater emphasis on the idealization of unhappiness by women does capture an important feature of the psychology of women in our society. At the same time, however, I must grant that this relatively greater emphasis is also a consequence of my having actively developed that storyline, among others, in my work with a number of women and of my having found it useful in helping them analytically to lead what were, for them, better lives. A similarly constructed conclusion applies to the pursuit of failure undertaken by many men. Thus, in this chapter I have been as much describing some aspects of my way of working analytically as I have been describing phenomena that should be available to any other analyst and that could be of some social significance, pertaining as it does to the prevalence of manifest depressiveness in women. The discipline of psychoanalysis would be advanced were more analysts to present their conclusions as both findings and creations, in this way getting beyond fruitless, naïvely objectivist, or empiricist arguments over the so-called facts of the case.

CHAPTER 7

Men Who Struggle Against Sentimentality

SENTIMENTALITY often turns out to be a key issue in psychoanalysis. And when it does, it is likely to come up in the context of a man's noisy or quietly desperate struggle *against* sentimentality, both his own and that of others. Those men who engage in this struggle regard sentimentality as a serious fault to be corrected or a great danger to be avoided. Typically, they do not recognize the potential of the phenomena they subsume under sentimentality for adaptive uses and consequences. I am referring particularly to men who present themselves in analysis as aridly obsessional, icily narcissistic, lovelessly depressive, brutally phallic, or psychopathically superficial. In other words, more than a few men, though by no means all or all to the same extent.

We analysts cannot fail to appreciate the fact that these men have grown up in a context of parents and others who have extreme and conflictual values of their own with respect to sentimentality and who, in one way or another, have tried to pass on these values and conflicts. Nevertheless, we cannot view the antisentimentalists' self-presentations simply as a matter of having been socially conditioned and forced into conformity. Geared as we must be to facilitating personal change, we do not view the child simply as a blank page to be written on by a pack of like-minded authors. We consider it more important to develop an understanding of how antisentimentality has figured in each child's attempt to resolve conflictual issues centered on sexuality and aggression and how it has been comprehended in the individualized terms of the typical unconscious fantasies of early childhood.

Usually, analyzing the struggle against sentimentality helps open the gate to a wide variety of repudiated but developmentally significant and even valuable strivings. Among other things, successful analysis of large-scale versions of this struggle leads to greater clarity about, and tolerance of, issues of gender identity, to more intense and stable relationships with others, to a fuller subjective sense of being alive in a social world and in a worthwhile way, and to a more continuous, inclusive, unembarrassed narrative of the analysand's own complex life history as a boy and man. In contrast, analytic impasses may develop when the analyst neglects to look into the lifelong activities that have gone into an analysand's conspicuous antisentimentality, or when the analyst fails, despite the best of efforts, to make headway against it.

For these reasons, an analytic discussion of men who struggle against sentimentality has implications not only for the general psychology of men, in which respect, for example, it will bear on what often seem to be their deficiencies of empathy and their fears of self-disclosure, dependency, and intimacy. This discussion also has important technical implications concerning both the analysis of defense and transference and the analysis of diverse aspects of emotional experience in general (Schafer, 1964). Additionally, certain significant countertransference issues may come to the fore in the course of analyzing this struggle, a topic to which I turn later on.

SOCIETAL CONCEPTIONS OF SENTIMENTALITY

Tastes and mores vary among individuals and social groups, and they change over time and with changing historical and personal circumstances or contexts. Consequently, the narrational boundaries of sentimentality are not clear or stable, and the common attitude toward sentimentality is not always predominantly or exclusively positive or negative. It seems that there can be no single, simple, satisfactory definition of the word, no definition that is timeless and value-free, and no such precise definition will be attempted here. At the same time, it can be said that a decidedly masculinist bias seems to pervade the uses of the word, as if somehow "feminine" should be central to its definition.

We cannot be satisfied with the dictionary that defines sentimentality as "excessive emotionality," for we must go on to ask: Who decides what is excessive and why or according to which values and ideals and in which circumstances? Usually, it is men who have decided, particularly men in power of some kind, those who are all the more likely projectively to empty their unwanted emotionality into women and powerless men and then to hold them accountable or to condescend to them, gallantly or otherwise.

Sentimentality has been and continues to be compared invidiously to autonomy, power, genuineness, rationality, and masculinity. Sentimentality tends to be linked to childishness, weakness, irrationality, victimization, failure, insincerity, and womanishness. Consequently, it should come as no surprise that the struggle against sentimentality often occupies a strategic position in the clinical analysis of men in our society. Today sentimentalism is also under ideological attack by some feminists: Alert to the social seduction of women into being sentimentalists and thereby becoming more easily exploitable by men as well as by other women, notably by their mothers, they view sentimentality as a trap.

SUBJECTIVE REFERENTS OF SENTIMENTALITY

To which features of emotional responsiveness do male analysands allude when they appear to be setting themselves against being sentimental? Commonly, these men subsume under sentimentality (or some key word, storyline, or image equivalent to it) being tearful, nostalgic, enthusiastic, thrilled, awed, or infatuated; also, yearning or pining for someone or being playful in an exuberant or silly way. They say such experiences are not rational or that they themselves have no reason to feel that way. They wish to avoid any suggestion that they are naïve or immature; they dread being labeled maudlin or self-indulgent; they cringe before the possibility of seeming foolish or womanly. Embarrassed or ashamed, they cover up, minimize, or attempt to dispel any incipient feelings and expressive behavior of these sorts. They fall silent; they speak with heavy irony or self-mockery; they become irritable, listless, or circumstantial. Alternatively, when faced with their own sensitivity, they quickly profess a hopeless attitude. One representative member of this group lamented, "What good does it do?" before he continued in an increasingly anxious manner to convey both a fear of falling apart if he unchained his sensitivity and a suspicion that the analyst was seducing him into a weakened position.

It is, however, always to be borne in mind that, in individual cases, only selected areas of sentimentality may be proscribed. For example, a man may tolerate sentimentality with respect to his feelings for women or mothers specifically but not for men or fathers, with respect to sadness but not exuberance. In these instances, it will be important to analyze the man's principles of selective response.

REGRESSIVE ASPECTS OF SENTIMENTALITY

A virtually inevitable storyline in this narrative of analyzing the struggle against sentimentality is this: struggle against regression. As regression is a term that can cover many different processes and phenomena, its application should always be individualized, for each male analysand will have his own configuration of specific regressive dangers. Although the main dangers I take up cannot be neatly distinguished from one another, considering them under separate headings can be useful to keep track of the varied emphases we encounter in doing analytic work. My headlines are these: daydreaming, being a baby, identification with the mother, anality, and latency-age boyishness.

Daydreaming

Daydreaming is a complex compromise formation that may be understood fully only by implementing the principle of multiple function (Waelder, 1930). It is not simply a means of erotic and egoistic wish fulfillment, as Freud (1908a) suggested. To one degree or another, it must also be retold in defensive, moralistic, and adaptive terms. But whatever relative weight we assign to these various components, however pleasant or unpleasant the daydream, and however manifest or latent its essential features, it tends to have a decidedly sentimental aspect. It is sentimental in the way it depends on simplistic idealizations and so is replete with naïve, even melodramatic renditions of success and failure, good and evil, safety and danger, and gratification and deprivation. Daydreamers are not hard-nosed; they are not engaged in cool and complex appraisals of self and others or of past, present, and future situations. Their daydreams feature illusions and do not represent the highest level of adaptive functioning of which they are capable. Some daydreamers are taking a refreshing holiday from external reality. Others are beating a hasty retreat from it. All are approaching life sentimentally.

For example, the analysand daydreaming longingly about the analyst over the weekend is sentimentally engaged in idealization, bracketing out the recognition that analytic life with the analyst is often disagreeable in various ways and so setting aside the ambivalence that inevitably pervades the analytic relationship. Similarly idealizing are those daydreams that feature persistent nostalgic longings for the family of their childhood, for in cooler moments, analysands recognize that this family was a source of much suffering. The case is the same when analysands are regularly thrilled by the praise of a superior whom they fear, scorn, or mistrust, and when they weep over a kind word said by a friend who, it is realized upon sober reflection, does not really understand that well or care that much.

Analysands who struggle against sentimentality are wary of what they regard as the undermining effects of daydream idealizations. In their eyes, the simplifications of daydreaming undo the unrelenting realism or irony and the absolute autonomy that they have worked so hard to achieve and on which their feelings of invulnerability and worthwhileness seem to depend. Consequently, they fear and condemn their regressive daydreaming; they want no part of illusion-fostering and illusion-filled emotionality. And because their negative attitude may have had significant adaptive consequences during their earlier development, such as fortifying them against never-ending traumatic disappointments, they may buttress their antisentimentality with painful reminders of grim alternatives.

Being a Baby

Very often, men imagine sentimentality to be a shift of functioning in the direction of being a baby. Babies are vulnerable to merging into others or, a bit later and analogously, melting mindlessly into symbols such as the home or the flag. In this context, sentimentality means being passive, helpless, yielding, or surrendering. These men fear that they will lose touch with reality and expose themselves in naked emotionality to violation, derision, and abandonment. The orality of this regressive move is suggested by the common link between sentimentality and being a sucker and swallowing things whole or, more euphemistically, lacking refined taste. These analysands find it frightening to seek comfort, as by weeping or pleading, or to accept help when it is offered, no matter how painful or terrifying reality may seem to them at the time. In their daily lives, they may deny their wives and children any chance to "mother" them, and in their analyses they repeatedly rebuff the analyst as a real or imagined benevolently "mothering" figure.

Identification with the Mother

For these men the regressiveness of sentimentality usually involves increased emphasis on intolerable identifications with their mothers. In their sentimental moments they feel womanish or perhaps girlish. On this basis they sense that a threat of homosexual responsiveness lurks behind their image of the sentimentalist. They sometimes claim to document this connection by referring to the blatant sentimentality that characterizes certain aspects of the gay community (for example, certain prominent figures in the entertainment world). The regressively intensified identification with mother may pertain to any one of a number of developmental phases: the mother as witch or smothering breast; the sick, suffering, raped, or castrated mother of the primal scene as envisioned by the phallic-oedipal boy; the mother as degraded woman (such as prostitute).

In one of its aspects, a desperately increased emphasis on rejecting this sentimentalized identification may serve defensively to assert masculinity. But it is not the masculinity of the primal father conceived as an indomitable, castrating phallic force. Freud (1921) described the primal father as the early and awesome ideal figure, a figure whose heights a person can never hope to reach. By implication, he is a figure with respect to whom, both fearfully and wishfully, a person is always something of a softy, a soft touch, a pushover, even a willing slave, in effect a castrate and sexual partner. Men live in the shadow of this figure, and for some it is a very long shadow.

In another of its aspects, an overemphasis on the danger of maternal identification may unconsciously accomplish a hostile and anxiety-relieving caricature of the mother whose emotionality, whatever its nature, stands for both her castratedness and her frightening castrating tendencies. And in a third aspect, this overemphasis may imply struggling against the wish to return, via identification, to a dyadic relation with mother from which father and siblings are excluded, that way to have her forever. What is lacking in these instances is the fearful male's recognition, tolerance, and moderated integration of the androgynous implications of a freer emotionality. What is present instead are some scattered attempts at compromise of subjectively irreconcilable extremes. But because he is convinced that those compromises can never be stable or satisfying, he must continue to aim for a totally one-sided result. This exclusionary emphasis on male gender often serves mainly as a screen for significant pregenital issues. I have already mentioned orality; anality, to which I turn next, is another such major pregenital issue.

Anality

The master psychosexual narratives of psychoanalysis lead the analyst to expect that anal ambivalence will be found to play a particularly important role in men's struggles against sentimentality. For it is a well-established interpretation of long standing that people in general and particularly those who are emotionally disturbed, construe emotionality in the terms of anal fantasy (see, for example, Brierley, 1951, chap. 2). They deal with emotions as with fecal matter—that is, both as dangerously sadistic expulsions or explosions and as shameful, dirty, messy incontinence. These ubiquitous fantasies are encountered in especially clear form in obsessional settings. We need not depend on the clinical analytic method to develop support for the claim that this equation is ubiquitous, for there exists an abundance of concordant anal jokes, colloquial sayings and metaphors, insults, rituals, myths, and fables of every kind. "I feel shitty" is a representative instance.

Thus, being well defended against sentimentality is unconsciously equivalent to having a clean diaper, while unrestrained sentimentality is like "crapping all over the place." "Crapping all over the place" is likely to express as much vigorous and torturing defiance as passive, erotic letting go and opening up. The "tight-assed" person is not sentimental, while the sentimentalist is a sentimental "slob."

In this context we encounter the well-known unconscious links between conventional femininity and passive anality; for example, to be masculine is to be impeccably toilet trained, as clean as an astronaut, as controlled as a drill sergeant. As one male analysand put it, when reflecting on the anal fantasy implied in his antisentimentality, "It's like denying I have an asshole."

Masculinist bias is plainly evident in the sphere of anality. "Don't be an asshole" conveys this bias. Implicitly, it is women who are "sentimental assholes." It is, by the way, not unusual for women to share this unconscious stereotype (as they do so many others) and, on this basis, to feel masculine once they stop being "sentimental assholes" and dare to maintain their dignity against all the seductions and assaults that are conducive to their behaving otherwise.

In the analytic relationship, a man's antisentimentality is likely to involve not only his enacting sadistically defiant constipation and his fearfully contemplating the possibility that analysis will reveal that his true sexual interest is in passive femininity and homosexuality. It may involve as well his attempt to seduce the analyst into performing symbolic anal rape in the form of pressing confrontations and interpretations of his defensive dealings with emotionality; perhaps he can seduce the analyst to make direct demands on him for emotional output, this amounting to the "analytic enema." Consequently, it is more than likely that working out and working through the anal meanings or uses of antisentimentality in the here and now of the analysis will render the entire realm of emotional experience more accessible to expression, understanding, and integration. Here I include such potentially adaptive phenomena as the release of strangulated grief, the spilling out of exhilarated exhibitionism, playfulness, and tenderness, and the bursting out of proscribed temper tantrums, competitiveness, and pride.

Before leaving the psychoanalytic storylines of anality, we must take account of feces as gift and, through the equation of feces and emotion, of emotion as gift. It is common to observe withholding of emotion as a means of inflicting feelings of deprivation and undeservingness on others. Withholding is also a means of denying that a person has needs that the other is satisfying; the antisentimentalists are very uncomfortable with the idea of being "dependent" on anyone for anything. They prefer the isolation of imperviousness and aloofness: Nothing "mushy" about that!

Latency-Age Boyishness

Boyishness plays a significant role in men's sentimentality and their struggle against it. I refer particularly to the emotionality of latency-age and prepuberty boys and to their play and playfulness. Under favorable developmental conditions, boys in this phase of development are passionately serious and passionately playful, often simultaneously so or in rapid alternation. They are not unduly threatened by latent homosexual and other such aspects of their functioning in this emotional way, and they are resilient when they have gone to extremes or when their experiments have turned out to be too exciting to be tolerated.

The man who struggles against sentimentality defensively introduces significant discontinuity into the life history potentially available to him. He does this by trying to renounce whatever limited boyishness he once enjoyed or suffered, as the case may be. He gives the appearance of having bypassed his boyhood. He presents himself as being unable to play or as too vigorously segregating work from play. For him, there is no play in work, and there is strenuous work in play. He participates in analysis in the same way. It is unthinkable to be simply playful before the analyst or with him or her. He would never entice the analyst into playful interaction. Those playful interactions that can and do take place are not tolerated well. He tends to be stodgy and humorless. A shared laugh is something to be coped with, and it may be used to discredit the analyst. At best, he substitutes telling jokes dryly for having open-ended fun. He has no heroes, just as he has no chum or buddy to comfort him or share experiences with him. He is set against the boy he has remained in his psychic reality, just as he is set against the woman, the toddler, and the baby.

LIFE HISTORICAL BACKGROUND

What kind of life historical background seems to be the matrix of this revolt against boyishness and all the other variables I mentioned earlier? I can summarize one family drama that in some cases seems to have contributed to the development of vigorous antisentimentality; however, I cannot claim that this drama is universal or that it sufficiently explains this particular outcome. But I do find some support for my account in a paper on tearfulness by Wood and Wood (1984); they present an account of a man's struggle against tearfulness that includes, in addition to phenomena of the sort I described earlier, some of the features of development I am about to describe.

In broad outline, it seems that, as boys, a number of these men had to cope with a disappointingly unresponsive and uncomforting mother, a woman who seems to have been depressed and also embittered and rivalrous in her relations with men and boys alike; further, they had to cope with an obsessionally rigid or narcissistically aloof, competitive father who regularly debunked his young son's enthusiasms and identificatory strivings for both closeness and autonomy. One analysand would imagine his father's voice saying "schmuck" or "good boy," depending on the waxing and waning of his own sentimental responses during the analysis. This is reminiscent of Kohut's (1977) emphasis on the damaging effects on healthy narcissism of unappreciative mothers and of fathers who do not tolerate well their being idealized and taken as models by their sons.

One of the functions that gets disrupted under those developmental conditions is what Hartmann (1956) discussed in another context as the testing of inner reality (see also chapter 1). Hartmann emphasized that it is misguided to equate rationality only with the testing of external reality. He argued that, from the analytic point of view, inner reality, with all its archaic, irrational, volatile, and otherwise extreme features, is as important a part of reality as whatever is of moment in the surrounding world. Here lies the response to the analysand's defensively despondent question, "What good does it do?" The good it does is to increase the analysand's readiness consciously to recognize and participate in his inner reality and to empathize with himself in that sphere (Schafer, 1964). On this basis, he may achieve what growth and mastery he can where that is needed. Because analysis helps people to view inner reality in this light, it gets to seem neither a horror to be avoided nor a disease to be cured; rather, it is a world to be transformed in its most shaky and disruptive aspects and to be enjoyed as it is coped with. To this consideration I might add another: Unconsciously, "inner reality," along with whatever else is "inner," no longer tends to be equated so readily with femininity, filth, and infantilism.

COUNTERTRANSFERENCE

What kinds of disruptive countertransference arise in the course of analyzing men who struggle against sentimentality? Here much depends on the analyst's relations with his or her emotionality in general and sentimentality in particular. We can expect that analysts who are still waging battles of their own either on behalf of sentimentality or against it will be especially prone to disruptive countertransferences in this sphere. They will identify too much or too little with one side or the other of their analysands' positions on affective experience. Subtly or obviously, they will devote themselves to ridding the analysands of their "diseased" sentimentality or their "unpleasant" antisentimentality rather than trying to understand why this or that mode of response has been favored. They may use an analysand's emotional experiences to immerse themselves vicariously and more comfortably than they could otherwise in experiencing the feelings they have difficulty tolerating and enjoying in their own lives. Alternatively, and with the help of projection, they may combat their own sentimental tendencies by a rigorously skeptical analytic approach to their analysands' sentimentality; on this basis they may neglect the developmental potential and relevance of sentimental responsiveness and thereby limit their own analytic effectiveness.

These departures from the neutral analytic attitude may be characterized metaphorically in terms of some of the psychosexual issues that were mentioned earlier. For example, orally, the analysand may be put on starvation rations or drowned in chicken soup. Anally, the analyst may be constipatedly clean, insistently enema-giving, or diarrheic with empathy. The countertransference may be homosexually seductive or castrating in a this-is-our-song atmosphere or rationalized as advocacy of the reality principle in an atmosphere of macho imperviousness. And so forth. In these respects it is well to recall the Scylla and Charybdis of analytic work sketched by Fenichel (1941): too much need on the analyst's part for volatile affect or too little tolerance of it.

The neutral analyst, the analyst who maintains the analytic attitude, will be enough at peace with his or her own sentimental tendencies to be able to participate through trial identifications in both the regressive features of the analysand's sentimentality and his antiregressive struggle against it. The analyst will not participate in this empathic way in order to implement or enforce any particular value other than the health-value of knowing reality inside out, as it were, for it is this kind of knowledge that helps the analysand work out less costly and painful solutions or compromises than those with which he came into analysis. In other words, the analyst's technical ideal is neither to conduct an analysis sentimentally nor to turn analysands into sentimentalists. It is rather to find ways to provide for sentimentality a better understood and less threatening place in the analysand's range of responsiveness and awareness. The analyst's ideal is an even-handedness in this realm as in all others (Schafer, 1983).

POSTSCRIPT

Of the many storylines I could have addressed or developed further but did not, I should like to mention two. One is the sadistic potential of the struggle against sentimentality, that component of the struggle that may be used to block empathy with others and to deny them their own emotional intensity and scope. The other storyline tells of the problems that may come up with particular force when an antisentimental male works with a female analyst: such problems as the transference conviction that the analysand is in the hands of an infantilizing, effeminizing, or incestuously seductive mother. In that context, the analysand uses the fact that the female analyst pays the least bit of active attention to emotional experience in the most defensive way to confirm the reality of the danger of regression and of all that regression means to him in analysis. I have noted versions of these problems frequently in the course of my supervising women doing analysis.

CHAPTER 8

Women Lost in the Maze of Power and Rage

THEMES of aggression and power pervade the accounts we hear in our daily work as analysts. Sometimes the stated or implied emotional violence is cold, as in the cruelty of prolonged withdrawal into silence; sometimes it is hot, as in burning rage and envy. Commonly, the analysand is presented in these narratives as the sufferer, perhaps reactively angry, perhaps passively resigned, but in any case victimized and in pain. And commonly, the exploration of these accounts of emotional violence seems to find its destination in the complex dramas of the analysand's family of origin. It is inappropriate for the analyst automatically to regard these painful accounts as altogether unreliable, for up to a point they are likely to enrich the treatment with useful information.

In order to work analytically, however, the analyst must also anticipate, and go on to establish, that much more is involved in the analysand's suffering than having been victimized by her or his family's unmistakably cruel or otherwise disturbing exercises of power. What is that "more"? It is likely to include the analysand's having become, over the course of development, either a seducer of sadism or, through identification, a ruthless wielder of power and a cruel victimizer of others, often in the most subtle way; or, as is true in many cases, both at once. Once the treatment is under way, the analyst gets to be included among those others who are to be seduced into cruelty and/or victimized themselves. Those analysts who can moderate the resulting countertransferences will not fail to note the ways in which these analysands feel frightened and penitent about resorting to masochistic and sadistic strategies. That is, these analysands may be understood to be pursuing this course of action unknown to themselves and in an acutely conflicted manner. Implied in this conflicted course of action are hidden loving kindness, desperate self-protection, and adaptedness to a history of family relations that required violent and perverse orientations to self and others. These orientations were the prerequisites for the patient feeling that she or he belonged and was not an outsider furtively looking in and not an object of derision.

Further, the analyst will recognize in each analysand's productions the activity of cruel internal objects. These are imagined internal figures or introjects that have been created chiefly in two ways: first, by the projective identifications perpetrated on, and accepted by, children whenever parents use them in an attempt to rid themselves of their unwanted bad parts or characteristics, and, second, by the sequence of the child's projecting his or her own cruel fantasies about others onto the others and then incorporating the bad figures that result from these unhappy creative efforts. In these fantasies, these incorporated cruel internal objects will finally fill so much of the "inner world" and so far establish an atmosphere of hostile surveillance and persecutory retaliation, much like an army of occupation, that in part they will stimulate continuous efforts at expulsion into or onto others (on an anal model, usually). Those who enter analysis as adults repetitively replay the painful interactions of their early lives and early fantasies; this they do in direct or inverted form, both with the analyst and with others in their current lives.

In this chapter I present a psychoanalytic summary of work of mine and some male supervisees with one such group of analysands. In this instance, "psychoanalytic" refers to work organized chiefly around both Freudian and object-relational analytic descriptions and interpretations of analysands' past and present lives, lives now being repeated in interpretable form in transferences and evoked countertransferences.

THE ANALYSANDS

The analytic work to be explored took place with a number of successful career women. Although these women seemed to be different from each other in many ways, the ones with whom I am here concerned shared a proclivity to get into painful relationships with narcissistic and sadistic men. The manifest content of these relationships showed them to be simply and extremely masochistic: These women seemed to lose the high level of cognitive, administrative, and social skills and the resourcefulness and poise that they typically manifested in their work; instead they became helpless, blindly repetitive, self-accusatory, and emotionally labile, seemingly addicted to their victimization, very often unaware of their rage at the way they were being treated, deficient or at least erratic and ineffective in their self-assertiveness, and greatly restricted in allocating responsibility for their interpersonal difficulties to anyone but themselves. All power seemed to have passed from their hands.

Typically, these women worked long hours in institutional settings, and it was mainly there that they developed their love and other significant social relationships. Not rarely, the love relationships were with older men, married men, or both; if not that, they were either with men on the rebound from broken marriages or disturbed love affairs or with men who, it seemed on reflection, could well have been married long ago but somehow were not, a fact that could have served as a warning but was ignored.

As a rule, these men were portrayed as hard-driving and highly successful, capable of being charming and of serving as helpful mentors; however, they were also ruthlessly critical, exploitative, and unfeeling. Even as colleagues, they were said to act like members of a club that excluded women from membership. These men made sure to look supercritically at the work contributions of any women, no matter how outstanding or profitable, to delay rewarding them with recognition and advancement in the institutional hierarchy, and to subject them to the harassment of sexist attitudes, language, and other provocations.

When they became the lovers of these women, these men rarely accepted responsibility for misunderstandings or hurts. Instead, they expected the women to accommodate to them and be available to them on short notice, even while they showered their victims with criticism for self-interest, unresponsiveness, and similar sins. And after the relationships ended, sometimes particularly after they ended, they found ways to harass and further torment their victims. It seemed then that they were determined to undermine the self-confidence and reality testing of these women and, more than that, to undermine their sense of having an ethical or moral center. Sometimes in these narratives, it seemed as if the men were engaged in brainwashing of the sort carried on by O'Brien, the torturer and soul-murderer of Winston Smith in George Orwell's novel *1984*. Moreover, the women went on clinging to their ex-lover tormentors, rationalizing their behavior as motivated by hopefulness or loneliness or as still trying to settle the score, perhaps aggressively but perhaps only reparatively.

Although I have presented no more than a composite picture of these entanglements, I believe that, sooner or later, each of these women presented one or another combination of its details convincingly, even if in an obviously one-sided manner. And yet, with respect to all of this apparent abuse and exploitation, consciously they characterized themselves primarily as failures rather than enraged victims and primarily as buffeted about by unkind, arbitrary fate rather than as driven uncomprehendingly to repetitions of being insulted and injured. These women were in a maze from which they could not find their way out.

Analysts cannot fail to be impressed by the declines in the level of functioning that are evident in the repetitive, self-abasing, and hopeless relations these women maintain with one man or, in some cases, with a series of men, in the painful confrontations they insist on reexperiencing, and in the prevalence of depression over rage or even enlightened self-assertion in response to the patent cruelty they describe at such great length and with so little variation. It therefore seems fully warranted to conclude that there is a lot more there than meets the eye and the ear.

On this understanding and after an appropriately careful initial screening, psychoanalysis was recommended as the treatment of choice. Apparently understanding of as well as accustomed to the long, hard grind of achievement, these women seemed quite ready to accept that recommendation. They agreed to the analytic procedure as the necessary disciplined approach to resolving their basic problems. Once the work was under way, however, they seemed mainly to want and often demand comfort and counsel rather than self-understanding. As befit the circumstances, they wanted directive help in gratifying their desires for love, marriage, family, personal dignity, and a career with recognition, for in their own eyes they were goodhearted women in dire straits, eager to be shown their mistakes, ready as ever in their high-achiever roles to go on learning how to perform excellently. In this respect they hardly made the most superficial distinctions between work and analysis. From this shift of emphasis alone, it could be inferred that preoccupation with the trials and tribulations of these current relationships served in one respect as a flight from the inner world of conflicted longings and in another respect as a clinging to an implied self-concept of the helpless infant, the good little girl in need of guidance, or the "victim."

ON WRITING ON THE THERAPY OF WOMEN: A CRITICAL PERSPECTIVE

I believe that those who write on the psychological therapy of women are obliged to give some account of how they view the historical/cultural conditions affecting the development of girls and women in family life, school, love, and work. Because these writings touch on the general psychology of women, they must somehow convey perspectives on the place of women in the world. Inevitably those perspectives will have political and ideological implications and consequences, some of them of great social significance. If this much is granted, it follows that these writings must also include some discussion of expectable countertransferential issues in the therapy of women; this is so because the author's social viewpoint is bound to contribute both to shaping the phenomena being reported and to the meanings and significance being attributed to them. Like any other countertransferences, those in question here, if attended to, will be potentially useful in both the therapeutic interaction and the reader's understanding. However, if they are screened out by defensive measures, they will limit and may even damage the treatment and the proper understanding of its text once it is written up. Certainly the close reader might not agree that my account of this work conforms closely to the analyst's stated intentions; nevertheless, these intentions are bound to play significant roles in the treatments being reported, so that there is something to gain, even if not everything, by every author's stating his or her position frankly.

Further on countertransference: I recognize that any discussion of countertransference may be overwrought or imbalanced to the point where it enacts unresolved or uncontained countertransference issues; however, it does not follow from this recognition that the mere calling attention to the play of historical/cultural factors in countertransference is itself a sign of countertransference. Indeed, I would venture to suggest that it is not only defensive but politically as well as analytically reactionary to argue that this kind of attention necessarily manifests countertransference, as if it were possible to elude completely the issues of culturally rooted countertransferences. Modern analysts are obliged to take these factors into account. Accordingly, before going further with my discussion, I shall summarize my perspective on the place of women in today's world, without completely neglecting some psychoanalytic insights that seem to me fitting in this context. I reserve for the next section my main comments on countertransference.

My summary is too brief to do justice to the complex issues being addressed; however, a comprehensive discussion would be so long and wide-ranging that it would overshadow this chapter's primary purpose and theme. Although brief, this summary is part of my effort to break with the now-discredited convention of writing as if it were possible, in areas of weighty social controversy, to be an utterly disinterested, value-free psychoanalytic observer of mental and behavioral phenomena. We may no longer claim that these phenomena are "out there in Nature," phenomena with a fixed essence waiting to be discovered and univocally described once and for all by an objective investigator.

To get now to the point. I believe that much of our social order has been arranged and is controlled by men whose attitudes toward women may be described as discriminatory, demeaning, and exploitative. I also believe that many high-achieving men may be characterized accurately as seductively manipulative, self-centered, and at least implicitly hard and cruel in their social relationships. Correlatively, the women here under study face in their work and their social lives great odds in occupational and social settings that too often neglect and even oppose their interests. These settings are continuations of the ones in which they grew up: gifted girls whose giftedness encountered at best highly ambivalent welcomes. In this respect, I believe the reality testing of these women was seriously compromised in their families and their surroundings, in that they had finally organized so much of their perception and feeling along the lines of depressive self-blame and low self-esteem.

Nevertheless, too much about these women's considerable assets and achievements would have to be ignored to settle quickly for the correct but limited social-psychological perspective within which they appear to be merely disadvantaged members of a sexist society. Although I agree that they are that, I would also emphasize that, in the sense most immediately relevant to psychoanalytic *therapy,* the maze in which they were lost was made up of the twists and turns and dead ends of their unconscious mental processes. These were the winding, entangled paths along which they distributed all the sadomasochism and all the dreams of omnipotence that flourished in the course of their growing up in their disturbed and biased family settings and social environment. Collaborating unconsciously with their persecutors seemed to be part of their lostness, and also part of their unconsciously devised strategy. That this was so became evident once these women began to benefit from the insights developed during analysis, when they found that in many instances they could renounce some habitual self-destructive courses of action, take previously inconceivable corrective or protective actions, and go on to enjoy more assertive and happier kinds of relationships and subjective experiences. They also found that they could elicit more respectful and warmer attitudes and actions—"bring out the best" in parents, siblings, and all those with whom they lived their lives at home and at work. It is not easy to apportion weight to the factors involved in these changes: decreased distortion, decreased provocation, and increased social poise and adroitness, together with efforts to "please" the analyst in the transference. There is, however, little reason to think that individual personal changes of any of these sorts can significantly and promptly reduce the general male chauvinism that continues to surround women in our society.

In these cases, although it would have been confusing and counterproductive to focus the analyses *exclusively* on the origins and dynamics of the women's unconscious, self-injurious collaborationism, it did seem helpful to elucidate as far as possible the complex part they had played and were now playing in their own *manifest* victimization. (For reasons that should become clear, I emphasize the word *manifest.*) It is on the results of this work of elucidation that I now focus. I do so despite my recognition that, to some of those concerned with these social-psychological issues, it will seem politically naïve or offensive to take this tack; to them it may still smack of blaming the victim. In my view, however, which I take to be the usual psychoanalytic view, treatment does not apportion blame; rather, it seeks to clarify the complex structure of tragic human situations in such a way as to facilitate the personal changes that could lead to the alleviation of neurotic suffering. In neurotic suffering, the social pathology of sexism plays its part mainly in the most indirect and elusive ways; and the victimizers, too, must be understood, both analytically and social-psychologically, as themselves victims of countless generations of every form of rage and power. Of more immediate consequence, however, is the recognition that, as a rule and tragically, chronic victims begin to participate in, and even to long for, further victimization, and themselves become victimizers of others as well.

THEIR MOTHERS

The principal clues, though not the only ones, leading to understanding the vulnerabilities and conflicts of each of these gifted women were established in the course of analyzing the relationship each one unconsciously maintained with her mother. By "her mother" I refer not to the mother as she "really" was, for, as modern historians acknowledge, the one and only "real" version of a piece of history can never be re-created. Rather, I refer to the mother of psychic reality—the figure the daughter constructed and experienced in an inevitable mix of fantasy, misunderstanding, and consensually verifiable fact and memory. Many negative aspects of this psychically real mother were repressed, and those that were not were denied or suppressed in the mother's physical presence; in the analysis, however, many of these negative aspects were readily described in the course of the analysand's complaining of always being victimized by her mother, even in her physical absence. Significantly, these complaints were regularly accompanied by, or followed by, guilty reactions, although often these reactions were repressed or projected.

Interpretively, it was helpful to accept for some time the analysand's stated or implied experience that the internal object was operating with a force of its own, that is, as an introject or what would be better named an imagined presence of shifting or uncertain location (Schafer, 1968b, chap. 4); only later in each analysis did it become both possible and desirable to interpret the patient's reviving this imagined figure in stressful situations, investing power in it through fantasy, putting it into operation, and then submitting to it. That is, ultimately this introject had to be analyzed as one of those quasi-delusional symptoms that are by no means restricted to the seriously ill or the so-called borderline cases.

To maintain some focus, I concentrate on two themes in the daughter-mother relationships. These two themes seem to be two sides of the same coin; at least they stood out as allied themes in the analytic work with these women. The themes are damaged self-esteem regulation and unconscious ambivalent identification with the dominating and intrusive mother. Before proceeding I must emphasize that although the mothers appeared to be demonic figures much of the time, they emerged over the course of the work as figures with noteworthy vigor, strength, color, and other assets on which the patient had built some of her own assets and to which the patient could relate in the search for a viable relationship with this most difficult, ambivalence-intensifying figure.

The mothers of these women tended to be extraordinarily intrusive, controlling, and critical. They were so ruled by shame that they were fanatically preoccupied with keeping up appearance. At times their preoccupation seemed to be barely in touch with reality, riddled with contradictions, and inevitably fragmenting in its approach to people and situations. Always on the lookout for flaws, these mothers would constantly and tactlessly raise questions not only about clothes, boyfriends, and physical appearance, but also about intellectual and cultural interests, need for solitude and privacy, and you name it. In their controllingness, they set up powerful barriers to any overt engagement with father, thereby limiting the daughter—of course, with the father's participation on the basis of his own unconscious conflicts—mainly to the daughter-mother relationship. Indeed, they used this one-on-one or dyadic strategy in the family to the point where they disrupted alliances among children, if there were others, or between the child and friends.

Usually, as it emerged, these mothers had themselves been victims of mothers even more mentally disturbed or disturbing than they were. Their own self-esteem was in ruins, and, in their conduct, they seemed to identify a good deal with their persecutory mothers. Persecutors in one perspective, they were victims in another, and links in a chain in a third.

On the face of it, these mothers so occupied the minds of their daughters—the analysands—that it seemed at first that the daughters had been blocked from setting up their own ego ideals or ideal selves; blocked, that is, from what traditionally would be called structure-building and direction-setting internalizations. When in love, the analysands did present themselves manifestly in just that way: so dependent on the affirmation of their lovers that they had no source of self-esteem of their own. Often their fathers had been compliantly, submissively, and self-defensively sidelined in the family, blocked from showing whatever fragments of interest and appreciation, normal fatherly seductiveness, and power and ideals they had available within themselves. Such factors might, if evidenced, have compensated to some extent for the mother's deprivations and depredations.

These daughters brought forth these growth-blocking experiences to account for how crushed they were by the callousness and abuse of their lovers and by the ultimate collapse of their love relationships. Without the love of their lovers, so they claimed, they felt they were nothing, even though they said they knew that, objectively, it was not so. At fault for all of this was primarily the invasive, overoccupying mother and only secondarily the sidelined father. It seemed that the analysands' development into a full-fledged positive oedipal phase had been severely limited; in the positive transference to their male analyst, after some initial pseudo-oedipal moves, these patients approached the entire realm of intimacy with a man with much guilt and anxiety and great readiness to regress. Freely felt love for a man seemed to add a new dimension to their lives that was simultaneously thrilling and threatening.

FURTHER COMPLICATIONS

These allegations and implications seemed to be true as far as they went, but they did not go nearly far enough. A host of other factors were defined as the analyses proceeded. For one thing, the constant love and appreciation of others were needed not simply for love's sake alone or for generalized intimacy or consolation, but also and mainly to drown out, refute, or show up the persecutory mother-presence.

Second, there were complex, unconscious phallic fantasies at play. In one respect, in her psychic reality, the high-achieving, good-girl daughter was serving as the compensatory phallus for a castrated mother, an arrangement that seemed to be designed to take care simultaneously of the castration fantasies of them both. In this respect, then, the daughter no longer seemed to be merely a passive tabula rasa completely covered with the mother's derogatory inscriptions. In a second and related respect, the daughter as upwardly mobile star proved to be arrogant and disdainful in relation to both parents and to men and, unconsciously and correlatively, the proud embodiment of an upwardly mobile penis—that is, an erection: someone who, or something that, would omnipotently subdue others, if necessary even through guilt-provoking tears and protestations of misery, and who would be furious and vengeful if turned back or away, though perhaps at first only feeling misunderstood and doubly betrayed. All of which is to say that a good deal of so-called inner structure could be ascribed to the patient: specifically, a grandiose self-image that involved identificatory participation in both the overwhelming force and the defectiveness of her apparently despotic mother-presence.

In both respects, therefore, each of these women was not so lost in the maze as she seemed on first telling. Indeed, it seemed to become clear and understandable that, in her transferences to the male analyst, the very idea of "truly" yielding to a man—that is, yielding at or close to what she felt to be her inner emotional core—was anathema to her. And in this additional respect, bound as she was to her mother, she seemed to take a stance toward men modeled on her mother's toward the father.

Again correlatively, the analysand's being a high achiever in the occupational worlds that traditionally are bastions of male authority and privilege was based in part on the phallic fantasy that she was in fact "one of the boys." Consequently, when she encountered professional barriers, her outrage and grief were based as much on her unconsciously imagining that she, along with her mother, was being castrated. Also involved were three other factors: those situational elements that repeated her disappointment in her father's relative inadequacy as protector and his emotional unresponsiveness; those elements that repeated the ultimate inaccessibility of her mother, for whom her occupational superiors, male or female, were stand-ins; and those elements that stemmed from powerful social traditions inimical to the well-being of women in love and work—the traditions that from early on convey and reinforce the tendencies of men and women to equate power and penis. Thus, these patients were up against much powerful destructiveness, both in their inner world and in their manifest daily life, the two realms being, as always, inseparable from one another.

Three more factors are significant aspects of these daughters and mothers. The first factor is the evidence that these analysands seemed to maintain loving, intimate, and enduring relations with at least one other woman. Although these relationships were usually in full flower before analysis commenced, they began to be used defensively in relation to the transference. They diluted the transference, for often the friend was the first to hear about significant emotional experiences and the first consultant on meanings and conceivable courses of action; the analyst was made to feel that he was merely one consultant among others, one who was even at a disadvantage, being neither an old and intimate friend nor a woman. He was put in his place by being displaced, as the father had been. This defensive use of friends could also be seen as acting out that part of the ambivalence felt toward mother that was loving, appreciative, and dependent while directing the split-off aggression toward the minimized analyst. This enactment also protected the patient from the dangers of attack and engulfment by the mother that would, she felt, surely result should she become totally involved with mother and show both sides of the ambivalence directly to her.

The second additional factor in the mother-daughter context is the deadening effect on emotional experience that could be traced largely to the mother's critical and possessive invasiveness. These mothers and mother-presences were experienced as constantly pulling the rug out from under the spontaneous enthusiasms of their developing daughters. The enthusiasms ranged from girlfriends, boyfriends, teachers, clothes, and makeup to intellectual interests and creative endeavors. These mothers had a devastating way of being unresponsive when they were not directly inflicting shame, guilt, or anxiety on their daughters, thus making them doubt even more their spontaneous feelings. As they grew older, these daughters came to inflict this affect-destruction on themselves. In this, they were identified with their aggressor-mothers. The identification served to lessen the shock of coming up against attack in the external world when unprepared for it and then impulsively reacting to an intolerant or unresponsive mother or mother surrogate and facing the consequences. The defensive strategy was peace at any price.

More than defense, however, the identification helped preserve an exclusive, totalistic tie to the mother; anything less was felt with terror to be a totally severed relationship such as was felt every time the mother failed to respond positively to her daughter's signs of growth and separate identity. Because the mother's influence continued to limit the range and depth of her daughter's investment in other relationships, the daughter lacked a developed context that would support a definite and affirmed identity of her own. Without the mother, the daughter would be alone and would be a nothing.

Consequently, when in treatment, these analysands backed off from excitement and the possibility of somehow getting excited. They were careful to maintain their own and their mother's rigid controllingness. But they were alive enough to sense the resulting deadness, which lowered their self-esteem further, even though, in self-contradiction, they also valued deadness as a barrier against the transference relationship. In one respect the analyst was put in the role of the persecutory mother; in another, that of the weak father; in a third respect, however, by consciously disclaiming their own aliveness, the analysands seemed to want to put the analyst in the role of the one who argued for life, liberty, and the pursuit of happiness, while they took the part of the other side of their ambivalence and clung to their controls and defenses and thereby to their invasive mothers and their identification with them.

Technically, the analyst had to do his best to maintain the fine balance between, on the one side, blindly accepting this projective identification laden with anxiety and guilt and, on the other, lapsing into a subdued, hands-off countertransference. Much of the time the important intervention was pointing out the analysand's attempting to create this no-win position for the analyst to occupy.

In addition to using women friends to split the transference and the ambivalent clinging to emotional deadness, I mention as the third additional factor *reparation*. In being the phallic completion of the crippled mother, the mother who herself had been wounded into cruelty by her own mother as well as by men and society, the daughter was healing her. She was making her mother whole, realizing her mother's many unfulfilled dreams through being a good-girl, high achiever. In that reparative role, it could not be acceptable to enter into a deep love relationship with a man experienced as such, for to do so would be to abandon her own mother, cripple her once again, and empty her out and depress her beyond what the analysand could bear. In this respect, love and guilt combined to reinforce the analysand's need to be omnipotent, in this context omnipotently reparative. However much each woman suffered in love and however abjectly she conducted herself outwardly in her heterosexual affairs and even in the workplace, in her psychic reality she carried power into the maze that was her life.

COUNTERTRANSFERENCE

The maze in which these women seem to stay lost is the maze of human tragedy, so much of which is necessarily beyond independent conscious reckoning. Consequently, progress in analysis is slow and painful, the work is arduous for the analyst as well as the patient, not every such patient gets deeply into treatment or continues it, and not every one of them emerges with the same types and amounts of gain. In my experience, however, analysis of the complex, androgynous, multivalent merger with the mother as it takes place in a sexist world often can make a significant adaptive difference. For the analyst, the work requires eliciting and dealing with much rage on many levels of functioning, with much manipulative and vengeful exercise of power, often enacted in the subtlest ways, and also with much maternal transference that sometimes is quite hostile and grandiose and sometimes blissful and only seemingly purely heterosexual.

This work requires much analysis of the countertransferences peculiar to working with acutely suffering, abused but powerful, successful, and exceptionally well-endowed women. For example, analysts may have the countertransference response of letting themselves be sidelined emotionally as the father had been all along, while at the same time, and still like the father, being the recipient of furtive and feebly erotic positive oedipal gestures and responses. Another example is analysts' countertransference response of wanting to assert their own force against the formidable latent power and control of these women—that is, not to feel the analytical equivalent of the "castrated wimp" stereotype or like the obligingly sidelined father—and to resort then to directiveness, emphasis, or more and more interpretation. Another countertransference features analysts' wanting to prove by shows of respect, support, warmth, and so on that they are not the narcissistic persecutory mother or a sexist male stand-in for her; also, that they are there to protect rather than neglect and to bind up wounds rather than inflict them or suffer them. This countertransference may touch at the center of the reasons why a person has become an analyst in the first place, and it is all the easier to rationalize if he shares the outlook on sexism in the world that I presented earlier.

Yet another countertransference may induce declarations of support for the patient's angry view of men and our sexist society. But this move will only make it harder to analyze the distortions and provocations that the patient has come to rely on defensively and through identification with the aggressor; specifically, it will obscure the play of these factors in the transference.

Sexist abuse and discrimination seem to be best dealt with as clear-cut trauma would be: acknowledged and used as an occasion to explore the unconscious meanings, all the pain and possible gratification, and all the fixation and resiliency unconsciously associated with that trauma. Of particular value is the demonstration to the patient of how she constructs the transference both to repeat and to repair the sexist traumatization. To proceed analytically in a less searching manner would be to join manifestly and countertransferentially an alliance with the abused analysand, a move that would leave in place the disturbances of reality testing and of self-enhancing adaptation. Thereby the analyst would be allowing the crucial, unconsciously maintained conflicts I have summarized to continue to limit the patient's mastery of problems and resumption of personal, autonomous development.

As always, every other kind of countertransference may be at play in these cases. I mention here only a few more, each of which inevitably narrows the analyst's interpretive range. Analysts may remain on only one psychosexual level, such as the oedipal or preoedipal or just the anal. They may stress only the positive (heterosexual) oedipal at the expense of the negative (homosexual) oedipal. They may focus too much on negative transference, in these cases on the woman's destructive, envious, castrating desires, thereby minimizing or dismissing her struggle against loving, admiring, idealizing, and submissive tendencies (in my experience as supervisor, a common countertransference). Also, analysts may disembody or desomatize the psychosexual factors and refer only to autonomy, dependency, trust, control, empathy, and the like, thereby playing down concretely oral, anal, and genital feelings and fantasies. (In this chapter, as I was not attempting a complete coverage of the analyses that were carried out, I did not go into these matters; anyone familiar with psychosexual theory can easily fill in the bodily referents of many of the major developments reported.)

THESE WOMEN IN LOVE: A BRIEF SUMMARY

Returning now to these women in love, or more usually desolate among the ruins of "love affairs," it seemed that their lovers, like the bulk of the other men they worked with, combined features of their mothers, their fathers, and the masculinized selves or body parts that they had projected onto these men. Their desolation and their excruciating pain combined oedipal and preoedipal features. It was *oedipal* in its (1) repetition of failure with father and confirmation of castrated status, all high achievement to the contrary notwithstanding; (2) providing positive oedipal gratification through playing the seductive but aim-inhibited role of the wonderful little girl; and (3) providing negative oedipal gratification in the sexualized union with mother. It was *preoedipal* in the centrality of the primitive merger with mother that unconsciously was played out in heterosexual relationships. With the undoing of that merger went loss of both the mother and her love and consequently the collapse of their joint grandiosity. In this light, much of their clinging to these men, much of their tolerance of criticism, demand, and abuse, involved repetition of the early projective-introjective relationship with mother, the seductively cruel, pregenital love relationship of early infancy. It was preoedipal, too, in the early guilt and reparativeness directed toward the damaged mother. Thus, their way of being in love with men could be viewed in its preoedipal aspects as helping them keep in check overt expressions of their multileveled omnipotence, rage, envy, and guilt, and at the same time obscure their relatively retarded individuation and engenderedness. All in all, their painful and costly victimization in this sexist world was therefore not without its rewards in defensive security against anxiety and guilt and in unconscious pleasure.

CONCLUSION

Although I believe my account of descriptive features and developmental and dynamic factors to be the valid outcome of helpful work with one subset of analysands, I do not claim to have laid out the necessary and sufficient conditions for a well-circumscribed disorder of living. Many of the factors I mentioned have turned up in the course of clinical work with women who presented themselves as the crushed, ineffectual victims of manifestly powerful, vain, and persecutory mothers. Also, some high-achieving women seem to attach themselves not to the sadistic-narcissistic type of man just described but rather to men they experience as passive and crippled on the surface, rather like the weak father and the handicapped mother, even though not lacking furtively sadistic and narcissistic tendencies of their own. The women who make this kind of object choice may have experienced less criticism and more idealization during their development. Further, the kind of pairing I have described may be encountered in relationships between men, between women, and in reverse form between men and women. And finally, I fully recognize that the intimate relationships of high-achieving women need not be deeply troubled at all. I have written here only about most of those who have come for analysis and seemed to show this one of a number of possible patterns of disturbance.

Whatever the limits may be on the generalizability of my report, it can, I think, be useful to clinicians in following the twists and turns of the unconsciously maintained mazes of power and rage in which women can lose themselves as they try to make their way effectively in our sexist world. Psychoanalytic work on this kind of tragic situation is of particular moment in our modern era of critical reexamination of relations between the sexes. For the female patients, it seems to increase thc possibilities of a liberated and fulfilling existence in the inner world and in society. And for all those who engage in critical inquiry, it may increase their range of understanding.

PART THREE

THEORIES AS MASTER NARRATIVES

CHAPTER 9

Reading Freud's Legacies

PSYCHOANALYTIC DISCOURSE AND MODERN CRITICAL THEORY

To give a reading of Freud's contributions and their development up to the present is to face the future as well as the past. Ostensibly, those who write or speak on Freud direct attention to the recent and remote past in order to develop an objective account of a legacy and perhaps to suggest what has been done with it. In this effort, however, they cannot hope to be simply descriptive. Like it or not, they are prescriptive at the same time, for, inevitably, they chart a future for psychoanalysis. I say so because I believe that all accounts of psychoanalytic history, however conventionalized they may be, are bound to place certain matters in the foreground, relegate others to the background, and ignore still others. On this understanding, historical accounts have to be imbued with their authors' value judgments. The narratives indicate what the authors hold dear, and it is through this implementation of values that they prescribe a future. In effect, the historian will be saying, "This is what psychoanalysis should be," and in the same breath, two related prescriptions as well: "This is the best way to talk about psychoanalysis," and, "This is the way to be or become a psychoanalyst."

If this much is accepted, then it can be added that the mode of telling prescribes allegiance to a particular discourse. A discourse is constituted in part by interlocking modes of establishing values and formulating and challenging truth-claims and in part by the practices that, it is believed, legitimize this discourse and are in turn legitimized by it. Therefore, to say of a discussion of Freud's legacy that it expresses one's aspirations for psychoanalysis is also to argue on behalf of specific values, truth-claims, and practices. This, then, must be true of the reading of Freud's legacy that I shall be presenting. Although my reading obviously owes a lot to familiar discursive traditions in our field, it also draws heavily upon what may be called twentieth-century Enlightenment.

I present this account because I want to convey my version of how we might try to situate Freud in the discourse of contemporary intellectuality. Intellectually, Freud was a child of the Enlightenment that dates roughly from the late seventeenth century, and we would, I think, all agree that it was in the context of the development of that Enlightenment that he tried to be up to date. In this "official" aspect of his effort, he provided a rationalistic, empiricist, objectivist account of his methods, the findings based on them, and his conclusions. He presented himself as working within the prevailing axioms and conventions of discourse of the natural sciences of his time. He also drew heavily on the content of what was, for him, contemporary psychology, anthropology, philosophy, archaeology, philology, and other disciplines, all of which were cast from the same epistemological and methodological mold.

In this discourse, language is taken unreflectively as a transparent medium of communication. It is not regarded as bound to person, time, place, culture, or specific conventions. Consequently, Freud did not regard the version of it he used to report his psychoanalytic work as having evolved in such a way as to express and serve primarily the interests of the white, male bourgeoisie of the Western world. Freud viewed language as a transparent and sufficient medium that is, however challenging its content may be, in harmony with the established order of things and what he called its "self-evident" morality.

But the terms of modern critical thought are not the terms of this earlier and still widely endorsed Enlightenment. In the newer context, language occupies center stage in theoretical thinking and research. Language is seen as that which makes the world that it tells about. Moreover, it makes this world through implicit as well as explicit dialogue; that is, it functions and has functioned always in a social context. Language now is a variable and not a constant; it is a message in the guise of a medium, a set of perspectives rather than a clear glass window on the world, an ideological process rather than an essence, a specific cultural net rather than a universal mode of exchange.

Additionally, it is an instrument of power to be wielded for good, as in therapy (usually), or for bad, as in racism and sexism. Therefore, I think it appropriate to try to situate Freud for our time, that is, amid the multiple perspectives made available by contemporary critical theory. Although my effort is incomplete, sketchy, and highly contestable, it conveys my allegiance to the idea of psychoanalysis as a discipline with an ongoing life.

To focus on the language of psychoanalysis requires paying particularly close attention to its dialogic nature. Equally important is the recognition that the practice of psychoanalysis is rooted in dialogue between analyst and analysand, between analytic teacher and student, and between colleagues. As so much is a matter of interchange, we may say that through dialogue psychoanalysis keeps coming into being. All the more reason to establish a dialogic context for this presentation.

To develop this context, let us consider first dialogue in relation to the general history of ideas. Progress in any discipline has always depended on continuing dialogue. Continuing dialogue over conflicting aspirations and truth-claims helps refine our notions of importance; our methods, samples, and arrangements of data; our logical tools; our conclusions; and always the rhetoric we rely on to make a case persuasively. Through dialogue, we also learn better how the opposition makes its case. Learning that, we then try to find common ground; failing that, we begin to develop more persuasive arguments for our point of view. In the process, once the questions being asked are modified, the answers will be framed differently, and even the subject of inquiry may be changed to whatever now seems to be more urgent or more fruitful than its predecessors. Goals are never set with finality. And taking into account all those contemporary dialogues aimed at connecting as well as contrasting the different perspectives associated with race, gender, and social class can only add further to the sense that the history of ideas, of theory and practice, is always in flux.

From what has already been said, it follows that the history of psychoanalysis should be written, read, and taught from this dialogic point of view. To give one example of the movement of dialogue: In reaction to changing times and interests, based in part on extensive philosophy-of-science debates over the problems of traditional metapsychology and in part on the widening scope of analytic perception and practice, which has been increasing the influence of Kleinian object-relational thought, we have been witness in the course of one generation to a spectacular change. Specifically, most psychoanalysts have shifted their discussions away from refined elaborations and critiques of the theory of psychic energy and the energic underpinnings of psychic structure; further, they have even been moving away from rigorous debates over the idea of structure itself and the explanatory value of structural concepts (Schafer, 1988).

The current trend seems to be to use the term *structure* descriptively. Used in this way, structure merely refers to whatever the observer pieces together into stable patterns of motives or modes of experience and overt conduct that are relevant to the thesis being developed. Implicitly, structure is no longer treated as a fixed essence of things waiting to be discovered, and analysts no longer are so preoccupied with the question of how it is ever possible for structure to come into existence, develop, and remain stable.

Instead, increasing numbers of analysts seem to find it more engaging and worthwhile to join dialogues that feature object relations and self experience and corresponding refinements in theoretical and technical conceptions of early development as it is reflected in the experience of transference and countertransference. In these dialogues, they weigh a variety of approaches to understanding and modifying psychopathology of every sort, and they emphasize particularly both the development and the disruption of their empathizing with archaic motives, fantasies, anxieties, and defensive shifts of orientation and experience.

Earlier I mentioned the need for persuasive rhetoric. Because rhetorical issues figure prominently in what follows, I should explain what I meant. If all cases are made through implicit or explicit dialogue, each case can be developed adequately only if its insecure or assailable aspects are recognized, explicitly confronted, and either persuasively justified or artfully dodged. In any event, the success of an argument depends to a noteworthy extent on rhetorical adroitness. Rhetoric is, however, not something people choose to use; every way of speaking or writing is subject to rhetorical analysis, and every way may be used more or less adroitly. Emphasizing and exploring how this is so is a conspicuous part of the linguistic turn in the recent history of ideas.

Consider this rhetorical perspective on psychoanalytic language: Much of the psychoanalytic literature is written in a drab style. I suggest that this style is a specialized and conventionalized rhetorical attempt to be persuasive. It attempts to be persuasive by creating an image of the writer as a reliable member of the Old Enlightenment: a neutral, value-free, countertransference-free, well-trained scientific observer; a genderless, raceless, classless expert delivering a monologue that gives all the appearance of having been stripped of rhetorical ploys. In part, this image is designed to instill a false sense of security in the reader. "Trust me," it says. And unquestioning trust is badly needed in many cases because it serves to blind the reader to two obvious difficulties that arise in connection with the detailed deterministic explanations usually featured in psychoanalytic publications.

The first difficulty is that those deterministic explanations cannot stand up to the simplest of *traditional* scientific tests, if indeed any such test can even be formulated. This difficulty arises because the testing of psychoanalytic propositions calls for a quite different approach to corroboration. The second difficulty is that the deterministic accounts do not satisfy the fictitious standard of perfect authorial disinterestedness, for usually it is easy to show that their author is trying hard to win readers over to his or her conclusions by more than the content and logic of the "findings" being reported. That *more* is a self-conscious rhetorical effort to be persuasive, and it is felt to be required because others working in the same area have either already presented persuasive arguments for other underdetermined conclusions or soon will.

I want to add an interpretation of defense to this account of the drabness of much psychoanalytic rhetoric. I suggest that this conventionalized drabness is an attempt to deny that there is much about Freud's creation of psychoanalysis, and thus of his legacy to us, that can be characterized as a triumph of vivid and masterful rhetoric. Freud wrote psychoanalysis: He wrote it in the teeth of powerful scientific opponents, and he wrote it persuasively. Consequently, in reading him, we cannot separate his content from what is widely acknowledged to be his powerful and beguiling, and sometimes even beautiful, style. Freud's winning language is now known, however, to have covered a multitude of shortcomings in his arguments. I can say so in this more enlightened and permissive period of psychoanalytic history without being thought to deny the least aspect of Freud's creative genius. Other writers on psychoanalysis, even those most closely identified with Freud, use their own rhetoric and so create more or less modified versions of the discipline.

My general point is that there is no absolutely specific and static Freudian essence. Nothing lies beyond any one writer's rhetoric and thus beyond the realm of implicit and explicit dialogue. Consequently, in order to assess properly each and every version of psychoanalysis, one must read it as a document situated in a personal context that in turn is linguistically situated in a historical and ideological context of dialogue.

FREUD'S MULTIPLE LEGACIES

All this said, how shall we begin to approach more directly the large topic of Freud's legacy? I begin by proposing that we give up the idea that there is just one legacy to sum up and assess, for in a world forever constituted anew through continuing dialogue, there can never be only one theoretical or technical legacy. There can only be legac*ies*, linguistic legacies, legacies that are theoretical through and through. Freud's texts will remain open forever to alternative readings and writings: scientific, literary, and cultural. In time, the absolutist writings and readings on theory and technique, with which we are so familiar and which still are published in official analytic journals, will become a thing of the past. Already they come across to some of us as narrowly doctrinaire and authoritarian if not old-fashioned bravura performances. In the perspective of the modern Enlightenment, it must be Freud's readers and Freudian writers who continuously co-create Freud's legacy. This they do by how they read his texts and by how and what they write. As the readers and writers change—and they do change—Freudian psychoanalysis changes.

Further support for this elevation of reading and writing can be mustered by any survey of single topics in the analytic literature, for it requires no strain to read each such segment of our literature as a battlefield of competing, incompatible, and newly triumphant claims concerning what Freud said, meant, intended, or laid the groundwork for. One example is the ongoing dispute over Freud's general orientation to psychoanalysis that is based on the assumption that there is a single best or correct way to translate Freud from one language to another: Was he scientific or humanistic? Does *Ich* mean "ego" or "self" or both? Another example is the often-repeated, authoritarian recommendation on how to settle disagreements: "Back to Freud!" When that recommendation is made as a simple absolute rather than as a prod to keep up one's reading of Freud, it suggests wrongly that anyone could hope to read Freud in an absolutely selfless, value-free, culture-free, nondialogic way and thereby reach not only the right answer for the moment but the one and only true Freud. "Back to Freud!" is perhaps the greatest rhetorical ploy of all. The advisor is saying "Back to *my* Freud; repress the rest."

What is the basis of these interpretive wars? It is not only that Freud was not always perfectly consistent or explicit in his creative work. Nor is it just that the rhetoric through which he created and conveyed his contributions ranged from the highly tentative, uncertain, apologetic, and ingratiating all the way to the virtually dictatorial, and ranged as well from the rigorously and mechanistically scientific all the way to the free-flowing and evocatively humanistic. Nor yet are these interpretive wars based solely on what is commonly recognized to be the influence of personality, training, and experience on the way readers read Freud and new writers write Freud. There is more to add to this list of undeniably important factors.

Here I discuss only one additional set of factors: those related to power. The adversarial readings and writings I have referred to have been based to a significant extent on both the *general* history of changing organizational conditions within the psychoanalytic movement and the *specific* history of official policy regarding the programming of meetings, the publication of articles in the analytic journals, the making of referrals to colleagues, and the selection of candidates. In these respects, it seems as if, at any one time, power has played a major role in deciding the truth about Freud's legacy. And this power has not always been attained and maintained through intellectual and clinical accomplishment and consensus.

It should come as no surprise that the play of power within organizations of analysts has figured importantly in the intellectual and professional history of psychoanalysis: The exercise of power is always with us as human beings. Psychoanalysis is no exception to this general principle, and the principle need not stimulate despair. In this regard it is not only hopeful but interesting that, necessarily, shifts do occur in the conditions of power and in the modes of its employment. These shifts are the result of dialogue that cannot be silenced. And correlated with these shifts are shifts in the intensity of the surveillance, discipline, and punishment of those who oppose or disregard the doctrines that the powerful try to enforce. It is these shifts that enable changes to be established in what has been taken to be important and true. Consequently, it may be said that the changes in power will always play an important role in the flux that characterizes the truths and the values of psychoanalysis. Consideration of Freud's legacy cannot be split off from the history of power.

Witness, for example, the relatively recent growth of interest in the preoedipal period, a period that was once not to be made too much of. With that growth of interest has come progressive articulation of the concepts of mothering, parenting, and selfhood; an ever-more insistent emphasis on understanding early aggression and early stages of guilt in treating extreme cases; and also special attention to preestablished adaptation, the acquisition of language, and early modes of cognition. Another example is found in the many competing and as yet unstable but terribly important modifications of what has been represented as the psychoanalytic truths about women and the importance of those truths for the general theory of psychoanalysis. Not one of these changes has taken place outside the arena of power; each has had to be fought for, and some are still being fought for and often fought over as well.

Power in new hands; power diffused and wielded differently; surveillance relaxed; professional discipline and punishment themselves under extreme suspicion, not to mention their curtailment by actual or potential intramural strifes and even lawsuits: These changes have allowed and fostered an altered set of facts of life in contemporary psychoanalysis. One new feature of today's freer psychoanalytic life is the tolerance, both genuine and feigned, of multiple and competing claims about what psychoanalysis is. Another feature is that, far from being considered monolithic, each contemporary school of psychoanalytic thought may be heard more accurately as a din of voices in argument over readings. No longer is it possible to claim legitimately to be presenting an exclusive, purportedly final or unarguable account of Freud's legacy.

I suggest that this pluralistic view of Freud's legacy, this view that there can only be legacies that are forever subject to change, is itself one of Freud's legacies. Although it is my impression that Freud always wanted to be in control of the development of psychoanalysis, I believe, too, that he also wanted his discipline to be open to challenge and improvement through revision. Even if he often seemed to want to be the absolute judge of proposed change, if not the prime originator of it, in his role as dedicated scientist, he recognized that in order for psychoanalysis to qualify as a science, its propositions should be forever on trial. Certainly he continually reviewed his own formulations and changed them. But in his wanting to have the last word, he revealed that he did not always live up to his own ideals, for it is one consequence of the open-minded scientific attitude that he espoused so well in other respects that there never can be a last word. No one ever can have the last word, because no investigator or writer can control history. Certainly no one can ever end it. No one can stop the ongoing dialogue. Any one language has its limits. Power and prestige have their limits. Closure will elude us forever.

No one can even dictate how a name is to be used. Freud, contrary to his wish, could not even own the word *psychoanalysis* for long. Although one may regret, as I do, the extreme diffusion of meaning of "psychoanalysis" in today's world, we cannot hope to halt or reverse it. Diffusion has already gone so far that, whenever "psychoanalysis" is used, we must wonder just what it refers to. In my view, the history of psychoanalysis has reached a point where it has become futile to argue over whether this or that and nothing else is the true or real psychoanalysis. Now it makes more sense to argue that only this or that specific idea or practice conforms to the version of psychoanalysis to which one is committed as author, teacher, thinker, or practitioner, or that it conforms to the version of it that a certain group of respected peers consider to have the longest and strongest tradition behind it or the greatest heuristic power. Today we must always be prepared to argue the merits of our chosen position. It was not always so, or so plainly a matter of choice of what to value and wish to transmit to the future. We must accept the idea that psychoanalysis is not property: It belongs to no one in particular. On this view, much controversy in psychoanalysis can be seen to be no more than pointless and history-blind debate over ownership.

FREUD IN THE HERE AND NOW

We cannot afford to neglect the transformations that take place in the dialogues that transmit psychoanalysis from one generation to the next. This consideration alone would compel us to regard Freud's legacies as ongoing processes. We may say that these legacies continuously come into being; they are constantly in transition; they do not remain identical to themselves. Or we may say that for every generation, Freud is always here and now, never there and then.

I suggested earlier that transmission of ideas occurs through a process that may be called a dialogue between Freud and his readers and writers. I want now to add that, phenomenologically speaking, in this dialogue Freud may be said to be constantly talking back to his readers. I have in mind the Freud who is always here and now. His constant presence is felt by those who keep restudying his texts without being locked into an infantile transference to him or to their teachers. They find that the texts are so rich that, as readers, they must continuously correct and supplement their earlier readings. The texts even provide reminders of how Freud paved the way toward analytic ideas that keep on being put forward as new, as truly modern, even as revolutionary and superior alternatives to his ideas. In saying this I am not implying that Freud knew it all, nor that he could have known all that he did know in the same way a modern analyst knows it, nor yet that he would approve of much that is now commonly accepted by those who call themselves classical Freudian analysts. Amazingly, however, there is a Freud who is felt by serious students to be holding up his end of a lively and invariably refocusing conversation.

This inexhaustible and zestful readiness for continuing dialogue with his changing readers is another of Freud's legacies. That there is a Freud who can be always present to us is attributable to his having written in a way that steadily invites the continuation of dialogue. In his welcoming aspect, he stands above many of his influential followers, specifically those whose tone suggests that we are being told what's what rather than being prompted to consider what's next. It is only in this processive and dialogical sense that the admonition "Back to Freud!" can have a nonauthoritarian modern meaning, the meaning that it is in the nature of the work never to be done.

FREUD'S TRANSFORMATIONAL DIALOGUE

Engaging as this contribution to dialogue may be, Freud made a far more fundamental one. I venture to claim that out of Freud's genius issued an altogether new form of dialogue. He made it possible for therapists and patients to engage in consequential forms of transformational dialogue that had never existed before. He showed therapists how to do things with words to help revise radically their patients' hitherto fixed, unconsciously directed constructions of both subjective experience and action in the world: to use words to change lives in a thought-through, insightful manner. No one before him had done anything as profound, comprehensive, skillful, basically rational, and effective. Of the many possible ways to describe this monumental achievement, I submit the following. Freud's clinical dialogue alters in crucial ways the analysand's consciously narrated presentation of the self and its history among people by *destabilizing, deconstructing,* and *defamiliarizing* it.

Before proceeding further, note that it is arbitrary to discuss these processes in sequence, as if they are logically and temporally distinguished; however, my account will, I think, be clearer if I describe each process somewhat differently and invoke each in a somewhat different context. Think of it as using different windows to look into the same room and never seeing things quite the same way. Also, although much communication goes on nonverbally, it is conventionally accepted that a *psychoanalytic* therapy requires bringing significant issues into verbal dialogue—psychoanalysis as the "talking cure."

To achieve the destabilization, deconstruction, and defamiliarization of the patient's narratives, the classical psychoanalytic dialogue uses the free-association method; frequent sessions for continuity; and sessions that last for most or all of an hour so that time is available for each day's dialogue to develop, double back on itself, seemingly cancel itself out, or otherwise enter into the larger treatment process. The classical psychoanalytic dialogue also features the interpretation of defenses against full expression and felt interaction. And with the help of the mixture of the "regressive" and "progressive" phenomena it elicits, it reconstructs the way in which the history of these defenses and their motives is grounded in the typical subjective danger situations of early childhood.

Because the life narratives with which the analysand has come for treatment are more or less stabilized by these defenses, the invaluable analysis of defense, insofar as it is effective, necessarily *destabilizes* them. The process destabilizes both the established stories of guilt, trauma, neglect, misunderstanding, and blissful, unambivalent love, and the stories that seem merely to have been put together spontaneously in the thick of the ongoing analysis. The patient develops a new slant on lives that have been lived and that are expected to be lived; at the least, the versions of lives that gain importance are far more complex, less rigid and one-sided, and more tragically and ironically constructed (Schafer, 1970a).

What now of *deconstruction?* The analysand's narratives are deconstructed through the analyst's steadily focusing on first, their internal contradictions, their being founded on displacements, condensations, and marginalizations, and their erasures of expectable, emotion-laden crucial life experience; and second, the hidden hierarchies of value in taken-for-granted polarities such as male-female, active-passive, and dominant-submissive. Psychoanalytic deconstruction brings out particularly the contradictory or otherwise incoherent types of overt and fantasized relationship that the analysand tries to develop with the relatively neutral and relatively opaque figure of the analyst. This deconstructive handling of transference clarifies the complex, unstable, and conflictual nature of the analysand's enduring attempts at self-definition and relationship. The analyst also takes up many paradoxical reasons for repetitious enactments of these often quite painful transferences. In principle, though for practical reasons not always in practice, nothing is taken for granted about any version of self, relationship, or reality in general.

Contrary to popular stereotype, however, deconstruction is not a lofty name for destructiveness and disillusionment. Psychoanalytic deconstruction makes possible new and sounder construction, in particular the construction of more fulfilling narratives of lives in progress. The analyst uses the analytically defined elements of narrative incoherence to begin to *retell* the analysand's presentations and to bring the analysand into the process of retelling, now in the terms of unconsciously developed and maintained conflict and taken-for-granted or well-rationalized compromise formation. At the same time, the analyst and analysand together construct *a* history for what Freud called the analysand's "conditions for loving," a phrase to which many of us today would want to add "conditions for hating" and "conditions for playing dead or empty." (It is to take account of narrative variation among analysts that I say *a* history, not *the* history.) Among the virtues of the new constructions are their being both more confident and more provisional than those they have replaced.

Certainly, any dedicated deconstructionist would approach even these new and provisional analytic narratives with an eye to their incoherent and contradictory elements. Being the kind of method it is, deconstruction accepts no self-exclusionary limits on its application. It recognizes that to develop its position it must use the very language whose basic coherence it regularly challenges. But here the therapeutic goals of the analytic dyad intervene: Analyst and analysand make a judgment, based on shared health values, that any attempt at further change at this time might create more problems than benefits or might just lack adequate momentum; it may also be judged that the patient is in a more or less adequate position to continue the work of analysis independently, as the need arises and to the extent necessary. At this point, the joint work of deconstruction and new construction comes to an end.

There is more, however; specifically, the *defamiliarization* accomplished by the analytic dialogue. In the therapeutic interaction, the analyst begins to retell insightfully, roundedly, and empathically much that the analysand initially has told and is telling naïvely, abjectly, seductively, or aggressively, and, in any case, defensively. By introducing new or revised or unexpectedly interdependent storylines as major amendments to the analysand's narratives or as supplements to them, the analyst begins the process of defamiliarizing them and here, too, engages the analysand in the process. The nature of life history changes; its variables and its conceptions of time and place, of process and progress, and of relevance continue to change. As the patient's sense of the "timeless unconscious" develops, established accounts of present circumstances and future prospects also become less familiar.

Secretly or obviously, the analysand always approaches with great trepidation these new ways of making history and the new versions that result from them. Consequently, much working through always remains to be done, both during the analysis and after its conclusion. Insightful mastery is achieved through the kind of repeated defamiliarization and working through that psychoanalysis alone is capable of effecting. With the sense of real life as an ongoing process, the patient is prepared to accept the fruits of these labors as always open to further modification.

In the foreground of these retellings is, as I have emphasized in several chapters, the figure of the analysand as an active party to bringing about much that initially is or was experienced in passive, frequently victimized terms. In this respect, the dialogue helps the analysand shift toward some form of assertive and responsible psychosexual and psychosocial maturity. In other respects, however, as in the case of hitherto denied or minimized trauma or abuse, the analysand remains no longer defensively omnipotent; now the patient is better able to accept that in many respects she or he has been, is, and will be more or less passive, helpless, needful, or yielding. In the latter respects, analysts often observe a beneficial reduction of grandiose inflations of self-esteem, guilt, independence, and imperviousness.

Freud taught us to see the action in apparent inaction and accident, but he taught us, too, how much of our sense of power and control is illusory, is compensatory fantasy that denies and reverses the powerful and sometimes dire necessities of the body. He showed us that we share with others in our world a great amount of helplessness over our life cycles. In this, as in all of his psychology—a psychology of unconscious conflict and necessary ambiguities and paradoxes that pervade human experience and action—he introduced a modern tone into our conceptions of tragedy and irony; after Freud, our understandings and narratives of human existence could never be the same. We may add this legacy to all the others.

DIALOGUE IN THE INNER WORLD

One outstanding feature of the analytic dialogue is its showing by interpretation that, both in the past and in the present, dialogic experience is never limited to two people present to one another physically. Far from it. Through analysis the analysand is able to develop and tolerate accounts of the dialogue that no longer feature exclusively or predominantly abstract tendencies, general patterns, habits, socially defined traits, and social existence defined only in the conventional terms of behavioral social interaction. Instead, the crucial analytic versions tell of a multitude of voices rising from his or her own imagined inner world as well as a multitude of inner-world voices that, by perception or projection or both, the analysand locates in the analyst or others in the surround. Ideally, analysis brings it about that this concordant and discordant chorus of voices is no longer obliterated or muted by repression and other defenses and no longer mislocated by projection. Once it can be heard clearly, it is accessible to sorting out. Each influential voice may then become clear enough to be traced back to early experience in real or imagined relations with others; at least, its power is reduced because it is recognized for what it is. Thus far I have spoken only of voices, but, of course, other powerful sensory images of the inner multitude, some of them purely kinesthetic, are often presented eloquently.

Particularly significant for the analytic narrative are all those fantastic, libidinal and aggressive, body-centered, emotion-laden elaborations and misunderstandings that young children regularly introduce into their experience of their relationships and then elaborate further over time. The sorting out of these features and sources is rendered especially difficult and time-consuming by the interplay of introjective and projective processes that, according to the analytic retelling, characterizes the analysand's unconsciously carried-out construction of experience both in the past and in the here and now of the analytic relationship. In other words, the interpenetration of inner and outer worlds and past and present worlds is extensive, often subtle, and regularly fluid, and its analysis can never totally eliminate ambiguity.

THE CENTRALITY OF PSYCHIC REALITY

These inner-world phenomena make up a large part of another of Freud's great legacies, specifically, his idea of psychic reality. That idea embraces much more than what is conventionally meant by subjectivity and its individual variations. In psychoanalysis, psychic reality begins with that conventional notion and goes on to include the analytically essential idea of unconscious fantasy that features all those twists and turns encountered in dreams and their interpretation.

Psychic reality refers to still more than that. It refers as well to individually different and persisting wishful but conflictual and compromised modes of *constructing* new experiences on all levels of development. It emphasizes how, unconsciously, people make and remake their own subjective experience, how they do so continuously—that is, when awake as well as asleep—and how, at later stages of development, they may have to exaggerate the weight and impact of their preserved accounts of early experience. Thus it is that they may be said to live in a second reality.

This second reality lies beyond conventional reality. In it space, time, and identity are in constant flux and disarray, so that then and now, there and then, no and yes, disturbing and insignificant, I and thou, all coexist, mingle, or change places; all may be reversed or fragmented or otherwise isolated from conventional rationality. Freud's dialogue centers more and more on this powerfully influential second reality. The dialogic chorus of voices is heard mostly there. The multitude of images resides there. The transference and defenses live in it. Dreams and screen memories portray it.

We do not dismiss as irrelevant or altogether inconsequential the "first" reality—by which I mean not one that necessarily originated earlier in time but one that is conscious, rationally organized, impersonal, and adapted to convention. For clinical purposes, however, it provides only a shrunken account of the analysand's mental activity and so is limited in its therapeutic usefulness. It is the largely unconscious second reality that emerges as the chief locale or scene of effective psychoanalysis.

THE SELF-REFLEXIVE DIALOGUE

Freud's new dialogue may be characterized in yet another way; it is a supplementary way in that this characterization rests on all that has come before it. It may be said that Freud developed a therapeutically consequential dialogue that, to a very large extent, is about itself. Basically, it is self-reflexive. However much the dialogue refers to other matters, such as past life history or current problems in work, love, and self-esteem, again and again it takes a self-referential turn. The focus necessarily and productively shifts to what was said or left unsaid in the analytic relationship and how it was or was not recounted, and when, why, and on what understanding. The focus also shifts to how each development is encased in a set of hopeful and fearful fantasies. Further, it shifts to the ways in which the formal features of the verbal and nonverbal dialogue may be construed either as attempts to remember and communicate with the analyst through enactment much material that has been deeply repressed or as attempts to introduce new material in order to refute or confirm interpretations already in play in the analysis. These formal features may even be construed in both ways: repeating the old *and* introducing the new. In any case, these communications are made mostly unconsciously.

There are, however, many ways in which a dialogue could be about itself; it is the *psychoanalytic* way that Freud devised and developed to a considerable degree, the way that I have been reviewing, that seems to me to be essential to the dialogue's therapeutic and transformational potential.

FREUD AND FEMINISM

It remains to take up briefly what I consider to be another of Freud's great legacies: his contribution to the further development of feminism. If we are to situate Freud in contemporary intellectual life, then we must consider him in relation to the profoundly influential, relatively recent revolution in critical theory that has been sparked by feminism.

I claim Freud for feminism even though it is now plain that he shared and implicitly endorsed much of the bourgeois sexism of his time. Among other things, he was dismissive of feminism itself. On the other hand, however, he was at least able to begin to transcend his biases in his more specifically psychoanalytic propositions. His curiosity and creativity did not stop at the borders of the mentality of the men he studied. However imperfectly and at times even woundingly he did it, by attempting to present women as fully human, by reversing the tendency to marginalize them, he participated relatively early in this century's process of restoring to them aspects of worth and dignity equal to those of men. This he did not only through the very fact of his studying women in their psychological development, dilemmas, and psychological ailments, but also through his clarifying the anxiety-ridden, conflictual basis of male sexuality, including the anxiety and aggression toward women that men express in their simultaneous fear, idealization, and degradation of them. This psychoanalytic "humbling" of men could not but elevate women to the level of fellow creatures. Freud did all this for women in the same way that he laid the basis for a deeper understanding of the prejudices against, and the mistreatment of, children, Jews, people of color, foreigners, the sexually unorthodox, and all the others included in the list of suspects usually rounded up for discriminatory treatment by the traditional white male community, whose world this Western one pretty much still is. A wonderful legacy, indeed! It is a legacy of liberating and humane ideas and a legacy of incredible boldness of vision and persistance.

FREUD AND THE HUMANITIES

In summing up I am impressed with the extent to which Freud's creation is rooted in the humanities. Freud was not prepared to consider any such possibility. He did not consider the humanist-existentialist aspect of his work suitable for theoretical purposes. Instead, he simply took that aspect for granted as a component of both clinical empathy and his novelistic feel for the language and the events of clinical work. For theory he turned to the scientific models of his day: Newton, Helmholtz, Darwin, and others in their line. These were men who had concerned themselves with the grand concepts of force, energy, structure, and mechanism; also with biological survival, adaptation, and evolution. They had taken for granted the account of the scientific observer as a totally detached, objective figure. In their tradition, Freud tried to construct the grand metapsychology that would establish psychoanalysis as a respectable empirical science.

Although it is historically and psychohistorically understandable, a number of eminent commentators have said that Freud's effort manifested misunderstanding of his own creation. Psychoanalysis did not follow the established models—not as a therapy, as a method of investigation, or as a theory of the human mind. It can even be claimed that Freud misunderstood the place of psychoanalysis in the roster of disciplines; for although it was, as he claimed, a psychology, psychoanalysis required a conceptual and methodological framework that did not then exist within psychology and is still kept in the margins of academic psychology. There were no frameworks anchored in relativistic, contextualistic epistemologies. Existential, structuralist, poststructuralist, and hermeneutic turns in the history of social thought had not yet been taken. Analytic and phenomenological philosophies were not available to help map out the linguistic and experiential realms in which psychoanalysis travels. Unavailable or unknown to Freud were modern explorations of the narrative, rhetorical, and dialogic nature of human communication and its role in the coming into being of differentiated self-object relations. In sum, the language of Freud's creation had to wait for the development of twentieth-century thought. He could have brought to bear the teachings of Nietzsche and thereby could have developed a more modern preliminary understanding of his work as deconstructive and narrative and so on; but he did not do so and later disclaimed any knowledge of these teachings—somewhat disingenuously, it seems, according to modern scholarship. On the other hand, it has taken generations of modern thought to see clearly just what Nietzsche was beginning to set forth, so that it is, I think, going too far to require Freud to have been on the cutting edge of the philosophical thought of his time, or even beyond it.

Ahead of his time in so many respects, Freud tried to be of his time—what else could he do?—and so he misunderstood himself. But in being ahead of his time, he facilitated some of those developments he would have needed to understand himself better, to be adequately understood by others, and yet to remain clearly open to continuing revision of those understandings.

That it is acceptable for more than one legitimate and arguable reading of Freud's achievement to exist was itself virtually unforeseeable and unthinkable in his time. Today we are better prepared to tolerate, if not accept, the pluralism that is the ground for my claim that we can speak of Freud's having provided more than just one legacy. By the same token, we are readier—at least intellectually readier—to accept the idea that our current readings of him will, in time, be superseded. We can, however, maintain some confidence that newer readings will not be modeled on the laboratory sciences or on simple evolutionism and organicism. The nineteenth-century versions of empiricism and naturalism are no longer dominant at the frontiers of the human disciplines. Doctrinaire adherence to the last century's narrow discourse and restrictive methods of proof no longer reigns supreme in psychoanalysis.

In conclusion, we may say that Freud invented a new discipline. Its roots and its branches extend into many realms of knowledge, and experts in every one of these realms—psychology, biology, history, anthropology, literature, and many others—may legitimately develop for their own purposes specialized perspectives on psychoanalysis, specialized applications of it, and specialized critiques of it. Nevertheless, psychoanalysis seems destined to withstand total appropriation by any one discipline. In this sense it will always belong only to itself. Fundamentally, it answers only to itself. Although Freud could not fully appreciate the gigantic magnitude and the special requirements of the texts he left for our perusal, he gave us tools and values that have helped us to appreciate those texts more than he ever could or did. It is for us to attempt to specify just what he bequeathed us.

CHAPTER 10

The Sense of an Answer: Clinical and Applied Psychoanalysis Compared

CRITICAL theorists in the humanities often enter into dialogue with psychoanalysis, taking note of both the bearing of their contributions on psychoanalysis and the uses they have found for interpretive precedents already established by Freud and other psychoanalysts. Although these dialogues vary with the critical theory or antitheory being espoused and the particular writer espousing it, they usually throw into question some or all of these psychoanalytic precedents.

Unlike these critical theorists, most clinical psychoanalysts (certainly most American psychoanalysts) continue to ignore these intellectual developments. To understand this difference of interest, it is not enough to make allowance for difficulty in the way of psychoanalysts combining close study of the work of critical theorists with their typically substantial amount of clinical practice, reflection on that practice, and efforts at psychoanalytic scholarship. Even when interested, analysts are daunted by the vast scholarly output of critical theorists and the great diversity among them. Analysts must struggle hard even to begin to understand the interdisciplinary excursions of the critical theorists, even harder to establish a preferred position of their own, and hardest of all to dare to join the conversation.

But no matter how daunting it is, never has it been more urgent for analysts to join these interdisciplinary conversations and confront (or confront anew) the epistemological and methodological presuppositions that ground, pervade, and control their own principles and practice of interpretation. Critical theorists have been arguing that all interpretation is inherently ambiguous, inconclusive, contestable, internally at odds with itself, blinding or repressive as well as illuminating, and dependent always on a specific context that is, however, infinitely revisible in scope and criteria of relevance. No less than the security of psychoanalytic interpretation is at stake. Consequently, psychoanalysts imperil their own discipline when they avoid dealing with what seem now to be the inescapable problems that inhere in finding things out, knowing them, understanding them, and communicating them—if it makes sense any longer to continue to refer to these activities as different from, and independent of, one another. And it is well for analysts to remember in this connection that those critical theorists who have explicitly or by implication questioned the grounds of psychoanalytic interpretation are not so much their enemies any longer as they are scholars studying the problems of *all* interpretation.

Simultaneously, it is incumbent on practicing psychoanalysts to contribute to interdisciplinary dialogues by writing about the way they arrive at and convey interpretations—what I call the sense of an answer. Their contributions are needed to offset a particular and growing problem: Typically, the interdisciplinary dialogues feature close readings of *selected fragments* of Freud's writings—usually, it seems, his *early writings,* as if only at the outset was Freud a true Freudian. In fact, however, Freud's writings and the received versions of them put forth by many later analysts no longer represent or control the practice of analytic interpretation to the extent that critical theorists often assume. By not recognizing this fact, theorists effectively deny psychoanalysis a history and so a future as well. It is a denial that can be only in the service of (in the eyes of psychoanalysts) an unconvincing economy, authority, and success of critical discussions of psychoanalytic interpretation.

Thus, what is lacking in the interdisciplinary realm are historically grounded and detailed versions of *modern* psychoanalytic work. How these versions relate to early Freud—or even to late Freud—is a subtopic in the history of ideas and therapeutic practices and is itself marked by considerable controversy. In this context, critical theory should live in the present; more exactly, it should not misrepresent the distant past as the dominant present.

As I see it, then, this chapter requires a section written from the standpoint of contemporary psychoanalytic practice, only then to be followed by a main text that searches for points of connection between this practice and the ongoing dialogues of critical theorists.

In the next section I present some workaday examples of clinical and applied psychoanalysis together with some comparative commentary on them. A fuller exploration of the common problems of these two types of analytic endeavor is presented in the section entitled "The Sense of an Answer." These common problems can be used to develop a livelier and broader context for considering psychoanalytic interpretation in relation to contemporary criticism than is now available.

Illustrations in the first section are sketchy. I set forth only enough to raise questions for my main text. First I present a conventional Freudian interpretation of part of the story of Snow White. After that I discuss two pieces of clinical analysis, one featuring interpretation of some prominent personality characteristics of women whose mothers appear to have been beset by severe narcissistic problems and the other featuring interpretation of the rhetoric of severely narcissistic men undergoing psychoanalysis. Instead of interpreting a fairy tale, I could have used psychohistory, psychobiography, analysis of the creative process, or some other familiar application of psychoanalysis. I hope that, by the end of this chapter, the reader is ready to grant that the fairy-tale illustration has served adequately as a point of entry.

SOME VERSIONS OF PSYCHOANALYSIS

Snow White

In the familiar version of the story of Snow White, she is sentenced to death by a vain mother-figure who wishes to be the fairest of all. Sentence is pronounced after this sinister stepmother has been told by the mirror on the wall that Snow White is fairer than she. Snow White is depicted as her innocent, passive victim.

Interpretation

This is a defensively disguised presentation of the daughter's positive (cross-gender) and aggressive oedipal aspirations and tribulations. This girl envies her mother's queenly feminine role, attributes, and sexual opportunities. In her wishful reality and by dint of considerable projection, she transforms her mother into a wickedly vain, envious, and vengeful woman who thinks nothing of destroying her own "innocent" flesh and blood. The supernarcissistic stepmother is now the split-off bad mother and the punitive maternal superego who, because she is greatly feared as well as loved, is useful to the daughter in strengthening the repression of her dangerously rivalrous oedipal wishes. Thereby, both the control of the daughter's aggression and the future of her relationship with the mother, whom she also loves and depends on, are assured, and the appearance of the daughter's passive innocence is maintained. At the same time it is unconsciously understood by the reader, who cannot but be oedipally guilty to some extent, that Snow White deserves to be punished for her rivalrous and matricidal impulses. There is no fooling the superego; like Jimmy Durante's nose and like the Shadow, it knows.

Freudian clinicians are familiar with this kind of life-historical narration by patients. Even when they allow, as Freud did, that many mothers do compete enviously and punitively with their daughters, they claim to know, or they confidently expect it to emerge, that in these narratives they are encountering a mixture of reality-tested and imagined object relations that have been given shape and content by the conflict of what traditionally they call instinctual drive derivatives and restraining superego and defensive structures. And with respect to the immediate clinical situation, they know (they say) that in these narratives they are encountering a blend of disclosure, warning, and resistance in the already forming transference. In these cases, sooner or later, analysts are prepared to "uncover" by interpretation some version of the core unconscious fantasy or storyline of Snow White. They have a sense that they have *the* answer to the question "What is wrong?"

But this sense of closure is not incontestable, for an object-relations analyst, one who more or less follows the lead of Melanie Klein (1964; see also Segal, 1964), hovers over the Freudian analyst, saying that that is not it at all; in fact, the Freudian analysis of Snow White is pretty superficial. Really, it is an obvious case of the daughter's projection of the aggression of the Death Instinct. The destructive daughter envies the mother's breast or goodness (her apple); envy leads by way of projection to spoiling the good breast (a queen with a poisoned apple); and the greedy incorporation of that now-bad breast results in the symbolic murder of the daughter by the evil introject. Snow White is a fairy-tale version of a universal unconscious fantasy that may have little to do with the attitudes and conduct of real mothers. The fantasy's principal source is in the paranoid-schizoid position of the first months of life. Only secondarily, if at all, does it involve actual experience with figures in the external world, and only in a tertiary way does it involve the Freudian Oedipus complex of a much later and less deeply anxious and guilty phase of development.

To complicate matters further, a self-psychological follower of

Heinz Kohut (1977) points out that neither the Freudian nor the Kleinian has been attending adequately to Snow White's experience of her narcissistically disturbed mother. This is the mother who does not or cannot provide that gleam in her eye—of appreciation, admiration, confirmation—that is essential to the daughter's growth of a cohesive self, a self with the impetus and direction provided by vigorous and defined aims. By looking only in the mirror—that is, at her own self—this mother consigns Snow White to the dead—to the realm of those with stunted, fragile, joyless, and inert selves. It is a case of the mother's poisonous lack of empathy and the daughter's arrested development and aimlessness.

What is one to do in this crowd before the analytic mirror? What should I do? Should I pick one line of interpretation, blind myself to the others, and declare that now I have the answer? If I did that, I would be deciding, on some combination of theoretical, temperamental, and professionally opportunistic grounds, to adopt a doctrinaire form of the identity of a Freudian, object-relations, or self-psychological analyst. Should I say instead "All of the above" and not worry about the intrinsic confusions of eclecticism? More than a few psychoanalysts do that, in a way that is evidently insecure, just plain flashy, or intimidating in its intellectual omniverousness and anal-retentiveness—or is it phallic exhibitionism or grandiosity? Perhaps I should just steer clear of applied analysis altogether and regard it as an inconsequential, inappropriate, inconclusive, hurtful and debased form of psychoanalysis. Or perhaps I should (as I have) involve myself in comparative analytic thinking-through of these three systems of thought—and maybe others as well? But if I did that, what ground would be left under my feet? Where could I find the authority for my work? How would I know what was real? How could I defend myself against the criticisms of colleagues? How might I arrive at the sense of an answer?

For many years I did mainly restrict my interest in any form of applied analysis, which I regarded as, at best, a poor relative of clinical analysis and something of a freeloader. Of late, however, my reading and my own clinical and theoretical efforts have led me to realize that I have been avoiding some serious issues that go to the heart of understanding the nature of any kind of psychoanalytic interpretation, and in this chapter I am beginning to try to correct the error of my ways.

Do I mean, as I just said, issues pertaining to *any* kind of psychoanalytic interpretation? Is it also difficult to understand the nature of *clinical* interpretation, and is the difficulty so much the same as the one I just brought up in connection with Snow White? I think so, and I am going to continue to try to persuade you that this is the case.

Severely Narcissistic Mothers and Their Daughters

The narcissistic mothers I have singled out for consideration are those who may be described as malignantly devoted to stunting not only their daughter's development of sturdy self-esteem but their capacity for satisfying relationships with their fathers, siblings, other girls and women, and the male sex in general—in other words, with everybody. These mothers are divisive in everything they do. They use the dyadic or symbiotic strategy of divide and conquer for all it is worth. Some of their daughters rebel through promiscuity, eating disorders, addictions, geographical flight, or some combination of these. Others—the ones I am concerned with here—stay and submit. In the main they become "good girls" and remain "good girls" of the latency-age type. They are reticent, easily embarrassed, and sexually and socially naïve, inhibited, and easily overstimulated. They are much like Snow White, except perhaps in some scattered, furtive, and rebellious sexual episodes that they themselves do not understand or take responsibility for. To the compassionate observer, they are the innocent victims of their mother's depradations, and the accounts of these depradations come across convincingly as so relentless and heartless that they may cause even the experienced clinician to wince or choke up on hearing about the horror of it all, a horror that includes witnessing the daughters' continuing attempts to idealize or at least defend these mothers.

How may we interpret psychoanalytically the life-historical narratives presented by these daughters? The Freudian view would have us say something like this. These daughters are conflict-ridden with respect to the libidinal and aggressive wishes that enter into their narcissism and object-relatedness. Out of anxiety, guilt, and shame they are hiding behind repressions, and they are yielding ambivalently to something between a severe maternal superego and a persecutory introject. They yield by becoming obedient, oedipally sexless, latency-type girls as well as, on a deeper level, passive, innocent, preoedipal infants. An additional factor is related to the positive libidinal strivings of these daughters: In living out their own fantasied castration by the phallic mother, they are able to identify with their fathers, whom they see as castrated victims of these mothers. Thereby they are able to adopt a partly gratifying androgynous position in the ostensibly simply horrible mother-daughter relationship and to cling to it tenaciously.

Or should the accounts of these daughters be interpreted, as earlier I interpreted Snow White, in the object-relational or self-psychological mode? At least in the schematic fashion I have been following, it would not be difficult to develop these alternatives—breasts both poisoned and made poisonous by the daughter's projections, glares rather than gleams in the maternal eye, and so on. How to decide? How to choose or synthesize? How to define oneself as analyst—as a being in the world, or in any world? How to tackle such large theoretical issues? Or should we as analysts try?

Can these analysands say anything to help analysts decide? Conventional psychoanalysts say they can and do; we have only to listen closely to analysands and be guided by what they say. Each school of psychoanalysis claims to be fairest of all in that it presents itself as based on listening that is far more acute, empathic, and rigorous than its rivals' modes of listening. But do psychoanalysts simply listen to analysands? If so, and despite large areas of agreement among themselves, why then do psychoanalysts disagree with one another so often and so strongly? Could it be that each of them is just interpreting the life-historical narratives of analysands in the same way he or she would interpret Snow White, that is, in an applied way and with ready-made interpretations? Could it be that analysts approach analysands as sets of stories to be retold in terms of the storylines provided by preferred analytic theories? These unsettling questions do not go away just because analysts repress or disavow them.

The Rhetoric of Narcissistic Men

Narcissistic men do not take readily or kindly to the analyst's interventions. They say, "I never thought of that," as if the first order of business is to determine who comes up with the ideas, or, if not that, to announce surprise that anyone else would have something of interest to say about them. Also, in response to the analyst's interventions, they say, "That could be," in a tone that suggests that they are going to weigh each puny intervention on a very grand scale of judgment before reacting to it. Often they repeat the analyst's interpretations some time after they have been made, not only as if they themselves have been the first to think them but as if they should be admired by the analyst for their achievement. They cannot hear or retain what the analyst says if he or she interrupts, speaks at any length, or develops a point along a line they have not initiated and authorized. They treat the analyst as something of a bore, with "bore" being defined, as in the old saying, as someone who is an expert in your own field. Often these narcissists say, "I don't know what this means" and "I can't figure that one out"; never once do they allow themselves even to think of asking the analyst for guidance or interested participation. In these cases, it seems for a long time that the analyst can aspire to be nothing beyond the status of a minor and intrusive expert.

What is the psychoanalytic meaning of this rhetoric? Are these men enacting in their transferences feeling castrated by their vain, competitive, and controlling fathers? Are they also victimized by their own pathological ego-ideal formation, a development that is attributable to the impossibility of their ever satisfying vain fathers who cannot take genuine pride in themselves and who undermine their sons by their ruthless competitiveness? Are these men also repetitively enacting in their transferences the life-historical story of how they had to develop defensive grandiosity in order to deal with the helplessness and hopelessness they felt in relation to their nebulous, masochistic, and ungiving mothers, the kind of women who are more than likely to be married to men of their fathers' type? And are they simultaneously enacting their full retreat from their oedipal desires for these mothers who, typically and obviously, are unhappy, isolated, and sexually unfulfilled in their marriages? Are the grandiose aspirations of these men being played out in spectacular feats of rhetorical and other control and controllingness that inevitably reek of anal sadism? Is their anality intensified by submissive wishes to be the castrated recipients of the love of their unreliably involved but idealized fathers? These men's narrations of their childhoods, their dreams and slips and defenses, their struggles with guilt and shame, their responses to Freudian interventions: All are likely to bear out these interpretive conjectures concerning the psychoanalytic import of their rhetoric.

And yet, to indicate only one alternative view, we could say that, in their rhetoric, these men are manifesting Kohut's disorders of the self as well as any analysand could. They are deprived and traumatized by mother and father alike of developmentally crucial empathic mirroring and holding up of attainable ideals. They have been forced into the compensatory construction of grandiose selves. In the analysis, they use their power of control to protect their fragile nuclear selves against further traumatization by the analyst who might make interpretations ill-suited to their inner experience and tolerance. Anal sadism is present as a by-product ("disintegration product") of their disturbance of self and not as a central dynamic. They are not so much conflicted as deprived, wounded, frightened, and self-protective. On this view, each of these men must use this rhetoric in order to survive with whatever self he can muster and to keep it on hold for that improbable future occasion when it might be safe to let it begin to grow. How well this self-psychological account fits these men, how warmly the less damaged of them will begin to receive it as time goes on, and how amply they will confirm it with more life-historical narratives of the same sort, provided that these interpretations are imparted to them slowly, perceptively, and empathically, and provided, too, that they are allowed to appropriate the interpretations in their own characteristic way for as long as they need to.

Again, we seem to have to confront the necessity of making a difficult choice. With regard to each clinical group, I have been applying the language and logic of different theories to roughly the same or similar descriptive phenomena. In each case, however, it could be said that it is as if I have been interpreting a story in a book or that I have simply been retelling one story in the terms of another. What is clinical here and what is applied? The disturbing questions of knowing and knowledge are present in clinical as well as applied practice. The sense of an answer eludes us. To get any further, we must, I think, take up questions of first-person speech, statements of intention, and the nature of the psychoanalytic dialogue and its interpretation. This I do in the next section.

THE SENSE OF AN ANSWER

Do psychoanalysts accept and rely on the authority of first-person speech? Does the pronoun *I* spoken aloud carry special weight in establishing the authentic presence of the speaker? Are the analysand's first-person locutions sufficient or even necessary for purposes of both grounding and verifying the analyst's interpretations? Is it essentially through what the analysand says aloud in the first person that the analyst arrives at the sense of an answer to analytic inquiries? If, in response to an intervention, the analysand says "That's not what I meant" or "That was not the result that I intended," is the psychoanalyst then required to revise the intervention? Is closure guaranteed by the analysand's assertions?

These questions may seem pointless to those familiar with clinical analytic work, as the obvious answer to each is no. Familiars know that, for one thing, speech may be inauthentic in its being deliberately or unconsciously misleading, incomplete, or biased. They also know that a good deal about what is in fact the case, according to conventional judgment, is communicated nonverbally through expressive movement, silence, and certain forms of acting out, and also communicated obliquely in narratives about others. And they know, too, that any of these other communications may contradict what is being or has been asserted explicitly in the first person by the analysand.

Additionally, familiars accept the conclusion Freud (1937a) reached in "Constructions in Analysis": An accumulation of indirect responses of various sorts, such as slips, dreams, reminiscences, and transferences, may add up to proof that a reconstruction of early experience is valid even though the analysand has produced no certified memory of that piece of personal history. And finally, these analysts know that at extreme moments in any one case, or as a rule in certain extreme cases, the analysand may be present in body but psychically absent or incommunicado. Thus, first-person speech is inherently problematic. To a noteworthy though lesser extent, this conclusion also guides ordinary social intercourse, where hearing is not always believing.

And yet it has been said, and it has often been implied, that there is all the difference in the world between clinical and applied psychoanalysis for, in applied analysis, "there is no patient to talk back." To refer to the patient who talks back is, however, to imply some debatable presuppositions. First, it implies that in doing applied analysis, analysts can have their own sweet way with the material at hand because that material is utterly passive and because there are no criteria for verification of applied analytic interpretations. Consequently, if the analyst is clever, applied analysis will be easy and safe to do. In contrast, so it is argued, the clinical analyst, confronted by first-person assertions and responses, cannot both do a good job and escape the rigors and deep experiences of clinical work. On this view, applied analysis is more like a flirtation, a rape, or a forced feeding than a total, interactive, and caring relationship. Additionally, reference to the patient who talks back presupposes that clinical interpretation is simply empirical, inductive, objective, and verifiable by known and independent criteria within the psychoanalytic dialogue; in contrast, applied analysis is a derivative and speculative enterprise that is parasitic on the clinically well-grounded theory of psychoanalysis. Thus, in the absence of a patient who can talk back, applied analysis is merely a monologue, not a dialogue with built-in, scientifically sound verificational feedback. It is lower in the hierarchy of psychoanalytic practice.

In making this case for back-talk, analysts are according a special place to the analysand's spoken words. They are granting much authority to the analysand's saying yes and no and to the confessions, disclosures, rememberings, and shocks of recognition that the patient delivers with the presumed authenticity of first-person speech. Indeed, analysts do often grant this same authority to their analysands when, in order to make their own written arguments more persuasive, they simply quote them to prove a point; it is common for an analyst to write, "As this patient put it so well . . ." and to follow with a quote whose unexamined "eloquence" is intended to put the finishing touches on an argument and establish the sense of an answer. For example: "Now I know that there was poison in Mother's kindnesses" or "It is better to be a star in the gutter than an undistinguished workhorse." In each case, that analyst is speaking or writing as if "that says it all." Not only is there a sense of *an* answer; this is *the* answer.

Evidently, then, analytic thinking about speech, interpretation, and verification presents inconsistencies or paradoxes. Something vital seems not to have been thought through. The comparisons of clinical and applied analysis that follow are intended to deal with this difficulty, and they involve some clarification of the theory of psychoanalytic interpretation, the relation of theory to practice in psychoanalysis, and the criteria of proof and truth that are customarily invoked in psychoanalytic work. Although what is offered adds up only to a small selection of observations, critical remarks, and suggestions, I do not believe that the consequences for our understanding the nature of psychoanalytic interpretation will be small in scale.

PSYCHOANALYSIS AS TEXT INTERPRETATION

For present purposes it is useful first of all not to take for granted any sharp commonsensical boundary line between clinical and applied analysis. Let us rather assume provisionally that there is only one psychoanalysis and that its practice encounters a variety of problems the nature of which depend on the details of the specific content being defined within the specific context being established. The methodological step I am urging requires us to concentrate on sameness rather than difference, congruence rather than divergence, interpretation in general rather than particularized versions of it. This is a psychoanalytic world without parasites or freeloaders. Taking this methodological step should help us begin to see clearly what clinical analysts have in common with those critics and critical theorists who, in recent years, can be said to have been having a love affair with psychoanalysis. Are these critics and theorists just being reckless romantics, frustrated creative writers, or emotionally deprived academics looking for thrills in applied analytic work, or are they (many of them), as I believe, engaged in fundamentally sober, even if often evidently ambivalent, common cause with clinical analysts?

Earlier I questioned the authority of presence in speech. I referred there to misleading as well as constructively communicative aspects of speech, silence, and other nonverbal actions in the analytic situation. At that point, I was already implying a perspective on the analyst at work, specifically that he or she takes everything in the analytic situation as a text that requires interpretation or that might, by suitable interventions, be developed to the point where it is enough of a text to yield to a psychoanalytic interpretation. Ordinarily, the analysand's professed intentions, while they must count for something, do not by themselves settle any question of analytic meaning or significance. Like any other text presented to the world, the analysand's text does not remain in his or her control. Once uttered or enacted, it becomes public property in the world of psychoanalysis and part of that world's possible histories. The analysand's declaration of intention is itself very likely to be taken as a text—for example, as defensive rationalization, a false lead, or a gesture of appeasement.

At most then, the analysand is used as a consultant on his or her utterances, and the consultation is itself considered to be further interpretable text. For the most part, this consultation is not carried out under the aspect of privileged opinion or insight; it is carried out by way of the analyst's interpreting the analysand's further free associations. Thus, the analyst treats the analysand in the same manner that many literary critics treat authors—with interest in what the analysand says about the aims of his or her utterances and choices, but with an overall attitude of autonomous critical command rather than submission or conventional politeness, and with a readiness to view these explanatory comments as just so much more prose to be both heard as such *and* interpreted.

Now, there is nothing psychoanalytically radical about this view of psychoanalysis as a form of text interpretation. In one respect, I am merely restating an analytic truism. The truism holds that, for purposes of developing insight through interpretation, we cannot rely simply or directly on manifest content or what is readily available consciously to the analysand. For instance, we do not interpret, let alone accept at face value, manifest dream content or accept the analysand's direct dream interpretations as conclusive communications about aims and meanings; similarly, we do not take the manifest wishfulness of a daydream as an unmediated or uncompromised expression of a primal wish. In another respect, I am only restating Freud's criteria for the verification of reconstructions: Verification is established by an accumulation of indirect or implicit responses, *the kind of responses that become evidence only upon interpretation, further analytic dialogue, and further interpretation.*

To take clinical analytic work as text interpretation is to establish the analyst as an influential co-author of the analytic text that is being interpreted. The text, in other words, is never fully delivered to the analyst; rather, it evolves out of the analysand's and the analyst's interpenetrating contributions. Increasingly, the two of them inhabit the text of the analysis; at times it seems that "cohabit" would be a better word for it. Cohabitation is what follows from throwing into question manifest content, including manifest avowals of intent and other such "explanations." In the end, the text and its interpretation are not altogether distinguishable. If, as I claim, I am merely restating psychoanalytic truisms, analysts should not find it difficult to grant this much about their work of interpretation. Yet many or most analysts still balk at accepting the ideas of text analysis and co-authorship when they are stated this baldly. It may seem to them to undermine their sense that *the* answer exists *in* the material and is to be *uncovered;* the latent lies *under* or *behind* the manifest; psychoanalysis is *depth* psychology; and so on.

To agree that analysts interpret interpenetrated or cohabited texts is to accord to constructivism and its corollary, perspectivism, an essential place in psychoanalysis and to put into permanent question the traditional psychoanalytic claim to the status of an empirical, inductive, objectively observational science. Constructivism and perspectivism are theoretical positions on what we can and should mean by "reality" or on the sense in which we can "know" reality. In constructivism, the world we claim to know objectively is not given directly to perception and reason. Rather, reality is constructed according to rules; these rules, though usually implicit, are ascertainable through critical study, no matter whether they are known as such to the subject or not. People follow these rules in observing or making observable whatever it is that they go on to say is in the real world. Broadly viewed, these rules are pretty much the same among members of the same culture and historical period, although the selection, comprehension, and application of the rules are more or less individualized. Hence the cultural diversity within conformity, or the conformity within diversity, that we generally acknowledge and more or less accept. The result is not reality plain but a perspective on reality or, more exactly, *reality by means of a perspective.*

According to this epistemological position, there is no coherent, sense-making way to approach a text. Indeed, there is no way to say what the text is that is to be approached, other than to construct reality by means of a particular perspective and to use consistently the language that manifests this perspective. However vulnerable the perspective may be to deconstructive demonstrations of its incompleteness and inconsistencies, and however much it may overlap other perspectives, it is distinguishable from them by criteria that are accepted by some segment of the critical community. On this basis, most members of the psychoanalytic community take Freudian, self-psychological, and object-relational perspectives to be different.

To present perspective in narrational terms: A perspective is made up of more or less coordinated sets of storylines that allow us to state in a comprehensible way what are being counted as relevant and significant facts. These sets of storylines also imply the special appropriateness of certain methods of fact-finding and indicate how best to use them. And the narratives they generate also enact the kinds of organization of facts that are to be considered legitimate, important, cohesive, and complete.

Instead of the terms *constructivism, perspectivism,* and *narration* or *storyline,* often other words or phrases are used to grapple with the same issues of knowledge of reality or how to arrive at the sense of an answer; these include *paradigms, models of the mind, leading metaphors,* or just plain *theory.*

Freudian theory specifies and authorizes certain technical methods for eliciting and defining certain phenomena and then organizing them serially and hierarchically within increasingly abstract levels of conceptualization and clinical generalization. Additionally, Freudian theory requires that all of this be done differently from the way analysts of other schools do it. For the sake of consistency, coherence, and completeness, and for the sake of a sense of Freudian identity, this requirement of difference has to be met. Self-psychological theory, for example, is very different from the Freudian: The self-psychological theory has no instinctual drives or primary stages of infantile psychosexuality; it has little or nothing in the way of defense or resistance, internalized object relations, and tripartite psychic structure. The phenomena elicited or defined by means of the self-psychological perspective are dependent on the unique integration and limitation of the technical procedures that it authorizes. Self psychology is rule-governed as is Freudian psychology, and the rules are different enough to establish its identity.

ANALYSTS AS CO-CREATORS

For the most part, in what follows I employ the Freudian perspective on constructing the psychological reality of human beings. More exactly, however—and to establish my general thesis this point cannot be overemphasized—I can remain only within one such perspective, namely, my own version of the Freudian perspective, as that is all I can reasonably claim to have. Other Freudian versions of the Freudian perspective differ from mine, with its definite object-relational coloring. This heterogeneity explains why at their meetings conventional Freudians continue endlessly to schedule panel discussions and symposia devoted to traditional concepts and problems, such as the meaning or nature of transference and acting out. It also explains why they disagree with one another at conferences and in their evaluations of colleagues and trainees. Conventional Freudian texts vary to some extent from one analyst to the next. Conventional analysts develop more or less different versions of the basic Freudian storylines of infantile psychosexuality, aggression, anxiety, guilt, self-esteem problems, danger situations, maturation, and so on. Consequently, interpretation is needed just to say what is essential to Freudian thought, and no one interpretation is the final one. We cannot avoid confronting the extent to which our assertions are saturated with perspectivism and constructivism.

If analysts co-create analytic data, if analytic observations make sense and attain significance only within a perspective, and if only by analysts' following, each in their own way, some more or less systematized and coherent set of basic storylines, then there can be no successful defense of the traditional Freudian image of "the analyst." In this image, the analyst is a straightforward inductive empiricist, an objective and independent clinician who simply observes what analysands set forth and draws the inevitable conclusions. Interpretation, then, is indistinguishable from inevitable conclusion and final closure. This image is, however, merely one of a number of possible images of the analyst, and to some analysts it has already become a joke. It depends on blindness enforced by anxiety before authority. That image may now be seen to be a naïve, precritical or unreflective representation of the analyst; it may also be seen to be a coercively repressive and anti-intellectual representation. It is the image found in the implicitly authoritarian rhetoric of what may now be regarded as the old school of Freudian analysis.

More important to note, however, is the more or less subtle way that image is presented in the polemical presentations made by members of *every* school of analysis. The fairest of them all: analysts who can still tell us confidently in each instance exactly what is what. They seem never to have heard of, or taken seriously, constructivism and perspectivism, visions or versions of reality, heterogeneity and self-contradiction at home as well as abroad. They stand for the image that all but some of the youngest analysts have grown up on, and so there is still widespread reluctance among analysts to put this image up in their intellectual attics along with self-preservative instincts, psychic energy, and certain sexist psychoanalytic generalizations that trivialize women in relation to men.

On the basis of the preceding discussions, it would be just as warranted to recommend viewing clinical analysis as a form of applied analysis as to continue viewing applied analysis as parasitic on clinical analysis, for clinical work is thoroughly, even if inconsistently, regulated by theory. Clinical interpretation makes manifest a prescribed perspective; it has its method, its language, and its own preferred sets of storylines. True, psychoanalysts present it as a plain fact that clinical analysis often facilitates personal change for the better, in whatever terms best suit the individual case. As an engaged clinical Freudian I would not contest that presentation. But the further claim is then made or implied that for this reason psychoanalysts occupy some position that privileges them to make and follow their own laws of knowledge and to ignore the history and current status of general theories of interpretation.

In contrast, I am arguing here that clinical analysis is not a thing apart and that nothing specific follows from presenting effected personal change in this way. That change is not an independent or unambiguous variable; rather, it is part of the initial conception of what analysis is. In other words, change alone cannot be used to validate clinical interpretations, for the final account of change, far from being theory-free, is shaped and presented in the terms of the methods, the storylines, and the interpretations of one or another psychoanalytic perspective. Each perspective, theory, or paradigm presents change at least somewhat differently. Owing to its regulative effect on technical practices, each perspective seems to bring about somewhat different types of phenomena, with theory-specific implications, that can be taken to indicate change for the better. This is why debate between schools of analysis over their relative effectiveness are never resolved and may be unresolvable, even if still worth debating for the clarity of systematic thinking they stimulate.

It is perhaps easier to see how the analysis of very young children may be regarded as a form of applied analysis. In that kind of analytic work, play and other behavior, much of it nonverbal, can be grasped and used analytically only by bringing to bear, on this less-than-ideal type of material, analytic theory that has been worked out much more thoroughly in the analysis of adults. The quality of being applied is also not too difficult to see in analytic approaches such as the old-fashioned kind of Kleinian and the cruder kind of Freudian and self-psychological approaches, in all of which we encounter tedious sameness in the occasions and contents of interpretive intervention. In the old-fashioned Kleinian case, we see particularly what other analysts regard as an overabundance and excessive depth of theory-dictated interpretation of rather limited amounts of material.

Hardest of all of the cases to see as applied (at any rate, hardest for me) is modern and subtle, though still theory-laden, Freudian clinical analysis and modern Kleinian analysis (see, for example, Joseph, 1989), which has relatively greater tolerance for prolonged ambiguity and freely wandering association and sustained interest in eliciting rather than imposing fantasy material, explores more fully spontaneous shifts of subjective experience and memory, and has greater interest, however ambivalent, in new theoretical possibilities.

What now can be said of that presumably privileged person, the patient who talks back? A case has already been made for the assertion that talking back does not encounter a passive, yielding, unquestioning analyst. Yes and no, right and wrong, yes but, not quite, that's off the wall, and so on: Analysts can always and do often take these responses by analysands as further analytic material. They try to do so in the thoughtful and artful way that Freud (1937a) began to outline in his paper on constructions in analysis and that he often illustrated in his case studies and clinical examples. That is, analysts can try to find some analytic interpretive way to assess the relevance and coherence of these responses by analysands and thereby convert them into evidence bearing importantly on interpretations that have already been made.

For example, a male analysand promptly forgot an interpretation that explained why certain repressions of previous analytic interpretations had been occurring. The interpretation was this: By his forgetting, he was acting out a fantasy of defectiveness. The analyst then transformed his forgetting this interpretation of his forgetting into further evidence in support of that very interpretation, and at that moment the analyst was transforming it into evidence in the crucial context of the transference. Subsequently, the analyst was able to construct the more developed interpretation that the analysand was enacting the fantasy of being castrated into defectiveness by the analyst's cutting interpretations.

An analyst with a different perspective might have transformed this forgetting of interpretation into something else. Kohut, for example, might have made it into evidence for two traumatizing effects: first, of the interpretation of repressive defense and the implication that the defectiveness was only a fantasy, contrary to the subjective experience of the analysand, and, second, of the implication that the analyst knows better than the analysand the truth of the analysand's self-experience. All these interpretations, being exceedingly unempathic, must have led to some further fragmentation of the analysand's fragile self and thereby to his inability to retain or retrieve the latest interpretation. Briefly, according to Kohut, the analyst's interpretation might be considered more of an assaultive rejection and devaluation than anything else, and the self of the analysand would be felt to be iatrogenically traumatized and fragmented.

Another example is that of the analysand who became very angry in response to an interpretation. The analyst used that response, along with other factors, as evidence that the interpretation's correctness was threatening to the patient and that this threat was being warded off by anger. In this instance, however, the anger could have been interpreted differently, even if still in keeping with the general Freudian perspective. It could have been argued that the anger showed the interpretation to be premature or that one of the effects of the previous interpretation had been to lift the repression of anger itself. And the angry response could have been interpreted in still other ways according to other analytic perspectives (for example, the interpretation was superficial or unempathic, therefore frightening or disappointing, and therefore angering in either case).

My examples are intended to suggest the extent to which evidence is created by analysis. Contrary to the empiricist-analyst's view, I believe that evidence is not served up on a platter, nor does it reach out to grab one by the throat. Although it is easy to note back-talk, it is difficult to prove unassailably or reach a firm consensus on just what it is that is being said. Psychoanalytic claims about what is being said and why (insofar as these are distinguishable) are essentially contestable.

Lest it seem that I am presenting the analyst as completely closed-minded once he or she has made an interpretation, I must point out that interpretations are often and appropriately offered conjecturally; the analyst delivers them in a way that implies that alternative, supplementary, or revised possibilities of interpretation are still open to consideration. The ideal analyst is well prepared to defer having arrived at the sense of any answer at all or at least to revise conjectures already tendered.

Let us return to more direct comparison of applied and clinical analysis to deal with another sense in which we can consider the statement that only in clinical analysis is there a patient who can talk back. In this other sense, the patient can talk back by showing change for the better, change for the worse, or no change at all, however each is defined in the specific case. For ease of exposition, I deal only with change for the better; this discussion should be readily applicable to change for the worse and no change at all without my spelling out those applications.

In connection with talking back by improving, it can be argued that, after all, analysis is a therapy; its goal is to help the analysand improve. In contrast, an artwork does not require therapy, and the goal of applied analysis is not so much to change the artwork for the better as to help its audience understand it and appreciate it better. Properly considered, the artwork does not talk back. But this argument is unhelpfully simplistic in that it does not do justice to the process and the results of both therapy and applied analytic projects, and it misconceives the relationship between an artwork and its audience.

I have already mentioned that there always has been and probably always will be room for controversy among analysts concerning the changes brought about by analytic therapy. Analysts would generally agree that among the forms of what they call resisting, there are flights into health, manic defenses, and transference cures, all of which may create false impressions of resolution of conflict and disappearance of symptoms in a lasting way. The analyst may therefore disagree with the analysand when the latter insists that things have improved greatly as a result of deeper understanding. The analysand's first-person testimony cannot be decisive in this respect.

Furthermore, analysts are likely to differ with one another in the way they apply such concepts as transference cure to a series of suggestive cases where more data are available than the analysands' explicit first-person testimony and the testimony of the treating analysts. And even when all analysts agree that there has been change for the better, they could not be expected to be unanimous about the degree of such change, nor would every one of them be likely to describe the change and explain it in precisely the same way, especially if they belong to different schools of analysis.

For example, conventional Freudians do not usually accept the benefits of self-psychological treatment as true psychoanalytic results, seeing them rather as the benefits of supportive psychotherapy or as transference cures. Self psychologists are quite ready to redescribe and reexplain the benefits of Freudian analysis in the terms of self psychology; they portray many of these benefits almost as accidental byproducts of good intentions hampered by poor technique based on poor understanding.

Furthermore, many of the changes in question are not measurable at all, for how can we measure subtle yet highly important improvements in the patient's quality of life, the patient's vision of reality, and his or her adaptation-enhancing integration of personal life-historical narratives? Upon reflection, therefore, it cannot be convincingly argued that talking back through recovery is a reliable and unambiguous feature of clinical analysis.

Turning now to the side of the artwork—say, a poem—we may question the flat assertion that applied analytic interpretation of a poem is not therapy. Following analytic interpretation of the poem (or for that matter following any other competent interpretation of it), the reader may better experience the poem's structural unity, richness of meaning, and potential impact, within the perspective provided. For this reason, we may legitimately say that the poem has become more alive and integrated, that it has been rendered available to enter into a more developed relationship with the reader, something more on the order of a mature, mutual, and modifiable relation of whole persons than one that features narcissistic aloofness and inaccessibility, schizoid weirdness, limitation to sexual organs, or something on that more disturbed and disturbing order. It would be arbitrary to insist that in consequence of interpretation only the reader has changed, for it can be argued that the poem changes with the reader as the reader becomes more expert. It is no longer the same poem. There is no determinate text of the poem. Markings on a page—the last resort of the anticonstructivist—are not the poem. The markings do not by themselves make a statement; they do not demand to be read or understood in only one way; they do not even sound.

On this basis, we may speak of interpretive recuperation or recovery of the poem. This idea is not new to literary criticism. Many of today's critics accept the proposition that a poem exists within the individualized relationship between it and the audience. Although their accounts differ in certain respects, they do agree that in necessarily interpreting in order to read at all, the reader becomes a co-author of the text. In making this argument, they have supplied the inspiration and background for my earlier argument that the analyst may be considered a co-author of the analysand's text. If, with the help of "applied" psychoanalytic understanding, along with other forms of understanding, the reader of the poem is better prepared to approach it as a particular kind of artwork than he or she might have been otherwise; if, in other words, the reader is an integrated and competent member of one or more definable interpretive and narrative communities and on this basis can draw on their conventions and observe their standards, then we might say that, in being psychoanalytically informed, the reader has been helped to bring about change for the better in both parties involved in the relationship. Among these features that are shared by psychoanalytic and other readings are the mixture of conventionalized and individual narrative and interpretive approaches and the therapeutic consequences of the work.

Furthermore, the artwork may be said to exert therapeutic influence on its critically prepared audience by introducing it to restorative perspectives on reality and restorative opportunities for subjective experience and understanding not previously available to it. Freud learned from Homer, Shakespeare, and Company, just as he made it possible for them to become more than they had ever seemed and for their audience to learn still more from them. Independent cases can be made for Freud's perspectival finding what was there to be discovered in literature, for his having re-created literature in his own image, and for a continuing interpenetration of and tension between both of these; and the same can be said for his contribution to the utterances of analysands.

There are those, however, who might still want to argue for an essential and hierarchical difference in favor of clinical work. They would point out that in clinical analysis talking back by changing for the better is a more important achievement. It is more important in that it concerns human welfare directly. Going further, they might also point out that in clinical analysis, but not in applied analysis, there is professional obligation to bring about this change.

Yet clinical analysts are not obliged to get good results, however those are defined. The clinical analyst fulfills his or her professional obligation by trying conscientiously to help bring about good results. Any feeling of obligation beyond that of making a good effort should generally be viewed as disturbed and disturbing countertransference involving some combination of guilt, overidentification with the patient, rescue fantasies, defensive grandiosity, and so on. And on their part, critical interpreters of an artwork have their own scholarly and technical obligations, too, even though the nature and extent of these are always being debated.

As to which kind of recovery is more important, that of a patient or that of an artwork, there is no way to adjudicate the issue except in terms of values or ideology that are not intrinsic to the psychoanalytic project. Clinical psychoanalysis does not prescribe the health values that it abides by once it begins by mutual consent; psychoanalysts do not properly exhort the general public to be in analysis. Moreover, we cannot hope to encounter universal agreements one way or another in this realm of judgments of importance.

Consequently, it is essential to reject the argument that the patient's talking back through recovery (or through personal disruption or stasis) distinguishes clinical analysis from applied analysis. At the least, it is warranted to reject that argument in its absolute, extreme, and unarticulated form. If we do not let ourselves be coerced by tradition into attending only to differences, if we focus on sameness as well as difference, we can see that clinical and applied analysis have in common co-creation and interpenetration of interpretable texts or of texts-as-interpretation. Clinical and applied analysis emerge as versions of one psychoanalysis, with no clear-cut parasitic relationship of one to the other. Both amount to the same work carried out under varied conditions. Clinical and applied analysts sink or swim together.

Although my conclusion is what earlier I recommended as a provisional assumption that could help us get on with the discussion, I maintain that I am not back where I started. Although I have not attained the sense of an answer, I have, I think, changed the sense of the questions that have arisen about applied analysis and stirred up some parallel questions about clinical analysis as well. But, of course, readers will not take my word for any of this, for they have been recreating this text from the time they started reading it. They will have been developing their own sense of an answer to my arguments and will perhaps have decided that it would have been better if I had formulated other questions and other answers.

CHAPTER 11

The Search for Common Ground

IN the contemporary psychoanalytic setting, where, as I showed in the preceding chapter, we are faced with considerable diversity of theory and practice, it can seem a most desirable goal to seek out some common ground on which all parties are standing and to maintain a sense thereby that all analysts, of whatever persuasion, are members of one basic discipline: psychoanalysis. But a search for common ground should be based on a shared and well-developed understanding of why it is a good thing to do, why it should be a rewarding thing to do, and how to go about it in a sound way. For, to begin with, a heterogeneous group of analysts would already have to be standing on some common ground before the idea of common ground could be discussed usefully. And in order to try to establish that preparatory common ground, the group would have to take up numerous issues of a linguistic, methodological, and ideological nature. Instead of any coming together, however, analysts continue to perpetuate a mixture of misunderstanding, ignoring, misrepresentation, and overeager rejection or accommodation, and instead of any systematic approach, they rely frequently on sheer assertion presented as argument and on much hasty and often severe supervisory critiques of the reported clinical work of respected colleagues.

The following remarks are intended to begin a systematic discussion of the issues. Although brief and incomplete, they do center on the thorny, if not impassable, way leading to useful discussion of the goal of common ground.

LINGUISTIC CONSIDERATIONS

In the clinical setting we must not be beguiled by manifest content. Upon searching the literature on the topic of common ground, we encounter another kind of ambiguous manifest content, namely, the words that make up technical and theoretical vocabularies. For example, consider the words *analyze transference*: These words must be taken as manifest content; both are treacherous words, treacherous because analysts of the same and different persuasions use them in association with too many different conceptions of childhood development; of psychopathology; of repetition and its basis, functions, and modes; of the uses of countertransference in defining transference; of the so-called real relationship with the analyst; of appropriate kinds and degrees of analytic activity; and so forth. This diversity of usage is all too evident in analytic writings, case conferences, and supervisory work. We must similarly regard as treacherous such other key words as *resistance* and *regression.* Consequently, to agree that analysts analyze transference, resistance, and regression amounts to little more than agreeing that they use the same words for whatever it is that they do do.

Words take on meanings through the practices in which they are used. Linguistic practices either presuppose contexts for words or try to establish these contexts as they go along. Thus, "transference" cannot be exactly the same word in the contexts of different clinical reports, for close inspection may show that in each case it has been placed in a different network of meanings. Instead of identity of meaning, there may be only family resemblances, if even that. We might have to stand very far back from individual propositions and practices to give mere family resemblances the appearance of identity and then lay claim to having searched out common ground.

For example, it could be regarded as certain that many clinical presentations manifest the analysis of transference in that they try to establish disturbing manifestations of past relationships in the present analytic relationship. And yet the conclusion that here there is common ground could be drawn only if we overlooked marked variations in clinical procedures and phenomena. Furthermore, after claiming common ground in the analysis of transference, what could we then go on to say? To what use could we put that claim? With so many specifics overlooked, the claim could not guide clinical work, nor would it be intellectually stimulating. Indeed, once familiar with details of the different schools of analytic thought, we could easily adopt the position of any one clinical case presenter and argue forcefully that when working from all other positions, we will be pursuing the analysis of transference in such a way as to make it less rather than more available to the patient's emotional experience and thus less available to relative resolution through insight. But where exactly would those critiques get us? Starting from any other position, we could arrive at another totalistic conclusion that repudiates the first.

It is, however, possible to point to some common ground. It is common ground not so much in the sense desired by those concerned with professional unity, but rather with respect to features that psychoanalysis shares with *all* investigative and interpretive disciplines. And it is to those features that I now turn.

METHODOLOGICAL CONSIDERATIONS

We can make more use now of the idea of manifest content. How do analysts transform manifest clinical content into useful analytic material? They do so by giving it a context or new context, thereby establishing and understanding it as something different from, or more than, it seemed at first. They derive that new context from what they have already defined and understood analytically about the patient's past and current life and the treatment relationship. Ideally, they get to understand both of these as presenting different versions of the same problems, for then the analytic versions of past and present problems in life and in analysis interpenetrate; having interpenetrated, these versions become virtually interchangeable in that fluid time/space of analytic accounts of unconscious mental functioning. In this aspect of the analytic method—the making, breaking, and remaking of contexts—there is *common ground* among the different schools of psychoanalysis. But, as modern literary studies show, to give only one interdisciplinary example, this ground, far from being peculiar to psychoanalysis, is a feature of all interpretive disciplines.

Also, an analyst's revisionary contextual work on clinical content is necessarily controlled by his or her theoretical orientation. Consequently, analytic understanding in the clinical setting can be the outcome only of a dialogue between analyst and analysand in which what the analyst comes prepared to look for both sorts out and shapes whatever is subsequently "found" or "presented." That understanding cannot be the report of a detached, uninfluential, and uninfluenced observer. The contexts provided for understanding in the dialogue convey the point of view of the analyst's theory. Through their engaging in what may be called spoken and unspoken dialogue, analytic interpreters do shape their observational data. *Common ground* again.

This interaction of observer and observed is widely recognized to be a feature of all investigative and interpretive disciplines.

Moving on to another set of methodological considerations, it must be emphasized that the analytic literature includes reports of analyses that are not closely comparable in detail, cultural setting, the nature of the clinical problems addressed, or the phase of analysis covered. Further, in these reports analysts seem to be working in rather different styles. For instance, they vary in how closely they stick to interpretations of the here-and-now transference and countertransference and how much regard they show for the analysand's defensive needs. These variations are evident within the analytic schools as well as between them, with the result that reports of clinical phenomena and interpretations cannot be compared with one another except in the most tentative or preliminary way.

Another methodological problem stems from the recognition that analysts write differently. It should be realized that, in reading case reports, analysts are not examining full analyses in anything like a direct fashion; rather, they are sampling written narratives of brief segments of analyses. Even when the published sample of process notes is quite detailed, much will have been left out or reduced in the interest of producing a followable, time-limited, thesis-specific, written narrative of an analytic process. Therefore, the reader would do well to resist developing the illusion that he or she can hope to draw definite and productive conclusions. That illusion would be comparable to the family myth, the myth about the family to which all family members subscribe in order to gain a conscious sense of interpersonal harmony and personal integration even though it will be to the detriment of their individual minds and hearts.

Much in the written report depends on whether, for both personal and professional reasons, the writer has aimed mainly to do a good job of representing his or her school of analysis as different from other schools or has chosen mainly to conform to the unifying aims of establishing common ground. In either case, the writer will have been writing with a systematic bias. Consequently, it is hard to assess precisely, fully, and with conviction the representativeness of every clinical report, however fine it may be as a clinical document.

I maintain that the contexts and aims of writing do so influence what gets to be written that single reports cannot serve as strong evidence for important conclusions. Here, too, in respect of limited representativeness of single case reports, divergent psychoanalytic approaches share *common ground* among themselves and with other disciplines.

Representativeness is a theme that helps us identify still more *common ground:* No school of theory and practice is so thoroughly thought through, integrated, monolithic, and binding on its members, none so static and controlling, that any one report issuing from it can be considered hard evidence of all of the school's principles and procedures. Moreover, each approach cannot avoid generating a set of potential limitations on its application and results, and each set of limitations will develop differently in specific clinical instances. As a consequence, there is continuing debate *within* schools over the representativeness of individual clinical reports. Unfortunately, the debates often turn away from the difficult methodological problem of representativeness and become judgments of the quality of this or that piece of work: "Inferior!" "Not real analysis!" or "Good job!"

IDEOLOGICAL CONSIDERATIONS

Ideologically, the search for common ground seems to me to imply a generally conservative value system in that it turns attention away from the creative and progressive aspects of the struggles between different systems of thought and practice. We may refer to conservatism with all due respect to the ostensible progressive intentions behind the search for common ground. Analysts know all too well that intentions and consequences are not the same thing.

My attribution of conservativeness is based on my belief that, in the realm of ideas and the practices in which they are realized, it is conflict that makes us both wiser and more creative. Sublimated aggression does have its wonderful uses: As well as being useful in defining the pros and cons of other approaches, it fosters adventurousness and constructive self-criticism, the kind of criticism that is required to do pioneering work and to recognize in one's own position those elements of incoherence, inconsistency, and incompleteness that stem from unexamined presuppositions and undefendable leaps of faith. The history of ideas shows that, sooner or later, in every system of ideas and practice, new frontiers will be defined and new problems internal to established positions will get to be identified and fought over. *Common ground.*

Ideologically, by valorizing the search for specifically psychoanalytic common ground, we are implying that differences are regrettable and should be leveled. Knowingly or not, we are then aiming for a single master text for psychoanalysis and an end to its history, and what could be more conservative than that? It is a high price to pay for the sense of professional unity. The progressive way—and obviously this is my contestable ideological preference—is to give up on the idea of a single master text and instead to celebrate and study differences and to continue to grow, as the field of psychoanalysis has grown, through unsettledness. Analysts should work with the sense that *their differences reveal all the things that psychoanalysis can be even though it cannot be all things at one time or for any one person.* The alternative is the blindness of conformism.

This progressive value is often deplored as one that leads to the chaotic relativistic situation in which anything goes, both technically and interpretively. But against this argument I would point out that, just like the members of other humanistic disciplines, analysts have been living with diversity for a long time, and it is abundantly clear that every major school of thought, every approach, every set of value-laden practices, has its own traditions, standards, and means of maintaining relative order as it matures. Also, whatever its problems, each psychoanalytic school of thought and practice has had things of value to teach about understanding and helping patients analytically.

PART FOUR

VERSIONS OF PRACTICE

CHAPTER 12

Another Defense: "First, the Bad News"

CLINICAL analysts often encounter a mode of behavior that may be designated "*first,* the bad news" and included among the narratives of defense. That narrative of defensive operations is the *clinical* subject of this chapter. After describing its typical forms of appearance during the analytic process, I present, first, an extended case example and then an account of the defense's manifestations during the termination phase of analysis. The theoretical implications of this material are reserved for a concluding section of this chapter.

The phenomena that may be redefined and organized by this narrative are certainly familiar to any experienced therapist. Many of these phenomena have already been taken up in the analytic literature, frequently under such therapeutically useful headings as negative therapeutic reaction (for example, Freud, 1923a, and Loewald, 1972), masochistic character (for example, W. Reich, 1933), and seduction of the aggressor (for example, Loewenstein, 1957). Under these headings we find references to the variety of efforts that analysands make, primarily unconsciously, to work up some anger, dispel some good feeling, produce a major or minor crisis, or even plunge themselves "mysteriously" into some depression or anxiety while they are on their way to the analytic session, in the waiting room, entering the office, or getting on the couch. Not only do they then present themselves as "bad news," they report and dwell on bad news at great length: their failures, disappointments, exacerbations of symptoms, and so forth. In each case this behavior is likely to be stereotyped and repetitive. The analyst learns, if only by fits and starts, not to get drawn into these self-presentations and these discouraging details as such; for often, and especially as progress is made in the analysis, it becomes apparent during each session that the news of the day as well as the emotional state of the newscaster are just not that "bad." The repetitively gloomy beginning soon seems to be serving the function of throwing a pall over the analyst and thereby blinding him or her to what may be called, in contrast, "the good news." In this one of its aspects, "first, the bad news" seems to be a defensive manipulation of the countertransference.

To the nonjudgmental analyst, of course, it is not a matter of badness at all, except perhaps in those first flickers of countertransference that indicate the action of the defensive manipulation. With reference to the analysand's psychic reality, however, it may be described as a case of "first, the bad news."

Case Example

My example is taken from the analysis of a young married woman of British origin. I have just returned from a week's vacation. During my absence, she began a new job. She also took an examination to qualify for advanced specialty training. Prior to the week-long break, much analytic time had been spent attempting to understand the intensely anxious way in which she was anticipating these two events. Connections with the transference, including those pertaining to the week's interruption, had been pointed out whenever possible. In the first session after my return she does not refer to my absence, and she alludes only vaguely and in passing to some uneasiness about having enjoyed the past week. She refers neither to her experience in her new job nor to how she had performed on the qualifying examination.

Saying that the details of various events are "nagging" at her, she goes on to dwell on the ups and downs, mainly the downs, of her personal relationships. In the midst of this account of her week, she lets drop again a hint that she had had some "great" times, but she then goes on to accentuate further only the negative, and she does so with considerable and mounting bitterness. She recounts in great detail how she attacked her husband for devaluing her as a marital partner and a woman; however, despite much circumstantial detail, she presents no specific or persuasive evidence in support of her charges against him. She succeeds in coming across as demanding, intolerant, and "nagging," particularly in relation to her husband. Although she throws in the remark that, on the basis of our previous work, she knows that she is criticizing him for "faults" that are hers, she does not slow the accelerating attacks on him.

On my part, I begin to respond silently with some countertransference, starting to wonder glumly whether the analysis of her presenting problem of depressiveness and inhibitedness will only eventuate in her becoming remorselessly vindictive. At this point, however, I realize that she is, so to speak, once again beginning to cast a spell over me. Under this spell, with which I am familiar in this analysis, I can no longer listen empathically or remember adequately; instead, I am moved to say something critical and thereby enter into a complex sadomasochistic interaction with her. By "something critical" I refer not to criticizing her in the conventional sense but to pointing out some problematic aspects of her account that I could know in advance she would take only as criticism.

Realizing all this, I begin to remember better. I recall once again that this mode of self-presentation has always been typical of the way she begins her sessions and that it used to be typical of her sessions from beginning to end. I also remember that it has deep roots in preferred patterns of interaction within her family. I recall, too, that recently she has been attempting to shift within her sessions from this "nagging" initial self-presentation to collaborative thoughtfulness. Often, though not always, when making these shifts she has used my comments late in the sessions reflectively rather than continuing her earlier pattern of treating even what I regarded as my most neutral or empathic comments simply as abuse or misunderstanding. In short order and with some chagrin I realize that in this session I have been observing an expectable regressive response to my week-long absence.

After much airing of her grievances, she reports a dream. In the dream she is chasing her husband with a cricket bat but ends up embracing him in an enfolding manner. To the bat she associates vampire and thinks of the subsequent enfolding as being demanding and possessive to the point of being devouring. To her husband's fleeing from her she associates to her sense that he has been trying to avoid a fight and that her attacks on him have been pressured, as if she has been clinging to them, as if she has been trying to drive him away. At this late point in the session, apparently continuing the reversal of her regressive "welcome," a reversal that was signaled by her dropping hints of good times and by her bringing up the dream and being prepared to give some associations to it, she changes her tone to her new-found thoughtfulness, and she asks me what I make of all the material of the session. Up to this point, I have been silent.

I decide to answer by taking up two factors: her defensive avoidance of manifest links to the transference and her unconsciously active, stereotyped attempt to seduce me into a sadomasochistic countertransference response. I say to her that she feels distant to me today, as in her making no mention of my absence and no mention of the new job and the examination on which we had spent so much time before I left. Not only distant from me, however, but acting as if she has been trying to get me to feel distant from her and dissatisfied with her as someone who is making no progress, as simply a "nag" who will not even tell me about her great times during my absence. She then acknowledges that she had come to this session wanting to tell me "the good news" but had felt embarrassed and didn't know why. She adds that during the past week she had been for the most part unusually generous toward her husband, and playful, too, bringing him a bunch of presents, some of them "silly." She had been pleased by this change in her behavior. She says she feels embarrassed to tell me this. With even greater embarrassment, she then confesses that for a change she had even felt hopeful about herself and had thought that she might be "well" before long. The session ends with her expressing concern that she had wanted to exclude the good news and establish hostile distance between us.

It seemed to me then that a collaborative atmosphere had begun to be reestablished; however, taking into account that this change had occurred only in the safety of the end of the session, and that it had been accompanied by much embarrassment and some guilt, I could only view it as a beginning. On her part, she had by no means given up her defensive use of "first, the bad news," and on my part, I had by no means made all the interpretations that were possible. For the time being I had limited myself to what, on the basis of previous experience with her, I thought that she could hear and use productively in this conflictual context.

Looking now at this session from the standpoint of the traditional taxonomy of defense, it is evident that in addition to repression and avoidance, she had made much use of projective identification, displacement (from the transference), and reversal of passivity to activity in the form of identification with the aggressor. And taking into account the induced, manifestly negative, incipient countertransference, it may be added that, more subtly, she had made a powerful attempt to reverse active sadism to passive masochism through seduction of the aggressor. What had helped me to advance the analytic work with this analysand from its earlier manifest phase of "bad news only" was my continually clarifying to myself how heavily she had been relying on this combination of defensive strategies for most of her life. It had helped me to sort out, reorganize, and then interpret what otherwise would have remained forbidding and impenetrably confusing manifest content. For the most part, however, it had not been useful to point out her defensive strategies as such; interventions of that sort usually served only to intensify manifestly negative transference responses.

What then could be taken up with her? Here, as I do not plan to embark on the history of the analysis, I merely summarize the major lines of interpretation that had proved useful up to this point in the work. Implied in her nagging, provocative orientation was her unconsciously fantasizing a masculine-phallic identity for herself. Not only did this identity alleviate her sense of humiliation, it played a central part in her complex preoedipal and oedipal relationships with both parents.

Unconsciously she had been struggling against identification with her mother. She portrayed her mother as unmotherly, repelled by instinctual expression on every psychosexual level, moralistic, snobbish, pretentious but unproductive, virtually anhedonic and unresponsive to exuberance, a stereotype of British propriety and snootiness as befit her socially insecure, upwardly mobile, provincial background in a blatantly class-conscious society. This struggle against identification contained the analysand's own strong aspirations to become a loving and sensual woman and to avoid her mother's allegedly barren existence. Unconsciously she experienced the forbidding imago of her mother as a major obstruction to realizing these aspirations, and she expressed her submission to this imago in her hating herself for maintaining these aspirations and in her hating me for pointing out anything that increased her awareness of them.

But, as would be expected, she had also assigned a central role to her unconsciously maintained father imago. She experienced her father as being exceedingly uncomfortable with her whenever the positive and mutual oedipal temperature in their contacts began to rise. At those moments, and often to forestall them, he would become withdrawn, irritable, hypercritical, and taunting in an anal-sadistic manner. Thus, for her, to be demonstrative, loving, and sensual only drove him away; more exactly, it incited him to engage her in sadomasochistic intimacies instead. Over the course of her development she had largely accepted his regressive terms; she had herself become an active initiator of sadomasochistic interaction with him. Quarreling was the currency of the realm. There lay her positive oedipal desires, and in her analysis she repeated these seductions endlessly in her paternal transference, just as she repeated her struggle with her mother in her maternal transference.

In this perspective, it could be understood that while in one respect her defensive strategy of "first, the bad news" was designed to drive me away, in another respect it was intended to engage me in a regressively debased positive oedipal interaction. Additionally, her defensive strategy repudiated her maternal identification and compensated her for her sense of humiliation; at the same time it played out that aspect of her maternal identification that promised to reproduce her mother's unhappy marriage in her own marriage as well as in her transference. She had to make the analysis and her marriage as joyless as the home in which she grew up.

Consequently, in the session I reviewed, she could not eagerly or demonstratively tell me about her great times. She anticipated that if she did tell me, she would lose me as the positive and accepting oedipal-level father I was just beginning to become for her; she would also lose me as a good mother, an alternative to the mother she had experienced, a figure I was just beginning to become for her as well. I would be pushed into contempt for her if she reported the generous, silly, fun times with her husband and if she manifestly welcomed me back with enthusiasm. She was protecting her newfound joy in her marriage and in her analysis. Her way of welcoming me back was to bat me around. And batting me around also expressed her intense oral deprivation, her wanting to suck life from me, which also meant incorporating my penis, thereby reinforcing her guilty view of herself as a devouring person.

Clearly then, in this case, "first, the bad news" was as much a matter of wish fulfillment and punishment, as much a matter of object-relatedness and adaptation as it was a matter of defense. In short, it had to be understood as a compromise formation, and bit by bit it was possible to interpret it to her in all its complexity as just that. But in order to get to this point, and in order to work this compromise through methodically, it was necessary to rely in my own thinking on the taxonomy of defensive strategies and transformations. It was also necessary to approach this compromise first as a defensive measure: This taxonomy and this emphasis on defense helped the two of us, as long ago it helped Anna Freud (1976) and her analysands, to become expert witnesses of the reenactment of a family drama that was being repetitively played out in the analytic relationship; it seemed to help lay down the storyline that could, finally, make a therapeutic difference in a potentially blocked analysis.

AT TERMINATION

A special version of "first, the bad news" is commonly encountered during the termination phase of analysis. In that phase we often see regressive shifts that seem to erase previous successful analytic work: Symptoms flare up, crises develop in good relationships, self-destructive behavior increases, and the transference in general assumes some of its most negative forms. All of which, to be sure, indicates difficulties with the pending separation and the need for working through issues of separation and loss. Here we shall be concerned with the way in which "first, the bad news" enters this picture.

Often the resurgence of regressive material appears at the beginning of the analytic sessions. In such cases, if the analyst either simply waits out these gloom-making reports and behaviors or with the help of a few judicious analytic interventions raises some questions about them, the analysands begin to tell and show that, in fact, they are themselves capable of significant resilience. They have, for example, already self-analyzed the regressive shifts, or they have limited the damage and taken steps to repair it; they show that they are not actually helpless, castrated, symbolically suicidal, or what have you. The session-opening gloominess is in part an attempt to seduce the analyst into a guilty and reparative countertransference; if not that, then it may be a seduction into a countertransference in which the analyst is to feel abandoned in response to the analysand's reversal of felt passivity to active withdrawal.

In some ways, this resort to "first, the bad news" resembles the adolescent's resorting to externalization of one part of a conflict over emancipation by provoking conflict with parents, in this way showing them to be unworthy of continued love and desire. In the case of the adolescent, this defensive shift probably involves an attempt to expel the incorporated parent, as if to show that all that has existed previously was a purely external relationship. The case may be much the same with respect to the analyst at termination.

In general, the regressive move is most usefully approached as a defensive measure. To a great extent, the improved patient cannot sustain that move and either gives away the game in upbeat dreams and parapraxes or gives signs of being in a good mood that contradicts much of the negative content. Sometimes the analysand just switches gears during the session. For example, in one case a dream was apparently reported in full as follows: *He was preparing to buy a $75,000 house that was quite broken down.* The analysand's associations led to the total cost of the analysis, which in fact was more than $75,000; 75,000 was also three-quarters, and that suggested that his life was three-quarters over, even though he was only in his thirties, a calculation related to his depressed parents' emphasis on their physical decline after the age of forty; three-quarters also stood for an incomplete analysis, and that implied disappointment in the analytic results. Only after this part of the work did the analysand go on to continue the dream report as follows: *He had rejected that house and he took one that was handsome, with lots of glass so that he could look outside and not be trapped in a wreck.* It was apparent then that the analysand had been setting up the analyst to fall into a gloomy mood.

In a sense, the patient in this example was showing rather than telling "bad news." Other ways of showing rather than telling include falling back on characterological rigidities that have been extensively analyzed and significantly modified prior to the agreement to move toward a termination date; also, increasing lateness or more frequent absences, the adoption of a "cured" bonhomie, and so forth. One analysand reverted to long, circumstantial, emotionally arid reports of daily events; fairly regularly, however, this analysand spontaneously began, within each session, to question this repetition and to understand it as a way of warding off the emotional experience both of mourning the analysis and of celebrating its achievements. As before, this analysand was trying to dull me and subdue any excitement or grief I might be feeling in order to keep us both in a state of being remote from one another, tightly controlled and protected; in this there was much repetition of anal-obsessive and oedipal prototypes.

Another analysand with massive guilt problems in relation to a fragile and overattached father found it necessary to resort to her characterological form of "first, the bad news" in order to reassure me that she was not about to abandon me and leave me stranded and depressed. She began being once again her "old self," that is, a good girl displaying her suffering and emphasizing how much she needed external supplies; it was she, however, who soon brought out this concern for me and who recognized it as a familiar defensive transference.

In another case, a female analysand resumed procrastinating in concluding certain significant and positive life changes, and she returned to secret forms of masturbation that we had analyzed as enactments of androgyny, specifically of having a phallic vagina that had no room for, or need of, a man's penis. Thereby she was denying both the value to her of her male analyst and, in her psychic reality, his potent analytic phallus and also her readiness to move on to a fulfilling relationship with a man of her own. In this instance, "first, the bad news" was a castration of the analyst and a return characterologically to the androgynous and ineffective boy-girl role she had played in relation to her father. All of which stood in marked contrast to many other experiences and activities of a more mature sort that she soon mentioned with an independently arrived at sense of self-contradiction and rapid insight into her responding defensively to our terminating.

On the whole, however, I would say that the most pervasive manifestation of "first, the bad news" is the one that accompanies felt progress *throughout the analysis.* In these instances, it is always a question of what is gained by apparently just submitting to the fear of getting well. What danger situation is being avoided by that submission? I have discussed this phenomenon in other connections as an attack on the analyst's empathy (1983), a fear of success or idealization of unhappiness (chapter 6), and in other ways as well, each of which will be found to have a complex inner structure, but each of which may yield to analysis only when recognized as a form of defense. As with my extended clinical example earlier in this chapter, there are different ways to tell this story of defense and so there are different stories to tell, each of which has its truth-value and therapeutic value. The choice among them, although never absolutely certain, is often guided by more or less subtle cues in the patient's associations.

THEORETICAL DISCUSSION

I have been discussing "first, the bad news" as a defensive operation, measure, or strategy. By using these terms I have attempted to illustrate several interrelated theoretical points. First, I have been highlighting psychoanalysis as a narrative enterprise, as Anna Freud (1936) did, though only implicitly, when she discussed identification with the aggressor and altruistic surrender as defenses, and as others have (for example, Bibring and her co-workers, 1961). Specifically, I have been presenting under the aspect of defense a number of complex configurations that include wish fulfillment, self-punishment, and adaptive efforts. Presenting these configurations under the aspect of defense clearly is an example of choice of narrative. Each defensive story of this complex type can be told differently: for example, as a compromise formation, as an illustration of multiple function, as an enactment of transference-countertransference fantasies that are briefly actualized through the patient's resort to considerable projective identification, or as the partially regressed expression of an intense bisexual oedipal transference.

Second, unlike Anna Freud's narrative, however, mine does not revolve around the assumption that there are "mechanisms of defense" that, in response to "anxiety signals," influence the workings of the "mental apparatus." Making that assumption and using those terms exemplifies adherence to Sigmund Freud's metapsychology, his mechanistic language for theorizing about mind and method, particularly as developed to its high point in "Inhibitions, Symptoms and Anxiety" (1926).

Elsewhere in this book (see chapters 9 and 10) I have characterized the metapsychologically developed theory of Freudian psychoanalysis as a master narrative with its distinctive storylines and rhetoric. My storyline of defensive operations is based on my previous work on action language and narration. On that basis I present the interpretable events of the analysis as actions of the analysand and the analyst, and I take up defense in the same way that I take up transference, countertransference, and repetition—as things people *do,* as the performances of agents.

Thus, the somewhat fanciful title of this chapter and its clinical focus should not be taken as a neglect of theory. In the context of psychoanalysis as a narrational project with both theoretical and clinical aspects, I present this chapter as an example of theory *in* clinical work. In this narrational context, no further theorizing is called for. A further step into a metatheory of some sort implies wrongly that clinical accounts are unprocessed "data," prescientific aggregates of observations, still to be refined into truth. That hierarchization seemed necessary to the Freud who remained faithful to his nineteenth-century scientific training and aspirations; it should no longer seem necessary to us one hundred years later.

CHAPTER 13

Psychic Reality, Developmental Influences, and Unconscious Communication

THE distinguishing feature of clinical analytic interpretation is its emphasis on psychic reality. That is, interpretation centers on the personal meanings that analysands ascribe, especially unconsciously, to events and actions in the past and present. Typically, these unconsciously ascribed meanings are organized in repetitive fashion around infantile conflicts, fantasies, and modes of thought and feeling. But interpretation deals not only with psychic reality. It is more exact to say that it involves a complex, subtle, and shifting distribution of emphasis on psychic reality, developmental influences, and unconsciously communicated messages. In this chapter I attempt to clarify some of the issues that arise in connection with this shifting distribution of emphasis.

To make the issue concrete, I focus specifically on how analysts take their analysands' representations of other people and how they deal with these representations in their interventions. By "other people" I refer to people other than the analyst and analysand, those whom the analyst encounters only through what the analysand says concerning them. I do not, however, neglect to consider how representations of other people are related to the analysand's self-representations and representations of the analyst. Representations of other people provide a good test case for the analyst's understanding and uses of psychic reality in relation to developmental influences and unconsciously communicated messages.

While what I lay out may seem to some readers obvious or customary, even elementary, I am not aware that the topic has already been dealt with in quite the way I deal with it. Much of my discussion is devoted to clinical instances and technical practices. I lead off with the analyst's primary focus on psychic reality alone; later on I amend that somewhat puristic account.

VIEWING REPRESENTATIONS OF OTHERS AS PSYCHIC REALITY

Usually (though some analysts would argue that it should always be so and others that it should be so only on occasion), analysts do not take analysands' representations of other people for granted. They do not hear them as reliable, valid, complete, factual statements. Instead, they take each statement about other people as a communication that bears on each analysand's psychic reality. This communication may be taken to be a narrative account of the analysand's subjective experience of these others. If so, it may be examined for what it tells about the analysand's unconsciously conflicted self—one or another of them (see chapter 2). Analysts may also take this communication as a displaced reference to an analysand's experience of the analyst, that is, as an unconsciously disguised manifestation of transference. In still another way it may be taken as a form of remembering the infantile past through selectively emphasized current experience. Or, finally, it may be taken as a projected reference, as in a dream, to some aspect of the analysand's unconsciously repudiated self-experience. Analysts may take representations of other people in any combination of these ways.

Consider, for example, the content of such commonplace statements as "My father is old." Apparently, this is a simple statement of fact. But instead of taking it as simple fact, analysts approach each such communication as a possible reference to unconsciously conflictual subjective experience and as possible displacement, life-historical background, or projection. In order to take it in any of these ways, analysts must first assume the following to be true. The allegedly factual world provides a plenitude of facts to speak of, and there is nothing inevitable about what the analysand selects from this plenitude and the narrative versions of these facts that he or she constructs. That is, the selective principles are not totally self-evident and beyond interpretation; rather they are interpretable expressions of the analysand's current conflictual position in the analysis. They say something about both the content and the mode of construction of the analysand's psychic reality in the here and now. They are facts without life or significance until they have been redescribed and given a context in the analysis. They have to be transformed into psychoanalytic facts.

Taking the representations of other people in this way, analysts promote a number of technically desirable consequences. These include, first, keeping open the possibility that over the course of analysis these representations will be revised and further revised through subsequent reversals of content or attitude and through filling in and the introduction of greater complexity. Greater complexity opens the door to interpreting the multiple functions served by representations of other people. Thus, the "old father" may get to be represented later as youthful, perhaps as competitively so, and unconsciously as murderously so. And from this later vantage point, the earlier "fact" stated simply as "My father is old" may be viewed as a defensive denial or reversal.

As a second desirable consequence of not taking any representation of others for granted, analysts avoid adopting an authoritarian or even authoritative position that they are experts on people and situations outside the analytic situation. Being cautious in this way, analysts are less likely to become dupes of an analysand's unconscious and defensive strategies or countertransference manipulations and are thus less likely to enact a role in the patient's fantasies, such as that of the omniscient conscience.

As a third advantage, analysts maintain neutrality by not taking sides in the analysand's conflictual situations. Were analysts to take any representations of other people as adequate or final, they would interfere with achieving a balanced appraisal of psychic reality. In accord with the principle of multiple function, a balanced appraisal features empathic appreciation of the analysand's needing unconsciously to work out complex compromise formations. In the long run, analysts' open-minded stance with regard to representations of other people testifies to their neutrality and interpretive competence even though, in the short run, the analysands may use it to attack analysts as unempathic and offputting, if not suspicious, or as taking sides with "the opposition."

How do analysts achieve these and other desirable effects on the analysis? One way is by indicating in those interventions touching on representations of other people that their comments are directed not at these others as such, but at the analysand's experience or version of them. They indicate that this experience or version is open to examination as a statement about the analysand's psychic reality. For instance, analysts say, "As you see her," "What you particularly want to emphasize about him," "The thing that stands out for me in your account of your father," and so on. Sometimes going further, analysts say, "You seem to be trying hard to limit me to seeing your mother as having no redeeming features, and I wonder why you need to do that," or "You have been bringing up many details that suggest you see your father as corrupt, even though you continue to insist that he is trustworthy, but for some reason you still do not acknowledge that other view of him," and so on. Analysts might go still further in some instances, saying, for example, "You describe her as if she is an erect penis," or "You make him sound like a fart."

In none of these instances do analysts simply speak out on what the facts are concerning these other people. If the analysand is threatened, hurt, or offended by this restraint, it indicates to the analysts that some defensiveness or transference problem needs to be taken up. Analysts may do this by pointing out the insecurity implied in the analysand's upset, and by going on to question the urgency with which the analysand is trying to get them to accept some version of another person in a way that is absolutely closed to exploration, interpretation, and revision.

Early in analysis, however, or during periods of crisis, it may seem to analysts that the best way to advance the analysis is to refer to other people without qualification—to speak, for example, just as the analysand has been doing, say of the father as being simply "withdrawn." As long as analysts do not get hooked on that unqualified representation, there will be opportunity later to introduce qualifications, saying, for example, "You felt he was punishing you by withdrawing," or "You felt you had driven him away." Usually this sequential accommodation is unnecessary, for ordinarily it is possible to be both tactful *and* noncommittal from the start. This can be accomplished by tone of voice alone, though it is risky to rely on implied messages; or by such prefatory remarks as "From what you say" and "If that is the case" may be used in passing. Or analysts may refer from the beginning to the father's "withdrawn aspect," to the impact of the father's "apparent withdrawal," or to the times when the father could only be "experienced as withdrawn." In general, it is better for the subsequent elucidation of the analysand's psychic reality if analysts do not use these early or crisis-based representations without some sort of qualification.

WORKING OUTSIDE OF PSYCHIC REALITY

But—and this is a big but, for here I begin to amend my puristic description—analysts do not always work within the confines of psychic reality. We see this in the reports of their work. We see it in statements, for example, that the father *was* withdrawn or sadistic, the mother *was* narcissistic or psychotic, the spouse *is* masochistic or depressive, and so on. And we see it in published interpretations of analytic material that are based on analysts' having taken certain representations of other people as certain, true, objective, factual. It would not be going too far to assume that these analysts have made comparable statements in the analytic dialogue itself; often, analysts explicitly report that this was so. Our next problem then is to fit this evidence into our schema of neutral, judicious, consistent analytic attention to psychic reality.

As a first step in dealing with this problem, we can acknowledge that, taking the analysis as a whole, analysts need not fastidiously qualify every remark touching on other people. There are three conditions under which unqualified interventions may be made with sufficient analytic security. The first is when the analysand is well into the analysis and has repeatedly and spontaneously demonstrated a reliable enough recognition that the focus of the work is on psychic reality. This means that pluralistic accounts of other people are the order of the day—and of the night, too—regardless of how "factually" things may be formulated moment by moment. The second condition is when the functions served by certain representations of other people in the analysand's defensive operations and transference have been repeatedly and productively analyzed. Analysts have gained confidence in these analysands' collaborative sense that it is important to grasp psychic reality. And analysts have gained confidence in their own grasp of these analysands' psychic reality as well. On this basis analysts do not need to be as analytically circumspect every moment; in particular, analysts are not as likely to be so concerned at that time with the hazards of countertransference, and so, appropriately, will feel free to make shorthand references to the characteristics of other people.

The third condition is when it seems that further entry into psychic reality requires the analyst to adopt a less detached or reflective manner, as with some schizoid patients at certain times. Then, analysts may refrain from introducing qualifying remarks and instead enter into a partial facilitating regression with the analysand to dreamlike acceptance of his or her narrative portrayal of other people. During these regressive excursions, analysts must remain alert to their own inclinations to become too insistent, enthusiastic, or vehement when referring to other people, for these inclinations may lead to disruptive expressions of countertransference, and they may stimulate destructive acting out. For example, simply to say "Your husband is taking advantage of you" or "Your partner in business is out to get you" might well stimulate destructive acting out.

Even when all these conditions have been met, however, analysts take a giant step away from psychic reality whenever they draw conclusions as to what these other people are really like or what they really did or are doing now. In taking this giant step analysts shift from a consistently genetic approach to a developmental-environmental-functional approach. The modern foundation for systematically understanding this shift was laid by Kris (1956b). The genetic approach focuses on the analysand's phase-specific, psychosexual fantastic constructions of reality, such as those Freud described in "Three Essays on the Theory of Sexuality" (1905b), "On the Sexual Theories of Children" (1908b), and many other papers.

In the genetic approach, analysts listen to representations of other people as to the manifest content of a dream. This way of listening is what I described earlier in my "puristic" account. In contrast, the *developmental-environmental-functional approach* (referred to as *developmental* for the sake of brevity) takes for granted certain biographical data concerning the analysand's early or current environment, the people in it, and the events that took place in it or are now taking place in it. Also taken for granted are events in the analysand's own bodily environment of a maturational or accidental nature. In this approach analysts listen to representations of other people as to a case history rather than as to a dream. Additionally, they listen in the role of diagnostician of cognitive functioning—its level, organization, and deformation.

The analysts' shift in mode of listening from the genetic to the developmental might not be readily apparent. For example, it might not seem to have occurred when an analyst continues to emphasize the primary importance of ascertaining what the analysand has made of these "actual" people and events. But this appearance is deceptive, for the analyst's viewpoint is that he or she knows what really happened or is now happening elsewhere in the analysand's life and is attempting merely to understand its elaboration or distortion in memory or report. The parents *were* obstructive, the husband *is* being withholding or guilt-provoking, and so on. What is the justification for analysts taking this stand outside psychic reality?

Taking this stand is justified, first of all, by the analysts' diagnostic estimate of the general adequacy and integrity of the analysand's cognitive activity. When this estimate is relatively high, analysts are more likely to ascribe some truth-value to reports of past and present actions performed by other people. Truth-value can be ascribed even when it is obvious that the representations of other people are being narrated in a way that is not altogether reliable—that is, when they involve defenses and transferences, as indicated by gaps, inconsistencies, glaring displacements, and apparently inexplicable emotionality. Nevertheless, analysts might still extract from these narratives that, for example, a boyfriend abandoned the analysand in a certain way or a girlfriend said she resented the analysand in a certain tone, and even that this action or tone was characteristic of this other person.

Analysts require some ground to stand on in order to make analytic sense of what is being reported in the analysand's associations; they cannot suspend judgment about everything. In this connection, analysts establish this ground by stepping outside psychic reality and making diagnostic judgments of cognitive functioning. In making these judgments analysts rely on versions of common human situations and cause-effect relations that are so highly conventionalized that they serve as standards of good reality testing, sound judgment, and adaptive functioning. Although there is always room for disagreement over these standards, for analytic purposes they are taken as generally applicable. At the same time, however, as I said, analysts are prepared for subsequent narrative revisions of what, for working purposes, it seemed safe or useful to accept as factual at an earlier or stormier time in the analysis.

A second justification of analysts' taking a stand outside psychic reality on the factuality of certain representations of others is their judgment that these representations meet the criteria of narrative good fit. Analysts use these criteria in piecing into analytically meaningful patterns various accounts of another person's actions. It would be a worthwhile task to attempt to spell out fully these criteria of good fit and their basis, but here I can mention only a few things.

As to their basis, criteria of good fit derive partly from conventional common sense or an analytically refined version of common sense, for analysts' idea of what hangs together in a story is founded on more than psychoanalytic understanding; it rests as well on conventions of coherence that are shared by analysts and analysands as members of a community of understanding. In addition, these criteria are based partly on analysts' empathic responses that have not yet been clearly conceptualized in the analysis. And they are partly dependent on the same kind of interpretive analytic synthesizing analysts use in making coherent sense of everything that is being produced by analysands in the analytic situation. In this last regard we must also bear in mind that even the coherence of an analysand's narratives of self-experience (for example, as "worthless") are not routinely taken for granted; they, too, require revision and synthesizing by analysts. For example, "I feel depressed" may refer more to anxiety than depression, particularly when an analysand fears to make an urgent request of an analyst.

One kind of good fit is based on a particular kind of correspondence or consistency. On the one hand, there are the analysand's versions of her or his actions in dealings with other people. On the other hand, there are accounts of the analysand's actions in the analytic situation itself that have already been jointly developed, provisionally accepted, and worked with. When these two sets of accounts correspond or are consistent with one another, a criterion of good fit has been satisfied—for example, a certain regularity of mistrustful reaction whenever the analysand encounters kindness.

Another kind of good fit is also based on correspondence or consistency. On the one hand, there is an analyst's conception of the analysand's problems and their developmental-environmental contexts. On the other hand, there are generally accepted analytic propositions about the way in which problems of this sort come into being or are strongly reinforced during development. For example, reports by the analysand of a father's sadism or passivity or a mother's narcissism or psychotic behavior are likely to be accepted as having truth-value when they conform both to developmental propositions concerning the effects of such parents on children and to the analyst's grasp of the analysand's problems. In accord with clinical theory, analysts accept certain developmental propositions as true and use them as tools to assess the extent to which reports of early "objective" reality correspond to or are consistent with the phenomena of the individual analytic interaction. For example, an analyst who is confident that the analysand is extremely schizoid will not accept glowing accounts of all early family relationships. These developmental propositions are not highly specific, but they do serve to set up some leading expectations. In relying on these propositions, however, analysts have temporarily stepped outside the psychic reality of the individual analysand in order to reenter it later with greater understanding.

In addition to estimates of cognitive functioning and of narrative good fit, there is a third warrant for analysts to draw conclusions about other people. This one, too, lies outside the psychic reality of an individual analysand. Analysts may be satisfied that an analysand is portraying others in a well-rounded way. This does not mean that analysts assume everyone in the world is equally well rounded in personality makeup; rather, they assume that there are analytically complex factors at work in everyone. Well-roundedness of representation is not always prominent early in analysis. In the beginning, other people are likely to be presented as simply good or bad in their natures and in their influence, or else they are presented as unpredictably totally good or bad. As a rule, only later on in analysis do representations of other people get to be well rounded. Then the representations convey some recognition on the part of the analysand that the actions of these others are complex, involving conflict, unconscious meaning, and compromise formations. We may say that, as a result of analytic work, others come to be portrayed as having their own interpretable life histories. This kind of narrative change may be tracked especially well in characterizations of parents.

Analysts do, of course, encounter some would-be superanalysands, those who deliver well-rounded representations of others from the start. These superanalysands will have to move from their judicious, well-balanced narratives of others to ones that are less defensively airtight and involve highly emotional simplifications before they can develop more wholly felt and convincing accounts of these other people. Whether any of these sequences occurs will depend on developments in the analysis of defense and transference.

Analyst can be sure of the truth-value of the now-complex representations of other people to the extent that equivalent and similar complexity characterizes an analysand's *representations within the analytic situation* of self and of the analyst. Again, therefore, correspondence and continuity play a major part in assessments of truth-value. And when this point is reached, analysts are able to shift freely and productively between comments on the analytic relationship and comments on the analysand's other relationships in the past and present.

The fourth warrant for the analyst's speaking of other people without qualification is the last I shall mention. As an analysis progresses, the analysand behaves differently in the analytic relationship. Some of the changes are based on worked-through insight. Concurrently, the analysand reports change or lack of change on the part of others in their reactions to the analysand's different mode of relating to *them* (see also chapter 1). Analysts are now in a better position to assign truth-value to these reports of variation or lack of variation in others' reactions. Analysts give evidential weight particularly to those reports that indicate a developing awareness of the ways in which the analysand is bringing about a *range* of variation in others: bringing out the best and the worst in them, their strengths and understanding, their symptoms and destructiveness. At this point, others are no longer being presented to analysts in a self-justifying way as completely static or unpredictable ahistorical entities. This principle of changed action and reaction holds even when others are reported in terms of personal extremes, such as unyielding passivity, depression, or mistrust. But as a rule it is impressive, as an analysis progresses, how many additional dimensions or features of other people do get to be brought out or made more definite by the analysand's analytically altered modes of interpersonal activity. And they need not all be benign features.

Analysts do not use all such changes in the representation of other people as a basis for saying "Now you see the world for what it is," for then they would be playing the arbitrary and condescending role of expert. Rather, analysts say or imply something like this: "These changes make certain things clearer about the way you needed to perceive and control others in order to fit them into this or that fantasy or to repeat this or that relationship from your childhood." Analysts may also use the changed narratives to raise fresh questions about the content and construction of the analysand's psychic reality. But still analysts are able to do so only after some temporary or oscillating departures from a position inside the analysand's psychic reality.

An important aspect of this shift from the genetic approach to the developmental, or from the psychic to the "actual," must be noted in order to develop further our understanding of the place of psychic reality in analytic work. The shift entails a second shift of emphasis from unconsciously constructed fantasy to *unconsciously carried on communication and reality testing.* Analysts do not doubt that such communication and its implied reality testing go on in every relationship. Taking these processes as fact or assigning truth-value to them is a necessary step in making the unintelligible intelligible through interpretation. We are able to say, for example, "You recognize how much your mother always wished you were a boy and not a girl." Freud recognized unconscious communication as one of the foundations of the analytic method as well as of the formation of the superego.

Consequently, in assessing representations of other people, analysts view the analysand as picking up messages being sent unconsciously by these others. In the present context, the messages that are picked up unconsciously deserve special attention. (Those that are picked up consciously or preconsciously may be important, but they present no special problem to interpreting analysts as they are more clearly presented as perceptions by the analysand.) For example, analysts may infer from certain representations of the mother that, unconsciously, the analysand has picked up the message that she wishes the analysand had never been born. Similarly, analysts may find it credible that the analysand has unconsciously picked up the message from father to mother that he would like to kill her or fears being castrated by her. Likewise, analysts may believe in the developmental "truth" of certain primal-scene representations; this may be the case when the representations seem to condense genetically based anal-sadistic constructions *and* unconsciously recognized, "actual" sadomasochistic pains and pleasures in the parents' relations with one another. And when an analysand's dream indicates unacknowledged recognition of an analyst's seductive or cruel countertransference, the understanding of the dream must include reference to what has been unconsciously communicated by the analyst and registered accurately, though unconsciously, by the analysand. We deal here not primarily with psychic reality, but with reality testing of "actual" communications.

Yet it does not follow from these points that, in this connection, analysts must shift the focus away from psychic reality more than temporarily. It remains essential that there be analysis of how and why the analysand elaborates further these results of unconsciously seeing, hearing, and understanding. In other words, analysts soon return to asking what the analysand makes of the analyst's seductiveness or cruelty, if these types of countertransference are in question. But even with all due regard for psychic reality, in the analysis analysts must step out of psychic reality somewhat in order to determine what that other person—in many instances the analyst him- or herself—is "actually" doing or feeling.

The word *actually* must always be put inside quotation marks, for there is always more than one analytically useful, realistic version of the observations in question. For instance, in the countertransference example I just mentioned, seductiveness and cruelty on an analyst's part are not necessarily mutually exclusive as realistic versions of any one countertransferential action. At one time the version to emphasize may be seduction; at another time, cruelty; while later on the analyst or analysand may include both accounts of the analyst's countertransference in a complex narrative. The complex narrative might emphasize the analyst's fear of the analysand's sadism and consequently his or her dealing with this fear through disarming efforts of an erotic or aggressive nature.

I am trying to bring out that analysts always employ a pluralistic view of what is real or actual (see also chapters 4, 5, and 6). The events in the analysis, like all other events, are available only in versions of them, and no one version states a significant fact in all its aspects. No one statement exhausts the so-called fact. Each version given by analyst and analysand is understood to serve certain functions in certain contexts, and thus gives rise to certain consequences rather than others. There is no nonnarrative set of facts for analysts to present with absolute authority. However, there are, as I mentioned earlier, some versions of events that are so highly conventionalized or consensually validated that analysts routinely use them as criteria of what is "real" or "actual." In principle, relying on convention in this way is not a mistake. Consequently, there are times when analysts rightly speak of what is "actual" or "factual" in connection with indications of unconsciously communicated messages and unconsciously performed reality testing. But, as I said, we should mean "actual" only in quotation marks, that is, within a commonsense or psychoanalytic convention of a binding sort.

With these perspectivist or pluralistic considerations in mind, we may return more judiciously to the immediate topic. It is important to pay the closest attention to what is unconsciously communicated and reality-tested outside the analysis and in the analysis itself. Regarding why the analysand engages in this communicative activity only unconsciously, analysts must assume that if an analysand has invested the cognitive functions being used with conflictual meaning of an erotic or aggressive nature, he or she regards that activity as dangerous. In other words, when the analysand has sexualized or aggressivized these functions, so that to use them in certain ways is to create a psychically real infantile danger situation, the analysand views that activity as fraught with danger. In psychic reality, reality testing may mean, for example, sexual peeping, seeing what is forbidden; and giving voice to the results of reality testing may be mentioning the unmentionable and so may mean rebellious and destructive attacks on parental authority or potency. Of course, the specific content may be the problem far more than the cognitive functions being used.

Also, by engaging in this activity and representing its results only unconsciously, analysands may be setting up analysts: Now analysts are the ones who are smart enough to see the "truth" and brave enough to state it explicitly, and so they continue to deserve being idealized by an analysand; or now analysts assume an analysand's guilt over reality testing by being the ones to state the "facts" and are to be blamed for that; or perhaps analysts will now be expressing some "truth" that corresponds to one side of an analysand's ambivalence, which the analysand can then vehemently refute as an "external" imposition. In these highly defensive contexts, it is always a question of who becomes the narrator as well as what the content of the narration will be. It should therefore be apparent that ignoring these unconsciously designed defensive maneuvers may seriously impede the analysis. Ignoring them may, for example, greatly limit analysis of self-castration and guilt in the transference.

In this connection, we should recall what Kris (1956a) emphasized when he discussed the theory of interpretation and insight. Kris emphasized in a most important way the analysand's preconscious preparation of material and the implicit demand for interpretation that is thereby established. What he did not emphasize, however, was that the implicitness of this preparation and of this demand might itself have to be interpreted as a sign of a defensive move within the transference. The analysand's psychic blindness to what he or she knows may be unconsciously manipulative as well as defensive.

Analysts frequently shift their focus of listening from the psychic reality of the analytic situation to what is "actually" happening in it, and then back again to psychic reality. Without this shifting or oscillating, the analytic work may become unbalanced. Analysts' ideas about what is "actually" happening play a vital role in defining transferences and defensive operations and thus in empathizing. I have been alluding to the need for analysts to oscillate between the genetic and the developmental perspectives in order to do well-balanced analytic work. This need to oscillate is evident, for example, in analysts' optimal handling of analysands' reactions to vacations. On the one hand, the vacation must be taken as an "actual" interruption, and sooner or later the psychic meaning of this event must be explored. Psychically, it may be an abandonment, a rejection, a flight, an exclusion from a tempting primal scene or orgy. On the other hand—that is, when analysts do not lose sight of psychic reality in its fullest sense—the "actuality" of the vacation's entailing separation or interruption will not be taken for granted, for analysts may or may not be absent during that time. In psychic reality analysts may be vividly present. Indeed, it is likely that analysands will continue to feel their analysts' presence during the ostensible separation and may even continue the analytic dialogue. This continued presence and dialogue may be represented as, for example, benevolently protective or savagely persecutory. And for defensive reasons these representations may wax or wane. Even though this sense of continued contact may be repressed, its derivatives will often be recognizable and interpretable by those analysts who can oscillate freely between psychic elaboration of "actual" events and psychically real negations of these events.

The issue is the same with presence as with absence. For example, an analysand may complain about lack of physical contact with the analyst, a lack that is "actually" the case and should be taken up at some point, and yet psychically the analysand may experience being held, contained, stroked, penetrated, or beaten in the absence of any "actual" physical contact. A "good hour" may be experienced as a good feed, a good spanking, or good sex. Insight may be experienced as gaining a penis of one's own or being penetrated by the penis of the analyst; if so, the experiencing of insight may be strenuously resisted or ecstatically asserted.

It is my impression that any imbalance in an analyst's mode of listening is more likely to be based on his or her neglecting the psychic reality of analytic presence and absence and overestimating the actuality of presence and absence, as well as of abstinence, verbal dialogue, or insight. Understandably, then, such imbalance often results in analyses that seem to be stalled, unnecessarily tumultuous, un-understandably passionate, simply tedious, or discouragingly intellectualized.

In conclusion, although it is by no means the only significant aspect of analytic work, analysts' handling of representations of other people shows the extent to which they are conducting the analysis in the oscillating but consistently analytic way I have described. It shows the extent to which analysts believe in the centrality of psychic reality while yet giving their due to developmental influences and unconsciously carried on communication and reality testing.

CHAPTER 14

Resistance: The Wrong Story?

I. "THE RESISTANCE" AND FREUD'S COUNTERTRANSFERENCE

The extent to which we value Freud's creation of psychoanalysis should be measured not by the tributes we pay to his genius—there has been no dearth of those—but by our entering into the very debate over his ideas that he himself frequently initiated within his writings. He did so in order to think through his ideas and then go on either to revise them and build further on them or reject them. The idea with which I am concerned here is "the resistance." I focus particularly on the narrative of resistance that Freud developed in his papers on technique (1910–1915). In that context, I present a recommended version of a modern technical approach to resistance wherein the analysis of countertransference replaces "the resistance" as a central factor in the analytic process.

Long before Freud wrote these papers on technique, as early as the "Studies on Hysteria" (Breuer and Freud, 1895), he had already constructed his essential narrative of defense: defense against psychic pain and defense in the service of an ego protecting its unity; and he had begun to dwell particularly on the ego's defense of repression. Yet, from the beginning of his psychoanalytic writing, he had also emphasized resistance as an independent force. By "resistance" he intended to convey the sense he shared with the patient that both of them were struggling against a negative force. To begin with, he considered it a force that stood in the way of remembering painful or traumatic memories. Freud's letters suggest that he encountered what he took to be the same negative force in his own early efforts at self-analysis.

As time went on, Freud presented this force as the cause of blocking of associations. More than the patient's conscious withholding, he emphasized in this regard the effects of the unconscious operations of repression. Because the resistance seemed to operate mostly unconsciously, much of the therapeutic struggle seemed to be against an invisible, often unfathomable force of great influence. In the main the patient experienced that influence passively; Freud inferred its presence from its limiting effects on the therapeutic process as well as the conscious effort it took to do the work of analysis. It was effortful to "overcome" it: Such was how Freud termed it repeatedly both before and in the papers on technique. He did, however, insist that the patient's passive subjective experience should not be allowed to obscure the insight that the patient was actively, albeit unconsciously, resisting. I believe that Freud's attraction to militaristic metaphors—weapons, slayings, battles, and so forth—was intensified by this sense of the analyst's waging a campaign against a devious, hostile, and relentlessly active force.

In his preanalytic clinical work, Freud had used hypnosis to gain access to disturbing memories. Soon, however, in a great leap forward, he realized that hypnosis merely bypassed the resistance and so ignored an essential player in the neurosis. He concluded that it was now essential to overcome the resistance rather than try to evade it. To this end, he began to rely on a combination of reassurance, didactic explanation of psychoanalytic principles and findings, exhortation, and physical pressure. His interest grew in the signs of resistance and, as time went on, in specific motives somehow connected to it; however, neither at first nor subsequently did he ever question the need to assume the presence in the therapy of that basic oppositional force. Nor did he abandon his technical emphasis on psychological pressure, reassurance, explanation, and other inducements to give up resistances against remembering; only physical pressure was abandoned. In the end, he accorded resistance equal place with transference when he stated that the analysis of both features defines psychoanalysis as a distinct method of therapy and investigation. Mainstream Freudian analysts have held to this account up to the present; over the years, much valuable experience has been facilitated and organized in its terms.

Notwithstanding Freud's productive start and latter-day developments, it is my purpose here to question the taken-for-granted need for the idea of resistance and the use that is made of it. I argue that the idea of resistance is diffuse and superfluous, too focused on relatively manifest content, and too dependent on theoretical propositions about the therapeutic process that no longer dominate sound Freudian analytic practice. Consequently, I consider the idea of resistance to be technically confusing. My second chief purpose is to suggest that, to a significant extent though not entirely, Freud's emphasis on resistance indicates that he had drifted into a generalized adversarial countertransference.

These two purposes are rather large to be served even in an extended chapter. Ideally, they should have the support of many citations of Freud's formulations. Nevertheless, I believe that I can make a case for my two claims without that support, even if only in broad outline.

UNINTEGRATED ASPECTS OF FREUD'S APPROACH

The first thing to emphasize in my critique is that, upon close reading of Freud's papers on technique, we can discern some retention of his preanalytic and early analytic technical attitudes and methods. In addition to his frequent references to "overcoming" the resistance, he writes of "clearing away" preliminary resistances as if they are difficult underbrush slowing down an expedition. Similarly, he recommends that the best response to expressions of distrust is to urge the patient simply to put that feeling aside and comply with the fundamental rule of free association and, further, to explain to the patient that distrust is merely a symptom, as trust is unnecessary to the analysis. Thus, he assumes that the patient can and should work analytically *in spite of* the resistance. In the same spirit, we find Freud writing of "working through" the resistance; here he means not the analytically sophisticated idea of working through, but rather merely the analysand's continuing to work *in spite of* both the feeling and the indirect evidence of noteworthy reluctance to do so. That is, I believe that he simply means "Do it anyway!" and not "How are we to understand your reluctance?"

To be complete, however, I should note that on the very same page where Freud mentions "working through" in this pressuring sense, he does begin to speak of "the working through of the resistances" (1914a, p. 155). We may take this small but significant revision of wording to be the beginning of his transition to the modern understanding of the idea. Nevertheless, I will venture to say that in these technical papers he had not yet arrived securely at that modern understanding. And I believe he never did. His attitude continued to favor pressing on *against* resistance and *in spite of it;* thereby he retained unanalytic impurities in his new analytic method.

Technically, this mixed analytic and preanalytic aspect of Freud's narrative is not just confusing, but superfluous. As I said, Freud already had in place his basic narrative of defense and a well-developed clinical idea of repression. His works on dreams, parapraxes, and jokes, written prior to these technical papers, show this to be so; even his earlier case reports show it. He could have made do quite adequately with the following schema: In the therapy, analyst and analysand are obliged to identify, analyze, and work through the repressive defense maintained by the analysand's ego. Freud could have taken this step even though he had not yet developed the later, far more sophisticated and balanced position implied by his 1923 (1923a) and 1926 theory of the ego with its motives and mechanisms of defense. But he was, I infer, too much in the grip of his own conscious subjective experience in doing clinical analysis: He felt that his way was being blocked by a powerful counterforce.

What can be surmised about this subjective experience? We may infer from his narrative that Freud saw his patients as failing to collaborate adequately in the treatment process. Specifically, they did not consistently associate freely in the manner he required of them, and their remembering remained spotty at best. As we know, Freud was banking very heavily on the method of free association to gain access to the pathogenic memories that he viewed as the analytically crucial content of the repressed. He believed that he could not reach his goal without breaking through the barrier represented by the infantile amnesia. He reasoned that the more he could do away with that amnesia, the more convincingly could he show his patients the disturbing memories organized around the conflictual infantile sexuality that unconsciously was dominating their current lives. The crucial insights concerned conflictual sexuality that was dominating their lives to the extent of necessitating the formation of their symptoms and symptom-like character traits. Freud believed that not only would those insights into their own histories, mental makeups, and current difficulties have a curative influence, they would also lead analysands deeper into their minds and thereby lead him to buried treasures of evidence to support and extend his theories of psychosexual development, neurosis, dreams, and the organization of the psychic apparatus. More than developing insights for his patients, he wanted to impress those insights on the world: the world he experienced as persecutory, keeping him under constant hostile surveillance. Here there was a basis for the significant generalized countertransference that I mentioned earlier.

I believe there is a discrepancy between Freud's ostensible therapeutic aims and his attitude toward his manifestly and implicitly uncooperative patients. In his papers on technique, his attitude toward his patients is not altogether impartial. Heavily invested in his own goals, he is defining clinical phenomena too much from his point of view. He writes as if he does not fully grasp or value his theory of repression in the service of the ego.

FREUD'S CONCEPTION OF ANALYZING THE RESISTANCE

But how, then, might we reconcile this reading with Freud's also going on to emphasize in these same papers the idea of "analyzing the resistance"? With this emphasis, he seems to be transcending the relative one-sidedness I have just proposed. To address this question, we must picture for a moment additional aspects of Freud's situation. It can be said with some justification that, in a way, the early teens of the century, when he wrote these technical papers, were also Freud's early teens as a clinical analyst. Relatively speaking, and notwithstanding the abundant clinical wisdom spread through these pages, it is still the peak time of Freud the Conquistador bravely invading a rich new world and tolerating opposition poorly. In this youthful role, he is not yet ready to be all that impartial; what he is ready to do is to attribute his own difficulties of understanding as well as the unevenness of his results to resistance being put up by the patient. In this respect, Freud's posture is not so different from one that today's analysts sometimes adopt, even when they are no longer analytic teenagers and have so much more intellectual sophistication about resistance. Analysts must still count on being constantly tempted to infer resistance when they do not yet understand what is being expressed or how to respond and when they are feeling disappointed in their results and frustrated by their patients.

Returning now to Freud's conclusion that it would be important to develop the idea of "analyzing the resistance," it must be acknowledged, first, that on the face of it, his emphasis on this technical principle sounds thoroughly and systematically analytic. I suggest, however, that it suffers from two major limitations. First of all, it seems to me that far too often what Freud means by this technical precept is limited to showing the analysands *that* they are resisting; for example, showing them that their passionate demands for the analyst's love serve the same purpose of blocking the uncovering of the repressed as their simply withholding associations or "failing" to associate or casually pooh-poohing interpretations. All such events and postures serve the resistance. Just this much *is* insight of a sort, provided that it can even be gotten across to the analysand convincingly. Even then, common experience has shown that it is insight that is very limited in scope, usually without great influence, and unstable in that it rests on a still-unanalyzed base of transference and unconscious defensive measures. Often it turns out that in that very insight there is much superficial acquiescence to the authority of the analyst as a transference figure. Freud was familiar with the phenomenon of veiled submission to his analytic authority; nevertheless, that submission seems to have had its appeal to him in his role as Conquistador. He referred to it favorably as "compliance" with his method.

The second limitation on Freud's conception of analyzing the resistance may be found in the inconsistent way that he deals with the dynamics of resistance. For one thing, he refers to those dynamics variously as the motives of resistance, the motives that stimulate the resistance into action or reinforce it, and the motives that the resistance puts to use for its own purposes. He also asserts that, like all other unconscious motives or wishes, the unconscious motives implicated in resistance have their own reasons to resist their becoming conscious; here he is referring to what he had postulated in earlier writings as the pull of the repressed, the so-called pull from below. Thus in this respect he is introducing yet another force—not a defensive one—into a narrative of resistance organized around repression. Additionally, he indicates awareness of the motives of secondary gain, in which connection he is bringing in an ego-based aspect of pleasure-seeking and thereby further compounding his ideas of repressive resistance. In support of Freud's variety of formulations, we could call on the idea of overdetermination or a view of resistance as a compromise formation, but I do not believe that Freud's writings support this rationalization of his conceptual diffuseness. "The resistance" retains its status as an elemental force and featured player throughout his writings.

More important than this diffuseness, however, is Freud's conceptual poaching on the territory of transference—which he did even before the technical papers. For example, in his study of Little Hans, he wrote that once he had enlightened Hans about his hostile and jealous feelings toward his father, he had cleared away Hans's most powerful resistance. Not his transference: his resistance! The background of this formulation is this: Among the motives implicated in men's resistance are, as Freud put it, fear and defiance of paternal authority and disbelief in it. Here transference and resistance lose their separate identities.

Then, in the course of writing these technical papers, Freud goes on to deepen his grasp of the erotic transference and the negative transference, and he begins to conceive of them largely as intensifying resistance: They are, he says, "accessory motives" that patients use to rationalize resistance. As such they protect patients by serving as warnings against the dangers of excess in emotion and its expression. In other places, Freud similarly suggests that these transferences are largely the work of the resistance; for example, they constitute destructive assaults on the analytic compact itself.

I believe that Freud had a sense of these new conceptual difficulties because he began to use that implicitly hyphenated concept "transference resistance." In my view, however, transference resistance is one of those bridge terms that, while perhaps useful as a very casual technical shorthand, cannot be explanatory in that it merely gives an awkward name to the conceptual problem and does nothing to solve it. Already then, I think, Freud could have subsumed all these phenomena, including even some core aspects of the erotic transference, under the negative transference—as analysts are likely to do today. He could also have included the technical challenge encountered and the effort required in dealing with these transferences among numerous other understandable issues in analytic work. This precisely is what he did when he took up transference and acting out: He continued to elucidate them brilliantly as he forged ahead. Not so for the resistance and the transference resistance, and the result was notable narrative unevenness in the quality of his technical papers.

FREUD'S NEGATIVE COUNTERTRANSFERENCE

I have been trying to show that in Freud's pioneering texts on the analysis of the dynamics of resistance, he introduced unclarity along with clarity. While the problem was not so important during the creative spells of genius, it is important for those of us who now constantly look at our patients through the eyes of this genius. I have just described the unclarity. On the side of clarity, I would say that, when taken together, these loosely organized motives and relationships have helped analysts recognize a set of interpretive possibilities by means of which they have often been able to reduce the so-called force of resistance and thus, in Freud's terms, help "overcome" it. The narrative is serviceable even if fundamentally flawed.

It is, however, not enough just to recognize this unevenness of quality. We must, I believe, go on to ask the following questions: Why did

Freud need to present resistance as an *independent* powerful force? Why was he so ready to take the common subjective experience of analyst and patient that analytic work is effortful as a crucial datum in and of itself? What can account for his failing to bring to bear his own understanding of the limited significance of manifest content, for, relatively speaking, the effortfulness in question lies in or close to the realm of manifest content: conscious or preconscious subjective experience that both indicates and obscures unconscious conflict?

We can say Freud was overresponsive to manifest content even after we take into account his recognition that the resistance also operates unconsciously and therefore requires its own interpretation before it can be, as he said, uncovered; there is, he said, resistance to the uncovering of resistances. Our attribution is warranted because frequently he describes resistance as phenomenon, not as theory or inference; for him, it is repression that is theory. It is also warranted because, in his view, resistance merely covers over the content he deems most important, that is, the repressed infantile sexuality. Functionally and descriptively, therefore, Freud's evidence of the resistance can be located as falling within or close to the realm of manifest content.

There is no denying that it takes effort to be alert to the myriad forms of transference and defensiveness, to think through ways and times to take them up, and, at the same time, to keep a firm grip on one's countertransference tendencies. Freud knew this, and, in broad outline, he taught us that this is so. Why then was he not ready to take this step: to subsume all these dynamic factors under the conflictual positive and negative transferences and the defensive operations of the ego. It was ground he had already prepared. Had he taken that step, he would have concluded that it is the analysis of both transference and the defensive ego that distinguishes psychoanalysis from other therapies. He would have seen the inadequacy and analytic inappropriateness of emphasizing so strongly uncovering "resistances" and exhorting the patient to fight them.

We come now to my proposed answer to my question about why Freud needed and remained stuck on the concept "the resistance" and his ideas about handling it: From the beginning of his creative labors, Freud remained under the influence of some negative countertransference. I suggest that because Freud felt he was in some sort of argument, he believed he had to introduce an adversarial orientation into his clinical and theoretical narratives. This proposed answer is consistent with the work of those authors who already have examined Freud's difficulties in his work with Dora: Finally alert to her adversarial transference resistance, as he would have called it later on, he still gave no evidence that he recognized the role of his complex countertransference in his conduct of the treatment and its outcome.

A MODERN ANALYTIC APPROACH TO RESISTANCE

To bring home my points about the limitations of Freud's attempts to work out what it means to analyze resistance and how countertransference may have entered into these attempts, I present next a brief, generalized sketch of what I consider a more adequate and less countertransferential modern analytic approach to the phenomena in question. In so doing, I also take a closer look at the way in which the diffuse, blurred, and superfluous aspects of Freud's narrative of resistance may facilitate and help rationalize countertransference in analytic work.

I believe that, in the most appropriate analytic approach, we as analysts hardly give any weight to the idea of resistance. Instead, we think in the general terms of transference and defensive operations. Specifically, we think in terms of enactments within the analytic relationship that are about the analytic relationship itself. These enactments can be taken as unconsciously devised communications; they communicate the fantasies that dominate the analysand's experience, unconscious as well as conscious, of the conduct of both parties to the analytic relationship. That experience and that conduct may concern every variety of self and object representation: loving, hating, suspicious, omnipotent, depressed, merged, lonely, sexually excited or frigid or impotent, sadistic, masochistic, and on and on. Analysts approach them as concrete manifestations of unconsciously elaborated transference fantasies.

On this view, we would take the withholding of associations that Freud emphasized so much not as a sign of resistance, as opposition that the analysand must acknowledge and overcome, but, for example, as an implied provocative move in the transference, perhaps a seductive move that enacts a sadomasochistic transference fantasy, or perhaps as an oblique reference to keeping a guilty secret in a transference enactment of guilty secrets from childhood. Analysts might adopt similar interpretive orientations to the analysand's attempt to be disarming by good behavior, or attempting to create distance by making direct attacks on the analyst's empathy, or trying to establish omnipotence by turning the tools of analysis against it or by doing "analysis" without help from the analyst.

Analysts view these and other such phenomena as communications that the patient must make repetitively and in many different guises. Analysts are always weighing the question of whether such enactments as being good, withholding, amorous, superficial, or in control of the analysis are now playing major parts in the analysand's life that it would be well to explore. Thus, far from its being dealt with as if it were an alternative to analysis, each line of action will be approached as a telling and a showing that might pertain, for example, to symbolic gaseousness or constipation, using a posture of innocence to disguise a guilty conscience, initiating a seduction, throwing out a hint that one possesses a stolen or a hidden penis, flaunting a flashy manic denial of one's own destructiveness, or parading cleanliness as a form of analytic godliness.

In every case, the clinical question about "the resistance" remains: How are we to understand the manifest or implied reluctance? The goal of understanding is a fixed constituent of the modern analytic attitude. As always, analysts continue to search for what is unconsciously conflictual, that is, for what has mixed defensive, gratifying, and self-punitive elements. And as always, there is no guarantee that analytic answers will be found to this question or that the analytic relationship will ever again change. But that uncertainty, too, and even that occasional total stasis will be made part of the subject matter of the analysis; instead of being seen as obstacles to be removed, they will be occasions for inquiry. In this respect, we do today as Freud did when, not long after he wrote his papers on technique, he reflected on the negative therapeutic reaction: Clinically, he saw that reaction as further analytic material bearing on the transference, he understood it as an expression of unconscious guilt, and he went on to install it in the foundation of his structural theory—that narrative in which the superego figures so majestically. Even then, however, he maintained his fixation on the idea of resistance, for, a few years later, he went on to name a new kind of resistance: superego resistance.

I do not present this formulation of a modern approach to analyzing resistance as original or singular. Although it appears in different analytic contexts, is expressed in significantly different languages, and is referred to with noteworthy variations in explanations and emphasis, this approach may be discerned in modern Kleinian object relations theory, Kohutian self psychology, and Freudian character analysis. It is also found in certain post-ego-psychological conceptual revisions such as I have been presenting in connection with what I have called the affirmative analytic attitude, action language, and a narrational and dialogic view of analysis (1976, 1978, 1981, 1983).

Fundamentally, each of these developments rejects the idea of an independent adversarial force that accompanies the analysis "step by step," as Freud said; and they all do so without denying that aggression, along with desire, self-protectiveness, and self-punitiveness, not only pervades every analysis but is its life-blood and is therefore one of its principal subject matters. And not one of these theories relies on the militaristic metaphors and storylines that Freud favored when describing the analytic relationship.

NEGATIVE COUNTERTRANSFERENCE: HELP AND HINDRANCE

In these alternative and affirmative approaches, when analysts begin to feel that they are engaged in an argument or a power struggle, they are prepared to realize that they have begun to shift out of the analytic attitude. Often they may understand that shift as a sign that they have been successfully manipulated into a countertransference that fits into the patient's transference fantasy. At that point they realize that some self-analysis of countertransference is required, not only to restabilize the analytic attitude but also to illuminate the analysand's current emotional status and aims. Under ordinary working conditions—that is, when analysts are not suffering severe countertransference for neurotic reasons—they will understand that the analysand is unconsciously enacting conflict or distress in the here and now of the analysis. The patient is involving the analyst in that conflict by stirring up adversarial attitudes and perhaps even a limited and discouraging view of the patient as uncooperative and in need of prodding and various blandishments to "get on with it."

By working in this way, contemporary analysts show that they value early stages of countertransference, seeing them as essential elements in the network of communication that evolves during every ongoing analysis. They do not automatically adopt the traditional but mistaken adversarial stance toward signs of countertransference; instead, they do as they do with signs of the so-called resistance: They take an analytic interest in them. Consequently, as well as asking the question How can I understand the patient's reluctance? today's analysts are likely to go on to question their own feeling that, at some moment, a struggle against resistance is taking place or that any kind of interpersonal struggle exists. By questioning themselves, analysts show their awareness that they may be beginning to play an assigned role in their patients' fantasies.

Carrying that inquiry further, they will search for ways in which they may be contributing to the stimulation of the patients' enactments by their own mode of construing and responding to the messages being conveyed from the couch. Many of these messages are sent in the form of enactments rather than words, and they are responded to in kind—by analysts' shifts in attention or morale, by flux in tone of voice and tempo of response, by one-sided interpretation, and so on. As we know, and as Gill (1982) among others has been insisting, that aspect of the analytic dialogue is all too easy to miss or misconstrue. I would, however, add a note of caution here: Often that here-and-now aspect of transference-countertransference interaction is fraught with ambiguity when it is noted, so that it is easier to raise questions about it than to answer them decisively and promptly. Still, analysts may clarify current problems in the analysis merely by raising such questions to themselves or on occasion with the analysand. I believe that analysts' ever-increasing alertness to and curiosity about early and implied signs of countertransference are becoming most important parts of the analytic dialogue. And so we may draw another important conclusion: *In place of the analysis of resistance, we may install the analysis of countertransference alongside the analysis of transference and defensive operations as one of the three emphases that define a therapy as psychoanalytic.* In this respect, analytic terminology has lagged behind practice.

DISCUSSION

When listening to an analysand, analysts are constantly ready to raise questions, as well as in time to suggest some answers, concerning what the analysand means by depression, anxiety, love, hate, abuse, guilt, desire, frustration, gratification, dependency, frankness, lateness, cleanliness, pride, truthfulness, and so forth. In this chapter I have been extending this methodological principle to the language of Freud's narrative of the analytic process, specifically to his use of "the resistance" and of other words, many of them militaristic, that he used in relation to that term. Reading Freud as I would listen to a patient—legitimately, I think—I have concluded that this language indicates a significant involvement of generalized negative countertransference on Freud's part.

It is not my intention to treat the word *resistance* as the culprit in analysis and to propose that it be eliminated. I recognize the usefulness of "resistance" for descriptive purposes, and I recognize, too, that the word is so well established in the clinical lexicon that it is not likely to be deleted. My claim here is different; it is that "resistance" is a perilous word to use emphatically and in an explanatory fashion, as when it is said that what distinguishes psychoanalysis from other therapies is its analysis of the resistance as well as the transference, and when it is said that resistance is the dynamic cause of a clinical phenomenon. This emphatic use distracts our attention from intrapsychic conflict and compromise involving defensive and self-punitive operations; it also distracts us from the analysis of countertransferences. Moreover, judging by how "resistance" is used, it seems destined to take on a strong interpersonal as well as a strong negative connotation. Neither fits a depth-analytic approach and both help rationalize negative countertransference positions that reduce empathic concentration on the patient's compromised strivings toward both psychic equilibrium and psychic change.

We might attempt to account for Freud's conceptual difficulties with "the resistance" by noting that he was in the throes of creative activity. Yet this suggestion establishes a questionable split between the throes of creativity and transference. It seems to me more consistently analytic to affirm that, in the heightened and fluid emotional states characteristic of creative work, it is *more* likely, not less likely, that strong transferential processes will be stimulated. I believe that when Freud advised against doing research on current treatment cases, he was doing so for the same reason, though it would be disruptive countertransference and not transference that would be the danger then. And when Ernst Kris (1952) discussed creative work from an ego-psychological point of view, he emphasized the regressive (and therefore inevitably heightened transferential) aspects of its inspirational phases. I would add that splitting Freud's creativity and countertransferences can only foster those submissive, idealizing attitudes toward Freud that have always interfered with the development of psychoanalysis.

My accepting the broad use of the idea of countertransference might be questioned. It might be claimed that as my usage fails to recognize the importance ego psychology accords to external reality, reality testing, adaptation, and ego autonomy, it signals a retreat to pre-ego-psychological reductive thinking. To this challenge I would reply that these ego-psychological factors have always been assumed and established within the framework of the analytic enterprise; clearly, they were assumed by Freud, Abraham, and others in their pre-ego-psychological days (see also Section II, below). These factors come into question only when they prove to be so pervaded by conflict and compromise formation that their reduction or impairment may be taken as equivalent to enactments that require interpretation (for example, lack of comprehension as a refusal to be fed or penetrated).

Consider, for example, the autonomy of ego functions. It should be remembered, first of all, that autonomy is *relative* autonomy; that is, it is never closed off to neurotic or regressive complications. We analysts regularly encounter, in work with relatively intact neurotics, striking instances of conflict-laden flux of reality testing and adaptation. Consequently, we have learned to be conservative in making unexamined assumptions about conflict-free therapeutic alliances and "unobjectionable positive transferences" (M. Stein, 1981). It is an important part of our analytic attitude to take nothing for granted in this realm as in all others. The issue of autonomy goes beyond the disruptive invasion of ego functions by conflict. Analysts should not split off countertransference from acceptably accurate reality testing or soundly approved moral values; here the assumption of autonomous functioning does not preclude a more complex analysis. "Reality" is known to be a good defense. It is also known that analysts who appear to be equally well adapted may still see the so-called same situation differently though not unrealistically; and it is expected that analytic inquiry could show that some significant elements of countertransference are contributing to these differences. Thus, in the clinical situation, even when it is recognized that the patient has correctly perceived a trait of the analyst's, even a countertransference manifestation, as a rule it is still best to keep the focus on the transference-significance of this piece of good reality testing. The timing, emphasis, mode of expression, and selectivity of whatever the analysand seems to have perceived correctly: All may signal significant transference and unconscious conflict. Truth, transference and countertransference are not mutually exclusive.

Finally, more should be said on the topic of enactment. Earlier in this chapter I indicated that enactment is central to my conception of the so-called analysis of resistance. I want now to add that I see enactment as a concept that can free analysts and, ultimately, analysands from the tyranny of the spoken word, specifically, from the conventional role of the spoken word as merely a conveyor of content and from verbalization as the only means of narration. The analytic dialogue and the analytic storyline are not developed solely by means of the verbal transmission of cognitive and emotional experience accompanied by familiar, semantically clear expressive movements. Under "enactment" we may include communication through the timing and manner of saying things and not saying things both within the analytic session and outside it; the use or nonuse made of interpretations; lateness, absence, symptomatic regressions and flights into health; and so forth. Enactment is a concept related to acting in, though it has the advantage of lacking the pejorative implication that acting in, like acting out, tends to take on—a mistaken implication in both cases but common enough for us to consider in this discussion.

Once freed from the tyranny of the spoken word and consistently thinking in terms of enactment, we can view the analysand as constantly working, not resisting work; further, we remember that the analysand is working in the only way possible, that is, in his or her own way, and we are prepared to recognize that, in part, the analysand is even hoping to be recognized as a co-worker, however ambivalent he or she may be about this collaboration out of fear, hatred, envy, despair, suspicion, or grandiosity. Seeing things this way neither guarantees nor precludes further progress in the analysis, but it is an affirmative way to take into account the details of the analytic process. That affirmative way sustains the analytic attitude against the hazards of disruptive countertransference. It also contributes to the flexible and tactful framing of analytic interpretations, the kind of interpretations that have the best chance of being heard as such by the analysand.

We have come far from Freud's approving reference to "compliance" with the psychoanalyst's instructions and far from his antagonistic narrative of resistance, with its unself-critical militaristic metaphors. In this respect as in many others, analysts have carried forward Freud's work of genius; continuing in the spirit of his labors, they have revised, extended, and enriched his technical as well as theoretical narratives.

II. A Clinical Critique of the Concept of Resistance

Here I extend my critique of the inclusion of resistance (as against defense and countertransference) in any formal definition of analysis, by presenting a series of clinical examples in which apparently resistive phenomena, once they were approached as further contributions to the analysis, yielded up a rich store of memory, affect, and conflict. I present these examples after some further comments on Freud's legacy and his technical discussions as a model for practice.

That Freud greatly valued the concept of "the resistance" he showed almost from the very beginning of his creative labors by being so preoccupied with the many problems of theory and technique he could include within its boundaries. He had already relied heavily on it in the "Studies in Hysteria" (1895), and in his great paper on transference (1912b), some seventeen years later, he spent much time on "the resistance." To understand this emphasis, we must imagine how important it was to him during those years to have developed the idea that, unconsciously, people seem to fight tooth and nail against the treatment and the very recovery for the sake of which they have come to the analyst in the first place. Gradually, Freud came to understand that it was necessary to analyze "the resistance" rather than just fight against it or to try to get around it. As I argued in the first part of this chapter, however, he never clarified and explored fully the idea of analyzing "the resistance," and he never recognized that "the resistance" is an optional concept rather than a necessary one; that is, it is only one way to describe some subtle as well as dramatic, superficially obstructive phenomena in the analytic process.

Freud prepared the ground for a modern understanding of analyzing resistance in his 1926 monograph, "Inhibitions, Symptoms and Anxiety." There he set down the crucial series of infantile danger situations. In psychic reality, these situations are carried forward unconsciously into the present. They require all of us always to rely on defensive activity. In that way, analysands carry into the psychoanalytic situation much of the motivation for "the resistance." After 1926, therefore, to speak of analyzing "the resistance" could only mean to explore the expression in the present of all the wishes and fears of early childhood and the means of coping and mastering that were developed over the years of the patient's life and have continued to be psychically real. On this understanding, we think of trying to use interpretation to reduce the anxiety, guilt, and shame that necessitate defensive activity and culminate in conduct that manifestly seems to be simply oppositional ("the resistance"). The analytic emphasis is on changing psychic conditions, not on removing anything and certainly not on fighting against it.

But if this is so, is it not the same understanding and the same practice that analysts engage in when they undertake the entire task of clinical analysis? Is it not also what they mean, or much of what they mean, when they speak of analyzing transference, or analyzing repetition, acting out, or the compromise formations that express unconscious conflict in general? If, in modern practice, "analyzing the resistance" seems to refer to everything in the analysis, then it loses its linguistic identity; it is different from nothing, so that, on linguistic grounds alone, the term can no longer be considered useful. Certainly, by the standards of ordinary common sense, patients do do things that manifestly seem to interfere with what analysts regard as the progress of the analysis. Yet it can now be argued that "the resistance" is no longer the best way to think about that conduct. There seems to be a contradiction between analysts' practices and the technical terms they use. As our next step, therefore, we must go on to ask how it is that "resistance" has continued to be an unquestioned ego-psychological Freudian term in psychoanalytic discourse.

I think there are many reasons for this continuing emphasis. One reason, but not the most important one, is analysts' idealizing submission to the authority of Sigmund Freud's eloquent way of writing. Another reason is that analysts have organized much experience, expertise, teaching, writing, and professional identification around "the resistance," just as they have around other traditional major terms, such as "the transference." A third reason I developed in the first part of this chapter: "the resistance" as the expression of a negative countertransference. Here analysts misunderstand as opposition the fact that analysands seem to be not cooperating in the analysis *in the way that analysts would wish or have expected or are demanding;* analysts wrongly think that analysands are following a course that in conventional terms is merely rebellious, limiting, unnecessarily puzzling, unresponsive, superficial, or irrelevant.

In the context of this third reason, I suggest that the problem may lie with the analysts in many instances, specifically in their not yet understanding what analysands are communicating by acting in this way. Perhaps analysts are witnessing old, unconscious, perseverative attempts at escaping or re-creating infantile danger situations. In that case, a patient, feeling endangered, thinks that this is the only safe way to act at this time. Alternatively, the analysand may be unconsciously enacting old patterns of family relations that are based on real and imagined, physical and emotional experiences with self and others, and the patient may even be trying to remember and communicate these very patterns to the analyst. Or perhaps it is a vicious circle in which an analyst's countertransference leads to one misunderstanding that results in more misunderstandings and finally brings about what seems to be a stalemated power struggle, in which case the analysand is protesting against the analyst's misunderstanding and the analyst's mistaken demands for a certain kind of behavior. These alternatives are not mutually exclusive, and other issues, too numerous to be mentioned, might also be involved in the disturbing and puzzling behavior of the analysand—or is it of the analyst?

CLINICAL EXAMPLES

As I said, if we were to approach the following clinical examples in the traditional manner, we would think of them as illustrating the workings of "the resistance," that force making for interference in the work of analysis. My intention, however, is to use these examples to bring out enough of the complexity and richness of the analysis to throw into serious question the usefulness of the idea of "the resistance." My examples, which are drawn from my own work and from that of some supervisees, vary both in how strong "the resistance" appears to be and in the form it takes. I have avoided extreme examples that would require long case studies to fit usefully into this discussion. Furthermore, as so much therapeutic work deals with less-than-extreme phenomena, it should be more useful to work the middle ground; as a rule, the extremes do not make the technical and conceptual issues clearer.

A Sluggish, Silent Man

Early in the analysis of a young man, there is a session in which the patient's thoughts seem to be unusually wandering. The analyst says nothing in response. The next day there comes a similar session in which his speech and manner are also so sluggish as to give the feeling of slow motion. Finally, after having remained silent for some time, the analyst comments that he does seem to feel sluggish today. He replies that he may be slowing things down. It is then suggested to him that, if so, he might be feeling threatened by something that he is afraid might come to mind unless he is careful. He tells then that, today, in a way that was unusual for him, he had briefly thought of skipping his analytic session, and he goes on to ask if being absent is a way to slow things down. In reply he is told that that is one of many things people do when they are worried about their sessions, so that the question to consider is what it is that he now fears. The analyst does not challenge his show of naïveté. The session ends here.

The next day he slowly brings out his being angry at the analyst. He knows in his head, he says, that the analyst was not criticizing him the day before, but he felt criticized anyway. It felt like his father's criticism: Usually his father would just fly into a rage, but sometimes he would just make one remark and fall silent and at times remain silent for days. The analyst then says that although his own having been silent as well as his remarking on his patient's sluggishness had made him angry, he had not said so at the time. (The technical point here is to focus first on his anxiety about being forthcoming in his sessions.) He says then that he realized he was angry only after the end of the session. To this it is replied that he must have been afraid even to be aware of it during the session, that he had dulled his awareness of himself just as he had dulled himself in response to his father. (That he had learned to dull himself as a boy he had related in earlier sessions.)

Next he tells about the violence of his father's rages and his own frightened reactive policy of make-no-waves, that is, of remaining quiet. The analyst says, "You kept your mouth shut but your resentments piled up with him, as they have with me." This leads him to tell about his having changed at puberty from an A+ student to one who failed his school courses and barely got by. His mind just would not work. The analyst comments then that he was trying to kill his mind in the same way he had just done here. "Yes," he says, "I just couldn't think. I also used to worry about my mother at that time, because he punished her when I disappointed him. And being in school, I was not at home to make peace between them." At this point, it is mentioned that he had told in the past that, at puberty, he had been sent to a certain private day school much against his will and only because his angry father demanded it. He spontaneously continues that thought, saying that there was rebellion in his attitude and that at that time he could see that form of rebelliousness in lots of the boys. "Hoping to flunk out, possibly," it is suggested, and he agrees, but then mentions again how preoccupied he had been with his father's verbal attacks on his mother.

This example could be considered simply as resistance, in fact, a double resistance: first the resistance implied in his wandering and dulled thinking, and subsequently his mental sluggishness based on unexpressed resentment and rebelliousness over what he took to be a critical demand. I remind you here that Freud cited fear and defiance of paternal authority as a dynamic of men's resistance—perhaps even *the* chief dynamic of their resistance—but I would say that much more than that problem with authority emerged in these sessions, and it emerged fairly rapidly. There were the issues of his use of silence and of his attack on his own mind as part of making no waves with the analyst, which was itself part of his transference from the dreaded father, a man who had often fallen into threatening silence. Both of these factors touch on the patient's unconscious identification with his violent father and his associated fear of his own violence. There was unconscious violence in his negative transference. These two factors—silence and mind-destructiveness—also fall under the heading of transference, which we must regard as a valuable contribution to the work of interpretation and reconstruction. Only superficially does it look like interference.

Additionally, the patient referred to what might have been an early school phobia centering on anxiety over his mother's safety while he was away from her. That phobia probably would have been based in part on sadistic primal scene fantasies, and his mentioning it now prepares the way for suitable transference interpretation of primal scene material and perhaps a need to protect the analyst, too.

Taking all of these references and plausible conjectures together, we might say that this analysand's wandering, sluggishness, dullness, and silence spoke volumes about his inner struggle to control his own turbulence and violence. Would any further understanding have been gained by labeling all this the analysis of resistance? I think not. Instead, I believe that using that term would have indicated some impatience and blindness on the analyst's part that could only be explained in terms of disruptive countertransference. And he would have been thickening the analytic plot with superfluous ingredients.

A Woman Tells a Disturbing Sexual Dream

This patient is a middle-aged woman from the academic world. In the session preceding the one I concentrate on, she had reported a two-part dream: In the first part she was in the analytic office naked; in the second, she knew that she had told the analyst something dishonestly but she did not know what it was. She then said she had found it very difficult to tell the dream because it suggested to her that she was having sexual thoughts about the analytic relationship. Her associations had then turned to her having a cold and how, over the preceding weekend, her mother, whom she was visiting, characteristically had made a great fuss about it. She also associated to the fact that she had been feeling more sexual interest in men lately. Because she had brought this up near the close of the preceding session, the analyst had limited himself to saying that her thoughts suggested that she was not clear whether she was feeling more sexual interest in him than she had before or was now wanting some mothering from him; it was also unclear why she would not want to talk about these topics.

The patient enters the next session with a smile. She says she is smiling because she had not been sitting in the waiting room as far from the door to the consulting room as she usually did, and she does not want the analyst to think therefore that she is overjoyed to see him again. Next, she thinks again of the two-part dream she had told the day before. She had thought a lot about it since yesterday's session, but now she does not want to reveal those thoughts because it is really for her analyst and not for her to interpret her dreams. She goes on to report that, although over the weekend she had wanted to get away from her mother's fussing over her, she is not concerned about wanting mothering from the analyst; rather, what she does worry about is that it would trouble him to be put in that position. She then says that in her relationships with men, being taken care of, being held, being close is more important to her than sex, and she thinks that this kind of feeling is true of women in general.

At this point the analyst comments that she is afraid he might take her interest in getting closer as an expression of sexual interest, and he reminds her of an insight that they had worked on in earlier sessions, specifically, that she picked men to get involved with whose character helped her avoid and deny the uncomfortable issue of sex. In response to his comment, she thinks of a female colleague in relation to whom, as in relation to her mother, she herself is supposed to be the sick, weak, needful one and in this way to help her colleague feel strong. This set of rules reassures her colleague that she is not a cold person. The patient goes on to say that her mother had been sickly as a child and had gone through some of the same experiences that she was now forcing on her daughter, the patient. She then wonders if she might be exaggerating her present illness, her cold. The analyst says that if that is the case, it would show her wish to make sure of his interest and concern. With some shame, she responds with the thought that if he had grown up under her circumstances, he would act as she does now. Clearly, she is feeling defensive at this point.

The analyst then offers a broader interpretive comment. He says that it must be a burden as well as a threat to her to appear to be well, as in showing her pleasure on seeing him again or offering interpretations of her own. To this she replies that in fact she is pleased that she is now so much more secure with him that she can feel good about coming in to see him, and she remarks on how different she used to be; nevertheless, she remains concerned that she has to be ill in order for the analyst to be warm and concerned about her. At this point, he adds that she is also afraid that he will misunderstand her showing any good feelings and closeness to be a sexual act. Throughout this exchange over her anxiety about being well and closer, she has been coughing a lot, as if her cold has gotten worse, but she leaves the session looking far more composed than she had when she entered, smiling comfortably but still guarded in manner. The analyst had not commented on her need both to bolster him and to protect him against her feelings, as that factor was not clear to him at the time.

I believe that in these two sessions this analysand was communicating her fear of getting well and being emotionally closer at the same time as she was showing that she was experiencing just those changes taking place in her. She had had to emphasize the negatives, such as shame, dishonesty, illness, and inability. For her, the danger was that the favorable changes would either chill the analytic relationship or overheat it, and they would bring about one or the other result because of the way the analyst would be affected both as a mother-figure and as a man. Thus, she had to disown parts of her self: her enthusiasm, her excitement, her gratitude, her wish to show herself and move closer freely, both emotionally and intellectually. Also, she would be dangerous.

To label her doing all this a manifestation of resistance would, it seems to me, miss the point badly. The analytic way to begin to think about it would be to frame these questions: What was she enacting in the transference that expressed her wishes, her anxiety, the nature of her danger situation, and her defensive strategies? What was her conflict? In one respect, the one taken up, it was the conflict between showing herself in a very alive way and hiding herself in illness, inhibition, and distance. In another respect, she was in conflict over trust. Could she trust the analyst to understand her, to understand not just her wishes but her fears and self-protectiveness as well, so that he would neither fuss over her excessively nor retreat from the possibility of sexual excitement in the new, more open encounter or else respond to it too strongly? Additionally, her manifest conflictedness, signaled by her increased coughing, was itself a bid for his analytic care of her in the role of patient, which is to say, his fussing over her by making interpretations and his having nothing to fear from her.

At the same time I would infer that her bringing this rich material is also a sign of her continuing to get well: better able to hear analytic interpretations primarily as such rather than in the terms of the restrictive maternal transference, though now also as worrisome indications of the analyst's being analytically/sexually aroused in response to her progress toward experiencing herself as a whole woman. In other words, I infer that, for her, moving forward has both sublimated and directly heterosexual implications, while moving backward or staying in the same place has implications of invalidism and oral subjugation mixed with omnipotent control. In this session, she has been enacting an unconscious conflict over which direction to move in and on which developmental level.

Therefore, it could not have been correct or helpful to think that she was resisting by forgetting part of her dream, by alluding to dishonesty, by withholding her own interpretations, and by clinging to the role of the damaged, anxious, and presexual patient. It was more to the point to think that she was both telling and showing where she was psychically at that moment in the analysis; in that way, she was contributing to the further progress of the work.

Delaying Acting on Insights

The patient is a young nursery school teacher, the divorced mother of several children. In recent weeks, one of the themes that was being followed was her avoidance of coming to her session in the short skirts and tank tops she might otherwise wear in hot and "sweaty" weather. Analytically, this avoidance had been related to her fear of sexual encounters with men. She has also been endlessly not acting on her wish to seek out situations in which she might meet suitable men. In the preceding session the analyst had remarked on her holding back from acting on the many insightful discussions they had had of all these problems, and he had proposed that they should give that delay of action some thought.

In the current session she soon brings up the idea that it is not helpful to patients to push them into actions they are not ready to take. The analyst replies that it seems she had understood his comment and question as a demand for action and that she now feels she is in a fight. She says that that is her feeling even though she understands rationally that he had not been making a demand for action. Then she remarks that she had noticed herself smiling when she thought that she was delaying taking action. Thinking about her smile now, she thinks of the derisive smile of a woman she met recently, and she says, "I don't like that thought; it's not quite it; I think now of play in connection with that smile."

At this point, inferring that open fighting is stating the theme of the moment in too strong terms, the analyst takes her cue and suggests that, by not making active use of the analytic work, she may be expressing her resentment through teasing him or keeping him dangling. She then mentions—or confesses—that she had bought an attractive, sexy dress during a recent shopping trip and was proud of it. He notes aloud that, in an earlier account, she had not mentioned the sexy dress. She then tells him once again that she becomes tense and anxious whenever a man becomes physically or emotionally demonstrative. He wonders aloud if she had been afraid that she might follow through sexually were she to make herself attractive and act flirtatiously. She agrees with that surmise and then notes an image that has come into her mind of her youthful, vain, attractive, competitive mother, and she goes on to think of how much her mother has always boasted of her own many conquests of men.

After critiquing her mother's vanity, she returns to her fear of sex.

She wonders why she is afraid, because, as she thinks about it now, it seems as if it would be soft and warm. She thinks that she has had a similar feeling whenever she reads anything in the popular press touching on psychology. She reminds herself then of an earlier discussion of her fearing to "take in" that reading and enjoy it because it felt too close and too sexual. She thinks next of sexual intercourse and how after its completion the man would withdraw and leave her feeling "empty." The analyst suggests that she fears she cannot keep that pleasurable experience alive, that somehow she will kill it and end up feeling empty. And would that not, he goes on to wonder, imply that she would feel guilty about the pleasure and gratification? That kind of guilt had, in fact, come up repeatedly during the analysis; typically, whatever first felt good within her somehow soon turned bad and became a reason to reproach herself. At this point, she spontaneously remembers that interpretive work, and she says she can see that she could or would do something bad to her good experience of sex. She concluded the session speaking of her negative perceptions of her sexual anatomy.

In this example, rather than taking as resistance her delays of action and her criticism of the analyst's calling attention to it, he took it as an opening to begin to explore, first, her aggression toward him, then her attacks on her own pleasures in sex as well as elsewhere, and then the guilt feelings that both stimulated these attacks and were increased by them. In the process there emerged new hints of her identification with her much-feared and vain mother and its entry into the analytic relationship in the form of subtly and derisively controlling the analyst. He did not take up this theme of identification now and in this context, even though it had already been touched on in other contexts, as it did not seem to be the appropriate time to do so. Nor did he refer directly to the many transference implications, having found it helpful to proceed a bit slowly with this woman. Overall, however, they were jointly busy clarifying how she was enacting significant parts of her basic transference. They were treating her associations as significant contributions to the analysis rather than as interferences with it. Far from being antagonists, they were collaborators.

Reluctance to Come to Sessions and Free-Associate

My last and longest example centers on the early phase of the analysis of a woman who, after having worked at relatively low-level clerical jobs, had obtained advanced business training and had been working her way up in a high-powered headhunter organization. Recently she had been assigned to a new and lucrative post there. A red-haired woman whose very good looks attracted men to her, the patient was already forty years old and recently separated from her husband. She began treatment feeling depressed over the breakup of her marriage to Ted.

By her account, she was the daughter of a hypercritical mother and a weak, unresponsive father. She seemed to have incorporated and elaborated a severe internal critic, in large part to master her mother's attacks on her. Her characteristically low self-esteem had fallen even lower subsequent to the breakup of her marriage. During her early oedipal years, she had been approached sexually on several occasions by an uncle. She remembered from those occasions her pleasure in his attentions, her fear, and her keeping it all secret.

My partial account of two consecutive analytic sessions would, I think, fit easily into any traditional writing or teaching about resistance in analysis. In these sessions, there were taken up or at least mentioned or mentioned again the following themes: difficulty in free associating, defensively making order, feeling emotionally frozen or dead, and playing a role in order to cover up her true self.

The analysand begins by saying that once again she felt reluctant to come. She does not know why, particularly because, as she thinks about it, the treatment has been helpful to her so far. Gradually she begins to indicate that she felt criticized. The analyst asks, "How come?" and she explains, "Because I am angry at myself because I'm still in the same place about Ted." He asks how she connects this to him. She answers that, in the previous session, he had said that she continued to use her preoccupation with Ted to ward off other thoughts and feelings. She was referring to his having said that he thought she felt very uneasy without a specific topic to focus on, as if threatened by the prospect simply of saying whatever came to mind, regardless of what it might be, and so had been dwelling somewhat repetitively on Ted, and he thought it important to understand what she feared. Now he says that having taken that comment as a criticism, her feelings had been hurt, but that both then and now, instead of being openly angry at him, she had on her own mentioned only her anger at herself. She sees that this is so and then recalls a three-part dream of the night before.

First, there was something about a freezer in the basement that had a door that would not close. Second, some children were climbing up the side of a house in which she had lived as a child; they were pulling up the blind on the window of the room her sexually abusive uncle had occupied when he lived with them. She was watching all of this from a house across the street. There was a woman lying on the bed in this now-exposed room; she looked like one of her sisters-in-law. The analysand hastened to emphasize that this woman was dressed, as if to make it clear that the dream was not about sexual peeping or exposure; the boys, she said, were just being naughty. The third part of the dream showed a row of cars double-parked; she and someone else were picking up the cars and putting them in a row inside the parking line.

The analyst asks for associations to this third dream segment. She says that in the dream she felt pleasure in making things orderly and then has nothing more to say. He then mentions pulling up the blind, and she adds that in the dream she thought her mother had come and straightened things out with the boys, and again trails off into silence. He mentions next the freezer with the door that would not close. First, she thinks that the things in the freezer would thaw out. Then she associates to how she has always used food to fill up her loneliness. She explains that her development has been filled with loneliness. Sometimes, however, when she was alone, she used to play with plastic puppets and would get very involved and very creative and her bad feelings would go away. As she talks about her chronically lonely feelings, tears run down her cheeks—a not unusual occurrence—and she takes some tissues from the box of large-size Kleenex beside the couch and wipes her eyes. She says that the thoughts and feelings that come up are disturbing to her.

The analyst then interprets that he thinks her reluctance to come to her sessions is connected to her having recently reported that she was experiencing some freeing up of her feelings. He comments that, on the one hand, that freedom seems to have an upside in reducing her loneliness and letting her feel closer to her creativity, but that, on the other hand, there is the downside of its being painful for her and making her afraid of her associations because of what they might lead to if she continues thawing out. Then, for the first time in the analysis, she acknowledges, "There is something frozen in me, even dead." In earlier sessions, she had only emphasized her need to feel loved, implying that she was full of warm feelings but had no one to share them with. The analyst ends the session at this point, and she leaves with a winning smile and, unusual for her, with a comment on the way to the door: She says, "I like your big Kleenexes."

The following session included further work on the dream. After first thinking she was going too fast at work and in her social life, and then mentioning her having deferred asking her mother questions about her childhood, as she had volunteered to do in an earlier session, she complains that her thoughts are all in a jumble and expresses her need for order. At this point the analyst says that what she has been bringing out also applies to problems she has been having associating during the sessions. Specifically, she feels a need to line up her associations in a row, as she can once she has a topic to talk about. The problem for her is to go freely with her associations, which seem so jumbled to her; they are a problem even though she understands, from what has been seen before, that the jumbled ones can be at least as useful as those involved in developing a topic.

Soon she is dwelling on needless worries and self-consciousness about her physical attractiveness, from the time she was an adolescent up to the present—needless because she is much admired and envied. The analyst comments on the implication that she is self-conscious about her being exposed and observed on the couch (the blinds being up in the dream), but that she does feel dead or frozen even as she reassures herself that she is attractive, and he suggests that there is a link between being "jumbled" and being sexually aroused. To this she responds, "No . . . well . . . yes, that's true, but I have found ways to excite myself in sex by having fantasies that I'm somebody else. I've done that for some years. I know that if I were thinking about myself, I would be unloved and rejected." She then says that her fantasies concern a woman being raped, degraded, and put on exhibition. She protests that she has been looking only for recognition and love, but the men in her life always put pressure on her to be sexually active: "They didn't force me exactly, but they manipulated me to engage in acts that required me to open myself up and be exposed and with nothing being returned. It was ultimate degradation."

It is time now to end the session, and the analyst chooses to comment on her anxiety, saying that all of this must color her experience of the way the analysis is set up; it could be contributing to her reluctance to come and to her not knowing what to talk about. It feels safer and terribly important just to talk *about* things and not to leave herself free to bring up these painful thoughts, feelings, and memories, and all the concerns that right now could refer to her and him.

In these two sessions, I would say, they were continuing the analysand's induction into analysis by clarifying her initial difficulties in coping with the analytic situation. She was experiencing the analysis in terms of her infantile and later childhood danger situations, including sexual pressures inflicted on her, as well as a persecutory mother, and that she was dealing with the analysis in the characteristic ways she had developed in earlier years. These ways included the incorporation of a hypercritical, degrading, controlling maternal figure, which now, through projective identification, she was beginning to locate in the analyst. Consequently, when he tried to help her reflect on her difficulties in the sessions, she could only hear him criticizing her for being a resistant patient, and she reacted with depression as a defensive cover for anger and with avoidance—her reluctance to come to the sessions. In effect, then, it was she who was introducing the idea of resistance, not he. Resistance was her way to understand her transference and her projective rendering of the analyst as a persecutory, withholding, and certainly unempathic figure.

Why did he not point out that, as her analyst, he was the voyeuristic, seductive, sexual abuser whom, on the one hand, she feared, resented, and desired to attract or be popular with by exposing herself and, on the other hand, wanted to keep composed and in line? Because they were in a very early stage of the work and she felt she was rushing and also under pressure; because she was very anxious and might easily hear him as making a sexual approach and be unprepared to cope with that; because at this point there was no way he could discriminate sexual "acting" from genuinely sexual content; because of the sadomasochistic and narcissistic loading of her sexual allusions; because it was the very end of the session, a time when he believed it best not to send the patient packing, as it were, after delivering disturbing interpretations; and because he had not yet put together consciously all the connections and implications that I am noting here. Consequently, he contented himself with pointing her toward the here and now in his concluding comment: It could refer to her and him. I regard this decision as contestable; it might have added to her difficulties. But I am presenting this example not to illustrate fine technique; rather, I am trying to show how much complex allusion to, and enactment of, here-and-now transference and defense there can be in attitudes and behavior that, traditionally, could be subsumed under "the resistance."

CONCLUDING COMMENT: WHOSE IDEA IS "RESISTANCE"?

In closing, I should like to supplement what I said earlier about the way in which "the resistance" has remained an unquestioned entry in our psychoanalytic lexicon. In addition to tradition and other such factors, and in addition also to its usefulness as a sign of negative countertransference based on lack of understanding, emphasis on "the resistance" may indicate that the analyst is being controlled by introjection of the patient's transference. Specifically, that emphasis may show that, through projective identification, the guilty patient is portraying the analyst as an unempathic, critical, ungrateful figure whose interventions are simply accusations of badness and noncompliance; in other words, the patient is saying or implying that it is the analyst who is accusing the patient of resisting. In this way, the analyst is to bear the burden of the patient's own self-criticisms and guilt feelings. In such situations the analysand's unconscious guilty transference might stimulate in the analyst some complementary hostile countertransference. In an effort at mastery, the analyst then might develop the conviction that there really is an essence "out there" and "in" the analysand, an essence that deserves to be called "the resistance" and requires to be analyzed as such, neutrally and at length.

I am suggesting, however, that it is more plausible to view this attribution of resistance as a mistake that takes the outward form of responding to manifest content as if it were depth material. In this one aspect, it is a mistake based on an induced disruptive countertransference. The analyst is not detecting another kind of force in the patient, a force, moreover, the analysis of which is on a par with the analysis of transference as a chief identifying feature of true analysis; rather, the analyst is playing an assigned part in the patient's projective enactment of transference. It is the kind of mistake that on the surface seems to be very analytic, while, in effect, it shows that the analytic work has been thrown off course. It might be said that the analyst has begun telling the wrong story about the analytic dialogue.

CHAPTER 15

Problems of Training Analysis

IT has been argued by Harold Bloom (1973), the noted literary theorist, that strong poets are bound to feel they have arrived on the scene of creative writing belatedly. Acutely aware of the great works already written by others, they have the sense that they are barging into the company of the true masters, those who have already laid out and explored the major poetic possibilities. Surrounded by all these exemplary figures and works, strong poets must suffer "the anxiety of influence." Consequently, while drawing strength from their predecessors, they must also struggle against these figures in order to find their own poetic voices and be bold enough to let them be heard. There is, Bloom emphasizes, a disturbing patricidal undercurrent in this struggle. The poet is yet another Oedipus.

I cite this conflict-centered account of creativity in a chapter on training analysis because it describes well the experience of becoming the kind of analyst who can work within the analytic tradition and yet come to do so in his or her own voice—in other words, become a strong analyst. There is a definite parallel between, on the one hand, the poet's struggle and, on the other, the analytic candidate's anxiety of influence vis-à-vis the training analyst, supervisors, other teachers, Freud, and the entire analytic tradition as embodied in the pantheon of great analysts. Ernst Kris, no slouch himself as a creative analyst, was so self-conscious and self-effacing in this regard—in Bloom's terms, so oedipally frightened, so engaged in shrinking back from any suggestion of parricide—that somewhere he described everything written by analysts subsequent to Freud as not much more than footnotes to the master's writings.

Psychoanalytic belatedness is not, however, just a matter of recognizing the genius of Freud's pioneering efforts and the contributions made by all those other analytic figures whom we have encountered personally or through reading and who have exerted a powerful formative effect on our own analytic development. Much of this sense of belatedness can be traced to transferences. We may say that the oedipal child has arrived belatedly on the scene of parental sexuality and procreativity. And we may add that the preoedipal child is a Johnny-come-lately or a Joanie-come-lately on the scene of nurturance and power, in all their threatening as well as reassuring aspects. This early experience of belatedness leaves all of us feeling forever that, after all is said and done, we have remained the kids of our parents and secondarily of our mentors and the authors we read during our training. Our most strenuous efforts to defend against this feeling through forgetfulness, relentless competitiveness, or grandiose fantasy can never quash it completely.

Each training analysis should take account of this mix of personal and professional belatedness. It should not, however, crassly reduce the professional purely to the personal. We do after all live in intellectual and social histories, too, however personalized our view of our place in these histories may be. It was of this consideration that Kris, who was an art historian to begin with, was so keenly aware. We do not make up our own ideas completely; nor do we invent our own practices. No one does and no one ever has, neither in art nor in psychoanalysis. But I am not sure that training analyses always include this complex taking account of the anxiety of professional influence; here I have in mind the facts that, in our field, fitting in is usually rewarded more richly than originality, fifty-year-old colleagues continue to be called young analysts, and many analysts suffer a malaise that renders them all too eager for someone else to inject novelty and explosive controversy into the arenas of theory and technique. Most likely, the anxiety of influence will be taken up in analysis in its personal aspects, such as the influence of dominant identifications.

There is, of course, much more to work through in a training analysis than professional belatedness and its associated anxiety of influence, and I shall soon come to some of the other requirements. At this point, however, there is more introductory work to be done. First of all, a brief note on my own sense of belatedness in writing on training analysis: A number of excellent papers have already been written on training analysis, and they have been chewed over in other excellent papers, so that taken all together, the analytic literature seems to have pretty much covered the ground. To appreciate this state of affairs, we have only to consult the reviews and presentations included in recent monographs on training analysis published by the International Psychoanalytical Association (1985, 1986). Perhaps, though, in joining the conversation, I may develop some of the important points more fully, vividly, or consequentially than has been done up to now. Also, I feel obliged to try to counterbalance some well-established positions that I consider problematic.

A second introductory note: To take training analysis as a topic is to plunge into the thick of every major psychoanalytic controversy—the clinical, the theoretical, the pedagogical, the ideological, and the political. And it is to thereby plunge into the metacontroversy over whether these five controversies are distinct or are so intertwined as to be inseparable, or are so much the same thing fundamentally that they add up only to one topic being approached in different ways. For example, in certain respects theory is a political matter; so is the selection of some training analysts and the selection and progression of some candidates. Phyllis Greenacre's (1966) well-known discussion of how certain candidates get to be "convoyed" through training implies the important role that analytic power politics may play in analytic education. To Greenacre's point, I add that convoying is often done by others out of respect for, if not fear of and to curry favor with, powerful figures in the field.

Further by way of introduction: A writer on this topic also plunges into the thick of the transference residues and transference crises of those readers who are analysts and analytic candidates. Their "reader response" cannot help but express strong feelings about their own analyses. More than other readers, they have axes to grind or wield and illusions to sustain. Accordingly, a certain amount of unfinished analytic business must be expected to color every reader's grasp of the argument. In fact, such unfinished business must have already colored this argument, though it is not for me to decide how that is the case.

Some notes on methodology: Because any one analyst cannot have treated many analytic candidates, and because each training analysis, if it is reasonably thorough and well conducted, is likely to have many unique features as well as some that remain ambiguous, it can be argued that no training analyst is in a position to come to general conclusions about training analysis. But this cautionary consideration does not lead to the conclusion that we should simply keep our mouths shut. In this respect, four sets of considerations should be taken into account. First, while no one analyst concludes a huge number of ordinary clinical analyses to the complete satisfaction of both parties involved during his or her entire career, that fact has not prevented many analysts from writing valuable papers and books on every conceivable analytic topic and at every point in their careers. Second, any one analysis provides so many repetitions and multilayered variations of the themes and problems that come to be central to it that it proves to be a gold mine of data once it has been subjected to circumspect, insightful, and systematic processing. In psychoanalysis, valuable conclusions are reached in ways that do not and cannot conform to traditional experimental models. Third, published papers and symposia as well as informal discussions among colleagues have already led to consensus on many points concerning training analysis.

The fourth and final methodological note concerns the reality that each school of analytic thought provides a good deal of standardized theory to guide analysts in preparing their interpretive expectations and storylines. These expectations and storylines help them establish their sense of what makes sense and how to make sense. The reality is, then, that analysts never do start their work with individual analysands from scratch; instead, and fortunately for everyone concerned, the analysts' degrees of freedom are limited, much of the way toward their clinical conclusions having already been paved for them. Consequently, clinical experience, including experience doing training analysis, can never be and need never be viewed as a powerfully forbidding independent variable. Also to be taken into account is the fact that training analysts do have to conduct their first, second, and third training analyses, and who is to say that these analyses are any less effective than those conducted by other, often much older training analysts?

On the basis of these four methodological notes, I do not regard it as presumptuous to address the fundamental, fascinating, and problematic topic of training analysis. I attempt to join the conversation by reviewing the circumstances in which training analyses are conducted and spelling out the influences those circumstances may exert on the analysand's transferences and the analyst's countertransferences, matters of common concern in analytic institutes.

THE INFLUENCE OF CIRCUMSTANCE

Training analyses cannot afford to neglect the extent to which they are significantly influenced by the complex interaction of intellectual, professional, and personal circumstances. These interactions constitute the context of training analysis. I assume a context of circumstance that obtains widely, though not universally, in analytic institutes. On the one hand, therefore, my remarks do not apply in equal force to all aspects of all training setups; on the other, they still apply to the average expectable training analysis.

What constitutes the fateful context of circumstance in which training analyses are conducted? The training analysis goes on during most or all of the candidate's training. The training takes place under the auspices of an institute. It is required that the training analyst be a carefully selected member of the faculty of that institute. Further, he or she does not submit reports to the institute on the candidate's problems and progress, does not participate in decisions affecting the candidate's progress, and avoids administrative and pedagogical discussions that might include news about the candidate's behavior and standing. By these means the training analyst and the institute attempt scrupulously not only to observe the rules of confidentiality but also to protect the analytic relationship against the intrusion of third-party observations and influences. They see that intrusion as obstructive and diverting. These, at any rate, are the ideals.

But even when the training analysis is conducted under conditions that approach the ideal, it is bound to encounter more than a few potentially disruptive circumstances. To begin with, there is the fact that the training analysis is required of the candidate rather than its being voluntarily elected by him or her. Moreover, everyone concerned expects the training analysis to play a major part in the candidate's attainment of professional competence, security, and identity within one school of analytic thought. These facts alone tend to augment—not create—the candidate's idealizations, negative therapeutic reactions, defensive identifications, and rebellious holding the analyst at bay. In other respects, the analysis will be regarded as an imposition; another course requirement; a chance to show that one is a good, compliant boy or girl; an enforced infantilization, castration, or brainwashing; an opportunity to defeat the oedipal parent; or, most likely, some combination or layered arrangement of these views. On this account, it may be said that because training analysis is institutionalized, it is even more problematic than the ordinary clinical analysis.

Adding to these problems are those that arise from the opportunities available to both candidate and analyst to observe one another and on occasion to interact outside the consulting room. And then there is the gossip about the analyst that is often imparted to the candidate by fellow candidates, colleagues, and friends: Ostensibly a friendly gesture made to a manifestly passive recipient, this gossip is most usefully understood analytically as an intrusive, controlling, voyeuristically seductive and hostile piece of acting out by all concerned. The analysand may be expected to use both the inevitable observations of the analysts in public and the gossipy information to rationalize transference fantasies and thereby make them all the more difficult to analyze. Here, as elsewhere, "reality" is being used in the transference defensively, seductively, and aggressively.

Additionally, in many instances publications and presentations by the training analyst are easily accessible. These, too, may be used by the candidate in a voyeuristically seductive and hostile manner and used, as well, as an intellectualized bulwark against frightening transference fantasies and reconstructed traumatic experiences. Of course, all of this "information" can also be used for some worthwhile reality testing (for example, the analyst's own life also contains problems), but that use never excludes problematic uses of whatever "knowledge" comes the analysand's way.

Into this part of the picture there also enters the relative status of the training analyst in the institute and in the world of analysis at large. Here there is not only much readily available and not easily avoidable information, but, as analysts hear from the couch, a good deal of misinformation as well. Among themselves, candidates often tend to compare the prominence and analytic conduct of their analysts, the lengths of their analyses, the intensity of their own joys and of their suffering during vacations and other periods of experiencing liberation and deprivation, their transferential loves and hates, and so forth. And often, as the training analyst hears all this and also remembers it from his or her own days as a candidate, it sounds as if the candidates are comparing fullness of breasts, lengths of penises, personal passion and lovability, grades on moral report cards, parental failures, nobility of suffering, and grace under pressure. The language, the metaphors, the attitudes seem loaded with infantile meaning. All of which is potential analytic material, to be sure, and so to be looked into empathically and carefully. But these contacts, revelations, distortions, and sometimes fabrications, which typically continue after termination of training analysis, are also bound to limit to some extent the type and degree of resolution of transference conflicts and defensive strategies. On this account, the end result may differ significantly from what is observed often enough in nontraining cases. These limiting circumstances cannot be ignored.

Training analysts, too, are subject to a variety of circumstances that act as pressures and temptations. For example, just about everyone at the institute seems to be looking over their shoulders and deciding how good they are. These observers may base their estimates of quality, often recklessly, on how insightful, responsible, clinically effective, or just plain attractive an analyst's candidates are or seem to be. They may also base these estimates on how long each training analyst's analyses last on the average, how warm each seems to be in public, and how highly rated as a teacher, a discussant, or analytic writer. Thus, training analysts swim in the same fishbowl as their candidates. Not only that, but like their candidates they are on display before an audience ever ready to make personal interpretations as well as professional judgments that can affect the training analyst's morale, general reputation, livelihood, and on occasion even friendships.

For present purposes, I need not go on enumerating circumstances that exert significant influences on the analytic relationship and process. I have been leading up to making a few main points about the understanding and handling of these circumstances, points I have already implied in my remarks on institute gossip and some other matters. My leading point in connection with influential circumstances is this: Everything in the analysis depends on the extent to which the training analyst keeps in focus the importance of developing psychoanalytic interpretations of what is brought up about these influential circumstances, and also of when and how it is brought up. It is generally agreed that it does not advance analysis simply or primarily to confirm or disconfirm claims to knowledge or to ignore the nature and force of the influential circumstances themselves. The analyst must develop interpretations of the candidate's unconsciously constructed, infantile perceptions of, wishful fantasies about, and defensive measures against these circumstances. As far as possible, the analyst approaches references to these circumstances as so much more manifest content. These references are material of the same order as the manifest dream. The training analysis depends on the analyst's never taking these circumstances simply or primarily at face value.

I am saying that everything depends on the importance the training analyst accords to that other reality, psychic reality. To put it more sharply, what is crucial is that the analyst understand that "external reality" is not even a psychoanalytic concept: For that reason I have avoided using the term, even though I recognize that words alone cannot be decisive in this respect. To the analyst, what is conventionally called external reality is something that can only be defined and understood *analytically,* that is, only after it has been worked out how the perceiver has processed it on many subjective levels and filtered it through dominant unconscious fantasies that have been organized in varied cognitive modes and in relation to varied psychosexual perspectives (Arlow, 1969a, b; see also chapter 13). What to the analyst is compelling, commonsensical external reality may not have that significance for the candidate, and vice versa. The reality that counts is the one that is developed through analysis. This respect for psychic reality is an essential component of the analytic attitude (Schafer, 1983).

Deferring for the moment consideration of the influence of countertransference, the crucial thing is that the training analyst believe in a relatively unthreatened way that, for the candidate, the training situation cannot fail to lend itself to family drama, fantasy, and reenactment: primal scenes; incestuous seductions, both heterosexual and homosexual; rapes, castrations, impregnations, and abortions; death wishes toward and from parents and siblings; enforced feedings, traumatic weanings, and starvation; constipation, incontinence, and enemas; abrupt abandonment and blissful mergings and reunions; imprisonment, slavery, torture, and rescue. You name it. The analysis of this material should be at the heart of training analysis. Seen in this light, the influential circumstances I have been discussing are not so much disruptive interferences as they are analytic opportunities, akin to those offered by dreams, daydreams, symptoms, and other such, to develop the analysis in depth.

It does help, however, to view this same material in another, darker light, for often it is not easily reachable, and once reached, not easily or fully analyzable. On this point, some analysts would disagree. They seem to believe that, because everything is open to analysis in principle, everything can be elicited and worked through in practice. They believe that if something can be talked about, it can be analyzed in a worked-through fashion. In some of his more heated polemical moments, Merton Gill (1982) seems to be such an analyst. So are all those training analysts who are altogether casual about their analytic incognitos. I am among those who reject this belief and the obtrusive conduct it can lead to. I believe, for example, that difficulties in analysis may become insurmountable when the stimulus of circumstance is unusually strong or prolonged, for then there is, in the analysand's psychic reality, so much seduction, hostility, and deprivation in the analytic relationship and, as a consequence, so much reason to cling to primitive defensive strategies, that even the most patient and clever interpretive work makes no evident headway against a candidate's transference and defensive moves.

A case in point are those situations that involve a candidate's becoming a favored analytic son or daughter or the persecuted victim of someone in analytic power; the candidate's being forced by confrontational tactics to deal with major and painful issues prematurely;

the candidate's being required to modify important career and family plans at critical points in his or her life cycle in order to be able to meet all the demands and pay all the costs of analytic education; and the candidate's being bound by training requirements to stay in analysis beyond the time when the analysis is ready to come to what seems, to analyst and analysand alike, its natural end. Factors such as these may so recapitulate oedipal victories and defeats and other contexts of overstimulation, deprivation, despair, and psychic pain that the candidate cannot be counted on, even with help, to draw and maintain necessary distinctions between the here and now and the there and then. It is generally recognized that excessive and unrelieved countertransference is dangerous to an analysis in large part because it renders unanalyzable many of the basic issues touched on within that analysis and perhaps within any subsequent analysis. I argue that that line of thought applies equally to any other strong and unrelieved stimulating or pressuring set of circumstances surrounding and invading an analysis. Interpretation has its limits.

In addition to overconfidence in the power of interpretation, a second attitude may lead to counterproductive effects on the training analysis. There are candidates who are subject to analysis in which the analyst uses egalitarianism in its most manifest and superficial sense as an argument in favor of a variety of conventionally free and open contacts and interactions, both in and out of the treatment room. In these instances, infantile wishes, fears, and defensive strategies may be so stimulated and seemingly gratified or confirmed in their nature by this analytic forwardness that their deeper aspects become sealed off from interpretation and working through. These candidates will emerge from training not having defined some fundamental, unconsciously maintained fantasies and not having experienced and mastered some essential conflictual issues. Consequently, they will be inadequately prepared to deal with these issues effectively when they arise in the analyses they conduct in their subsequent independent careers. Sometimes this egalitarianism is rationalized as a way of not infantilizing, enslaving, abandoning, or castrating the candidate. Ultimately, however, this way of thinking is nonanalytic or even antianalytic in principle, practice, and consequence, in that it conveys an analytically naïve faith in the power of conventionalized social conduct. That faith latently encourages further repression of infantile desire, fantasy, and conflict and further minimization of psychic reality; also, it often encourages certain forms of dramatic acting out. And countertransferentially, it may manifest some sadistic seductiveness that plays on the candidate's masochistic tendencies at the same time as it sugarcoats them.

THE TRAINING ANALYST'S COUNTERTRANSFERENCES

It is not the candidate alone who is subject to situationally intensified turbulence in psychic reality. Like the candidate's, the training analyst's turbulence, though it is not created by the circumstances of the training situation, may be very much intensified by it. In response to this intensification, the analyst may use defensive strategies and construct conflictual perceptions and fantasies of the same general sort as the candidate does. For instance, the analyst may develop his or her transferences to the figures who make up the institute, including all the candidates and not just the one on the couch; these transferences will then surely enter into or reinforce the training analyst's countertransferences to the candidate of the moment. Analysts have, however, learned to live with these countertransferences—at least, to try to live with them by interpreting their disruptiveness so as to provide information about the analysand: what is being enacted and why and so forth.

At their best, analysts are also alert to their characterological countertransferences, those that Annie Reich (1951) discussed so helpfully in her basic paper on countertransference. Characterological countertransferences originate in the dynamics that led in the first place to a person's having chosen the career of therapist and analyst. These dynamics continue to play a part in the analyst's relations with analysands. To varying degrees, these countertransferences have voyeuristic, reparative, sadomasochistic, paranoid, perfectionistic, and other such features. They can add significantly to the analyst's motivation, stamina, steadfastness, perceptiveness, empathy, range of skill, and personal style of working. But at the same time, in that they are still rooted in their infantile conflictual soil, they can make of every one of these motivations a jungle of confusion and obstruction. Therefore these characterological countertransferences are mixed blessings or, at best, fortunate falls from the grace of neutrality.

Well-analyzed and thoughtful analysts get to know a fair amount about those characterological countertransferences during their own training analyses. They get to know a lot more about them subsequently in the course of doing independent analytic work, provided that they pay open-minded attention not only to what analysands have to say about their experience of being analyzed by them but also to what they themselves experience in doing analysis. Doing analysis is never entirely free from the influence of the dynamics that led to this career choice. No "work ego" is altogether autonomous, nor should we hope for anything different, for in this respect the nuclear dynamics of talent and trouble are the same. As Freud (1937b) noted in

"Analysis Terminable and Interminable," however much our own analysis may help master the seriously deleterious consequences of these nuclear dynamics, the vulnerabilities linger on and with them the defensive measures they have necessitated, albeit in less extreme forms. Much earlier (1913), Freud had emphasized the resistances that are put up by those already working as therapists and dealing with the resistances of their own patients.

As I mentioned, during a training analysis conducted in the stressful and transference-laden circumstances of institutional training, the process can be said to be institutionalized from the first. In the training analyst, the institutional setting may stimulate characterological countertransference continuously. Consequently, in order to stay on top of things, the training analyst must keep on trying to take account of his or her transferences to figures in the local analytic world, all the other analysts in his or her pantheon, and all the protagonists in the theoretical and technical controversies in the field of analysis. Through transference, the institute itself becomes a good but also bad family and home. The training analyst functions in a social system that lends itself to the enactment of every kind of family drama, and its being drama in a fishbowl means that it all takes place at very close quarters and under the pressure of the incestuous, voyeuristic, exhibitionistic, and hostile tendencies and conflicts of all concerned. It might be called analytic theater in the round.

Within that social system, the training analyst will feel that the ranks of the anointed do not include some who are deserving or who are friends who take their exclusion badly, while these same ranks do include others who are thought to be unfit, unlikable, or just too different to be *sympatico.* The system or family will seem to distribute power and recognition unevenly and sometimes capriciously. It will have its share of pretense, pretentiousness, overweaning ambition, factionalism, toadies, and ostracized heretics, mavericks, and incompetents. In these respects and contrary to our hopes and perhaps our illusions, the world of the institute proves to be not all that different from the so-called real world.

In a characterologically based response to all these impressions, involvements, and perhaps disappointments and resulting bitterness, the training analyst may overemphasize some factors in each training case and minimize others. To give one set of examples—one that is especially important for the vitality of our field—I mention that the training analyst may overreact to originality, seeing it simply as dissident acting out of oedipal rebellion and parricide or as incorrigibility based on pathological narcissism or defective ego functioning. That same training analyst will take too readily and too generously to the conforming candidate who makes no waves and so neither adds to the analyst's professional and personal insecurity nor rocks the institutional boat.

A rigidly conforming candidate is defending by remaining consciously blind to the overcharged and often contradictory circumstances in which training takes place. In this regard, the candidate's defending may also amount to being on "good behavior" in order to get through and out of training, much as if he or she were serving a sentence. In this there may be much splitting of transference as well as defensive idealizing of, and surreptitiously identifying with, the analyst; thereby the candidate limits him- or herself to presenting only a "false self" for analysis. Exceptionally difficult to eliminate through analysis are the unconscious fantasies on which this defensive strategy is based. This problem will be all the harder when these fantasies seem to be amply supported by observations of such questionable administrative and clinical practices in the institute as "convoying" or its persecutory opposite. For purposes of the training analysis, it becomes especially important, through appropriate interpretation, to help free the candidate's sense of reality with regard to the practices that prevail in the institute and also to liberate his or her capacity for expressiveness and adaptive action (not to be confused with passive acquiescence) within this system.

There is a notable alternative to quashing originality and perceptiveness while rewarding conformity. In the name of empathy, antiauthoritarianism, and the fostering of creative self-expression, the analyst may be so keen on originality that, out of countertransference, he or she encourages the displacement of every kind of negative transference onto the institute or the field of analysis generally. This evasion is accomplished by not analyzing what it means to the candidate to be using originality as a way of warding off analysis itself, when that is the case. In question here is analysis of the student's ambivalent, envious, and parricidal transferences, for in the guise of independence of mind, the candidate may act out the role of serving as his or her own womb, breast, paternal phallus, and fount of analytic wisdom. This is the role of the one-person tradition, the child prodigy, and, in time, perhaps the crucified savior. Much more than the assertion of talent and originality will have entered into the candidate's conduct.

It is worth emphasizing that this sort of self-generative fantasy of the talented may be analyzed to death or counterproductively fostered by neglectful handling. Of more general significance, however, is the question of how institutionally reinforced characterological countertransferences inevitably color the analyst's responses to manifestations of independence of mind. These high-spirited manifestations, which in the long run can be fostered in the analysand only by effective analytic work, may along the way develop into barriers to further analysis. Their becoming barriers may be due simply to the candidate's defensive use of them, but it may result from the training analyst's countertransferences to content that bears on conformity, individuation, or group belongingness; most likely, it is due to some complex combination of all these factors.

Who is to say that in the end a certain amount of limit-setting on analysis by the analysand should not be tolerated and respected? Do analysts know that much about what in the long run makes for a good-enough analyst or enhances a creative one? Can analysts generalize across all candidates in these respects? Can they even hope to eliminate completely all barriers and blindness? While there is no substitute for sustained analytic attentiveness, the line between attentiveness and hypervigilant and perfectionistic coercion is fuzzy and shifts from one case to the next. Certainly, institutionally reinforced characterological countertransferences can get in the way of tolerating this ambiguity, in that they exert a pressure on the analyst to try to turn out what looks unquestionably like a "finished product."

It has been much discussed whether training analysis should have as its general goal producing a "finished product," that is, a recognizable, acceptable, and safe member of the analytic community that is providing the training. In my view, it goes against the basic conception of psychoanalysis for the analyst to have any such analytic goal. Here I leave aside questions pertaining to the carefulness and correctness of the process by which candidates are selected. Thereafter, however, the best way to turn out a good-enough analyst in each case is simply to do the best clinical analysis we can; the rest should be left up to the candidate and the remainder of the training. In other words, the best way to show concern as an analyst and the best way to discharge our responsibility to the discipline of psychoanalysis to which we have committed ourselves is to reject the unanalytic role of watchdog, enforcer, or cautionary moralist; for in this role the analyst becomes at one and the same time a seducer and a superego figure.

Certainly it would strain analytic credulity to think that the candidate's departing significantly from the analytic community's prevailing orientation and ethics will never come up for analysis in the form of conflictual experience within the transference and erratic action outside it. Even so, successful analysis of this deviationism requires that the training analyst have a flexible conception of what is required for an analyst to have "the right stuff"; otherwise, he or she shows a lack of confidence in analysis itself and in the candidate's future and independent use of the analytic experience.

Contrasts to my position are, however, plentiful. To give only one example: In Edith Weigert's (1955) excellent paper on the problems of training analysis, after wisely and frankly discussing numerous countertransference problems, she ended with what I regard as a thinly veiled countertransferential sermon on the exemplary figure the training analysis should produce. The contrasting position I advocate is neither easy to arrive at nor simple to maintain consistently, but I do recommend it as an ideal. It is, however, an ideal way of working analytically, not some idealized end result.

I believe that all the countertransferential difficulties I have been mentioning have been steadily increasing as a result of the rapid increase in the number and variety of schools of thought on analytic theory and technique. It seems that attitudes toward rigorousness, constraint, tradition, and sometimes even integrity have become both more controversial and more casual among those entering training. And it seems to be true, too, among prospective patients. Consequently, candidates are more likely than ever before to view as so many manifestations of empathic failure, tyrannical rigidity, elitism, and repressiveness the devoted efforts their elders make to maintain the conventional rigorous standards of the past and to do so in the customary way. Today, conventional respect for continuity of ideals and practice is often regarded as uncritical submission to "the establishment" or to "the medical model." Candidates may even minimize or block reading the analytic literature during training. And candidates' increased awareness of countertransference as a discussable issue may be used to question disturbing interpretations of transference.

Thoughtful training analysts, struggling to adapt their old bearings to changing times and mores, need not be less secure analytically on this account, for being provisional rather than certain is consistent with these times. But if they are more insecure, they are more likely to react countertransferentially to the new ambiguities of transference, defense, and acting out, and also to those ambiguities having to do with becoming one's own person as a result of effective analysis.

To these considerations it might be retorted that it has ever been thus; many members of each older generation are disheartened and perhaps offended by what they see as the waywardness of the young. I will, however, venture to mention an alternative view: The rate of change has accelerated in recent years, and traditional modes of quality control have become a problematic of psychoanalysis rather than an ostensible given. I say "ostensible" because I believe that some amount of generation gap in values and practices is inevitable and that, except for the denials and repressions of candidates and the unconvincing official proclamations of unity and stability by the psychoanalytic bureaucracy, nothing has ever been totally "given" in psychoanalysis.

I further believe that the accelerated rate of change in values and practices has increased the countertransference hazards facing training analysts. The undecidability of many technical and interpretive issues has become a more prominent circumstance of analytic work (Schafer, 1985a). For this reason, it has become useful to explore the fantasy meaning to the analysand of the undecidability of important analytic issues. In this connection, countertransference may show itself in the analyst's being either wishy-washy or inflexible or alternating between the two. When the analyst is too indecisive or too quickly comes to traditional conclusions, the candidate will not be initiated adequately into an essential segment of contemporary psychoanalytic work, namely, dealing consistently with qualitative and quantitative ambiguity in clinical, theoretical, and professional matters of great moment. In this area of concern, however, there is not likely to be a general consensus among training analysts and certainly not among candidates.

Before closing, I want to take up one more important aspect of countertransference. Mention of this factor is required by my discussion of heterogeneity in the field of psychoanalysis. It is arguable that increased psychoanalytic tolerance of heterogeneity has resulted in a relative shift of emphasis away from superego analysis and toward pre-superego analysis or analysis of forestages of the superego (for example, introject experiences stemming from early object relations and also disturbances in the formation of self and object constancy). Consequently, the tolerant training analyst, being less prone to the countertransference of overexactingness, a countertransference that can be experienced in a well-defended way by the modern candidate only as accusatory, punitive, and untimely, is not likely to develop a sustained focus on oedipal rebelliousness and oedipal guilt in the transference.

There is, however, an upside to this change. By being more open to the analysand's archaic types and levels of experiencing and functioning, the analyst is less likely to pressure the candidate into presenting an ordinary oedipal self that is in some crucial respect a false self. It will be a false self not because there is nothing oedipal there to analyze, but because too much is then left out of the analysis that pertains to atemporal, dyadic, intensely physical experiences of being shattered, empty, abandoned, persecuted, depressed, paranoid, anxious, and traumatically overstimulated. The new openness broadens the scope of the individual training analysis to include more of the candidate's preoedipal madness. True, this gain in breadth may for its part be at the cost of adequate superego analysis, and with it, of course, of oedipal issues and all that is associated with them. I am inclined to think that this is the price paid for the sensitive aspects of the work of Kohut (1984) and his followers.

Taking these changes into account, we may go on to specify an "equidistance" in the analyst's neutrality other than the equidistance from id, ego, and superego that has been recommended traditionally. Now we must aim to be equidistant from oedipal and preoedipal issues. It is not that analysts have neglected to position themselves that way; rather, it is a matter of emphasizing explicitly another facet of neutrality.

In some cases it may be inevitable that getting deeply into the preoedipal will slant the emphasis mostly away from the oedipal. In my view, the language and the narrative organization of the entire analysis and the corresponding shape of the analytic relationship may not be able to include full and equal representation of both phases of development. To repeat a point that cannot be overemphasized: Not everything interpretable in principle can be effectively worked through in practice. Where it seems that a choice must be made, I believe that, as a rule, it is desirable to go for the more archaic and to entrust beneficial modification and future growth of useful superego functioning to the analysand's strengthened preoedipal functioning or "ego," which is, anyway, the foundation for adequate superego functioning. It should be borne in mind in this connection that, throughout the history of psychoanalysis, many analysts have had to seek second or sometimes third analyses to deal with all that has been left out of a first, "correct" Freudian analysis biased toward oedipal and superego issues. But, as with so many other analytic issues, I cannot simply assert that the criteria for decisions of this type are very clear or easily generalizable across cases. The problem of how to work through important issues adequately on all levels of development is easier to mention than to manage with complete confidence.

In these last remarks, I have not wandered as far from countertransference as it might seem. Suppose, now, that the training analysis is centering on preoedipal issues. Then such concepts as the analyst as a new object, the holding environment, the depressive position, and the like seem inevitably to recommend themselves. In practice, the consequence is that all the doors open wider to disruptive experiences and expressions of countertransference, whereupon the training analyst may make poorly rationalized, ad hoc, premature departures from his or her own version of the traditional technical baseline.

Many analysts seem to have decided that they must relate more openly and variously to their analysands than even the most liberal published versions of the tradition seem to allow. They believe that a method that is limited almost totally to interpretation and its judiciously managed preliminaries—listening, questioning, confronting, and clarifying—is inadequately responsive to all the clinical manifestations of early developmental damage, arrest, and tension; rather, it has become something of an obstruction to fundamental analysis (see, for example, Loewald, 1960). Their experience seems to tell them that their analysands do not develop confidence that the analyst is fully and empathically there for them, available for whatever nutriment is required in psychic reality: merging, holding, mutual incorporation, as well as identification. Not through dramatic enactments but through subtle manifestations of presence, analysts can foster that confidence and enable the hampered and overwrought analysand to tolerate, and get to understand analytically, early infantile terror, rage, paranoia, depression, withdrawal, and hypochondriasis. Failing that sort of thoroughness on the part of the analyst, the analysis may become a pseudoanalysis in which the analysand plays the part of a good blind boy or a good blind girl. Consequently, that candidate's future analytic patients may well not get at, or be helped to get beyond, their own preoedipal wastelands. And so on down through the generations.

On the other hand, as I have already indicated, analysts who work with greater presence are exposed to their own increased emotionality and disruptive countertransferences. Then they may too readily and rigidly play the role of good mother or father, or soother and rescuer, and neglect the more traditional, formalized, relatively impersonal approaches to castration anxiety, penis envy, womb and breast envy, sadomasochistic anality, and supergo savagery; instead, these analysts may favor sentimentalized and externalized rapprochements and good cheer. It is, I believe, quite a widespread characterological countertransference to want to improve on one's own parents and to do so as a way of all at once getting revenge on them, making reparation to them, and obtaining vicarious and belated gratification from them. It is not easy for analysts to maintain perspective on this countertransference when working responsively with preoedipal material, and it is here that characterological countertransferences may rule the day.

Controversies that have been going on for a long time in this more tolerant era of psychoanalysis may revolve not around hard evidence but around the pros and cons of radically different characterological countertransferences and the "clinical experience" they have shaped and which is now used as hard evidence. Perhaps that is one main reason why these controversies over technique do not seem to be decidable by theoretical argument, clinical example, and the rhetoric of panel discussions.

I feel that I am closing this discussion of training analysis belatedly, having wandered all over the map in spite of my efforts to maintain the interrelated foci of circumstance and countertransference. And yet I cannot escape the sense that I am closing too soon in that I have scarcely done justice to any of the major issues I have taken up and to alternative points of view. My story of training analysis is not the whole story, but I think it is one that should be told as I have told it.

CHAPTER 16

Psychoanalysis, Pseudoanalysis, and Psychotherapy

I believe the following: What is sometimes presented as Freudian psychoanalysis proves on close examination to have many of the features of eclectic psychotherapy. What is ostensibly psychoanalytic psychotherapy may prove to have many of the features of Freudian psychoanalysis. Some analysts doing psychotherapy get more analysis done, at least with certain patients, than other analysts do in carrying out conventional analyses. And some patients in psychotherapy get more analysis done, at least with certain therapists, than other patients get done in psychoanalysis proper; in this case it may be argued that that therapy deserves to be called psychoanalysis even if it is, to a purist, imprecise and incomplete. After all, how many analyses meet an ideal standard of purity and completeness?

There may be advantages, then, in treating the three therapeutic categories in this chapter's title as therapeutic approaches that differ in degree rather than kind. However, to focus on differences of degree does violate the assumption made by many or most analysts that the three are distinct categories. We encounter here some of the difficulties presented by *narratives of difference.* Typically, these narratives are developed in a manner that is decisive and perhaps even severely judgmental: "That's not analysis at all!" "That's wild analysis!" "It's merely psychotherapy!" and so forth. These narratives of difference are told in official presentations, such as in the "best" journals or the comments of their referees as well as at meetings and in informal shop talk. But they rest on the arbitrary assumption that all analysts would agree in specific instances; it is arbitrary in that actually it is analysts who are criticizing one another's work in just these terms. In the short run, the judgments that usually prevail are those that are voiced by analysts with the most power (by reputation or professional office). Additionally, these arbitrary narratives of difference discourage further thought, and that should be considered their most serious fault. Finally, these strict divisions and judgments seem to suggest that the necessary criteria are already clearly formulated and readily available, when actually, I believe, each judge may, if pressed on this score, encounter difficulty in laying out an adequate and persuasive supporting argument and then, explicitly or implicitly, may resort to the unsatisfactory pronouncement: "I know it when I see it!"—at which point the authoritarian impulse stands naked before us.

In order to approach the three "categories" as headings for stories of difference of degree, we must, it seems to me, begin with a general summary of an ideal standard for clinical psychoanalysis. Only then and in relation to this standard might we take up the others. To proceed in this manner is to develop a position in terms of comparisons rather than self-evident absolutes: "pseudo" as compared to what? and so on. It should not be expected, however, that this comparative approach will eliminate all difficulties with drawing sharp distinctions. We would, for example, still have to ask such questions as these: If wild analysis is a form of pseudoanalysis, how far can we go in making interpretations before being judged "wild" rather than being accepted as intuitive, or creative, or highly individual in style but still sound? Also: If insubstantial analysis is another form of pseudoanalysis, how accepting of a specific patient's limited capacity for change, such as that referred to by Freud (1937b) in "Analysis Terminable and Interminable," should we be before being classified as conducting an insubstantial analysis? Even to begin meditating on these questions will plunge us into some formidable problems in methodology and epistemology. My narratives of difference will venture that far, especially in connection with my contention that the extravagant promotion of short-term dynamic psychotherapy may be a form of pseudoanalysis: venture that far, not so much to attempt to arrive at compelling conclusions as to establish some of the groundwork for genuine and productive debate in this vexing area of clinical judgment.

PSYCHOANALYSIS

My list of general criteria for Freudian psychoanalysis begins with the steady fostering of a free-associative atmosphere. To foster this atmosphere the analyst must maintain a neutral, receptive, and interpretive stance. The analyst's primary focus of interpretation must remain on unconsciously devised defensive operations and enactments of transference and countertransference. Transference enactments are best taken up extensively and not hastily reduced to experiences and fantasies of early life; by "taken up extensively" I refer to full development in the here-and-now relationship, although I do not exclude the analysis of displaced transference enactments so long as these are not being used as substitutes for engagements in the here and now. Interpretation will be guided by the search for conflict and compromise formation under the umbrella of the principle of multiple function. The analyst will use the genetic and developmental approaches of psychoanalysis to strengthen the analysand's interest in a coherent, psychoanalytically meaningful history of her or his conflictual constructions of psychic reality in the past: all, however, as leading into a better grasp of the present. In the process, the analysand will develop more or less intense, complex, primitivized, and repetitive transference reactions to the analyst that will warrant the designation *transference neurosis* so long as it is not seriously contaminated and rigidly reinforced by the analyst's own countertransferences and so remains interpretable as being based on the analysand's self-expressive fantasies.

Analysts recognize that the analytic process is not defined simply by the analyst's interventions, for there are many noninterpretive elements in the analytic situation, such as being listened to attentively, nonjudgmentally, and empathically. Leo Stone (1961) has reviewed many of these noninterpretive factors. The analyst's theory of the therapeutic effects of analysis will, accordingly, take these noninterpretive elements into account. Also to be taken into account are the many noninterpretive elements inherent in interpretive activity itself: implications of attentive and concerned listening; concerns with tact, timing, and dosage; a willingness to participate as well as observe; and a readiness for empathic experience as well as deliberate reflection. All these elements convey a special kind of relatedness that itself may move the therapeutic process forward in ways both visible and, for the time being at least, invisible.

Further, analysts assume that the therapeutic process cannot be defined as analysis just on the basis of what they think, say, do, or intend—that is, by their methods and goals. Neither will they define an analysis just by the procedural arrangements of frequency and use of the couch, length of treatment, emphasis on the fundamental rule, maintenance of a relative incognito and abstinence so-called, and other frequently mentioned desiderata of analytic conduct. Nor will they define analysis just by what the person who has come for help calls it, wishes it to be, or believes it to be. After taking all of these factors into account—which we should—analysts go on to ascribe a crucial role to the kind of participation in the process that the patient is ready to develop: the changes that he or she is prepared to seek, undergo, and understand analytically, and the method she or he is prepared to tolerate and use. As I indicate soon in taking up pseudoanalysis, these questions of readiness apply to the analyst, too, though ordinarily not at all to the same degree as to the suffering but as yet unanalyzed patient.

In turning next to pseudoanalysis and then to psychotherapy, I am adding to the exposition of my general view of psychoanalysis.

PSEUDOANALYSIS: THE WILD AND THE INSUBSTANTIAL

I use the term *pseudoanalysis* to refer to a number of cases that share only one feature: They represent themselves as analysis in form and substance despite their either violating the principles of psychoanalysis in some fundamental way or giving only the appearance of being analysis. In the former group are the varieties of wild analysis; in the latter group, analyses that exist in form but not in active process. Both groups are not so rare as one might wish.

Wild Analysis

Wild analysis as a characterization of interpretive therapy makes sense only within the context of one or another system of psychoanalysis, for what is wild in one system may not seem to be so in another and vice versa (Schafer, 1985a). In this chapter, as my context is my version of contemporary Freudian analysis, I refer to wild analysis without further systematic contextualization (see also Schafer, 1985a).

The characterization *wild analysis* is usually reserved for the making of interpretations that are neither warranted by the material at hand nor invited by the analysand's basic, even if erratic, acceptance and use of the analytic method and the collaboration it calls for. Usually, the charge of wild analysis is made when the analyst rapidly makes deep interpretations of unconscious conflict or hastily engages in reductive reconstructions. In a general way, this kind of work seems to refer to the id so called. In my view, however, the designation *wild* should apply equally to superego- and ego-centered interpretations and reconstructions and also to relatively superficial issues and deep-lying issues. The crucial factor should be that the intervention is unwarranted by the evidence available and inappropriate to the patient's state of preparation for that kind of intervention. Accordingly, I divide wild interpretations into structural types—id, superego, and ego—even though I recognize that in practice none of these types is pure. Rather, I am referring to differences in emphasis and explicitness.

To begin with the most familiar: Wild id analysis is illustrated by hasty, ill-founded, tactless interpretations of kindness as simply a reaction formation against anal sadism, curiosity as primal scene voyeurism, and demandingness as an expression of exaggerated orality or of psychological emptiness. Similarly wild are mechanical interpretations of political radicalism as simply or mainly oedipal revolt, of a woman's feminism as simply or only an expression of penis envy, or a male feminist's beliefs as showing his self-castrating identification with penis-envious women.

Wild superego analysis is exemplified by hasty, ill-founded, inappropriate interpretations of unconscious guilt and need for punishment, of primitive object-related fantasies of damage or retribution (as superego precursors), and of the apparent absence of guilt as being due to defective superego development.

Wild ego analysis may take the form of too quickly and narrowly interpreting intrasystemic conflict, such as that between ambition and humility. It may simplistically make interpretation in terms of past and present interpersonal conflict only. It may accept representations of other people at face value and use them in interpretation, as if the analysand is bound to be a reliable informant. Often it is evident in discussions of ego autonomy, a conflictless sphere of the ego, and sublimation. In my opinion, many discussions of nonconflictual and nontransferential therapeutic alliance also qualify as wild ego analysis.

We must also recognize complex forms of wild analysis, such as early, overly specific, comprehensive, deterministic formulations of psychodynamics. These implicitly omniscient formulations cannot amount to much more than intimidating and indoctrinating the patient and perhaps additionally, irrationally supporting the analyst's confidence that he or she understands and is adequate to the occasion. The material with which analysts work cannot be shown to support this kind of intervention; it is intervention by formula or preconception, and it rides roughshod over the ambiguous and often unclearly interrelated phenomena of analysis. It also ignores the evidence that the same material can be interpreted in a number of ways, depending on one's school of thought and one's predilections within that school.

A special instance of interpreting wildly and by formula may often be observed in reports of time-limited dynamic therapy. At their best, these time-limited therapies do not pretend to be anything more than a limited form of applied psychoanalysis. Often enough, they can help reduce acute suffering, eliminate some symptoms, improve impaired functional efficiency, and make immediate life crises more manageable. In many cases changes of this sort are very helpful to the patient. But an analyst would have to insist that these therapies cannot provide an adequately rich account of how these beneficial changes have come about; nor can these therapies specify convincingly and in depth what, in each instance, these changes mean to the patient. Only on the basis of the general and specific methods and theories of psychoanalysis could we even begin to hope to provide that account. Even then, that account would have to remain tentative because the methods and theories require recognition that time-limited work eventuates in such a limited sample of phenomena that it cannot support decisive formulations. Even full analyses do not seem to provide data that are entirely adequate to explain their own effects: Witness disagreements among Freudian analysts on this score.

In narrational terms, the overexcited proponents of time-limited dynamic therapy have been using the master narratives of psychoanalysis to tell the story of an activity that does not meet the criteria of psychoanalysis that I just mentioned. As a crude analogy, it might be said that it is like telling a musical comedy as if it were grand opera, or perhaps that it is confusing fast food with a gourmet meal.

Analysts cannot accept the claims of Malan (1979), Davanloo (1978), and others that their short-term or sector therapies can bring about the worked-through insights and so-called structural changes that are distinctively psychoanalytic. However impressively stable and extensive the changes wrought by these therapies might seem, they cannot take precedence over the theory and methodology of psychoanalysis. If we accept this theory and methodology, we must assert that, in their inner makeup, changes wrought by short-term therapies cannot be the same as psychoanalytic changes; they can only resemble them superficially. Any other conclusion effectively junks psychoanalysis and its long and complex history. And so we might say that the ardent proponents of brief therapies are advocating not just wild clinical analysis but wild theoretical analysis: They make too free with theories and their histories and too free with the hard-earned methodology and interpretive resources of psychoanalysis. They lay claim to legitimacy and a respectful hearing on the basis of their seeming to deal adequately with transference and resistance and in this way to be meeting Freud's announced criteria for the conduct of psychoanalysis. However, their claim is fundamentally mistaken in that it does not meet the spirit of Freud's succinct (in my opinion, too succinct) definition of psychoanalysis, the spirit that can be recognized only in the context of *all* of Freud's writings about the psychoanalytic process and the psychoanalytic theory of human mental processes.

In order to remain consistent with the master narratives of psychoanalysis (true to its theory), we would have to speculate that the benefits brought about by time-limited therapy are based on some mixture of the following. Within limits, clarification of problems brings about significant relief and increased adaptability. Faltering defenses are buttressed by intellectualization. Wild analytic interpretation of basic conflict frightens the patient into a flight toward health or into a more obscure form of neurosis. Transferential, possibly masochistic submission to the dominating superego figure of the therapist leads to apparent cure. And so forth. Although speculative, these ideas conform to observations repeatedly made by analysts in the course of conducting the most careful and lengthy analyses. Patients are constantly, though mainly unconsciously, on the lookout for these alternatives to worked-through insight and change, and on the lookout, too, for opportunities to enact their core problems and their transferences rather than come to understand them and modify them.

I have gone into these methodological and epistemological aspects of the claims for time-limited therapy not to dismiss it from consideration, for as I have already asserted, that approach does have its clinical uses and occasions. Rather, I want to indicate that psychoanalysis is to be regarded as more than a specific, empirically focused technique. Psychoanalysis provides a systematic point of view on all clinical practices, even those of behavior therapy, so many of which have been promoted as superior alternatives to psychoanalysis. Whatever its internal variations, psychoanalysis is a well-established tradition, an organized basis for attempting to understand, a way of constructing the world it tells about through application of its master narratives and the storylines they generate. And it is also a way of reserving judgment on what appear to be phenomena it cannot incorporate. In all these ways psychoanalysis has laid claim to being a basic discipline.

In order to debate clinical matters rationally, instructively, and productively, we must have a systematic point of view. Such a viewpoint is an epistemological necessity. Without it, we can make only obvious or disguised pronouncements based on inadequate or irrelevant observation and personal power, and in the field of psychoanalysis we already have had far too much of these unhealthy practices. Emphasis on dramatized data and personal authority relies for its effectiveness on manipulating the audience's transferences. Freud said that one should never underestimate people's inner irresolution and their craving for authority, that is, their readiness for submissive transference. Analysts are not exempt from this generalization; if anything, the anxiety-arousing aspects of therapeutic work make us vulnerable to these transferential manipulations, thus the advantages of having been treated in depth ourselves. The therapist's transferences aside, however, we should not aspire to eliminate rhetorical persuasiveness from our debates, and we must not pretend to work with altogether unambiguous data. Consequently, it behooves us to develop our narratives as systematically and persuasively as possible. In this way, we can orient our audience both to the goals we are using our narratives techniques to reach and to what these goals require us to certify as significant facts, plausible arguments, and noteworthy results.

Once the system is in place, it takes precedence over new, apparently discrepant findings. If Freudian theory changes, it is because in its existing form it cannot meet the challenges raised by some new findings, no matter how much these challenges are redefined in terms of the theory itself. Even then, however, the theoretical changes that are made are designed to *repair* the theory rather than replace it; they bring the theory up to date, so to speak. For example, Freud's (1914b) reconsideration of the phenomenology of psychosis launched his new systematic account of narcissism in which the role of ego instincts began to give way to libidinal contributions to ego development. It was a change that was still recognizably part of the development of Freud's system of psychoanalysis. And in turn, that theoretical change played a part in Freud's (1923a) later revision and further development of ego psychology and his introduction of the structural point of view. Still, the fundamentals remained the same: drives, defenses, conflict, infantile sexuality and amnesia, primary and secondary process, unconscious mental processes, and so forth. Theory continued to take precedence: It shaped the "data" needed to assure the theory's value as well as to broaden, deepen, and articulate it further, and in some cases to help get rid of its unnecessary complications and glaring faults.

Insubstantial Analysis

Analysts are familiar with those would-be analysands who, though they lie on the couch five times a week and talk at length, hardly ever associate freely. Only occasionally do they hear the analyst's interventions as anything but criticism, exploitation, or guidance. And they seldom seem to accept the idea that thoughts, feelings, and behavior can be interpreted neutrally as having crucial, unconsciously conflictual libidinal and aggressive meanings. These are meanings that must be, on the one hand, traced back to the past and, on the other, shown to have entered into every significant, real or imagined interaction with the analyst. Only then will they be *analytic* meanings.

Given that these would-be analysands have the requisite intelligence and mental intactness for analysis, their unresponsiveness to analysis must be understood as a manifestation of a stand-pat strategy that is too powerful to be dealt with analytically. By standing pat, they are indicating that, unconsciously, the analysis and the prospect of personal change constitute too much of a danger situation for them. They are unprepared to tolerate the ambiguity, the open-endedness, and the plain distress of the free-associative atmosphere with both its progressive and its regressive pressures. Analysts say finally of those who take this position unyieldingly that they are unanalyzable.

Often it is these would-be analysands who break off the analysis; sometimes the analyst must do so. Sometimes, however, the analyst maintains the analytic format, correctly or incorrectly, in the belief that it gives much-needed support to a fragile personal integration. Such instances are likely to be static, insubstantial, pseudoanalytic relationships that may continue for many, many years. On the one hand, this static nature may be a manifestation of an unanalyzable, ambivalent, dependent transference, or perhaps of sugar-coated, exploitative, sadomasochistic collusions into which the analyst has entered. On the other hand, however, it may be a manifestation of the analyst's judiciously arrived-at understanding of the would-be analysand's primitive needs for support through frequent contact in an analytic format. Thus it is not easy to distinguish competent from incompetent procedure, though it is all too easy for third parties to become hypercritical despite their inadequate evidential base.

Other would-be analysands' unresponsiveness takes a form that is not blatant. Manifestly accommodating themselves to the analyst's need to go on as if doing analysis, they play at the part of analysand. Latently, however, their appearing to fall in with the analyst's interventions gets to be recognized as a means of warding the analyst off:

Ready compliance is usually an unconvincing response to the analyst's interventions.

The danger of successful analytic pretense becomes particularly great when the analyst departs from the reserved Freudian model and becomes overactive and personally obtrusive. I am referring to those analysts who insistently confront, clarify, and interpret, no matter what is considered: the transference, defensiveness, the patient's current life outside the analysis, the infantile past, or some combination of these. The overactive analyst believes that sooner or later this inevitably obtrusive way of working must be effective. There are many reasons why an analyst may hold this belief in the ultimate triumph of interpretation, among them narcissistic strivings for omnipotent mastery, guilty emphases on reparation, and intolerance of feelings of boredom or helplessness. Analysts with these problems may then rationalize overactivity on the basis of some sort of questionable theoretical and technical dogmatism, such as the centrality of early infantile experience and the patient's need for contact or "holding." It does not help these analysts make a strong case when they point out that the verbal content of their interventions seems to be of a conventional analytic sort and seems to be corroborated by the analysand's responses. A one-sided attempt at analysis does not qualify as a Freudian analytic dialogue. It is correctly regarded as a miscarriage of analysis, what I call one kind of pseudoanalysis.

Many or most analyses, of course, include periods that give the appearance of pseudoanalysis; these are periods during which the analysand implicitly draws a line on further insight and change or the analyst falls behind the analysand's progress. However, so long as they are no more than intermittent periods of analysis, they do not justify the designation "pseudoanalysis" or "insubstantial." But not all pseudoanalysis is ascribable to the analysand's analytic limitations. All too often it is the ill-equipped analyst who promotes pseudoanalysis by dealing inadequately with transference and its allied defensive measures. It may be that this analyst's emotional limitations require him or her to work at too great a distance from the emotional immediacy of the here-and-now transference relationship and situation. In these instances, the analytic pair will collude unconsciously to maintain the appearance that they are engaged in analysis.

Fuller discussions of the part played by analysands in developing insubstantial analysis can be found in the extensive literature on resistance; the part played by analysts, in the extensive literature on disruptive countertransference. Here I intend only to begin drawing the contrast between psychoanalysis and pseudoanalysis and to suggest that it is a topic that deserves careful reflection and investigation.

Before turning to psychotherapy as the third major designation, it would be well to juxtapose insubstantial and wild analysis, the subvarieties of pseudoanalysis. In many instances, insubstantial analysis may not be all that different from wild analysis. What the two may share is a disregard of the analysand's defensive operations. This disregard may be most evident in those instances when the analyst is busily interpreting or knowingly attempting to "break through" or defeat "resistance." It may still be the case that the patient is warding off these interpretations, too, doing so perhaps by superficial accommodation that the analyst fails to recognize. The analyst is being wild in that he or she is interpreting *at* an unprepared patient and not talking *to* a truly collaborative one. The problem may persist even after the analyst recognizes that the patients is only being accommodating and interprets *that* to the patient. As I said, these would-be analysands may have to hear almost everything in a fixed way, including these new interpretations of defensiveness, and thereby remain able to block dreaded insight and basic change.

As Freud (1910a) emphasized in his discussion of wild analysis and in many other places as well, someone may know something intellectually and yet not know it in the transforming way that is characteristic of analytic insight. Interpreting *at* an unprepared patient conveys analytic content that is dead and, most likely, deadening. Freud was saying that interpretation cannot do anything and everything. That this is so amounts to one more important reason why analysis is to be thought of as a matter of degree: The analyst always and necessarily finds out how far and in which ways each analysand will be able to use the best of interpretations (see Freud, 1937b).

PSYCHOTHERAPY

There seems to be no limit on the ways in which psychotherapy can be practiced. Even psychoanalytic psychotherapy—our present concern—comes in many flavors. We encounter in this respect a formidable obstacle to discussing psychoanalytic psychotherapy in relation to psychoanalysis. With so much variation, it makes no sense to set up a hypothetical or ideal norm. Such a norm can still be set up for Freudian analysis, as I have done earlier in this chapter, despite the variations in that sphere of practice.

As I indicated earlier, nothing necessarily stops the psychotherapist from working analytically and well. By this I mean that the psychotherapist can maintain a neutral, consistent, but unpressuring focus on transference and countertransference and defensive measures, both in the here and now and in relation to their origins and transformations over the course of a lifetime. And nothing necessarily and totally prevents the patient in this context from associating relatively freely; working on dreams, daydreams, transferences, and defenses; developing some elements of a transference neurosis; and developing some important insights on the basis of limited change and then changing further and perhaps profoundly. On this basis, and provided that they are not time-limited, the therapist and patient may get a good deal of analytic work done even when they meet twice a week and face-to-face. This effect is more likely to be achieved when the patient is someone who could be in analysis were it not for life circumstances that preclude that arrangement.

Such an effect is far less likely to be achieved when the patient will accept only a more structured and limited format despite the fact that life circumstances do not preclude a conventional Freudian analysis and despite the therapist's best efforts to resolve the difficulty through interpretation. In this instance, the patient's unyielding decision to limit the work, sometimes just by refusing to use the couch, is most likely to signify quite desperate defensiveness, possibly involving significant paranoid tendencies. In any case it will be based on anxiety, guilt, fragility, or rigidity, and most likely also based on environmentally supported patterns of gratification and protection that the patient wishes to keep hidden from the therapist's scrutiny. No one can say with confidence that such patients are ill-advised to set these limits on the therapy.

Now, suppose we take into account all the factors I have mentioned. Suppose that analysis is always a matter of degree, that much of what passes for analysis is pseudoanalysis, that some psychotherapy is very like analysis proper, and so forth: Why not just call any psychoanalytic psychotherapy *psychoanalysis?* Recognizing that psychoanalyses themselves vary in effectiveness, where could we draw the line between them and comparable psychotherapies? I believe that there are two major reasons for retaining the distinction between psychoanalysis and psychotherapy, even though many cases seem to fall in an ill-defined intermediate area.

First, the aggregate of Freudian theories requires that some such distinction be drawn. If most or all of the traditional conditions of psychoanalysis are not being met, it is unlikely that the therapy will achieve the altered and facilitative mode of functioning required of both participants. This altered mode of functioning has been described in various ways. One way of putting it is that the participants cannot achieve enough of the required, sustained shift toward a more dreamlike or primary process mode of functioning. At best, they will only sample this mode; at worst, they will simulate it by dint of much intellectualization and more or less wild analysis. Only to a limited degree will the analyst be able to establish a fluidly receptive and responsive mode of participation in which listening predominates. As for the patient, he or she will not have the frequent and regular opportunity, the safety, and the situational pressure that promote shifts toward those more primitive forms of self-expression that provide access to unconsciously persisting, infantile, conflictual material. Then the phenomena and the results of the process cannot be quite the same, and the problems of interpretation and working through cannot be identical. And if the same is true of some analyses, then it would be better to recognize a border zone or gray area between the two approaches than to collapse the distinction entirely. Better for what or for whom? Better for analysts who should be paying attention to the degrees of analysis achieved in their psychoanalyses proper, and on that basis better for all their current and future patients.

In this perspective, psychoanalytic psychotherapy might be characterized as another form of limited or incomplete analysis. It is limited or incomplete not just in the sense that, with respect to a hypothetical ideal, every analysis is, but because the design of the therapy must lead to different expectations of the process. I do not question that psychoanalytic therapy can be enormously helpful. What must be recognized is that any combination of reduced frequency and continuity; face-to-face work; the therapist's more active, discussionlike participation; and other departures from the traditional psychoanalytic format militate against the process being the same as traditional analysis.

From this point of view, I am critical of certain psychoanalytic psychotherapists for being overambitious. Out of too much therapeutic zeal and inadequate appreciation of the rationale of the psychoanalytic method, these psychotherapists decide—recklessly, I would say—to get as much conventional analytic work done as possible. I say "reckless" in that they do not take seriously the constraints imposed by departures from the traditional psychoanalytic format and its rationale. Instead, they freely and hurriedly make ostensibly analytic interpretations on the basis of whatever cues come up. Frequently they engage in interpretation of manifest dream or fantasy content, of incidental expressions of attitude by word or deed, of unprocessed reports of life historical experience, and of other such material. In these respects, they are behaving in the same way as the practitioner of wild time-limited therapy.

A more subtle but equally problematic form of wildness may be practiced by the psychotherapist who, on the basis of a diagnostic appraisal of severe ego weakness, recommends a face-to-face therapy rather than a psychoanalysis, and from then on presents the patient with an extremely reserved, noninterventionistic, pseudoanalytic posture. In so doing, this therapist may leave the patient to flounder unproductively and often quite painfully and self-destructively. It is as if this therapist (usually male, in my experience) has decided that he at least will behave "analytically" even though the patient cannot, reasoning that it is better for at least one of them to proceed "correctly" than for neither of them to do so. I would call this conduct wild in that it adopts an inappropriate analytic approach to a patient who cannot be prepared for it.

Decisions are not always easy to make in this respect. Certain psychotherapy patients seem to do best if they are left pretty much on their own. These patients tend to get paranoid or depressed if, as they experience it, they are invaded and demeaned by conventional therapeutic interventions.

Many instances of psychotherapy meet few, if any, of the criteria for psychoanalysis. In these cases, we should not even speak of psychoanalytic psychotherapy. An example is when the therapist deliberately and manifestly meets needs, such as those for advice, reassurance, relief of ignorance; introduces personalized comments; and explicitly accepts severe limits on exploration and disclosure. It is also the case when the patient cannot enter into the free-associative atmosphere and when the patient's conception of the entire process thoroughly excludes exploration and interpretation of psychic reality. If analysts are providing this form of therapy, they will still be guided by psychoanalytic considerations so far as possible; in such cases it follows only that the analysts practice supportive therapy, not that it is psychoanalytic therapy.

There is a second reason to maintain the distinction between analysis proper and psychoanalytic therapy. This reason concerns training and professional standards. If the distinction is abandoned, what is to stop someone who has undergone a limited form of psychoanalytic therapy from claiming to have been analyzed and to have met the requirements for analyzing others, often then using the couch, free association, and frequent sessions in the attempt? Those who deny the distinction would perhaps say, "What does it matter, as long as he or she has had an analytic experience?" Again, the Freudian analyst would be required to fall back on the aggregate of Freudian theories and say that, in all likelihood, the therapist is not optimally prepared to conduct full-scale analyses in the modern manner.

CONCLUDING REMARKS

In conclusion, I emphasize that the fundamental factor determining what is to be called analysis, pseudoanalysis, and psychoanalytic psychotherapy is the analyst's understanding: specifically, his or her understanding of the kind of dialogue that is being carried on in the consulting room and his or her understanding of the mutative effects and the limits of this dialogue. Often, perhaps typically, this understanding develops only over the course of the work. That this is so is entirely consistent with the set of general and specific theories of psychoanalysis, for psychoanalysis is the basic discipline of finding out in depth. Among other things, it is a way of finding out in each individual case what can be found out, what is being found out, what is beyond understanding and influence, and what, after all is said and done, must remain undecidable.

Not that "finding out" is merely a matter of common sense; rather, it is primarily a matter of adhering more or less systematically to the master narratives we subscribe to, as we show by following the storylines laid down by these master narratives. In practice, the tension is always between finding out in the empirical sense and looking for the factors that fit our narrative expertise; that is, between on the one hand uncovering, discovering, and recovering, and on the other hand constructing the interpretations that are appropriate to our methods and narrative preparedness.

CHAPTER 17

Narrating Psychotherapy

I. TALKING TO PATIENTS

Talking to patients is a resource that, in my observation, psychoanalytically oriented psychotherapists neither draw on as often nor employ as masterfully as they should. Of the many reasons for this limitation, I emphasize only one now—the psychotherapists have uncritically fashioned their therapeutic activity in terms of the so-called psychoanalytic model. According to this model, psychoanalysts limit themselves to making interpretations; otherwise, they remain as nondirective as possible. They neither instruct nor speak personally because they believe that instructing their patients will intensify their resistances by encouraging them to intellectualize and, further, that speaking personally or emotionally will contaminate the analysis of the transference. Those who rely on this model reveal an inexact understanding of the subtle and complex rhythms in a psychoanalyst's work: nondirectiveness and active curiosity, laissez-faire and forcefulness, neutrality and emotionality.

Yet even from this corrected model we might safely draw only one guideline: Psychotherapists will usually facilitate exploration mostly by listening thoughtfully and intervening mainly when they can impartially point out and perhaps interpret those expressions of major conflict that become clear in the conscious and preconscious communications they receive. Although I do not question the value of this guideline, I do want to stress that by honoring in this way the artificial and inappropriate psychoanalytic model, psychotherapists have not systematically considered the resource of talking to patients and, therefore, have not yet understood, tested, and mastered this technique.

In the following account of psychotherapeutic work, I describe and explain two major aspects of talking to patients: talking pedagogically and talking personally. Both are aimed at facilitating investigation and refining understanding. They are not, in my opinion, universally applicable. As I have found them especially useful when doing time-limited therapies, I refer mainly to those therapies, although I believe that my suggestions apply more broadly than that.

TALKING TO PATIENTS PEDAGOGICALLY

Psychotherapists never start from the beginning with any patient. They already know a great deal about all patients prior to acquiring any factual information about each one. They know a lot about the psychological development and existence of human beings of both sexes. Even in an opening statement the therapist could—though rarely would—impart to a patient all sorts of things about her or him. Yet therapists would not on that account necessarily be offering gratuitous remarks; that is, universals that, because they fit everybody, communicate nothing, however much they might impress the recipient.

For one thing, few people will know as much as psychotherapists do about these "universal" factors and their interrelationships; in this matter, most patients are as amateurs to professionals. Second, when patients are working within the realm of their greatest conflicts, they are hardly likely to maintain intact and consciously available the knowledge they do have; they cannot be expected to keep their trials and tribulations consistently in perspective. Third, we must grant that the fact that something is believed to be universal does not render it insignificant; for example, it is universal, relevant, and significant that all people need oxygen to live and that all adults were once children, and it may be very much to the point to emphasize these propositions in certain therapeutic or other contexts. And, finally, we know that, to the extent that they are neurotic, patients are locked into static existential positions as a result of their having closed off large portions of their world of subjective experience. On this account they are always decidedly ambivalent about reducing their emotional hardships; they see that change as requiring them to modify their valuations and their categories of understanding and to resume, after so long a time, the personal development they have viewed as so dangerous. The business of psychotherapists is to help patients understand and master their chronic fears of pleasure, change, and development, and their preferred ways of coping with these fears, in order to live in subjective and objective worlds more open but not as unstable than those they have settled for. Incidentally, these few points about knowledge and change convey some of the insights available to psychotherapists before beginning therapy with any patient.

Psychotherapeutic knowledge of the patient is both general and specific. *General* knowledge includes:

1. The *complexity* of human problems: the place in these problems of "mixed feelings" and multiple perspectives, especially with respect to the psychotherapy itself.

2. The *continuity* of these problems: the idea that one repeats them throughout one's life, including in psychotherapy, however consciously painful they may be.

3. Their *coherence:* the usual relationships among problematic situations, experiences, and actions that the patient is likely to isolate from each other in her thinking.

4. The *significance of fantasies,* both fearful and wishful, mostly unconscious in their archaic and most threatening aspects, and usually sexual or aggressive, or both, and simultaneously self-directed and other-directed.

5. The *significance of defense,* especially patients' readiness to overestimate the extent to which independent conscious reasoning about their major psychological problems can be consistently objective and influential.

Specific pretherapeutic knowledge includes the various problematic modes of responding emotionally that are regularly associated with certain types of events or certain periods of life. On the basis of this knowledge, psychotherapists are able to say a good deal about any past or present absence or extremeness of these modes of action or reaction. In those common instances, they are far from being limited to puzzlement and the asking of questions. Therapists have knowledge of: various forms of desire, frustration, fear, aspiration, and rage that occur regularly during specific phases and typical circumstances of development; the pervasive importance of self-esteem, anxiety, and guilt; inescapable fears of loss and the prevalence of strangulated grief; and the many developmental conflicts surrounding the questions of masculine versus feminine, passive versus active, and success versus failure—whatever these words are understood to mean in specific cases and whatever the master psychoanalytic narratives they employ in their work.

I cannot overemphasize that in doing brief exploratory psychotherapy, therapists are working at a decided disadvantage—as are the patients—because on the one hand the patients are usually relatively unprepared for psychotherapy, while on the other hand only a short time and a limited number of visits are available in which to achieve any insight and consolidate any change. It is important that psychotherapists not be pressured by these facts into acting hurriedly—such as engaging in wild analysis to "get results." Nevertheless, it may be argued that under the circumstances, and *always following the narrative leads patients provide,* therapists can offer their patients some helpful instruction in the work to be done. By offering instruction, I do not mean delivering an orientation lecture; nor do I mean producing a set of demonstrations. Rather, I mean leading patients to appreciate those vantage points most likely to be useful in considering the problems they present. Their "instruction" can extend a patient's sense of relevance, grasp of the kinds of questions that must be asked about personal problems, and access to the kinds of information it will take to answer these questions productively.

Let me put it another way: Must patients in brief psychotherapy discover for themselves everything about the conduct of their own treatments? Must they shape every aspect of the work? Will their own sense of autonomy and their own conflict-revealing way of shaping the treatment still not have adequate scope even after their psychotherapists have offered their pedagogic efforts? I am confident that their problems will emerge with some clarity, especially in the form of engaging in defensive operations and enacting transference, so long as psychotherapists remain genuinely receptive to these responses. We may also expect that patients will feel no disrespect in these pedagogic efforts beyond what they would inevitably feel in connection with any of their therapists' actions, such as silences, questions, and authoritative pronouncements.

Consider, too, that effective exploration requires a framework of security based on both a working relationship with a nonjudgmental psychotherapist and some grasp of the nature of the work to be done. The patient never feels more alone than at the beginning of psychotherapy and is never more in need of some kind of bridge to the therapist in order to stop perseveratively defending against the dangers of self-exploration in the presence of an enigmatic stranger. The psychotherapist's imparting some general and specific knowledge about the patient, sharing some insights, and doing so in a way that can be genuinely empathic: These are means of both educating the patient and securing his or her position within the therapy.

Consequently, these efforts may help launch a brief psychotherapy auspiciously. It may be only on this basis that patients who initially are shy, guarded, doubt-ridden, or otherwise "shut in" or "bogged down" will be able to begin the work productively.

Each of these insights is an introduction to understanding rather than a well-developed understanding. Before it can be very useful, it will have to be detailed and qualified in terms of subjective experience and overt behavior, both in the past and in the present.

A representative list of these insights: "It's frustrating to be always looking after a lot of younger brothers and sisters." "A defeat like that is bound to be depressing." "A girl can't be indifferent to her parents' getting divorced." "It's the kind of guilt that you'd never want to admit to yourself." "People often find it disturbing to get sexually excited beyond a certain point and so they deny that they are excited at all—even to themselves." "You couldn't have always despised your father." "If you got that depressed over it, you could have been quite angry but unable to face that fact." "There's probably some connection between your guardedness with me and your general mistrust of people." "Your mother sounds like the kind of woman who would burden her children with the feeling that they have to protect her mental stability or else feel terribly guilty." "Your beginning to menstruate must have been filled with meaning for you."

In one way, statements of this sort say a good deal. They may even be so threatening to the patient that, in particular cases, psychotherapists will be well advised to refrain from speaking out in this manner, at least for a long time. And yet they may still be characterized as introductory, for the psychotherapist is not saying flatly that they apply to the patient or, insofar as they do, just *how* they apply in his or her case—how intensely, predominantly, conflictually, consciously, or consequentially, with respect to specific situations. In our role as psychotherapist, we think about such things while listening; in saying them aloud, we are literally thinking aloud. And yet thinking aloud is not the same as presciently saying "You are thus and so"; "This means thus and so"; "The important connection is this one"; "The crucial context in your past is that one."

At this point, the following question might be raised: What happens when a patient—say, a female—says that this imparted information does not apply to her? In other words, what if she will not be instructed? The answer, simply, is that the therapist—say, another female—stands her ground, the ground she truly believes she knows on the basis of her training, experience, general understanding, and, most important, her immediate self-awareness. If nothing else, she does know what she thinks, even if it is only that she is confused and does not know what to think. In standing her ground, she does not, of course, twist her patient's arm for a confession. But in some useful way she might say that she finds the patient's disclaimer surprising, and she might surmise that perhaps the patient has some need to deny to the therapist and even to herself that she feels a certain way or has a certain expectation or aspiration. Alternatively, the therapist might say there must be some other factors peculiar to the patient's situation that would help account for her being different in this respect. Or she might say a number of other things to continue the dialogue, or she might just wait silently while the patient continues to resonate to her initial remarks. No matter whether the patient agrees, disagrees, elaborates, disgresses, or flounders in uncertainty, it is likely that her reaction can be construed in a way that further defines the best questions and answers for this treatment. And it is always possible that the patient will go on to bring out another, perhaps altogether unsuspected factor that becomes the one to work on. This factor will be a welcome correction of the psychotherapist's surmise. I must emphasize in this connection that there is all the difference in the world between thinking aloud and being a know-it-all. Actually, the know-it-all's insecurity, vanity, and impatience will preclude the development of any sustained and deeply felt therapeutic dialogue. As in so many other connections, a respectful, collaborative attitude makes many difficult things possible.

In effect, I am describing one version of an approach recommended by Anna Freud (1936) in a discussion of child analysis. She suggested that the child analyst, not having the free associations of adult analysts to work with, looks for the distortion or absence of the expected affective responses as equivalent material on which to base his or her interpretations. The brief psychotherapist must adapt to a similar limitation in a similar way.

I have mentioned that taking this approach entails risks. The chief risk, of course, is that of encouraging patients to intellectualize. Additionally, therapists have to worry about stimulating a general intensification of the frightened patients' defensiveness through forewarning them of what is yet to come as well as seeming to demand tacitly that it *must* come if the patients are to prove themselves "good patients." Further, there is the risk of the therapists' imposing their thoughts on the patients or blocking or muddying the spontaneous development of their material. We must also consider a seduction to collaboration, a seduction that may erotize the work and obscure the patients' hostile reactions to it. And then there is the risk of intensifying the patients' idealizations of the psychotherapist as omniscient. All these risks endanger the prospects of the patient's understanding and later acting on what often proves to be indicated—the need for a more intensive and extended psychotherapy.

Earlier I mentioned that thinking aloud serves both as a supportive personal bridge and an illuminating pedagogic introduction or guide to exploratory psychotherapy. But there are other sides to thinking aloud that may advance the therapeutic work. For example, it conveys an unambiguous offer to share the work of exploration, and it establishes a suitably provisional or tentative mood for the therapy. Far from being consigned to the role of a passive object by psychotherapists eliciting information from them and then directing statements at them, patients are invited to join the therapist in discovering and framing the statements that might make a therapeutic difference to them. In this there is something that counteracts or exposes defensive passivity, ingratiating compliance, and extravagant idealization; there is also something in it that tends to make future, more ambitious therapeutic efforts increasingly understandable and acceptable to them.

And, with regard to seduction, I would ask whether it is more than the limited seduction Freud (1913, especially pp. 139–141) recommended when he advised building a positive working transference before attempting very much in the way of definite interpretation. Although it is true that a psychoanalysis, unlike a brief therapy, provides the time and opportunity to analyze the erotic overtones of this seduction, I do not think that psychoanalysts usually spend much time on this part of the work; it is so much more urgent, fruitful, and time-consuming to attempt to analyze the inevitable and basic infantile erotic transference and the defenses against it, factors that remain influential up to the very end of the psychoanalysis. Consequently, we should be careful not to exaggerate the risk to brief psychotherapy of a patient's reacting, probably unconsciously, with some erotic excitement to the invitation to therapeutic collaboration.

In offering these introductory insights, psychotherapists manifest both their expertise and their ignorance. They need not touch their fingertips, gaze at the ceiling, and ostentatiously muse aloud, seminar-style. They should not gun down their patients psychologically with rapid-fire, decisive interpretations; the offers they make should be offers than can be refused. As a rule they will avoid extended clarifications of their and the patient's roles in the therapy; instead, they will mainly wait for the anxious questions and disrupted communication that will give them a chance to demonstrate in action, through their steadfastness and curiosity and preliminary understanding, what it is to work with a psychotherapist and how the roles of the participants are as much the preoccupation of therapy as they are its framework. And, finally, they will not engage in those hasty, indiscriminate, presumptuous, "soupy," and frightened attempts to be empathic that some psychotherapists, especially novices, make with the hope of achieving quick, forceful, and comfortable therapeutic relationships. A solid therapeutic relationship is hard to develop and is arrived at in unanticipated ways; its goodwill can never be altogether counted on. It certainly cannot be described as the psychotherapist's being steadily and comfortably at one with the patient; tensions and lapses of contact are bound to occur. I return briefly to the topic of empathy in the next section.

The point of emphasis in any psychotherapy is the importance of patients' developing some skill in conducting their own continuing investigations of their lives and, through learning and identification, doing so with a constructive, self-supportive attitude. Certainly patients will almost always intellectualize and idealize to some extent, and probably they will be stimulated to intellectualize and idealize even more by the psychotherapist's utilizing pedagogic moves. But if therapists are not extremely interested in intellectualization or being idealized, and if their instructive comments make exploration more possible and thus more secure and informed, then their instructive efforts will promote change through understanding at least as much as they will create barriers to it. Probably more. The conduct of therapy, it must be borne in mind, is always a matter of weighing one thing against another and making complex, not altogether certain, choices. Claiming to know the one way that is the right way and the one interpretation that is *the* interpretation has no place in sophisticated and responsible work. There is too much we do not yet understand.

TALKING TO PATIENTS PERSONALLY

In many psychotherapies, therapists do not make enough use of speaking personally to the patient. Although it is easy to say that the type and degree of the therapist's "self-expressiveness" has to be suited to each patient's needs and tolerance, we do not know very much about making these estimates and adjustments. For too long we have been content automatically to use a fundamentally *impersonal* diction: It seems so safe and effective, so tried-and-true. But working *only* in that way no longer seems adequate to the variety of situations we encounter or arrange. Certainly being compelled to work in that way should be a cause for concern.

Next, taking as our model now a male therapist working with a male patient, we may ask, "What is the difference between the psychotherapist's saying to his patient 'You are not making yourself clear' and 'I don't understand you'?" There is no doubt more than one difference, but the one I want to emphasize is that the first intervention sets the therapist apart from and above the patient as his judge, however benign. Speaking thus from on high, he brackets himself off from a true interaction. It hardly captures the difference to which I am referring to think of it, in Phyllis Greenacre's phrase, as a "tilted relationship" (1954, p. 674). In this connection Harry Stack Sullivan's (1940) preferred response to a psychotic patient's disclosure of a hallucination might be recalled: "I don't see it" rather than "It isn't there." Sullivan viewed speaking personally as the therapeutic response of choice. I believe that therapists should speak personally in some measure in all psychotherapy. Such behavior supports every patient's speaking of and for himself while at the same time it clarifies that there are difficulties in the way of his doing so. The fact that the therapist freely makes certain personal declarations enables both therapist and patient to engage each other beneficially in the task.

The same difference in interaction obtains between the psychotherapist's saying "You must have felt awful" and simply saying "How awful!" A therapist could not have uttered the first response genuinely without having previously or simultaneously responded in the "how awful" way. Why, then, should the therapist bracket him- or herself off by referring only to how the patient "must have" felt? This customary form of empathizing is inherently uncertain, overcautious, or condescending, and its effect is to create undesirable distance in the therapeutic relationship. Therapists detach themselves even more questionably when they simply ask "How did you feel?" upon hearing one of the terrible things therapists so often hear from their patients—or one of the thrilling things they sometimes hear. It does not explain the bracketing-off response to point out that horror stories and thrilling stories are often told manipulatively, for example, as plainly erotic or masochistic seductions or subtle attacks on the therapist. If it is clear that they are being told in such a way, psychotherapists can say so (if they decide to say anything at that point); if it is not clear enough, they will have time to get to it, perhaps in not more than a few minutes. They do not compromise their position by responding simply and directly to these grim or gratifying accounts, and there is no sound basis for their losing their poise upon discovering that they have been "had." Why should they? Indeed, how have they been "had"? Were they so thrilled with their previous empathic response? Were they unusually overidentified with the patient? Were they falling back on the same defenses as the patient? Do they pride themselves on being absolutely unmanipulable or unfailingly correct? If any of these, all the correct therapeutic diction in the world will not save the therapy.

It is true, however, that when speaking freely in the way I mean, psychotherapists tend to experience the situation more emotionally than when speaking otherwise. At one time or another, they must expect to experience more "choking up," giddiness, irritability, anxiety, and other emotional responses than they are used to or secure with. This significant, unsettling, enriching, and perplexing complication of therapists' expressiveness deserves an extended discussion in its own right. Obviously, psychotherapists will be better able to keep their balance while interacting emotionally in this endeavor if they have had, or are having, the benefit of a personal psychoanalysis and some well-supervised professional experience.

Here are a few more illustrative contrasts: "I am wondering what that could be about" as against persistently remaining thoughtfully silent. "Congratulations!" as against "You must be very proud of yourself." "I don't feel at ease somehow and I have a hunch you are trying to get me to feel that way" as against "You are trying to make me ill at ease." "That's a helluva way to live" as against "Your life does not seem very satisfying or easy." And "I'm not surprised" as against "That might have been expected."

The statements I favor are those whereby psychotherapists speak directly to the patients. They are not telling the patients everything, of course (I know there are psychotherapists now who would challenge my "of course"); actually they are telling patients very little. They are simply saying what they might ordinarily say on the kind of occasion to which they are responding. They are speaking in ordinary good faith. Any sophisticated observer would wonder at a therapist's *not* responding in that way, at least silently or privately. After all, the expectations of response that apply to the patient, which I mentioned earlier, ought to apply in some measure to the psychotherapist as well. What I want to emphasize is that it may help the treatment considerably if psychotherapists respond aloud or publicly, that is, directly to patients. Their doing so may be all at once supportive, enlightening, and highly evocative. And by enhancing the exploratory dialogue through not placing brackets like armor around themselves, they do not preclude their monitoring the effects on them of making these approaches to intimacy and going on to regulate them if necessary. They are not in an either/or situation in this regard.

As there are many kinds of people practicing psychotherapy, there are many ways of speaking personally as well as pedagogically. I am not prescribing a specific style or language.

To say that the self-expressive remarks are introductory and incomplete is not to damn them. For example, "I am wondering about that" is basically quite noncommital and undeveloped; it must be said in a certain way to be engaging and open-ended. Essentially, the remarks I recommend differ from the others in not having been "professionalized." They have not had their evocativeness needlessly sacrificed. In speaking for and of themselves, psychotherapists establish personal presence—that quality that seems to grease the wheels of all therapies. And their being sensitively and informedly selective in what they say does not compromise the authenticity of their remarks—only the pretense of total frankness could do that.

It need not be argued here that psychotherapists may and do communicate nonverbally all the time. Their attitudes toward patients and the current material may be suggested, if not fully revealed, by tone, timing, attentiveness, mood, and so forth. Thus, a smile, a frown, a quizzical look, and the like may do some of the recommended work of personal expression in the service of investigation. But the risk of being misunderstood by a patient, which is anyway a continuous one, is increased in proportion to a therapist's reliance on nonverbal communication. Nonverbal communication is inherently more primitive, ambiguous, and fluid than words in sentences, which organize and establish a more definite record. Heavy reliance on nonverbal communication is also a way of being emotionally evasive, for, as we all know from our personal lives, we can hardly exaggerate the emotionally evocative potential of the spoken word and the dread that restricts our saying some of the things dearest to us or otherwise important to the conduct of our lives. Here again the psychotherapist is not in an either/or situation.

The idea that there is some one naturally spontaneous way of conducting oneself in any relationship is psychologically indefensible. Indeed, according to my observations, most of those psychotherapists who allegedly talk "naturally" to their patients and who might think my recommendations altogether unnecessary do not do so in the optional, selective, and investigatory sense I have suggested. Rather, they do it routinely, that is, most or all of the time with most or all of their patients. They are, in fact, relying on what I call force of personality—an eclectic mixture of interpretation, warmth, guidance, reassurance, firmness, exhortation, and other deliberate or unwitting manipulations of transference potentials. Usually they seem to be doing so in order to bring about corrective emotional experiences within the therapeutic relationship, and, if so, they tend to rationalize their actions by making the questionable assumption that the patient will transpose this experience to the rest of his or her life in a stable and satisfying way. In some instances this strategy seems to gratify the therapists' needs for excitement and activity, to allow them to engage in the vanities of the "wise man" or "guru," or simply to avoid the tensions of sustained exploratory discipline and its frustrations. It cannot be denied that this stereotyped, basically controlling, and repression-reinforcing conduct often leads to their patients' experiencing symptomatic relief. So many things do! But what it cannot lead to is the kind of insight and change that may be generated by a genuinely exploratory psychotherapy.

II. The Termination of Brief Therapy

Supervisors of brief analytic therapies cannot fail to notice how often, during the termination phase, all the gains that have been made earlier are seriously threatened, compromised, or lost. But as these developments do not invariably and automatically forecast the outcome, they cannot be written off as due merely to the superficiality of the therapy, the illusion of improvement based merely on intensified defense and transference gratifications, and the inevitable power of infantile unconscious conflict. We do, of course, expect these undoubtedly powerful limiting and regressive influences to be operative during any therapy, including psychoanalysis, and we do expect them to be difficult to define precisely and fully, and especially difficult to modify for the better in brief therapy. But merely to acknowledge these points and then suspend further inquiry and reflection is to do injustice to patients and therapists alike.

Recognizing that there are various ways of practicing brief analytic therapy, I limit myself here to the way I have practiced it and taught it. After describing that way briefly, I discuss the kind of changes it seems to bring about, the crisis that frequently develops around termination, and the problems of the therapist in dealing with this crisis. Then I return to closer examination of the changes that seem to occur, and I conclude with some remarks on the problems of validating the claims made for brief analytic therapy. It may well be that I am merely covering ground that is well known; my experience, however, is that what should be well known often is not, even in the best training centers, and that, even if it is well known, there are always further important points to be explored, clarified, or debated. My narration may make its own contribution.

BRIEF ANALYTIC THERAPY

By brief analytic therapy, I mean therapy in which the patient is seen individually, once a week, for about fifty minutes, in face-to-face verbal interchange that is focused on the patient's difficulties in his or her life in general and in the therapy in particular; and I mean therapy that continues for some months, perhaps for as long as a year. Such therapy is more or less clearly time-limited, as is often the case in clinics and other institutional settings and also in private work due to limited funds or motivation or rapid increase of defensiveness once some relief is experienced and the prospect of deeper involvement looms (Ernst Prelinger, personal communication).

In this therapy the therapist—say, a woman—tries to establish as much of an exploratory or investigative atmosphere and discipline as possible. She is particularly alert to signs that the patient is having emotional difficulty in the therapeutic relationship. I mean especially difficulty of the sort that entails anxiety, guilt, or shame and the evident withholding, circumventing, or dissimulating of certain experiences on account of these relational difficulties. In other words, the therapist pays special attention to manifestations of conflict, defense, and transference. Mainly she indicates this attentiveness in the form of noting aloud and perhaps raising questions about these manifestations. In this regard, sexual and hostile feelings and dependent feelings are touched on or alluded to or named directly, along with anxiety, guilt, and shame. The pace, directness, and persistence of these interventions are regulated by considerations of tact, anxiety tolerance, the patient's reaction (as it can be reasonably surmised) to these interventions, and other considerations familiar from classical psychoanalytic technique.

Often the approach is indirect, following displacements and other detours. There is no hurry to explain anything, either in terms of current life issues or in terms of genetic antecedents, as what matters most is the drawing out of unarticulated, undeveloped phenomena and especially the difficulties in the way of that articulation and communication. The patient—say, a man—is helped to describe what his life is like for him—especially along the lines made familiar by psychoanalysis, as mentioned above. Elaborate or far-reaching interpretations usually are not be attempted. A kind of psychoanalytically informed phenomenology is developed. When the patient raises practical questions, such as requests or demands for advice or intervention in his outside life or even in his conduct in the sessions, the therapist generally encourages reflection on the nature, implications, and background of, or reasons for, the request or the dilemma to which they pertain, or reflection on the feelings that accompany those requests and demands, or the feelings of the therapist they seem designed to stir up or play upon. But in so doing, she remains flexible and does not attempt to play out in full the "incognito" of the clinical psychoanalyst, itself often exaggerated both within and outside the field of psychoanalysis.

Ordinarily, psychotherapy of this sort requires a patient who is reasonably intelligent, capable of some reflectiveness, able to verbalize, and not acutely psychotic or agitatedly near the edge of psychosis or in an extreme life crisis in which family, community, or legal figures are active. In other words, it requires a patient who ideally should be—or at least could be—in analysis but who, for whatever reason, will not or cannot undertake analysis. Typically, such patients complain of inability to work or enjoy work, uncertainty or moderate despair about their course in life, neurotic symptoms, attacks of anxiety or moderate depression, or unsatisfactory relationships with parents, peers, members of the opposite sex, children, teachers, or supervisors at work. They are people with acute psychological problems who knowingly have come for psychological therapy, although, on account of their defensiveness, they are not always equally clear about that or equally cooperative in those terms. Some borderline psychotic patients can be worked with in the way described, though often with a different mode of developing understanding—a mode I cannot elaborate on here.

CHANGES DURING EFFECTIVE THERAPY

Now, what typically happens as an effective therapy of this sort goes along? The following is a composite picture; there is considerable individual variation. What is most clear is that the patient develops a more definite and more comprehensive idea of the scope, multiplicity, and complexity of his problems. He discovers symptoms and inhibitions he never acknowledged consciously, as well as attitudes and feelings of all sorts—dread, remorse, resignation, mistrust, overweening pride, and also hopeful, tender, sentimental, compassionate, adoring, and loyal sentiments that he formerly would have blushed too much or wept too much to acknowledge. In one sense, he comes to realize more fully the extent of his illness. But, in another, he realizes the extent of his human existence, with its suffering and its possibilities, both enlarged in his subjective experience and objective view. Most of all, and especially through his examination of his problems in the therapeutic relationship, he may begin to realize something of the extent of his active participation in bringing about the difficulties that to begin with he experienced passively, such as his social isolation, his alienation from his family, his failures in sex, his poor performance at work, his dismal outlook itself. In this way, he discovers the centrality of personal conflict in his existence.

It is impressive that, as these changes take place in the patient's conception of himself, often by dint of and with the accompaniment of much suffering, he begins to feel better and to function better. His symptoms diminish in scope and persistence; his mood improves; his social and sexual relationships are enhanced. It seems that it can be a gain just to be able to recognize one's neurotic misery.

A skeptical observer of psychotherapy might easily challenge that all these changes can take place when no exploratory work of the sort I described has been undertaken or on account of factors other than the exploration itself. I do not think this challenge succeeds, however; while people do certainly get to feel and function better in response to all kinds of interventions or noninterventions, including simply being on a waiting list for therapy, the terms in which they are better and in which they view their being better and the context in which they are better vary considerably. The enlarged appreciation of activity in apparent passivity, for example, or the coexistence of enhanced suffering and doubt *and* pleasurable and effective living—all accompanied by an increased sense of meaningful conflict—is not typical, in my view, of the other types of improvement.

The test of these changes comes as termination approaches, for, as I mentioned, it then appears as if all were built on sand. Then, with the patient apparently as depressed, morose, provocative, or helplessly symptom-ridden as when the work started, the therapist may well wonder whether the patient's enlarged and active view of his life was worth anything. Much escapes understanding at this point, and where understanding fails, resentment flourishes. The therapist may then justify her negative countertransference as appropriate to the passive aggression of the patient or to his masochism or negative therapeutic reaction. She may blame the superficiality of the therapy. She may develop inclinations to extend the therapy; clearly, she rationalizes, it is too early to stop; a few more sessions beyond the cutoff date should turn the trick. Or she may determine that now, finally, she must replace or at least greatly modify her neutral investigative approach with a display of personal feeling; that will save the day . . . she hopes. Here are all the signs of a relationship and a job in crisis; some serious sorting out of issues and assumptions is necessary in order to avoid the kind of cruelty in failure that marks the course of such crises and their attempted resolution.

THE THERAPIST'S POSITION AT TERMINATION

The therapist is observing a regression, of course. It is very similar to the regressions repeatedly observed by the classical analyst in ongoing, effective analyses, and as such it is by no means a cause for despair. Like everything else in treatment, rightly construed, the regression teaches something about the current difficulties of the patient and their history. It helps matters considerably if the therapist does not falter at this point but continues the work of investigation. Among other things, at least in her own thinking, she must keep track, as best she can, of the various oral, anal, and phallic meanings that the patient attributes to termination (for example, being weaned abruptly, being put down in disgust or pushed away in horror for being too "instinctual" or "animal"), together with the defenses against recognizing these meanings and the feelings associated with them. In order for this to occur, however, the therapist's own narcissistic investment in therapeutic results must be of a certain sort and not go beyond a certain point in intensity. Above all, she must realize that her ideal should be to do the best she can and not necessarily to get "results." I shall discuss this further later.

But more than a narcissistic demand for "cure" is at issue here. It is during termination that all the unspoken promises, expectations, transferences, and defenses on the part of both persons in the therapeutic relationship may come to light: all their fundamental assumptions about illness and human existence, and about the role and duty and merit of therapists as well as their satisfaction and pride in their work; and all the collusions by which issues were skirted during the therapy. All are asserted in such various and devious ways that patient and therapist can easily be bewildered and disheartened. The objective assessment of change, of the course of the work and of its reasonable prospects, then suffers considerably.

Among the problems that emerge is that of facing the limitations of what therapy can do. These limitations concern the therapist in quite a powerful personal way. Through them she must recognize that her effectiveness as a healer is quite limited, which means that important narcissistic ideas about herself and ideals for herself are seen to be forcefully contradicted by experience. The roots of these ideas and ideals lie in infantile fantasies of omnipotence, which no one ever renounces completely. Most likely these ideas and ideals played an important part in her having chosen to become a therapist. These ideas and ideals concern valuing activity greatly over passivity (at least with regard to other people's problems!) and, in the extreme, "choosing" to be omnipotent rather than helpless, a savior rather than a destructive force, and/or a breast of infinite capacity rather than a ravenously hungry parasite. On this account, the terminating patient, who is still saddled with problems—and perhaps, through regression, with apparently accentuated problems—and who quite likely is expressing dissatisfaction with the therapist, is bound to become very much of a disappointment and threat to her. This problem is often increased by the patient's increased recognition of the extent and complexity of his problems, which seems also to be, as I mentioned, one of the beneficial achievements of the brief psychotherapy.

Because it is too complex to go into here, I only mention in passing the additional problem introduced by the therapist's reluctance to give up her relations with patients she has gotten to know and to be able to feel with and for. One of the best protections against disruptive countertransference responses to the terminating patient is a reasonable and stable sense of one's own goodness. I mean "goodness" in two senses. The first sense is goodness as a therapist in terms of having offered something good, having made a sincere effort, and having achieved some results (if that is the case) under very disadvantageous conditions—and brief psychotherapy *is* work under disadvantageous conditions. The other sense of goodness is the archaic or infantile sense that, on the whole, one is a worthwhile, benign person, whatever one's faults and limitations. Here I am in a way adapting Edith Jacobson's (1964) point about the "good but also bad mother" who constitutes the necessary constant object representation the child must achieve for his or her satisfactory development. I am also speaking of the fact that the child and, later, the therapist herself is a "good though also bad person." If the therapist's self-confidence is lacking or easily undermined in this regard, the vicissitudes of termination are bound to get to her and she is likely to intensify the crisis of termination rather than turn it to advantage.

It is in this context that all the unspoken understandings, mutual transferences, and collusions that I mentioned earlier are relevant, for they are all temporary expedients that the therapist adopted to protect her narcissistic vulnerability. For, contrary to what she may have suggested or declared, the therapist is not, cannot be, and should not try to be endlessly and totally dedicated to the ultimate welfare of particular patients. Nor is she able to effect any and all desirable changes that she may have vaguely promised, or always to feel and act with equal understanding, acceptance, and benevolence toward her patients.

The therapist requires a corresponding view of patients as "good though also bad." During crises, such as the one at termination, it is the "good," at least in the sense of hoping to become more of a person, that is so easily lost sight of by patients and therapists. And it is here where a foundation of patience and steadiness is required.

I mentioned earlier that among the possibly disruptive factors at termination are certain assumptions about illness and human existence. Many therapists, and in my view many analysts, too, do not like to face the prospect—I would call it the fact—that irrationally based or neurotic problems are not entirely eradicable by the best of therapies; that there is more to it than, as Freud put it, freeing people from neurotic miseries so that they can deal more effectively with the inescapable objective miseries of existence; that, in other words, what we call illness and what we call human existence are not sharply and clearly separable, except in textbook definitions. There is no doubt that many people can be helped by therapy to assume more stable, effective, and satisfying positions, and certainly less anguished positions. However, there is no evidence that all infantile neurotic problems are totally and finally resolvable; certainly they are not resolvable through brief therapy.

All of this has disturbing implications for therapists, for, in terminating with their—at best—partially improved patients, they must face again the prospect that their own lives are only partially improvable. Especially in the United States, I think, with its traditionally unbounded melioristic enthusiasm and expectations, this is a difficult prospect to deal with. Progress is almost a state religion. Psychotherapists must resist such naïve enthusiasm, in order to maintain the proper *scale* as well as perspective. These are essential to good work, especially during the doubt-ridden crises of termination. Perhaps, above all, psychotherapists must believe in the great difficulties in the way of significant changes and in the great value to their patients of their symptoms and other problems, however much the patients may consciously wish to be rid of them. These difficulties and the value of symptoms are among the great lessons taught by psychoanalysis.

I cannot prevent the various exaggerations and misunderstandings to which these brief remarks on a very complex and emotionally arousing subject are vulnerable, but I can go on to discuss two very important, though limited, accomplishments that not infrequently are observed in brief psychoanalytic psychotherapy. A clear conception of these changes and their value can be a powerful support against the doubts and disappointments that can fill the air during termination. Affirmations are, after all, still in order.

FURTHER REMARKS ON CHANGES DURING BRIEF THERAPY

I have already mentioned two of the changes that may occur during brief therapy: (1) the patients' recognition of the extensive and complex nature of the problems with which they are dealing; and (2) their recognition of the activity on their part that has contributed to bringing about and continues to support the existence of these problems. And I have pointed out that these changes, though burdensome and painful in some ways, seem to have a liberating and strengthening effect. I particularly emphasize the extent to which these gains depend on consistent attention having been paid during the therapy to the discomforts and disruptions of rapport and collaboration with the therapist—that is to say, to the anxieties, dishonesties, evasions, flights, and manipulations in which the patient has engaged in response to the anxieties of the therapy situation. In principle, these anxieties must be those at the core of his disorder or at least offshoots of them. These discomforts and disruptions are heightened by irregularities in the schedule of appointments, such as absences, holidays, lateness, and interruptions, and by the relative briefness of the therapy itself. They are reinforced by the therapist's role, which is, on the one hand, relatively unstructuring so far as specific topics are concerned and, on the other hand, relatively leading with regard to the focus on the phenomenology of experience, the so-called internality of the patient's existence, and especially the implications of "inner" conflict of purpose, goal, or value in what appear initially to be simply problems with a past or present unaccommodating surrounding world.

The patient is made uncomfortable by the therapist's role and the procedure it defines because they threaten his or her accustomed modes of defense and adjustment. But what *is* the procedure that is defined? In one crucial respect this procedure is an invitation and a pressure for patients to become more fully acquainted with themselves and to achieve and experience the discovery of themselves in the medium of communicating with another person. It is precisely this discovery in a medium of benign relationship that all patients, in their own ways and for their own reasons, have grown to feel hopeless about. They anticipate that the discovery will be unbearable and the disclosure of it either intolerable in itself or intolerable as the certain cause of a forthcoming traumatic response by the other person, the therapist. This hopelessness is at the core of a radical discontinuity or fragmentation of patients' knowledge about and tolerance of themselves. They have blinded themselves to themselves; they have lied to themselves about themselves; and, to maintain these blind spots and lies, they have given up both major achievements of their past lives and major possibilities in their current and future lives. They have a stake in seeing their lives as incomprehensible or chaotic, however dismaying that may be.

But now, in the therapy, with the support of the benevolent but tough-minded curiosity of the therapist, and in order to pacify the therapist and to be loved by him or her in the transference, patients begin to explore, organize, and express, whereas before they had felt it was hopeless to begin anything along that line. They *discover*—often actually rediscover—and they *connect* and *express* fear, hate, shame, desire, sentimentality, pride, aspirations, and longings. They see that these emotions do matter to them, that they are endurable, and that their difficulty with the emotions and their way of dealing with that difficulty are understandable, manageable, and revisable. At least they make a beginning in that direction. And to some extent patients see that, rather than being unique to the therapy situation, these tendencies and difficulties are virtually a distillate of chronic problems in major relationships of their lives. I cannot overemphasize that the core problems in question are not fully defined and certainly not resolved. Often patients only glimpse the problems and possible solutions. Nevertheless, something new and vital has been added: the possibility of doing something about the problems that have begun to be defined in a new and more organized and hopeful way. The redefinition itself makes activity and hope more acceptable to patients.

Thus, the hopelessness is qualified, tempered, even questioned as a premise. With that, patients can envisage the possibility of becoming more whole and understandable beings. And while at best it is only a beginning, it is a beginning that seems to make a big difference in a patient's view of the situation. Here, a little seems to go a long way, especially if the patient is still young. Though it is correct, it does not go far enough simply to say that we are observing a "realignment of defenses."* And it is not just that patients see that they have been active in bringing on their own misery, whereas they thought they had been merely passive. They see, too, that they can also be active in another way that alters their past, present, and future, all at once.

This reference to altering the past serves as transition to the second of the two additional accomplishments I said were possible through brief therapy. I should also mention transitionally another remark I made earlier: that patients' radical discontinuity and fragmentation of their knowledge about, and tolerance of, themselves may be reduced as their hopelessness is reduced. That discontinuity or fragmentation is essentially cross-sectional. The point I am leading up to is the reduction of a longitudinal or historical radical discontinuity or fragmentation. What is at stake is interrupted personal development due to the patient's having resorted to massive repression, denial, or other defense in earlier times, in order to deal with intolerable life situations. Such life situations may include the death or psychotic breakdown of a parent or sibling, severe injury or protracted illness, parental conflict and divorce, the birth of a sibling, or cruelly dishonest, exploitative, or seductive parental behavior in relation to the future patient. It is not unusual for therapy to establish that, in connection with such disruptions of life, a major relationship that was filled with feeling—good feeling as well as bad—was ostensibly broken off on the initiative of one or the other or both persons involved, and that there followed an attempt by the future patient at thoroughgoing repudiation, repression, or isolation of all that had gone before. In that predicament, a patient then rewrites his or her history: for example, "I *never* loved him," or "If I did love him, I was *deceived* and *shouldn't have,* and in any case I *don't* any more," or "It wasn't *really* love." Therapists, who are familiar with these disillusionments and disclaimers, know that they do not really work: The anguished love persists, the denied emotion is all the more threatening and painful because it is not faced and lived through, and it is all the more costly to the personality as a whole because the defense invariably necessitates a breakdown in the patient's sense of historical continuity and authenticity and restricts the kind of relationships and feelings that are tolerable from then on. Typically, this restriction means consciously avoiding relationships and feelings that are reminiscent of the repudiated ones, while unconsciously repeating endlessly the worst aspects of those very relationships and feelings.

I am thinking, for example, of several young women who had "irre-

*Mentioned by Anna Freud at a staff conference.

vocably" broken with their fathers, to whom they had once felt very close. In one case, the father had been seductive and exploitative; in another, cruelly depressive; and in a third, sadistically overcontrolling and paranoid. These women were now caught up in one or a series of quite unsatisfactory relationships with men who were, in fact, not unlike their fathers. As a therapist, I could not question that these three women had been much abused in one form or another. But I also could not help seeing how tied they were to these fathers and how hampered in their relationships to other men and to themselves as individuals, by their continuing repudiation of tender, admiring, hopeful, and sentimental feelings for them. Of course, ambivalence at such close quarters and of such intensity is terrible, and people just do not bear it well. During therapy in these and similar cases, it is sometimes possible to bring about some reexperiencing of the continuing positive feelings for father, mother, sibling, or self by paying particular attention to the warding-off positive feelings toward the therapist that arise in the therapy hours, especially at times of crisis, separation, and, most of all, termination.

I say "most of all, termination" because the potential for virtually every significant human emotion resides in the termination situation—assuming, of course, that the patient has formed some felt relationship with the therapist, with its inevitable transference components. The ideal termination would explore all these emotions—for example, feelings of deprivation and longing, guilt and unworthiness, gratitude and envy, triumph and defeat, love and betrayal, disappointment and elation, rage and grief—from all levels of psychosexual and ego development, insofar as they are accessible and significant. But it can be useful, within the narrow limits of brief psychotherapy, to explore one or two of them, and then only in a limited way. These feelings are or should be the ones that are most recognizable at the time, for in all likelihood they are emotions that patients can best tolerate dealing with at that time. They are not the root problems, there to be dealt with directly, though most likely they are offshoots of them.

And so therapists have an excellent opportunity to demonstrate that patients are understanding the termination in the terms of key conflicts that have been identified during the therapy; are actively and arbitrarily setting that interpretation on it; are fragmenting themselves cross-sectionally and longitudinally in so doing, just as (according to the therapy up to that point) they have done at critical junctures in the past; and thereby are again reducing the possibilities of their very being. Then gratitude, love, regrets, and sober appraisal of continuing problems are more likely to be mingled in patients' communications and are likely to be experienced and conveyed more directly than it might have seemed they could ever be when therapy began. This change may not come when expected, and it may not last more than a few moments. But, however confused and conflictual it may be and however oblique and brief, this change during termination demonstrates the effectiveness of the therapeutic work.

Often patients are able to begin to appreciate the value of long-range, perhaps more intensive therapy or psychoanalysis. They may, however, need the skillful guidance and support of the therapist before they can face and act upon their further therapeutic needs. And if they do so, then, as I mentioned in chapter 1, all this ground will be worked over in much finer detail and greater depth, quite frequently with invaluable benefit for the patients.

VALIDATION

I said earlier that I would finally discuss the problem of validation of the claims made for brief therapy. I shall not dwell on this point, for I do not know what would constitute validation other than the event itself—that is, the experience of therapy and its termination. The issue is one of historical understanding rather than reliance on any behavioral science test. If we put together the available observations and accounts of past history, plus the gist of interventions during therapy and responses to them, plus some common sense and clinical generalizations, we have a narrative understanding of what the therapy has been like for the patient and what has changed; we are guided and satisfied by criteria of intelligibility, cohesiveness, and economy of exposition along certain storylines. We also know that a life crisis has been traversed or reduced with less damage and perhaps more gain than might well have been the case without therapy, given the presenting picture. This is historical understanding.

By *validation* it might be meant proving that the therapy *always* gets results or the *same* results. As no such claim has been made, no such proof need be developed. Rather, what is claimed is that certain people more or less make certain types of gains or undergo certain types of limited change in response to this therapy.

Validation may be used in the sense of providing an answer to the question of how lasting are any of the changes or benefits that are attributed to this therapy. I think that *in principle* that question is unanswerable, for it would require another course of therapy to elicit the data necessary to answer it. How else, for example, could we ascertain that a benign identification with the "lost" therapist not only took place at termination but survived for so many months or years? And there cannot be another course of the same therapy, just as we cannot step into the same river twice, because history is irreversible; the same patient is not there to treat twice, nor is the same therapist there twice, though two people answering to the same names as before might be there. The "same" data are not available. And certainly life circumstances do not persist psychologically in exactly the same way, even if they seem the same to an outside observer. It will be a question of another story to tell. Questionnaires and interviews cannot do this job.

Or *validation* might mean proving that the changes that have occurred can justifiably be attributed to the therapy or, more ambitiously, to particular aspects of the therapy, such as the relationship, the interpretations, or even, in the extreme of ambitiousness, to *an* interpretation. Again, I think that *in principle* that question is unanswerable by the methods of behavioral science, for, rightly understood, the question itself is one of historical understanding. Good historians who share certain assumptions about method and conceptualization can agree on matters of historical understanding; so can good clinicians *in their context* and for quite similar reasons, as I have argued in chapters 9 to 12 particularly. It is that kind of truth we are dealing with. Ultimately, it is the truth of psychoanalysis, which, from the time of Freud's work on, has usually been misconstrued as that of an actual or potential behavioral science.

CHAPTER 18

Analytic Love

AMONG the writers of note in the recent history of psychoanalysis, few have a narrative voice that is immediately felt to be distinctive. Hans Loewald is one of these. Winnicott, Erikson, and Kohut are others. Because Loewald's is a distinctive voice, it does not allow us to pick over his utterances casually or to center on just one of them, thereby to elude the man himself. His voice resists appropriation through reductive synopsis and definition. Although it is consistently meditative and modest, it does what any distinctive voice does: It insists on speaking through us. As we continue to listen, it engages us in the process that Loewald has returned to again and again—the process of internalization: And, as a direct developmental consequence of internalization, it engages us in the unending process of emancipation from internalized authority.

In his now-classic paper, "On the Therapeutic Action of Psycho-Analysis" (1960), Loewald proposed that, in the course of analysis and as the more regressive transferences are analyzed and diminished, the analyst emerges as a new object for the analysand. In one way, this narrative turn is not difficult to grasp and accept, especially not these days, some thirty years and several analytic generations after Loewald ventured to publish it. We would be inclined to follow the storyline that when analysis is effective, it frees the analysand to develop toward levels of integration higher than those reached so far. This development occurs in the field of the analytic relationship. The primary and forever influential precursor of the analytic field is the field of the mother-infant relationship, the field in which development necessarily and fatefully originates. In both fields, first the mother and later the analyst represent a higher level of being, relating, and mutual definition of selves; they hold out their higher level and create a tension relative to more primitive levels, thereby giving direction and focus to the developmental strivings of the child and, later, the patient. We might say that they make of these relationships growth fields. Consequently, in growing as never before, the analysand enters into modes of relationship with another person—the analyst—that he or she has not yet attempted, maintained, or integrated. A new kind of relatedness is now felt to be not only possible but necessary, safe, and gratifying. On this understanding, then, we would enter into Loewald's narrative and agree that a new kind of significant object has come into existence, and that, along with that object, there has come a new self which in significant measure reflects that object's perceptions.

The analyst is a new object also in the special pattern of interests, capacities, functions, ideas, and emotional experiences that he or she offers to assist this growth process. Included here are the analyst's readiness to engage in partial regressions to the analysand's response level, when and where indicated, in order to help free up, through understanding, empathy, and interpretation, the analysand's growth potential. Here Loewald continued to draw parallels to (not advocate literal copies of or replacements for) the infant's mother. And in this connection especially, we get a clear view of Loewald's consistent and brilliant inclusion in his narrative of the preoedipal phases of development.

Looked at historically, these were bold narratives to put forward to the ultra-conservative Freudian audience that prevailed around 1960. Contained in the storyline of the analyst as a new object were a number of significant modifications of the then-received Freudian theory of psychological development and neurotic psychopathology. Loewald was putting forth a master narrative of development in an interpersonal and experiential field: In this field drives, for example, are to be regarded as products of differentiation rather than primary forces that seek out objects to discharge themselves on or through. In contrast, conservative theory holds that drives bring into being relationships where, to begin with, none have existed. Loewald's precursors and contemporaries in this connection include Sullivan, Fairbairn, Erikson, Winnicott, Kardiner, and Heinz Hartmann (in his work on adaptation specifically). In Loewald's narratives, drives are no longer where we begin; they are something between a mode of experience and a developmental achievement, though they retain their propulsive role. Simultaneously, Freud's reflex-arc model of drive stimulation and discharge is thrown into question, and human beings, or the selves of human beings, emerge as social and interactive from the first. Additionally, the analytic patient is now to be viewed primarily from the vantage point of arrested development (arrested both in the interpersonal sense and the experiential sense). In a departure from Freud, the patient's ego is no longer to be regarded as a developed ego with focal areas of fixation and regression. It is only within this radically revised context that we can fully appreciate Loewald's narrative of the analyst emerging as a new object for the analysand. The easily accepted, commonsense view of a new object (for example, "finally a kind-hearted mothering person") does not do justice to Loewald's contributions.

It was in this context that Loewald went on to refer to analytic love, that is, the analyst's love for the patient. Loewald did not seem to mean heightened disruptive countertransference in the usual sense, although as he made plain in his discussion of transference, he would be the first to say that this love includes transference in relation to the patient; it includes transference in the same way that every relationship presupposes or requires transference. (Recall here Freud's [1915c] similar discussion of transference love.) Nor does it seem that he would rule out some heightening of countertransference in connection with the analyst's facilitative, technically less constrained, empathic regressions and identifications with the analysand, especially when working in the context of preoedipal issues. I believe, however, that Loewald was aiming at something more than these factors when he referred to analytic love. He approached his goal when he wrote, for example, of holding in trust the ego core or potential self of the analysand through all the trials of analysis; he approached it when he referred to the analyst's seeing the patient as more than he or she can yet conceive and thereby taking on the responsibility of safeguarding a future for that person. And he expressed his meaning in full force when he wrote the following distinctive passage:

> Scientific detachment in its genuine form, far from excluding love, is based on it. In our work it can truly be said that in our best moments of dispassionate and objective analysis, we love our object, the patient, more than at any other time and are compassionate with his whole being.
>
> In our field scientific spirit and care for the object flow from the

same source. It is impossible to love the truth of psychic reality, to be moved by this love as Freud was in his lifework, and not to love and care for the object whose truth we want to discover. All great scientists are moved by this passion. Our object, being what it is, is the other in ourselves and oneself in the other. To discover truth about the patient is always discovering it with him and for him as well as for ourselves and about ourselves. And it is discovering truth between each other, as the truth of human beings in their interrelatedness. (1970, pp. 297–298)

To develop further the sense of Loewald's references to analytic love, it will help to turn to a poet, specifically Rilke writing about Cézanne. In a letter to his wife, Rilke is describing his efforts to comprehend the artist Cézanne at work. Cézanne's work has just burst on his consciousness in a way that makes him feel, as he says, "I must change my life."

Here now is Rilke, in a translation by Joel Agee:

We also notice, a little more clearly each time, how necessary it was to go beyond love, too; it's natural, after all, to love each of these things as one makes it: but if one shows this, one makes it less well; one *judges* it instead of *saying* it. One ceases to be impartial; and the very best—love—stays outside the work, does not enter it, is left aside, untranslated; that's how the painting of sentiments came about. . . . They'd paint: I love this here; instead of painting: here it is. In which case everyone must see for himself whether or not I loved it. This is not shown at all, and some would even insist that love has nothing to do with it. It's that thoroughly exhausted in the action of making, there is no residue. It may be that this emptying out of love in anonymous work, which produces such pure things, was never achieved as completely as in the work of this old man. (1907, pp. 50–51)

I suppose that in this passage Rilke was writing about his own artistic aspirations as well as Cézanne's way of working. I further suppose that Rilke was also doing a piece of creative writing of his own about love as well as artistic creativity. I mention these suppositions to indicate my belief that there is no one right way of delivering Loewald's meaning or anyone else's meaning, though there are some ways that can serve much better than others.

Taken together, these two narratives of love in work—Loewald's and Rilke's—may serve as model renderings of an essential component of the engaged analyst at his or her best.

REFERENCES

Arlow, J. 1969a. Unconscious fantasy and disturbances of conscious experience. *Psychoanalytic Quarterly* 38:1–27.

———. 1969b. Fantasy, memory, and reality testing. *Psychoanalytic Quarterly* 38:28–51.

Bibring, G. L.; Dwyer, T. F.; Huntington, D. S.; and Valenstein, A. F. 1961. A study of the psychological processes in pregnancy and of the earliest mother-child relationship. *The Psychoanalytic Study of the Child* 16:9–72. New York: International Universities Press.

Bloom, H. 1973. *The anxiety of influence: A theory of poetry.* New York: Oxford University Press.

Brenner, C. 1981. Defense and defense mechanism. *Psychoanalytic Quarterly* 50:557–569.

Breuer, J., and Freud, S. 1895. Studies on hysteria. *Standard Edition* 2:1–309. London: Hogarth Press, 1957.

Brierley, M. 1951. *Trends in psychoanalysis.* London: Hogarth Press.

Culler, J. 1975. *Structural poetics: Structuralism, linguistics, and the study of literature.* Ithaca, NY: Cornell University Press.

Davenloo, H. 1978. *Basic principles and techniques in short-term dynamic therapy.* New York: Spectrum.

Erikson, E. 1950. *Childhood and society.* New York: Norton.

———. 1956. The problem of ego identity. *Journal of the American Psychoanalytic Association* 4:56–121.

Fenichel, O. 1941. *Problems of psychoanalytic technique.* New York: Psychoanalytic Quarterly.

Fish, S. 1980. *Is there a text in this class? The authority of interpretive communities.* Cambridge: Harvard University Press.

Freud, A. 1936. *The ego and the mechanisms of defense.* New York: International Universities Press, 1946.

Freud, S. 1895. Studies in hysteria. *Standard Edition* 2. London: Hogarth Press, 1955.

———. 1899. Screen memories. *Standard Edition* 3:299–322. London: Hogarth Press, 1962.

———. 1900. The interpretation of dreams. *Standard Edition* 4 and 5. London: Hogarth Press, 1953.

———. 1905a. Fragment of an analysis of a case of hysteria. *Standard Edition* 7:3–122. London: Hogarth Press, 1953.

———. 1905b. Three essays on the theory of sexuality. *Standard Edition* 7:125–243. London: Hogarth Press, 1953.

———. 1908a. Creative writers and day-dreaming. *Standard Edition* 9:141–153. London: Hogarth Press, 1959.

———. 1908b. On the sexual theories of children. *Standard Edition* 9:205–226. London: Hogarth Press, 1959.

———. 1910a. Wild psycho-analysis. *Standard Edition* 11:219–227. London: Hogarth Press, 1957.

———. 1910b. A special type of choice of object made by men (Contributions to the psychology of love I). *Standard Edition* 11:163–176. London: Hogarth Press, 1957.

———. 1911a. The handling of dream-interpretation in psycho-analysis. *Standard Edition* 12:89–96. London: Hogarth Press, 1958.

———.1911b. Formulations on the two principles of mental functioning. *Standard Edition* 12:213–226. London: Hogarth Press, 1958.

———. 1912a. On the universal tendency to debasement in the sphere of love (Contributions to the psychology of love II). *Standard Edition* 11:177–190. London: Hogarth Press, 1957.

———. 1912b. The dynamics of transference. *Standard Edition* 12:97–108. London: Hogarth Press, 1958.

———. 1912c. Recommendations to physicians practising psycho-analysis. *Standard Edition* 12:109–120. London: Hogarth Press, 1958.

———. 1913. On beginning the treatment (Further recommendations on the technique of psycho-analysis I). *Standard Edition* 12:121–144. London: Hogarth Press, 1958.

———. 1914a. Remembering, repeating and working through (Further recommendations on the technique of psycho-analysis II). *Standard Edition* 12:147–156. London: Hogarth Press, 1958.

———. 1914b. On narcissism: An introduction. *Standard Edition* 14:73–102. London: Hogarth Press, 1957.

———. 1915a. The unconscious. *Standard Edition* 14:159–215. London: Hogarth Press, 1957.

———. 1915b. Instincts and their vicissitudes. *Standard Edition* 14:109–140. London: Hogarth Press, 1957.

———. 1915c. Observations on transference-love (Further recommendations on the technique of psycho-analysis III). *Standard Edition* 12:159–171. London: Hogarth Press, 1958.

———. 1915d. Thoughts for the times on war and death. *Standard Edition* 14:274–300. London: Hogarth Press, 1957.

———. 1916. Some character types met with in psycho-analytic work. *Standard Edition* 14:309–333. London: Hogarth Press, 1957.

———.1918. The taboo of virginity (Contributions to the psychology of love III). *Standard Edition* 11:191–208. London: Hogarth Press, 1957.

———. 1919. A child is being beaten. *Standard Edition* 17:175–204. London: Hogarth Press, 1955.

———. 1920a. Beyond the pleasure principle. *Standard Edition* 18:1–64. London: Hogarth Press, 1955.

———. 1920b. The psychogenesis of a case of homosexuality in a woman. *Standard Edition* 18:140–172. London: Hogarth Press, 1955.

———. 1921. Group psychology and the analysis of the ego. *Standard Edition* 18:67–143. London: Hogarth Press, 1955.

———. 1923a. The ego and the id. *Standard Edition* 19:3–66. London: Hogarth Press, 1961.

———. 1923b. The infantile genital organization. *Standard Edition* 19:140–145. London: Hogarth Press, 1961.

———. 1925. Some psychical consequences of the anatomical distinction between the sexes. *Standard Edition* 19:243–258. London: Hogarth Press, 1961.

———. 1926. Inhibitions, symptoms and anxiety. *Standard Edition* 20:77–174. London: Hogarth Press, 1959.

———. 1930. Civilization and its discontents. *Standard Edition* 21:59–145. London: Hogarth Press, 1961.

———. 1931. Female sexuality. *Standard Edition* 21:223–243. London: Hogarth Press, 1961.

———. 1933. New introductory lectures on psycho-analysis. *Standard Edition* 22:3–182. London: Hogarth Press, 1964.

———. 1937a. Constructions in analysis. *Standard Edition* 23:255–270. London: Hogarth Press, 1964.

———. 1937b. Analysis terminable and interminable. *Standard Edition* 23:211–253. London: Hogarth Press, 1964.

———. 1940. An outline of psycho-analysis. *Standard Edition* 23:141–207. London: Hogarth Press, 1964.

Gill, M. M. 1976. Metapsychology is not psychology. In *Psychology versus metapsychology: Psychoanalytic essays in memory of George S. Klein,* ed. M. M. Gill and P. S. Holzman, 71–105. *Psychological Issues* Monograph 36. New York: International Universities Press.

———. 1982. *The analysis of transference. Psychological Issues* Monograph 53, vol. 1. New York: International Universities Press.

Glover, E. 1931. The therapeutic effect of inexact interpretation: A contribution to the theory of suggestion. In *The technique of psychoanalysis,* by E. Glover, 353–366. New York: International Universities Press, 1955.

Greenacre, P. 1954. The role of transference: Practical considerations in relation to psychoanalytic therapy. *Journal of the American Psychoanalytic Association* 2:671–684.

———. 1966. Problems of training analysis. *Psychoanaltic Quarterly.* 35:540–567.

Greenberg, J. R., and Mitchell, S. A. 1983. *Object relations in psychoanalytic theory.* Cambridge: Harvard University Press.

Greenson, R. 1954. The struggle against identification. *Journal of the American Psychoanalytic Association* 2:200–217.

Grossman, W. I. 1967. Reflections on the relationships of introspection and psychoanalysis. *International Journal of Psycho-Analysis* 48:16–31.

———. 1982. The self as fantasy: Fantasy as theory. *Journal of the American Psychoanalytic Association* 30:919–938.

Grossman, W. I., and Simon, B. 1969. Anthropomorphism, meaning, and causality in psychoanalytic theory. *The Psychoanalytic Study of the Child* 24:78–114. New York: International Universities Press.

Hartmann, H. 1953. *Ego psychology and the problem of adaptation.* New York: International Universities Press.

———. 1956. Notes on the reality principle. *The Psychoanalytic Study of the Child* 11:31–53. New York: International Universities Press.

———. 1960. *Psychoanalysis and moral values.* New York: International Universities Press.

———. 1964. *Essays on ego psychology: Selected problems in psychoanalytic theory.* New York: International Universities Press.

Horney, K. 1924. On the genesis of the castration-complex in women. *International Journal of Psycho-Analysis* 5:50–65.

———. 1926. The flight from womanhood: The masculinity complex in women as viewed by men and by women. *International Journal of Psycho-Analysis* 7:324–339.

———. 1932. The dread of women. *International Journal of Psycho-Analysis* 13:348–361.

———. 1933. The denial of the vagina. *International Journal of Psycho-Analysis* 14:57–70.

International Psychoanalytic Association. 1985. *Changes in analysts and their training,* ed. R. S. Wallerstein. Monograph Series 4.

———. 1986. *The termination of training analysis: Process, expectations, achievements,* ed. A. M. Cooper. Monograph Series 5.

Jacobson, E. 1964. *The self and the object world.* New York: International Universities Press.

Joseph, B. 1989. *Psychic equilibrium and psychic change: Selected papers of Betty Joseph,* ed. E. B. Spillius and M. Feldman. London: Tavistock/Routledge.

Kernberg, O. 1975. *Borderline conditions and pathological narcissism.* New York: Jason Aronson.

———. 1982. Self, ego, affects, and drives. *Journal of the American Psychoanalytic Association* 30:893–918.

Klein, G. S. 1975. *Psychoanalytic theory: An exploration of essentials.* New York: International Universities Press.

Klein, M. 1964. *Contributions to psycho-analysis.* New York: McGraw-Hill.

Kohut, H. 1971. *The analysis of the self: A systematic approach to the psychoanalytic treatment of narcissistic personality disorders.* New York: International Universities Press.

———. 1977. *The restoration of the self.* New York: International Universities Press.

———. 1984. *How does analysis cure?* Chicago: University of Chicago Press.

Kris, E. 1952. *Psychoanalytic explorations in art.* New York: International Universities Press.

———. 1956a. On some vicissitudes of insight in psychoanalysis. In *Selected papers of Ernst Kris,* 252–271. New Haven: Yale University Press.

———. 1956b. The recovery of childhood memories in psychoanalysis. In *Selected papers of Ernst Kris,* 301–340. New Haven: Yale University Press.

———. 1975. *The selected papers of Ernst Kris.* New Haven: Yale University Press.

Lakoff, G., and Johnson, M. 1980. *Metaphors we live by.* Chicago: University of Chicago Press.

Loewald, H. 1960. On the therapeutic action of psycho-analysis.

International Journal of Psycho-Analysis 41:16–33. Reprinted in *Papers on psychoanalysis,* by H. W. Loewald, 221–256. New Haven: Yale University Press, 1980.
———. 1970. Psychoanalytic theory and psychoanalytic process. In *Papers on psychaoanalysis,* by H. W. Loewald, 277–301. New Haven: Yale University Press, 1980.
———. 1972. Freud's conception of the negative therapeutic reaction, with comments on instinct theory. *Journal of the American Psychoanalytic Association* 20:235–245. Reprinted in *Papers on psychoanalysis,* by H. W Loewald, 315–325. New Haven: Yale University Press, 1980.
Loewenstein, R. L. 1957. A contribution to the theory of masochism. *Journal of the American Psychoanalytic Association* 5:197–234.
Macmurray, J. 1957. *The self as agent.* London: Faber & Faber.
Malan, D. H. 1979. *Individual psychotherapy and the science of psychoanalysis.* London: Butterworth.
Orwell, G. 1949. *1984.* New York: Harcourt, Brace.
Rado, S. 1956. *The psychoanalysis of behavior.* Vol. I of *Collected papers 1922–1956.* New York: Grune & Stratton.
Rapaport, D. 1967. *The collected papers of David Rapaport,* ed. M. M. Gill. New York: Basic Books.
Reich, A. 1951. On countertransference. *International Journal of Psycho-Analysis* 41:16–33.
———. 1953. Narcissistic object choice in women. *Journal of the American Psychoanalytic Association* 1:22–44.
———. 1954. Early identifications as archaic elements in the superego. *Journal of the American Psychoanalytic Association* 2:218–238.
———. 1960. Pathological forms of self-esteem regulation. *The Psychoanalytic Study of the Child* 15:215–232. New York: International Universities Press.
Reich, W. 1933. *Character analysis.* New York: Touchstone Books, 1974.
Reik, T. 1941. *Masochism in modern man.* New York: Farrar & Rinehart.
Ricoeur, P. 1977. The question of proof in psychoanalysis. *Journal of the American Psychoanalytic Association* 25:835–872.
Rilke, R. M. 1907. *Letters on Cézanne,* ed. C. Rilke, trans. J. Agee. New York: Fromm International Publications, 1985.
Sandler, J., with Freud, A. 1984. Discussions in the Hampstead Clinic of A. Freud, *The ego and the mechanisms of defense. Journal of the American Psychoanalytic Association* 31 Supplement:19–146.
Sandler, J.; Holder, A.; and Meers, D. 1963. The ego ideal and the ideal self. *The Psychoanalytic Study of the Child* 18:139–158. New York: International Universities Press.
Schafer, R. 1960. The loving and beloved superego in Freud's struc-

tural theory. *The Psychoanalytic Study of the Child* 15:163–188. New York: International Universities Press.

———. 1964. The clinical analysis of affects. *Journal of the American Psychoanalytic Association* 12:275–299.

———. 1967. Ideals, the ego ideal, and the ideal self. In *Motives and thought: Psychoanalytic essays in memory of David Rapaport,* ed. R. R. Holt, 129–174. *Psychological Issues* Monograph 18/19. New York: International Universities Press.

———. 1968a. On the theoretical and technical conceptualization of activity and passivity. *Psychoanalytic Quarterly* 37:173–198.

———. 1968b. *Aspects of internalization.* New York: International Universities Press.

———. 1968c. The mechanisms of defense. *International Journal of Psycho-Analysis* 49:49–62.

———. 1970a. The psychoanalytic vision of reality. *International Journal of Psycho-Analysis* 51:279–297. Reprinted in *A new language for psychoanalysis,* by R. Schafer, 22–56. New Haven: Yale University Press, 1976.

———. 1970b. An overview of Heinz Hartmann's contributions to psycho-analysis. *International Journal of Psycho-Analysis* 51:425–446. Reprinted in *A new language for psychoanalysis,* by R. Schafer, 57–101. New Haven: Yale University Press, 1976.

———. 1972. Internalization: Process or fantasy? *The Psychoanalytic Study of the Child* 27:411–438. New York: International Universities Press. Reprinted in *A new language for psychoanalysis,* by R. Schafer, 155–178. New Haven: Yale University Press, 1976.

———. 1973a. Action: Its place in psychoanalytic interpretation and theory. *The Annual of Psychoanalysis* 1:159–196.

———. 1973b. The idea of resistance. *International Journal of Analysis.* 54:259–285. Reprinted in *A new language for psychoanalysis,* by R. Schafer, 212–263. New Haven: Yale University Press, 1976.

———. 1974. Problems in Freud's psychology of women. *Journal of the American Psychoanalytic Association.* 22:459–485.

———. 1976. *A new language for psychoanalysis.* New Haven: Yale University Press.

———. 1978. *Language and insight: The Sigmund Freud memorial lectures, University College London, 1975–1976.* New Haven: Yale University Press.

———. 1981. *Narrative actions in psychoanalysis. Heinz Werner lecture series 14.* Worcester, MA: Clark University Press.

———. 1982. The imprisoned analysand. In *The analytic attitude,* by R. Schafer, 257–280. New York: Basic Books, 1983.

———. 1983. *The analytic attitude.* New York: Basic Books.

———. 1985a. Wild analysis. *Journal of the American Psychoanalytic Association.* 33:275–300.

———. 1985b. The interpretation of psychic reality, developmental influences, and unconscious communication. *Journal of the American Psychoanalytic Association* 33:537–554.

———. 1988. Discussion: Panel presentations on psychic structure. *Journal of the American Psychoanalytic Association* 36 Supplement:295–314.

Segal, H. 1964. *Introduction to the work of Melanie Klein.* New York: Basic Books.

Smith, B. H. 1980. Narrative versions, narrative theories. *Critical Inquiry* 7(2):213–236.

Spence, D. 1982. *Narrative truth and historical truth: Meaning and interpretation in psychoanalysis.* New York: Norton.

Stein, M. 1981. The unobjectionable part of the transference. *Journal of the American Psychoanalytic Association* 29:869–892.

Stone, L. 1961. Notes on the noninterpretive elements in the psychoanalytic situation. *Journal of the American Psychoanalytic Association* 29:89–118.

Sullivan, H. S. 1940. *Conceptions of modern psychiatry.* New York: Norton.

Thalberg, I. 1977. Freud's anatomies of the self. In *Philosophers on Freud: New evaluations,* ed. R. Wolheim, 147–171. New York: Jason Aronson.

Waelder, R. 1930. The principle of multiple function. *Psychoanalytic Quarterly* 15:45–62, 1936.

Weigert, E. 1955. Special problems in connection with termination of training analysis. *Journal of the American Psychoanalytic Association* 3:630–640. Reprinted in *The courage to love: Selected papers of Edith Weigert, M.D.,* 264–275. New Haven: Yale University Press, 1970.

Werner, H., and Kaplan, B. 1963. *Symbol formation* New York: John Wiley.

Wilbern, D. 1979. Freud and the inter-penetration of dreams. *Diacritics* 9:98–110.

Winnicott, D. W. 1958. *Collected papers: Through paediatrics to psychoanalysis.* New York: Basic Books.

Wood, E., and Wood, C. D. 1984. Tearfulness: A psychoanalytic interpretation. *Journal of the American Psychoanalytic Association* 32:117–136.

Woolf, V. 1924. *A room of one's own.* New York: Harcourt, Brace.

CREDITS

Chapter 2 was originally published in *Psychoanalysis: Toward the Second Century*, edited by Arnold M. Cooper, M.D., Otto F. Kernberg, M.D., and Ethel Spector Person, M.D., Yale University Press. Copyright © 1989 by Yale University. Reprinted by permission.

Chapter 3 was originally published in *Psychoanalysis & Contemporary Thought*, 10, 319–346. Copyright © by Psychoanalysis & Contemporary Science, Inc. Reprinted by permission.

Chapter 4 was originally published in *Journal of the American Psychoanalytic Association*, 1974, 22: 459–485. Copyright © International Universities Press, Inc. Reprinted by permission.

Chapter 5 was originally published in modified form as "Impotence, Frigidity, and Sexism," in *Language and Insight*, Yale University Press. Copyright © 1978 by Yale University. Reprinted by permission.

Chapter 6 was originally published in *American Psychologist*, 39: 398–405. Copyright © 1984 by the American Psychological Association. Reprinted by permission.

Chapter 9 will also appear in Smith, Joseph H., and Humphrey Morris (eds). *Telling Facts: History and Narratives in Psychoanalysis.* Baltimore: The Johns Hopkins University Press, 1992. Vol 13 of the series *Psychiatry and the Humanities.* Copyright © 1992, Forum on Psychiatry and the Humanities of the Washington School of Psychiatry.

Chapter 10 was originally published in *The Future of Literary Theory*, ed. Ralph Cohen, 1988, published by Routledge, Chapman & Hall. Reprinted by permission.

Chapter 11 was originally published in modified form in *The International Journal of Psycho-Analysis* (1990) 71: 49–52. Copyright © Institute of Psycho-Analysis. Used by permission.

Chapter 13 was originally published in *Journal of the American Psychoanalytic Association,* 1985, 35: 537–554. Copyright © International Universities Press, Inc. Reprinted by permission.

Chapter 17, I, was originally published as "Talking to Patients in Psychotherapy." Reprinted with permission from the *Bulletin of the Menninger Clinic* Vol. 38, No. 6, pp. 503–515. Copyright © 1974, The Menninger Foundation.

Chapter 17, II, was originally published as "The Termination of Brief Psychoanalytic Psychotherapy," in the *International Journal of Psychoanalytic Psychotherapy* (1973), 2: 135–148. Reprinted by permission.

Chapter 18 was published in modified form as "Internalizing Loewald" in *The Work of Hans Loewald,* edited by Gerald I. Fogel, 77–90. Northvale, NJ: Jason Aronson, 1991. Reprinted by permission.

INDEX